INCLUSIVE DEVELOPMENT IN SOUTH ASIA

This book examines the multi-layered aspects and the complexities of inclusive development in South Asia based on recent data and using innovative methodology.

The book offers an analysis of the existing ground realities in terms of economic and inclusive development, presenting relevant discussion and findings. It discusses lower castes, tribes, religious/ethnic minorities, and other socially vulnerable people, as well as gender, rural–urban, and educational disparities in South Asia, and highlights that all these issues are interrelated. Structured in two parts—Spatial Dimensions, Labour, and Migration, and Social Dimensions and Beyond Inclusion—the chapters present emerging new concepts related to socio-economic and inclusive development and use effective and valid methods and methodology covering the ground realities-based information and secondary data-based analysis. Evaluating the extent to which inclusive development has been realised in South Asia, the contributors explore a new approach towards the concept of 'inclusiveness' by drawing on the experiences of the diverse societies in South Asia.

An immensely useful contribution to the analysis of different economic and social issues in different countries in South Asia, focusing on inclusivity, this book will be of interest to researchers working on South Asian Politics and Development Economics.

Toshie Awaya is Professor at the Graduate School of Global Studies, Tokyo University of Foreign Studies, Japan.

Kazuo Tomozawa is Professor at the Graduate School of Humanities and Social Sciences, Hiroshima University, Japan.

Routledge New Horizons in South Asian Studies

Series Editors:

Crispin Bates, *Edinburgh University*

Akio Tanabe, *University of Tokyo*

Minoru Mio, *National Museum of Ethnology, Japan*

Sustainable Development in India
Groundwater Irrigation, Energy Use, and Food Production
Edited by Koichi Fujita and Tsukasa Mizushima

The Dynamics of Conflict and Peace in Contemporary South Asia
The State, Democracy and Social Movements
Edited by Minoru Mio, Kazuya Nakamizo and Tatsuro Fujikura

Caste and Equality in India
A Historical Anthropology of Diverse Society and Vernacular Democracy
Akio Tanabe

Language, Identity, and Power in Modern India
Gujarat, c. 1850–1960
Riho Isaka

Indian Economic Growth in Historical Perspective
The Roots of Development
Late Prof. Haruka Yanagisawa (ed. Tsukasa Mizushima)

The Rural-Urban Nexus in India's Economic Transformation
Tsukasa Mizushima

Inclusive Development in South Asia
Edited by Toshie Awaya and Kazuo Tomozawa

For a full list of titles please see www.routledge.com/Routledge-New-Horizons-in-South-Asian-Studies/book-series/RNHSAS

INCLUSIVE DEVELOPMENT IN SOUTH ASIA

Edited by Toshie Awaya and Kazuo Tomozawa

Routledge
Taylor & Francis Group
LONDON AND NEW YORK

First published 2023
by Routledge
4 Park Square, Milton Park, Abingdon, Oxon OX14 4RN

and by Routledge
605 Third Avenue, New York, NY 10158

Routledge is an imprint of the Taylor & Francis Group, an informa business

British Library Cataloguing-in-Publication Data
A catalogue record for this book is available from the British Library

Library of Congress Cataloging-in-Publication Data
Names: Awaya, Toshie, 1957– editor. | Tomozawa, Kazuo, 1962– editor.
Title: Inclusive development in South Asia / edited by Toshie Awaya, Kazuo Tomozawa.
Description: First Edition. | New York : Routledge, 2023. | Series: Routledge new horizons in South Asian Studies | Includes bibliographical references and index.
Identifiers: LCCN 2022033149 (print) | LCCN 2022033150 (ebook) | ISBN 9781032303710 (Hardback) | ISBN 9781032303727 (Paperback) | ISBN 9781003304760 (eBook)
Subjects: LCSH: Economic development—South Asia. | South Asia—Economic policy. | South Asia—Social policy. | Minorities—South Asia. | Marginality, Social—South Asia.
Classification: LCC HC430.6 .I495 2023 (print) | LCC HC430.6 (ebook) | DDC 330.954—dc23/eng/20221122
LC record available at https://lccn.loc.gov/2022033149
LC ebook record available at https://lccn.loc.gov/2022033150

ISBN: 978-1-032-30371-0 (hbk)
ISBN: 978-1-032-30372-7 (pbk)
ISBN: 978-1-003-30476-0 (ebk)

DOI: 10.4324/9781003304760

Typeset in Times New Roman
by Apex CoVantage, LLC

CONTENTS

FIGURES

TABLES

MAPS

PREFACE AND ACKNOWLEDGEMENTS

'Inclusion' is a concept/perspective that has become one of the indispensable aspects when we consider development themes. It shows that we have been dissatisfied with narrowly conceptualised economic growth and intolerant of not only economic but also social inequalities. With the background of a global pandemic, which revealed clearly the existing disparity between the privileged and the vulnerable, and intensified the social divisions among people, 'inclusion' has become even more important.

This volume is based on the papers presented at the international symposium titled 'Inclusive Development in South Asia' held at Tokyo University of Foreign Studies (TUFS) on 15–16 December 2018. This was one of the symposiums organised under the project called 'Integrated Area Studies on South Asia' (INDAS-South Asia), which has been supported financially by the National Institutes for the Humanities (NIHU) since 2016.

This project is characterised by the collaboration of scholars from multiple disciplines. Reflecting this, the contributors to this volume are experts trained in various academic fields. At the symposium, we did not set out with a guiding definition of 'inclusive development.' Although we admit the danger when a concept expends out of control and loses its analytical power, we believe that contentions surrounding the definition and various approaches themselves are meaningful.

We are indebted to numerous people for assisting in bringing out this volume. First, we wish to thank our colleagues in the INDAS-South Asia project and all participants in the symposium. This joint work has been always fun and stimulating. We would especially like to thank Maya Suzuki, Asuka Murakami, Lin Chen, and Yutaro Katsumata, research associates at the Center for South Asian Studies at TUFS and the Center for Contemporary India Studies at Hiroshima University, for their valuable assistance in organising the symposium and preparing this volume. We are also grateful to the series editors, Akio Tanabe, Minoru Mio, and

Crispin Bates, for their timely support and Dorothea Schaefter at Routledge for her understanding and generosity. Lastly, both editors acknowledge with gratitude the patience and cooperation of the contributors.

We hope the debates about 'inclusion' across disciplinary and geographic borders will continue.

Toshie Awaya and Kazuo Tomozawa
Tokyo and Hiroshima, 2022

ABBREVIATIONS

AISHE	All India Survey on Higher Education
ASI	Annual Survey of Industries
BANBEIS	Bangladesh Bureau of Educational Information and Statistics
BIG	Basic Income Grants
BSUP	Basic Services to Urban Poor
CA	Cluster Analysis
CPI	Consumer Price Index
EFA	Education for All
FDI	Foreign Direct Investment
FFEP	Food for Education Programme
FSEP	Female Secondary Education Project
GCM	Global Compact for Migration
GER	Gross Enrolment Ratio
GSDP	Gross State Domestic Product
GSVA	Gross State Value Added
GVA	Gross Value Added
HSA	Hindu Succession Act
HSC	Higher Secondary Certificate
ICT	Information and Communications Technology
IHSDP	Integrated Housing and Slum Development Programme
ILD	Institute for Liberty and Democracy
INI	Institutions of National Importance
IOM	International Organization for Migration
JNNURM	Jawaharlal Nehru National Urban Renewal Mission
JSC	Junior School Certificate
LARRA	Land Acquisition, Rehabilitation and Resettlement Act

MGNREGAS	Mahatma Gandhi National Rural Employment Guarantee Act Scheme
MHRD	Ministry of Human Resource Development
MPCE	Monthly Per Capita Consumer/Consumption Expenditure
MSJ	Multipurpose Society for Justice
NCEUS	National Commission for Enterprises in the Unorganised Sector
NCR	National Capital Region
NEG	New Economic Geography
NREGA	National Rural Employment Guarantee Act
NSDP	Net State Domestic Product
NSO	National Statistical Office
NSSO	National Sample Survey Organisation
OBCs	Other Backward Classes
PCA	Principal Component Analysis
PDS	Public Distribution Scheme
PSC	Primary School Certificate
RSS	Rashtriya Swayamsevak Sangh
SCs	Scheduled Castes
SDGs	Sustainable Development Goals
SEWA	Self Employed Women's Association
SEZ	Special Economic Zone
SFEP	Stipend for Education Project
SSC	Secondary School Certificate
STs	Scheduled Tribes
UBI	Universal Basic Income
UIDSSMT	Urban Infrastructure Development Scheme for Small and Medium Towns

CONTRIBUTORS

Toshie Awaya is a professor at the Graduate School of Global Studies, Tokyo University of Foreign Studies. Her research interests include South Asian modern history, gender history, and social movements. Her recent publications are the edited volumes *India Gender Studies Handbook* (with Takako Inoue, 2018, in Japanese) and *The Voices from the Margin, Contemporary India, 5* (with Riho Isaka and Takako Inoue, 2015, in Japanese).

Eric Denis is the current director of the Géographie-cités Lab, Paris 1 Panthéon-Sorbonne University, French National Centre for Scientific Research. His research interest is urban studies with a focus on spatial analysis, systems of cities, small towns, land-use changes, and poverty in India, Egypt, and Sudan. He is one of the editors of *Subaltern Urbanisation in India: an Introduction to the Dynamics of Ordinary Towns* (2015).

Satish Deshpande is a professor at the Department of Sociology, Delhi School of Economics, University of Delhi. His research interests include caste and class in contemporary India; the history, theory, and practice of social theory; and issues of language in the social sciences. His most recent books are the edited volumes *Sectarian Violence in India: Hindu-Muslim Conflict, 1966–2015* (with Sanjay Palshikar, 2019) and *The Problem of Caste* (2014).

Binod Khadria is a former professor of economics and education at Jawaharlal Nehru University (1995–2018). In 2017–2018, he held the inaugural Indian Council for Cultural Relations (ICCR) Chair at Rutgers University, USA. His fields of research include economics of education and international migration. He is the author of *The Migration of Knowledge Workers: Second-generation Effects of India's Brain Drain* (Sage 1999). His recent publications include *The*

Sage Handbook of International Migration, London (co-editor, 2019) and *World Migration Report 2020* (co-editor, 2019).

Junko Kiso is a professor at the Faculty of Global and Intercultural Studies, Ferris University. Her research interests are in socio-economic development, employment, labour, and informal sector in India and Bangladesh. Her research works include *Indian People and Their Labour in Economic Development* (2012, in Japanese), 'Job Loss and Job Opportunities of Factory Workers in Ahmedabad: Flexible Labour Rethink' (2008).

Tatsuya Kusakabe is an associate professor at the Center for the Study of International Cooperation in Education, Hiroshima University. His research focuses on an impact of educational development in rural Bangladesh and on creating Muslimness in unrecognised madrasas in South Asia. He played the role of the section editor of *Handbook of Education System of South Asia* (2021).

Kentaro Kuwatsuka is a professor at the Faculty of Business Administration, Ryukoku University. His research interests include the servitisation of regional economy, spatial organisation of economic activities, and the role of technologies in regional growth. He has published some papers and articles on these and related themes in Okinawa, Singapore, Thailand, and India.

Nivedita Menon is a professor at Centre for Comparative Politics and Political Theory, Jawaharlal Nehru University, Delhi. She is the author of *Seeing like a Feminist* (2012). Apart from research papers in Indian and international journals, her previous books are *Recovering Subversion: Feminist Politics Beyond the Law* (2004) and *Power and Contestation: India after 1989* (with Aditya Nigam, 2007, 2nd ed., 2014). She also has two edited volumes *Gender and Politics in India* (1999) and *Sexualities* (2007); and a co-edited book *Critical Studies in Politics. Exploring Sites, Selves, Power* (2014).

Kazuyo Minamide is an associate professor in the course of Global Studies at Department of English, Kobe College. Her research interest is in educational influence on people's life courses in Bangladesh from anthropological approaches. In this field, she has several publications including her recent edited book *Millennial Generation in Bangladesh: Their Life Strategies, Movements, and Identity Politics* (2022).

Sae Nakamura is an associate professor at the Graduate School of Arts and Sciences, The University of Tokyo. Her concerns are broadly aimed at themes in cultural/medical anthropology with a focus on ageing and care in Sri Lanka and Japan. Her recent publications include *Communicative Body: An Ethnography of Home for Elders in Sri Lanka* (2017, in Japanese) and 'Fiction in the making of intimacy in old age: a case from Sri Lanka,' *Contemporary South Asia* 29–1 (2021).

Tatsushi Nemoto is an associate professor at the Department of Sociology, Bukkyo University. He has been working on issues of Dalit movements and revival of Buddhism in India after 1956 from an anthropological perspective. His recent works include *An Ethnography of the Post-Ambedkar Era: Buddhists and Dalit Movements in Contemporary India* (2018, in Japanese) and 'An Analysis of the Religious Expressions of Shurei Sasai that Shape *Kokū*,' *Cultural Anthropology*, 86–3 (2021, in Japanese).

Seika Sato is a professor at the Faculty of Liberal Arts, Teikyo University. Her interests centre around gender, labour, and minorities in Nepal. She is the author of *Conversing with the Yolmo Women: An Anthropology of Life/Story in Nepal* (2015, in Japanese).

Ai Sugie is a senior lecturer at the Graduate School of Letters, Kyoto University. Her research explores the social changes in rural Bangladesh and reconsiders the concept and practice of 'development' by an ethnographic approach. She is one of the authors of *Kinship and Family among Muslims in Bengal* (2021) and *Perspectives on Geographical Marginality Volume 4: Rural Areas between Regional Needs and Global Challenges* (2019).

Kazuo Tomozawa is a professor at the Graduate School of Humanities and Social Sciences, Hiroshima University. His research focuses on India's industrialisation and formation of labour market from the viewpoint of economic geography. He is one of the editors of *Structural Transformation in Globalizing South Asia: Comprehensive Area Studies for Sustainable, Inclusive and Peaceful Development, Senri Ethnological Studies 96 (National Museum of Ethnology, 2017).*

Shuji Uchikawa is a professor at the School of Economics, Senshu University. His research focuses on India's industry policy from the viewpoint of economics. His recent work is 'Caste Membership, Business Access, and Social Mobility among Indian Apparel Manufacturers,' *Economic and Political Weekly*, 52–22 (2017).

INTRODUCTION

'Inclusive Development' in South Asia

Toshie Awaya and Kazuo Tomozawa

What is 'inclusive development'?

The term 'inclusive development' has gained popularity in recent years. The United Nations' 2030 Agenda for Sustainable Development adopted in 2015 has inclusion as a core item alongside sustainability, as conveyed by the impressive slogan 'leaving no one behind.'[1] Meanwhile, the World Economic Forum, which promotes the market economy, has also released the Inclusive Development Index, placing importance on inclusive growth.[2] Notably, inclusion is now an agenda among national governments, corporations, and grassroots organisations. With the neoliberal economy sweeping the globe since the 1990s, besides the criticism of the current intensification of disparities causing social inequality and disruption, it is somewhat recognised that excessive wealth disparities could be barriers to the further capitalistic development itself and that it is necessary to improve the economic as well as social conditions of the poor.

In developmental economics, the nature and content of 'development' have been understood in various ways. In this field, before 'inclusive growth' came to the mainstream in the discussions on economic growth of developing countries, including those in South Asia, we can find several trends starting with the stance that pursuits achieving economic growth first and foremost, and expects its trickle-down effects, to the 'pro-poor growth' perspective (Ali, 2007).

While economic development aimed at increasing GDP has benefited certain sections of people and regions, the expected 'trickle-down effect' has not turned out to be effective enough at improving the living conditions of a vast number of the poor nor has it eliminated existing disparities. Critical of this, the 'pro-poor growth' argument that emerged in the 1990s pays more attention to eliminating poverty and promoting welfare of the poor. Amartya Sen's capability approach and argument of 'development as freedom' are also located in the trend critical of

DOI: 10.4324/9781003304760-1

the GDP-centred conceptualisation of economic growth (Sen, 1992, 1999). Following these trends, it was in the 2000s that the concept of 'inclusive growth' emerged. This concept is believed to be more comprehensive and wide-ranging in the sense that its goal is to improve the living conditions of the poor and socially vulnerable communities, including women and ethnic minorities, and to move towards the realisation of an economy and society wherein no one is excluded from the benefits of growth.

What the term 'inclusion' should mean or what elements are considered essential, Klasen (2010) pointed out, still remains elusive. Does it mean inclusion in processes or inclusion in outcomes? Does it mean the absolute or relative alleviation of poverty?[3] Who is the target of inclusion efforts, decided solely by income or other criteria? Thus, unsurprisingly, researchers have not succeeded in arriving at a mutually agreed definition of inclusive growth. For example, Ranieri and Ramos (2013) identified key elements in the definitions used in 14 previous studies on inclusive growth. The authors found that 11 definitions included the element of correcting inequality, 9 referred to poverty reduction, 6 mentioned economic growth, 5 alluded to capability/empowerment, 3 definitions referred to productive employment and opportunity, 2 mentioned social protection, and 1 alluded to gender inequality, access to infrastructure, participation, targeted policies, basic social services, good governance, barriers for investment, and benefits of growth. Thus, the reduction of poverty and inequality is believed to be a critical foundation for inclusive economic growth, and in this sense, some elements of pro-poor growth, which precede inclusive growth, are included in the concept of 'inclusive growth.' What distinguishes inclusive growth from pro-poor growth is, first, that while pro-poor growth emphasises equality of outcomes, such as a decline in the rate of poverty or the proportion of the poor population, inclusive growth emphasises participation in the processes of human development. Thus, a variety of contributing factors, such as empowerment, opportunity, productive employment, access, and formal and informal institutions (de Haan, 2015), that can play a crucial role in improving these factors are included in the definition of inclusive growth, thereby lending it multidimensionality. Second, while pro-poor growth tends to focus exclusively on the poor, the range of inclusive growth concerns extends to the entire citizenry of a nation and its regions (global at the largest), while paying more attention to the disparity of various units or regions.

The elements that create inequality/disparity are often structurally determined and inherited across generations. Attentive to these aspects, inclusive growth is perceived to move beyond the narrow definition of economic growth and poverty reduction to broader sociocultural inclusion, with an emphasis on equity. In this respect, 'inclusive growth' and 'inclusive development' are often used interchangeably.[4] Still, note that the importance of 'growth'/'development' itself is confirmed and conceptualised in the capitalist framework. Capitalist or not, this volume addresses the idea of 'inclusiveness' in the widest sense.

Inclusion/Exclusion

In the international context, the Indian government reacted early in adopting inclusive development as a national development strategy. During Manmohan Singh's first administrative tenure, inclusive growth was the basic principle of the 11th Five-Year Plan (2007–2011). The plan's central vision was 'to build on our strengths to trigger a development process that ensures broad-based improvement in the quality of life of the people, especially the poor, Scheduled Castes/Scheduled Tribes (SCs/STs), Other Backward Classes (OBCs), minorities, and women.' A similar vision was essentially adhered to during the second Singh administration[5] and by the subsequent Narendra Modi administration.[6] This emphasis on inclusiveness was backed by the perception that India's economic growth since the neoliberal reform in the early 1990s—or as some believe in the 1980s—has not produced trickle-down effects, but rather widened economic disparity, with little benefits to the poor. It is not a coincidence that the 2000s are characterised by a series of rights-based legislations, such as the Right to Education and the Right to Information.

Various problems with India's unprecedented economic growth over the last 30 years have been pointed out (Dréze and Sen, 2013). For instance, in response to the government's claim that the proportion of the population below the poverty line has declined in India, critics have underlined that the said bracket has been set too low. Kannan (2014) and others have highlighted that if the global poverty standard was applied, the proportion of poor people in 2004–2005 (Kannan regards this sector as 'common people') would have reached 77%. Kannan further pointed out that poverty was disproportionately experienced by Muslims and those positioned lower in the existing social hierarchy, for example, SCs/STs and OBCs. According to him, the Indian economy after economic liberalisation experienced the process of 'inequalising growth' (Kannan, 2014).

Some reports note persistent economic disparities in India. For instance, India ranked 62nd among 74 developing countries listed in the Global Economic Forum's Inclusive Development Index 2018, a finding reported as 'shocking' by the Indian media at the time of the announcement.[7] When we look at 'inclusion,' one of the three indicators used in that Index—the other two indicators are 'growth and development' and 'intergenerational equity and sustainability'—India ranked even lower, at 72nd place.[8]

Inclusive development is not a theme monopolised by development economics. Many studies have discussed inclusive development in non-economic domains, such as the social, educational, gender, and political spheres.[9]

The concept of inclusion is closely linked to the opposite concept of exclusion. If studies focusing on exclusion themes are added, the volume of the literature on inclusion/exclusion greatly increases. Studies addressing the issue of exclusion in India have become even more relevant against the backdrop of the intolerance and violence towards minorities caused by the rise of the Hindu Right since the 1980s and the economic disparities arising from the progress of neoliberal economies.

As an exhaustive survey of these studies is not possible here, we will touch upon only some of the contentious areas.

In South Asia, where diverse religions coexist, 'minority' communities are often subjected to social, political, and cultural exclusion/discrimination. There are numerous studies confirming that Muslims and Christians, considered 'Other,' have been the targets of attacks from Hindu nationalist forces since the 1980s. The fact that Sachar's report pointed out the relative 'backwardness' of the Muslim population in India is also fresh in the memory (Government of India, 2006). Concrete examples of Indian Muslims' exclusion are found in Shaban (2018) and Jeffrelot (2019), to cite only a few. Notably, the Centre for Equity Studies has published the India Exclusion Report, in which 'adverse inclusion' is also accounted as 'exclusion' (Centre for Equity Studies, 2016). As a specific example, one could imagine a situation in which 'tribes' are subsumed into the mainstream economy, and consequently, lose their livelihood (see Chapter 12 in this volume). A similar issue was taken up by Amartya Sen in an examination of the concept of 'social exclusion' (Sen, 2000; Nevile 2007). Sen acknowledged the usefulness of the term 'social exclusion' which focuses more on relational aspects compared with his own idea, that is, poverty as the deprivation of capability. Sen also referred to the phenomenon of 'unfavourable inclusion'—similar to 'adverse inclusion' described earlier—and problematised the nature of inclusion.[10] In other words, when discussing inclusion, it is necessary to critically analyse and evaluate *who are included to what and how they are included.*

Numerous studies are available on the social inclusion/exclusion of Dalits and lower castes (Mosse, 2018). Given the controversies regarding the implementation of the Mandal Commission's recommendations to extend the reservation to OBCs under the V. P. Singh administration and the increasing expansion of Dalit intellectuals' intervention (cf. Rawat and Satyanarayana, 2016; Arya and Rathore, 2020), aspects of caste-based exclusion have been discussed from multiple angles (see Chapter 10 in this volume). Specifically, one of the foci has been the education field, particularly in that of higher/English education, since English knowledge is regarded as a lever of social mobility (Deshpande and Zacharias, 2013). The 2016 suicide of Rohith Vemula, a PhD student at Hyderabad Central University, tragically exemplified the issue of the 'exclusion' of Dalit individuals in higher education institutions (see Chapters 4, 8, and 9 in this volume).

Economic reform and its impact are another highly debated issue. Does it open a new space and possibility for Dalits to be free from exclusion/discrimination? (Deshpande, 2011). Prakash (2015) and Harriss-White et al. (2014) point out the various discriminations faced by Dalit and tribal entrepreneurs. In contrast, Prasad (2008) and Kapur et al. (2010) argue that global capitalism and market economies disrupt the caste regime and provide an opportunity for the upward economic mobility of Dalits. However, a consensus has not been reached (see Chapters 5 and 6 in this volume). The debate on whether caste is declining or resiliently working as a structure favouring the already privileged castes in the inclusion process of economic and social participation will remain for a considerable time.

Chapters of the book

This volume is the outcome of the international symposium 'Inclusive Development in South Asia' held at Tokyo University of Foreign Studies (TUFS) on 15–16 December 2018. Here, researchers from different disciplinary backgrounds have adopted a multifaceted approach to 'Inclusion' issues. Though their methodology varies, readers will notice that many chapters are based on long-term field research, which allows the researchers to gain a nuanced understanding of the grassroots level reality of the 'inclusion/exclusion' process experienced by common people. Further, the limitations and shortcomings of current discussions on 'inclusion' are also pointed out, especially in the last two chapters.

The volume is divided into two parts: 'Spatial Dimensions, Labour, and Migration' and 'Social Dimensions and Beyond Inclusion.' The first four chapters of Part 1 discuss 'inclusive development' in contemporary South Asia mainly from the spatial perspectives. These chapters present a fresh understanding of spatial relations, spatial structure, and regionally diversified development.

In Chapter 1, Kazuo Tomozawa, an economic geographer, focuses on widened regional disparities between states in India. The distribution of relatively prosperous states is confined to western and southern India (Tomozawa names it 'India's Banana'). To better understand this situation, the author examines the location pattern of leading manufacturing industries. The automobile industry was thus noted to form an 'auto crescent' that encompasses the National Capital Region (NCR) of Delhi and has a spatial pattern most closely resembling that of the aforementioned 'Banana.' Tomozawa's investigation of the NCR indicates that contract workers, who have become a dominant workforce, mostly originated from a 'contract workers' belt' extending from Uttar Pradesh to Bihar, constituting mainly younger men of a socio-economically vulnerable working class. The relationship between the auto crescent and the contract workers' belt appears to have formed a centre-periphery structure. The author concludes that this structure may have an impact on the spatial divide of contemporary India's national economy.

In Chapter 2, using principal component analysis (PCA) and cluster analysis (CA), Kentaro Kuwatsuka analyses India's spatial structure, focusing especially on work opportunities, which are crucial when considering inclusive employment growth. District-level data in the B-Series Economic Tables of India's 2011 Census provides the basis for these analyses. The author identifies six principal components and finds that 'diversified work opportunities in metropolitan regions' scored high in metropolitan regions such as Mumbai, and in widely dispersed districts between Delhi and Punjab. Kuwatsuka uses CA to further characterise five regional types of work opportunities utilising four principal components with high eigenvalues. The author also demonstrates that the emergence of metropolitan regions is a crucial determinant in the modification of India's spatial structure after the economic reforms of the 1990s. These findings support the hypothesis proposed by Okahashi (2015), who emphasised that the mega-region functions as a core part of the nation.

In Chapter 3, Eric Denis proposes the concept of 'subaltern urbanisation,' which emphasises the importance of small towns, and horizontal (contra hierarchical in the planetary urbanisation model) and diffused development of cities. By identifying four types of settlements (influenced town, micropolis, market and/or administrative towns, and census towns), the author highlights the varied nature of small-town development trajectories. In these trajectories, Denis underlines the agency of local actors and the innovative solutions they deploy, as well as the 'politics of classification' of towns. The author posits 'subaltern urbanisation,' which is not hierarchical but horizontal, as a possibility for an inclusive development path. This chapter and the preceding two chapters should be read together to get a new picture of the dynamics of inclusion/exclusion in the process of urban space creation.

The recent spread of education, especially at the primary level, in Bangladesh is generally acknowledged, as Chapter 8 also confirms. In Chapter 4, Tatsuya Kusakabe instead focuses on secondary level education and asks how the rural inhabitants, the poorer section in particular, in Bangladesh have utilised their education credentials over the course of their lifetimes. The author analyses the changing faces of level of education and job opportunities among four clusters of villagers (upper, upper-middle, lower-middle, and lower classes) based on ten years of long-term comparative research of two villages: one in a remote rural setting and the other in a suburban rural setting. Kusakabe finds that the connection between job opportunities and the growth of the education system has been strengthening in the case of a suburban village. The author thinks that people in remote rural areas have to wait for a more favourable socio-economic environment to be motivated. Further, Kusakabe points out that the rise in meritocratic social mobility of poor people through the education system—one aspect of inclusive development—is a new phenomenon in the lower-class suburban rural setting.

The next three chapters examine inclusive development in the labour market and migration scenes (inland and international).

In Chapter 5, based on the author's long-term field survey in Ahmedabad, Junko Kiso discusses 'jobless inclusiveness,' defined as inclusive growth without a corresponding sufficient increase in employment with 'decent work' conditions. The author first analyses the life trajectories of factory workers (managerial and clerical staff, technical staff, production workers, and contract workers) employed in the organised sector of the manufacturing industry to ascertain the inter- and intra-generational history of inclusion and exclusion in the labour market from the 1990s to the 2000s. Kiso points out that even though income increased in general, once they lost formal jobs, it was difficult for them to find jobs in the formal sector. The author then similarly analyses the socio-economic mobility of informal sector workers in the slums. The findings show that caste background and educational resources greatly affect both categories of workers. Finally, after describing the limits of jobless inclusiveness, Kiso asserts that it is important to increase productive employment and decent work, and improve the education and skills of human resources to effectively use the demographic dividend and realise inclusive growth in India.

Migration opportunities and remittances are sometimes considered crucial ways for the poor to improve their quality of life. The next two chapters discuss this theme. In Chapter 6, Shuichi Uchikawa focuses on migration in India, which depends on various factors in rural and urban areas. The author emphasises that migration opportunities and benefits are not equally shared. Lower-income households cannot bear the initial costs and risks of migration. In contrast, highly educated migrants from high-income groups experience greater income growth than those from low-income groups. Uchikawa opines that 'inclusive development' expresses the goal of several policies. The present conditions are not conducive to achieving the goal in the short term. However, the author also stresses the importance of paying attention to the long-term gradual change in the socio-economic structures of rural areas. For instance, in Bihar, migration has improved the bargaining power of agricultural labourers vis-à-vis landlords and the previous asymmetric relationship between these players has weakened in the last three decades.

In Chapter 7, Binod Khadria discusses the exclusion and inclusion in South Asia caused by international migration. Using the 'hubs and hinterlands of migration' model, the author conceptualises a simple distinction between inclusion and exclusion: some countries have emerged primarily as destination hubs for the inclusion of migrants from within the region, while others experience exclusion as hinterlands from which migrants originate. Following the examination of several dimensions of migration in eight countries in South Asia, Khadria questions whether and how a trans-South Asian diaspora policy can drive inclusive migration through several key objectives of the Global Compact for Migration (GCM).

Part 2, 'Social Dimensions and Beyond Inclusion,' examines the issues of inclusion in education, caste, and gender.

Education has been recognised as a crucial factor in the inclusion process. In Chapter 8, Satish Deshpande focuses on the recent phenomenon of 'massification' of higher education in India. After confirming the growth of this trend over the last few decades, the author offers a detailed examination of several features of this 'great expansion' by meticulously using the All India Survey on Higher Education reports and data from the National Sample Survey Office. Deshpande focuses primarily on the extent to which higher education has offered access to hitherto excluded social groups/classes (such as women, SCs/STs, and Muslims) and brought about equality among those groups. The author's analysis reveals that the recent expansion of higher education has increased the inclusion of disadvantaged groups, especially women. However, that inclusion stops at the level of 'enrolment inclusion.' Deshpande points out that equality in higher education is still hindered by the cost of education, which is getting high due to the privatisation of education under the neoliberal reform and the resulting unequal access to high-quality education. In other words, class, caste, and gender still matter.

While Deshpande focuses on higher education in India using statistical data, Kazuyo Minamide's analysis in Chapter 9 is based on long-term field surveys in

Bangladesh. The author's long and deep involvement with research subjects helps in understanding the ambivalent and complex relationship between these subjects' aspirations for 'a better life' and an often-frustrating reality. Minamide first demonstrates that primary education in Bangladesh has dramatically expanded under the slogan 'Education for All' and that the 'first educated generation' is creating the foundation for the country's large-scale rapid economic growth, predominantly in the export-oriented garment industry. Yet, the author points out that inclusion in the education system goes along with inequality in the quality of education as well as uneven access to secondary education (and beyond) and job opportunities. Minamide is also critical of neoliberal ideology that emphasises 'individual responsibility' for one's failure. Drawing on rich anthropological fieldwork, the author probes members' perceptions of their life course and suggests that they rationalise their unsatisfactory reality by considering their circumstances to be 'temporary.'

In Chapter 10, Tatsushi Nemoto discusses Dalit activities in Maharashtra. Since Dalits are considered as a typical example of a socially excluded group, the inclusion and exclusion of Dalits in various fields have been studied extensively. Instead, by proposing the perspective of 'becoming Dalit,' Nemoto attempts to go beyond existing arguments. The author examines the inclusion process not from the viewpoint of dominant castes but from that of Dalits and of the non-Dalits who interact with Dalits. The author elaborates this perspective as a powerful and future-oriented shift by drawing on Deleuze and Guattari's argument of 'becoming minoritarian,' and Dalit feminism theorisation. The empirical cases examined by Nemoto include inter-caste marriages and a 2013 drinking water purification project launched by a Buddhist Dalit organisation in a village in Nagpur district. In the latter case, this organisation's Buddhist Dalit activists provided chemically purified water to villagers, including caste-Hindus, at a low price. The activists' narratives describe the project to be based on the egalitarian principle in the Indian Constitution drafted by Ambedkar, with the goal of bringing about social change and 'respect' towards Dalits. In contrast, caste-Hindu beneficiaries justified receiving drinking water from Dalits by referring to the concept of 'equality before God.' Nemoto observes that although the project created some interaction between Dalit activists and non-Dalit villagers, their respective concepts of equality remained disconnected. In the case of inter-caste marriages, the author closely examines narratives with a focus on non-Dalit women who married Dalits and discovers a critique against multiple patriarchies and a move towards 'becoming Dalit' as a transformative open space.

The image of the Muslim woman is a contentious terrain, especially in the contemporary world after 9/11. Muslim women are sometimes depicted as victims oppressed by a misogynistic Islamic orthodoxy. Against this background, in Chapter 11, Ai Sugie first argues that Islamic discourses are diverse and warns that the purported 'Islamic norms' could be male-centred interpretations. The author analyses one of the women-centred Islamic education movements in Bangladesh, *Talim*. This is a weekly Islamic lecture delivered to the neighbourhood women by a female teacher in a local house. Based on field research on two *talim* gatherings, the author analyses the profiles of attendees, the content of lectures, and the interactions between lecturers and attendees. The findings show that *talims* provide women with a 'place of their own' where they can assemble, free themselves of daily chores, and exchange information and opinions. The author further underscores one subtle but important difference between sermons by male preachers and *talim* lectures by women: the former demands only unquestioning female obedience to male authority. Sugie is careful enough to not easily conclude that *talims* are enhancing Muslimahs' (Muslim women's) status in society or nourishing their faculty to criticise the male-dominated social structure. However, the author emphasises the possibility of Muslimahs' inclusion into existing male-centred 'Islamic discourse' space by participating in *talims* and the resultant transformation of it.

In Chapter 12, Seika Sato examines the situation of Janajati (indigenous people) and Dalit women in Nepal. According to Sato, the value of '*desh vikas*' (developing the nation) has been pervasive as 'nation credo' in Nepal since the 1950s, and the demand for inclusion, based mainly on ascribed categories, is a recent trend. The author's main interest is whether the development practice of '*desh vikas*' has made Nepali society more inclusive. Sato explores this question with a special focus on Janajati and Dalit women, who are positioned at the intersection of exclusion based on both gender and caste/ethnicity. After examining their statistical profiles drawn from the National Social Inclusion Survey (2012) and the contradictory discourse regarding these two groups, Sato confirms that Janajati and Dalit have been represented as the ambivalent 'Other.' Sato then proceeds to describe women's own engagement with development, which is characterised as 'not being developed,' 'being developed,' or 'suffering from development.' The author notes that Janajati and Dalit women's engagements with development are 'not being developed' and they are excluded from it; moreover, even when they are 'getting developed,' for most it simply means the inclusion 'at the bottom' of the 'national developmental order.' In the most catastrophic cases of 'suffering from development,' women's traditional livelihoods have been impaired. Finally, the author examines the inclusion of Janajati and Dalit women in the process of democratisation, specifically in the context of recent constitutional reforms and identity-based electoral politics. The author concludes that the question of whether its development practice has made Nepali society more inclusive for Janajati and Dalit women is in flux.

The last two chapters critically engage with the concept of 'inclusive development' and suggest an alternative perspective. In Chapter 13, Sae Nakamura raises the fundamental question of whether the conventional logic of inclusivity can effectively deal with the real, distinct, and sometimes unavoidable differences that exist in the human condition. The author's doubt stems from the inexorable asymmetrical power relationship in every human interaction. After critically appraising arguments of inclusion and exclusion vis-à-vis ageing, such as the 'successful aging movement'—which is increasingly gaining influence with its neoliberal rhetoric—the author explores the socio-economic reality of *vädihiti nivāsa* (old age home) in Sri Lanka, where Nakamura conducted anthropological research as a volunteer staff member. *Vädihiti nivāsa* can be regarded as an example of 'exclusion' in the sense that it is a place where only the poor and elderly without familial support are compelled to spend their final days. However, Nakamura also provides more complex meanings of actual life there. The author describes how two asymmetrical relationships, one between a donor and a recipient of dāna—a donation in the form of food and other goods—and the other between a resident and floor staff, are overcome or transformed in various ways. Nakamura's argument proposing *vädihiti nivāsa* as 'a place for encounters,' where 'the contingency of life' is acknowledged and mutuality is fostered, alerts us of the mostly unconscious preoccupation with 'productivity' in the discourse regarding inclusive development.

In Chapter 14, Nivedita Menon makes a strong plea for going beyond capitalism, unsettling the contemporary discussion on inclusion, specifically in the capitalist framework. The author's argument begins with a critical survey of positions supporting cash income grants, either in the form of a Universal Basic Income (UBI) or Basic Income Grants (BIG) proposed by left-wing and neoliberal economists. According to the author, while neoliberal economists consider cash income grants as a means of replacing social welfare schemes, left-wing scholars fail to recognise this argument and presume capitalism as 'inescapable and omnipresent.' By tracing the changing land rights policies of colonial and postcolonial regimes, Menon identifies a recent move to bestow equal land rights to women (Hindu Succession Amendment Act of 1956) and entitle land rights in general as the 'long process of turning land into a commodity.' According to the author, this process is encouraged, as capitalist transformation and taxation require all forms of property to be completely alienable and transparent to the state. The author concludes with fundamental propositions that demand introspection. For example, Menon asserts that a new concept of 'work' distinct from 'labour' is required that includes any work performed by humans and non-humans with elements of self-creation and without exploitation. Menon also contends that one should pursue '*collective* forms of property and *use rights* in property,' not 'an individual-centred capitalist regime of property.'

Further remarks

The beginning of the twenty-first century has been characterised by widening disparities and social divisions across the world. We observed that the global pandemic has intensified this trend. Rather than merely creating an atmosphere of intolerance or outright hatred, social divisions have made actual violence increasingly entrenched and directed at those considered to be 'others,' as typified by the 'immigration' issues encountered in Europe. While the slogan of the Occupy Wall Street movement, 'We are the 99 percent,' was impactful in critiquing the injustice of income disparity, those within the 99 percent do not constitute a homogeneous group. As discussed in Butler's series of provocative works, while 'the precarity of life' is widely felt, precarity itself is unevenly distributed; some are entirely excluded, abandoned, and denied 'grievability' (Butler, 2004, 2009, 2015). If we borrow Ambedkar's well-known expression of 'graded inequality' that characterises the caste system, we could state that contemporary societies are in a state of 'graded inclusion.' What we need is to sharpen our discourse on the truly meaningful implication of inclusion, and discuss and create the conditions under which everyone can survive, especially when facing worsening environmental problems. In such a situation, the substance of 'development' would also need to be recalibrated. What kind of development are we going to pursue?(Gerber and Rina, 2018).

Notes

1 United Nations, *Leaving no one behind: the imperative of inclusive development, Report on the World Social Situation 2016*.www.un.org/esa/socdev/rwss/2016/full-report.pdf (accessed September 27, 2022)
2 World Economic Forum. The Inclusive Development Index 2018: Summary and Data Highlights www.weforum.org/reports/the-inclusive-development-index-2018 (accessed September 27, 2022)
3 See Saad-Filbo (2010) and Kannan (2014) for criticism of inclusive growth as understood by the World Bank and others; the latter assumes that inclusiveness is achieved once 'absolute' poverty is reduced, although they incorporated pro-poor growth arguments.
4 For a discussion on the need to strictly distinguish between 'inclusive growth' and 'inclusive development,' see van Gent (2017) and Kannan (2014).
5 The philosophy of the 12th Five-Year Plan (FY2012–FY2016) was 'Faster, More Inclusive, and Sustainable Growth.' To be precise, faster growth was supposed to be promoted through the development of economic infrastructure, inclusive growth was guided by the improvement of basic social services and the improvement of productivity in rural areas, and job creation was to be realised through both factors with the aim of sustainable growth which is attentive to the environment. This kind of policy agenda can be found and claimed in various places.
6 However, it is not that the elimination of social inequality has not been set as a goal in previous Five-Year programmes. A continuity does exist (Hirashima et al., 2011).
7 Nepal is ranked 22nd, Pakistan 47th, Bangladesh 34th, and China 26th.
8 An Oxfam report about extreme wealth distribution—India: extreme income in numbers. www.oxfam.org/en/india-extreme-inequality-numbers (accessed September 27, 2022)
9 Japanese scholars' contributions to the debate are not small. While Hirashima et al. (2011) analysed a wide range of topics in relation to the inclusive growth policy that first appeared in official Indian documents in 2006, Nawa (2017) highlighted the inclusion theme in Nepal.
10 The term 'unfavourable inclusion' is also used by Prakash (2015) to analyse the economic and sociocultural obstacles that Dalit entrepreneurs experience.

References

Ali, I. (2007). *Pro-Poor to Inclusive Growth: Asian Prescriptions*, ERD Policy Brief Series, No. 48, Manila: Asian Development Bank.

Arya, S. and A. S. Rathore eds. (2020). *Dalit Feminist Theory: A Reader*, London and New York: Routledge.

Butler, J. (2004). *Precarious Life: The Powers of Mourning and Violence*, London and New York: Verso.

Butler, J. (2009). *Frames of War: When Is Life Grievable?* London and New York: Verso.

Butler, J. (2015). *Notes Toward a Performative Theory of Assembly*, Cambridge, MA: Harvard University Press.

Centre for Equity Studies (2016). *India Exclusion Report 2015*, New Delhi: Yoda Press.

de Haan, A. (2015). "Inclusive Growth: Beyond Safety Nets?" *European Journal of Development Research*, vol. 27(4), 606–622.

Deshpande, A. (2011). *The Grammar of Caste: Economic Discrimination in Contemporary India*, New Delhi: Oxford University Press.

Deshpande, S. and U. Zacharias eds. (2013). *Beyond Inclusion: The Practice of Equal Access in Indian Higher Education*, New Delhi: Routledge.

Dréze, J. and A. Sen (2013). *An Uncertain Glory: India and Its Contradictions*, Princeton: Princeton University Press.

Gerber, J.-F. and R. S. Raina eds. (2018). *Post-Growth Thinking in India: Towards Sustainable Egalitarian Alternatives*, Hyderabad: Orient Blackswan.

Government of India (2006). *A Report: Social, Economic and Educational Status of the Muslim Community in India*, New Delhi: Cabinet Secretariat.

Harriss-White, B. et al. (2014). *Dalits and Adivasis in India's Business Economy: Three Essays and an Atlas*, Gurgaon: Three Essays Collective.

Hirashima, S., H. Oda, and Y. Tsujita (2011). "Introduction: Inclusiveness in India: A Challenging Strategy for Growth and Equality," in Hirashima, S., H. Oda, and Y. Tsujita eds., *Inclusiveness in India: A Strategy for Growth and Equality*, Hampshire: Palgrave Macmillan: 1–32.

Jeffrelot, C. (2019). "A *De Facto* Ethnic Democracy? Obliterating and Targeting the Other, Hindu Vigilantes, and the Ethno-State" in Chatterjee, A. P., T. B. Hansen, and C. Jeffrelot eds., *Majoritarian State: How Hindu Nationalism Is Changing India*, Noida: Harper Collins Publisher: 41–67.

Kannan, K. P. (2014). *Interrogating Inclusive Growth: Poverty and Inequality in India*, New Delhi: Routledge.

Kapur, D., C. B. Prasad, L. Pritchett, and D. S. Babu (2010). "Rethinking Inequality: Dalits in Uttar Pradesh in the Market Reform Era," *Economic and Political Weekly*, vol. 45(35), 39–49.

Klasen, S. (2010). *Measuring and Monitoring Inclusive Growth: Multiple Definitions, Open Questions, and Some Constructive Proposal*, ADB Sustainable Development Working Paper Series No. 12, Manila: Asian Development Bank.

Mosse, D. (2018). "Caste and Development: Contemporary Perspectives on a Structure of Discrimination and Advantage," *World Development*, vol. 110, 422–436.

Nawa, K. ed. (2017). *Taisei Tenkanki Neparu niokeru "Housetsu" no Shosou: Gensestuseiji, Shakai-jissen, Seikatsu-sekai (Aspects of "Inclusiveness" in Nepal during the Change of Regime: Discursive Politics, Social Practices, Life World)*, Tokyo: Sangen-Sha. (in Japanese).

Nevile, A. (2007). "Amartya K. Sen and Social Exclusion," *Development in Practice*, vol. 17(2), 249–255.

Okahashi, H. (2015). "Kukan Kouzou No Keisei to Hendou (Formation and Transformation of Spatial Structure)," in Okahashi, H. and K. Tomozawa eds., *Taito Suru Shin Keizai Kuukan, Gendai Indo 4 (The Emergence of New Economic Space, Contemporary India 4)*, Tokyo: University of Tokyo Press: 29–51.

Prakash, A. (2015). *Dalit Capital: State, Markets and Civil Society in Urban India*, New Delhi: Routledge.

Prasad, C. B. (2008). *Markets and Manu: Economic Reforms and Its Impact on Caste in India*, CASI Working Paper Series No. 08–01, Center for the Advanced Study of India, Philadelphia: University of Pennsylvania.

Ranieri, R. and R. A. Ramos (2013). *Inclusive Growth: Building up a Concept*, IPC-IG Working Paper, No. 104, Brasilia: International Policy Centre for Inclusive Growth.

Rawat, R. S. and K. Satyanarayana eds. (2016). *Dalit Studies*, Durham and London: Duke University Press.

Saad-Filbo, A. (2010). *Growth, Poverty and Inequality: From Washington Consensus to Inclusive Growth*, DESA Working Paper No. 100. New York: United Nations.

Sen, A. (1992). *Inequality Reexamined*, Oxford: Oxford University Press.

Sen, A. (1999). *Development as Freedom*, New York: Alfred A. Knopf.

Sen, A. (2000). *Social Exclusion: Concept, Application, and Scrutiny*, Social Development Papers No. 1, Manila: Asian Development Bank.

Shaban, A. ed. (2018). *Lives of Muslims in India: Politics, Exclusion and Violence*, 2nd edition, London: Routledge.

van Gent, S. (2017). "Beyond Buzzwords: What is Inclusive Development? Synthesis Report," https://includeplatform.net/wp-content/uploads/2017/09/Beyond-buzzwords.pdf. (accessed September 27, 2022)

PART 1

Spatial Dimensions, Labour, and Migration

1

THREE SPATIAL LAYERS OF THE INDIAN ECONOMY

Regional Disparities, Industrial Locations, and Labour Market

Kazuo Tomozawa

1 Introduction

Since the turn of the century, India has experienced rapid economic growth, emerging as the sixth-largest economy in the world behind the United States, China, Japan, Germany, and the United Kingdom. Since 2005, India's real GDP has continued to grow by more than 5% per year, except for 2008 (during the global recession). This strong economic growth has been beneficial to many people and regions. Nevertheless, has it been able to improve the living conditions of poor residents sufficiently? Has India narrowed the gap separating haves from have-nots? Has it reduced regional disparities? To contribute to discussion of these questions, economic geographers must, from the viewpoint of inclusive development, elucidate the national economic spatial system that has been emerging in India under this strong economic growth.

This chapter presents exploration of this theme, particularly addressing India's industrialisation. During Japan's higher economic growth period, industrialisation within the country accelerated the formation of a huge industrial area: the Pacific Belt. Cities in the belt were able to improve their economic conditions and gain population because of a strong inflow of workers from other areas. However, non-metropolitan regions exhibited increased economic dependence on the belt. This structural framework of the spatial system of the Japanese economy has long persisted. In India, economic growth in recent years has not necessarily been driven by industrialisation, but industrialisation is expected to play an important role in creating employment. Inclusive growth is a central idea adopted under the 11th and 12th Five-Year Plans: the 11th extending from April 2007 through March 2012 and the 12th extending from April 2012 through March 2017. Employment in the manufacturing industry has played important roles in facilitating the extension of benefits of economic growth as it ripples through society. The 'Make in India' policy proposed by the present Modi administration also aims to realise high

DOI: 10.4324/9781003304760-3

economic growth rates and expand employment opportunities by transforming India into a global manufacturing hub. Consequently, expanding employment in the manufacturing industry has been emphasised in India's policies.

However, the trend of non-regularisation or informalisation of the industrial labour force has intensified since the turn of the century (Himanshu, 2011; Barnes, 2015). Informalisation has two aspects. First, industries in India are formally divided into formal (or organised) and informal (or unorganised) sectors. The bulk of the expansion of employment in India's industrial labour market results from tiny-scale factories or workshops positioned in the informal sector. Second, non-regular employment has expanded in the formal sector (Chaubey, 2008) because non-regular and contract workers are becoming more common in modern industries (Neethi, 2008; Verma and Awasthi, 2010) such as automobile manufacturing (Barnes, 2018). Tomozawa (2017) sought to explore meaning of non-regularisation of the industrial labour market, mainly by addressing contract workers in the automobile industry. His survey was done in IMT Manesar in 2014, a large industrial estate in the National Capital Region (NCR) of Delhi. It is 32 km distant from Indira Gandhi International Airport via Gurgaon city. He found that most contract workers had come from a 'contract workers' belt' extending from Uttar Pradesh (UP) to Bihar. For further discussion, the following two research questions have been raised in this chapter. First, what spatial system of the national economy has produced the contract workers' belt? This is the main topic of this chapter. Second, for contract workers, are there any positive outcomes from entering this unstable labour market?

The framework of this study is simple but clear: three spatial layers associated with India's economy are explored: regional disparities, industrial locations, and the labour market. After describing their features, the structure that has linked these three layers is discussed. Additionally, this study specifically examines how contract workers are striving to take advantage of India's industrialisation under the given structure, based on a field survey that the author conducted in 2016.

2 First layer: regional disparities

The per capita net state domestic product (NSDP) is often used as a criterion indicating disparity in economic development between states in India. India's per capita net national income (NNI) was Rs. 103,870 in FY 2016 (at FY 2011 prices), which was accompanied by huge regional gaps. The highest per capita NSDP, Rs. 375,550, was recorded in Goa. It was 11 times the amount of the lowest: Rs. 34,409 in Bihar. Map 1.1 portrays a distribution of the per capita NSDP. The east–west and north–south lines through the Betul district of Madhya Pradesh (MP), India's geographic centre, are also drawn on this figure to illustrate the regional disparities. Comparison of north and south, except for Delhi and its neighbouring states, reveals that the value of the criterion is higher in the south. Comparison of east with the west shows that the value of the criterion is higher in the west. In this manner, north–south and east–west economic divides have appeared across India as a whole. Specifically, states of northeastern India have exhibited poor economic conditions. This lagging development of the northeast has been observed widely since the 1980s. The concept of 'BIMARU,' which expresses the poor economic conditions of Bihar, MP, Rajasthan, and UP in the mid-1980s, is well known. Because Jharkhand, Chhattisgarh, and Uttarakhand were formed by partitioning Bihar, MP, and UP, respectively, in 2000 and because Rajasthan has raised its economic position in recent years, the term BIMARU is rarely used today in India. Nevertheless, the lagging economic development of the northeast has continued to the present day, apparently indicating that some mechanism is causing it.

How are the regional disparities displayed in Map 1.1 related to India's economic growth after the turn of the century? To respond to this question, the change

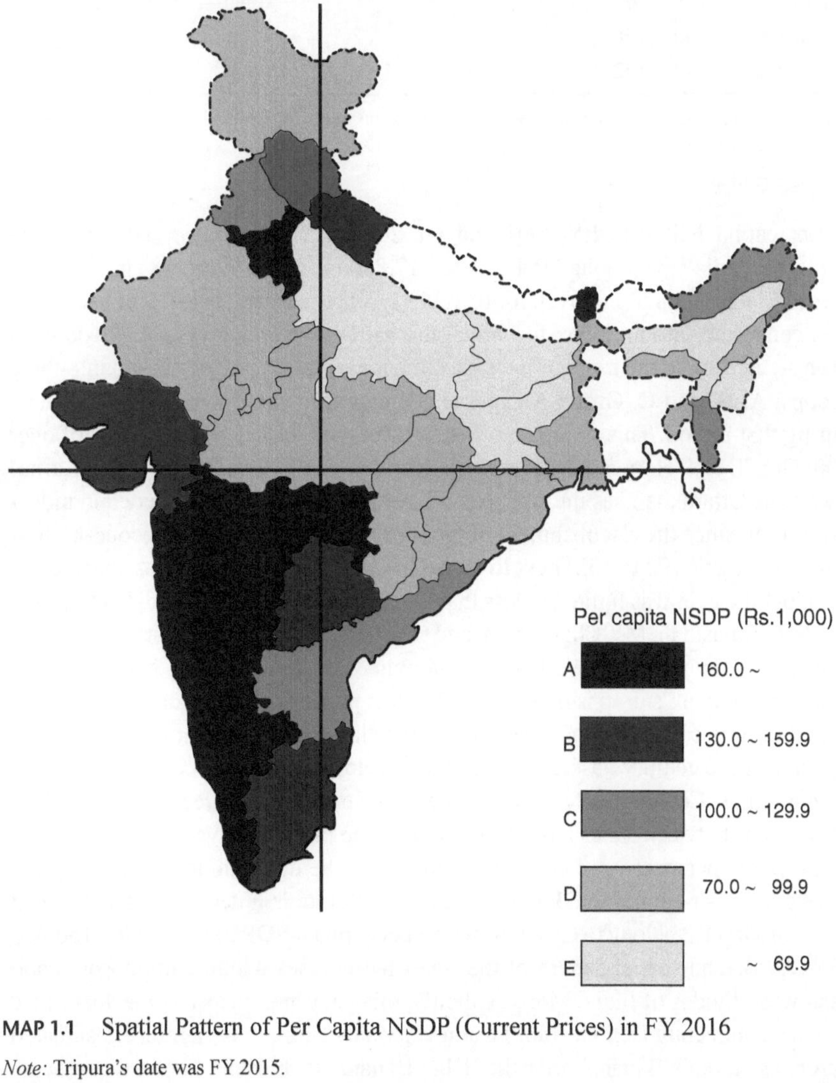

MAP 1.1 Spatial Pattern of Per Capita NSDP (Current Prices) in FY 2016

Note: Tripura's date was FY 2015.

Source: Ministry of Statistics & Programme Implementation.

TABLE 1.1 Change of Per Capita NSDP in Main Indian States

Group A			*Group B*			*Group C*		
	2001	2016		2001	2016		2001	2016
Goa	248	362	Himachal Pradesh	138	145	Punjab	163	124
Delhi	245	290	Rajasthan	80	89	West Bengal	100	80
Haryana	147	173	Madhya Pradesh	71	72	Jammu & Kashmir	84	75
Maharashtra	137	159	Chhattisgarh	70	81	Assam	74	65
Kerala	118	157	Odisha	62	69	Jharkhand	62	58
Tamil Nadu	118	144				Uttar Pradesh	55	49
Gujarat	111	151				Bihar	35	33
Karnataka	100	156						
Uttarakhand	92	152						

Note: Per capita NSDP of each state was converted into an index for which the national average was set as 100 each year.

Source: See Map 1.1.

in per capita NSDP in FY 2001 and FY 2016 in major Indian states must be explored. India's per capita NNI was Rs. 17,800 (at FY 1999 prices) in FY 2001. It rose to Rs. 103,870 in FY 2016. In Table 1.1, the per capita NSDP of each state was converted into an index for which the national average was set as 100 each year. According to the trend of the index, the main states are categorised into three groups: A, B, and C. Group A experienced a gain of more than 20 index points during that period. This group comprises states with an index in FY 2001 of over 100: Goa, Delhi, Haryana, Maharashtra, Kerala, Tamil Nadu, Gujarat, and Karnataka, plus Uttarakhand as the sole exception. Uttarakhand has succeeded in industrialisation since the establishment of the state. In fact, it shows the second-highest index point gain (92 to 152) next to Goa. Group B also experienced an index point gain, but the gain was limited to less than 20. States in this group include Himachal Pradesh, Rajasthan, MP, Chattisgarh, and Odisha. Group C includes states that have lost index points: Punjab, West Bengal, Jammu & Kashmir, Assam, Jharkhand, UP, and Bihar. Punjab's drop is noteworthy, but this paper does not address this matter. Based on this categorisation, one might infer that India's economic growth since the turn of the century has accelerated the development of the economically prosperous states. Economically weaker states have experienced weaker growth. As a result, gaps between states have widened over the past dozen years.

From the perspective of economic geography, the distribution of the states that have a high per capita NSDP with a high growth rate is noteworthy. The hatched states in Map 1.2 belong to Group A, with a per capita NSDP exceeding Rs. 150,000 (FY 2016). The spatial pattern of the states harmonises with the north–south and east–west divides of India. More explicitly, this pattern is shaped somewhat like a banana, connecting Delhi to Tamil Nadu via Maharashtra. It is therefore designated herein as 'India's Banana' after the 'Blue Banana' of Europe. For further discussion, the reason for the coexistence of the northeast and India's Banana must be

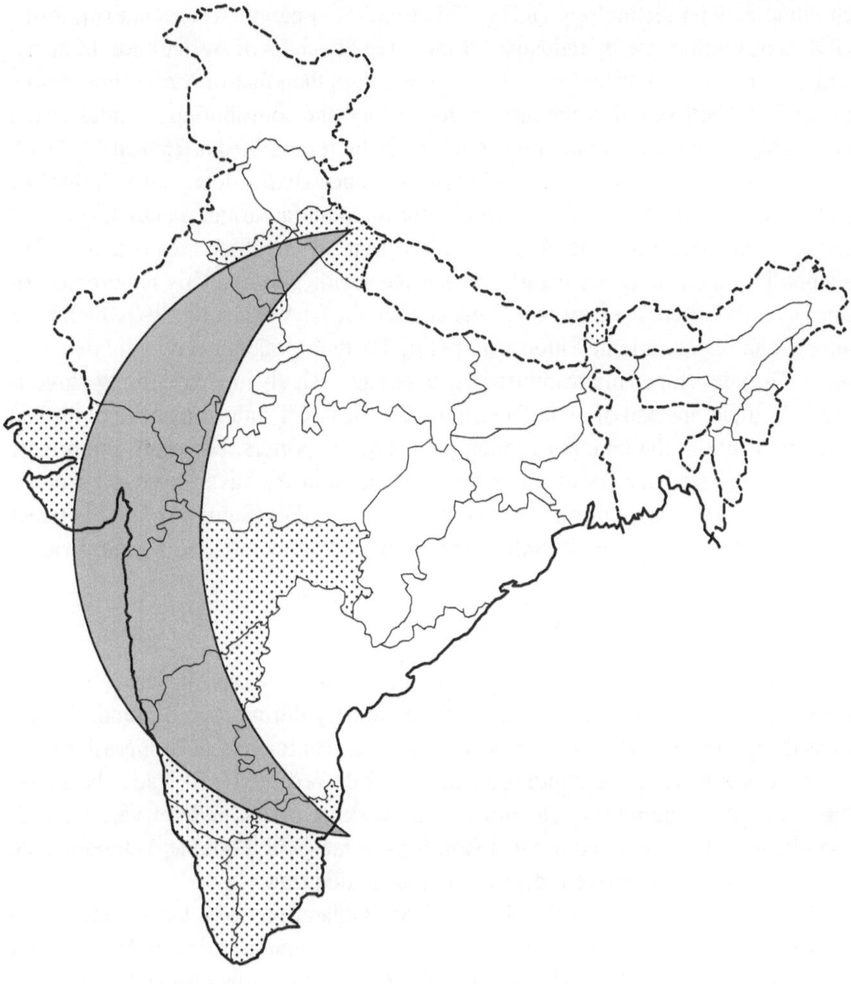

MAP 1.2 India's *Banana*

Note: Hatched states belong to Group A (in Table 1.1) with per capita NSDP exceeding Rs. 130,000 (FY 2016).

better understood. At the same time, existing relations between the two regions should be clarified. This paper is an introductory note for that purpose.

3 Second layer: industrial locations

What is the driving force of India's economy? As Japan has demonstrated, economic growth is usually driven by a rise in industrial production. In China and Southeast Asian countries, industrialisation has been driving economic growth. However, India's economic growth has been recognised as largely dependent on development of service industries, especially those of information and communications technology (ICT). This trend is apparent when confirming the GDP contribution rate by industry. Of the three divisions of Agriculture, Industry, and Services, the contribution of Industry was less than that of Agriculture before the mid-1990s. Even after the turn of the century, the contribution of Industry did not change much: it accounted for less than 30%. It remained at 26% in FY 2013. In contrast, the contribution rate of Services has been expanding yearly. It reached 59% in the same FY. The contribution rate of Manufacturing, a sub-category of Industry, has been hovering at 15–16% in recent years, which means that India's economic growth depends greatly on service sector growth. This feature constitutes a major difference between China and Southeast Asian countries, which have adopted an export-oriented industrial policy for their national economic development. They developed many industrial estates aggressively to secure foreign investment. In India, instead of manufacturing industries, ICT industries have played an important role in the national economy as major exporters. However, the private and the registered sectors of the manufacturing industry have improved productivity rapidly and have raised their contribution to GDP (Sato, 2017). This paper therefore specifically examines the location of leading manufacturing industries.

Trends in industrial locations

First, one must understand changes in industrial locations in India. Johnson (1983) briefly described the location of the industry during mixed economic systems using the *Annual Survey of Industries 1972*. He found that Maharashtra and West Bengal were in outstanding positions, followed by Tamil Nadu, based on three indicators: number of factories, total working hours, and net value added. Simultaneously, he pointed out that Bombay-Thane (with Pune) and Hooghlyside were India's representative industrial regions at that time.

After economic liberalisation in the 1990s, Gujarat gained a large share of the whole of India's industrial activities and rose to the same position as Maharashtra and Tamil Nadu by FY 2001, although West Bengal's status dropped drastically. Gujarat succeeded in industrial development because of the establishment of large-scale oil refineries. Both Gujarat's share of India's total industrial output and net value added grew to 10%. West Bengal's share of both indicators fell below 5%. West Bengal faced a decrease in industrial investment from the latter half of the 1970s to the 1980s and confronted a long-term economic depression. Even after liberalisation, it failed to attract foreign direct investment because of frequent labour disputes and the communist state government regime. Some local business groups shifted their production facilities to other states. These negative elements are thought to have severely affected the state's performance in terms of industrial activities.

In FY 2015, India's total industrial output was Rs. 68.6 trillion. The total number of persons engaged in industrial activities was 14.2 million. Both indicators display a similar spatial pattern (Map 1.3), with a high correlation coefficient between them (r=0.918). Maharashtra, Gujarat, and Tamil Nadu are situated in the top three for both indicators. The state-wise percentage composition in FY 2015 was similar to that of FY 2001. Rapid growth of India's economy after 2001 has

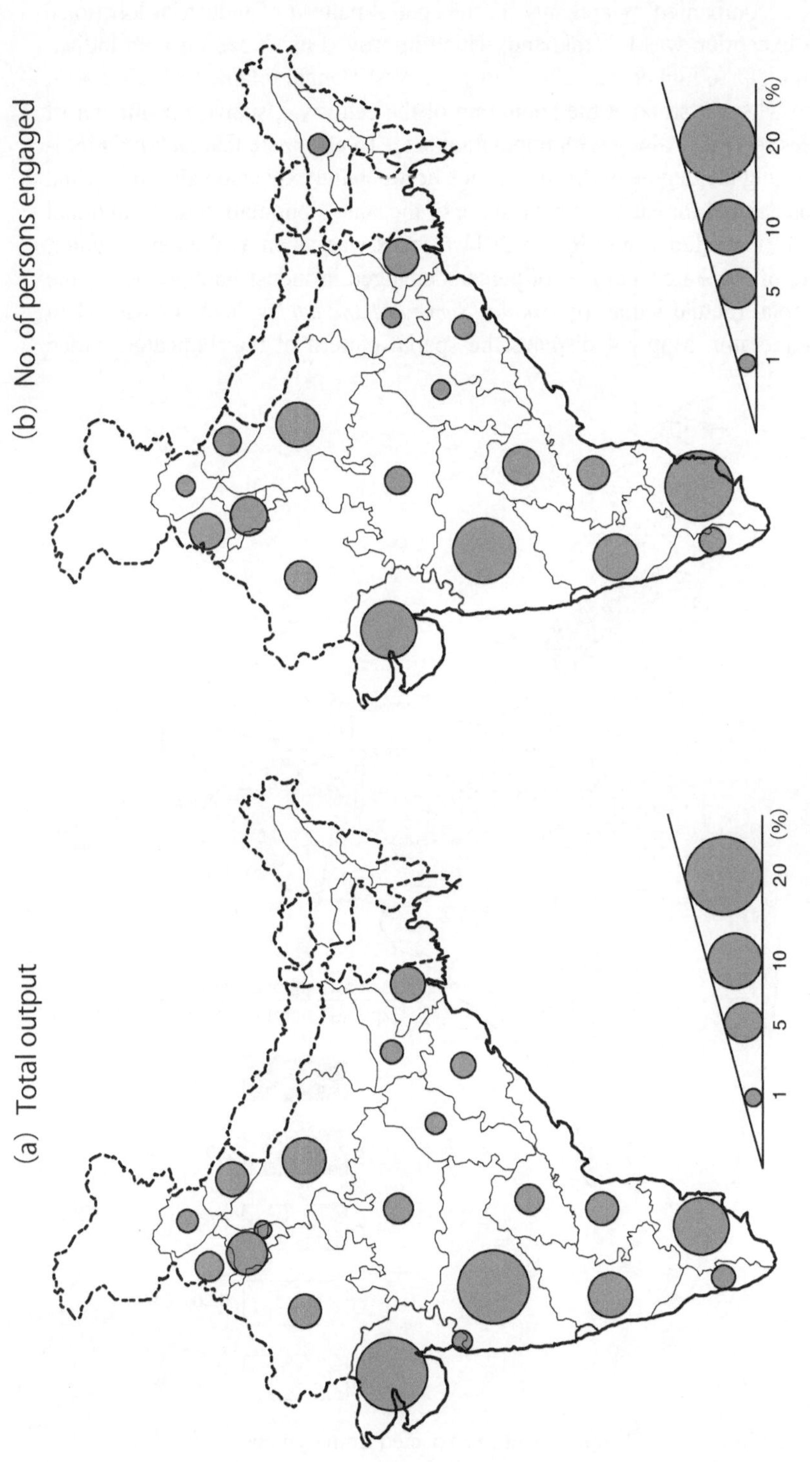

MAP 1.3 Total Industrial Output and Number of Persons Engaged

Note: Values less than 1% are not displayed.

Source: Annual Survey of Industries 2015–2016.

not been accompanied by a change in the spatial pattern of industrial locations. The sole exception was Uttarakhand, which improved its shares for both indicators from 0.5% to higher than 2%. However, West Bengal retained its low status, similar to where it stood at the beginning of the century. Usually, the number of employees increases along with population size. To eliminate this factor, an indicator denoting the degree of the divergence between the expected value and actual value was created for each state; the share of the state's population to the national population (expected value) by the 2011 Census was taken as the denominator. The share of the state's number of persons engaged in industrial activities to the national total (actual value) by *Annual Survey of Industries 2013–14* was taken as the numerator. Map 1.4 displays the spatial pattern of that indicator, which

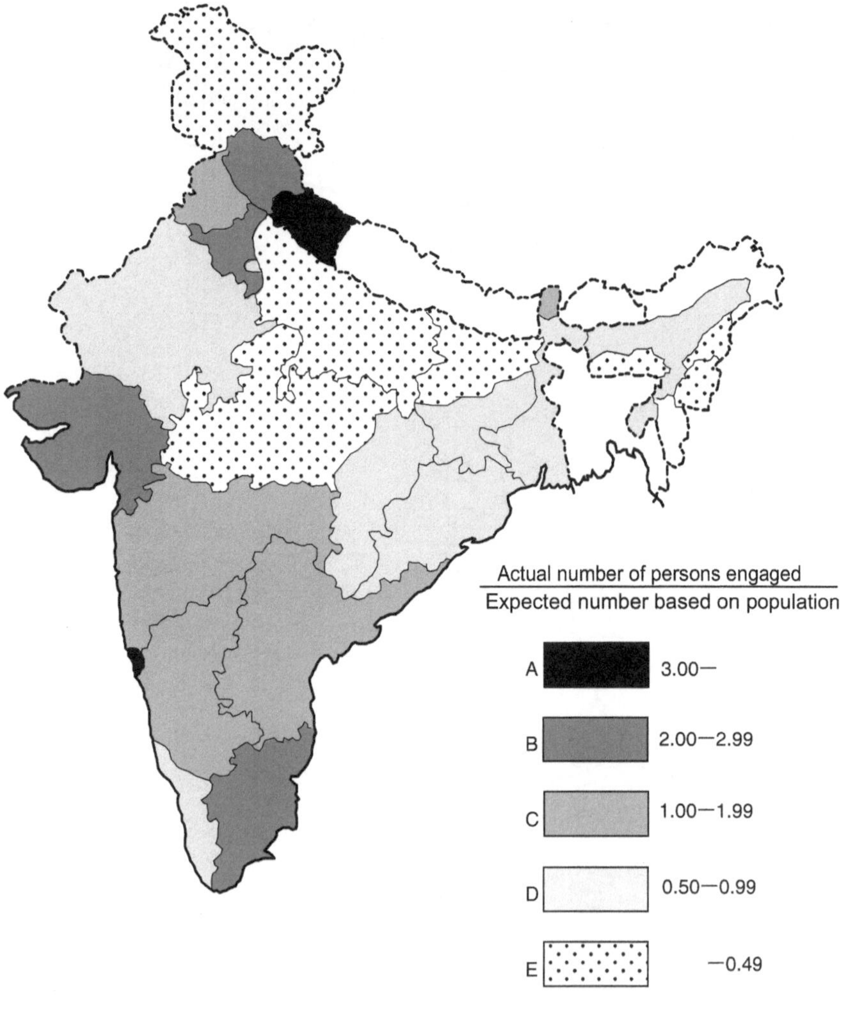

MAP 1.4 Ratio of Actual Employment to Expected Employment

Sources: Census of India and Annual Survey of Industries.

resembles the pattern for per capita NSDP. States with lower scores of these indicators are located primarily in the northeast. Particularly, Bihar's score is the lowest at 0.1, followed by UP and MP at 0.4, which means that fewer than half of the expected industrial workers work in these states. In contrast, states in India's Banana record higher scores, exceeding 1.0, except for Rajasthan. As a whole, the spatial distribution of the indicator (the population-adjusted number of industrial workers) shows a harmonic relation to that of regional disparities in India. Therefore, industrial location is probably effective for discussing economic disparities among states in India.

Industrial locations of main industries

Table 1.2 presents percentage shares of the top six Indian industries in FY 2015: food and beverages (12.7%); coke and refined petroleum products (11.4%); basic metals (11.3%); chemical and chemical products (8.2%); motor vehicles, trailers, and semi-trailers (7.1%); and textiles (5.1%). Each accounts for at least 5% of the total industrial output. Industries that process raw materials are dominant in India. The chronological change in these industries' output is also displayed in Table 1.2, as indexed with 100, representing the level in FY 2001. The index of all industries rose to 681 in FY 2015. Based on 'all,' the top six industries are divided into two groups: a higher growth group (motor vehicles, 1,231; basic metals, 897; and coke and petroleum, 810) and a lower growth group (food, chemicals, and textiles). The author has confirmed the location pattern of the higher growth group.

NIC-19: coke and refined petroleum products

An example of this industry is a petroleum refinery, which is generally located near an oilfield or at an import terminal for crude oil. About 35% of India's crude

TABLE 1.2 Top Six Industries in FY 2015

	Share (%)	*Index*
Food products and beverages	12.7	619.4
Coke and refined petroleum	11.4	809.6
Basic metals	11.3	872.9
Chemicals and chemical products	8.2	397.6
Motor vehicles, trailers, and semi-trailers	7.1	1230.6
Textiles	5.1	457.0
All	–	713.0

Notes: Share: Percentage of total industrial output.
Index: FY 2001 is 100.
Source: Annual Survey of Industries.

oil production is derived from the Mumbai High oilfield, which is 176 km off the coast of Mumbai. Some oilfields exist in Rajasthan, Gujarat, and Assam. Additionally, India imports crude oil from Persian Gulf countries. India's main oil refineries are located in Gujarat (Jamnagar and Vadinar) and Maharashtra, the top two states (Map 1.5(a)).

In India, before the liberalisation of 1991, the key oil refining industry was operated by the public sector exclusively. Even today, although more than half of production is contributed by the public sector, the private sector has been playing an important role. For example, Reliance Industries and Essar Oil have established large-scale refinery plants with state-of-the-art technology in Gujarat, endowing the state with a competitive advantage in the industry. However, this industry is not labour intensive: employment opportunities are few, especially considering the production volume. The number of jobs created by this industry, 143,000, is the least among India's top six industries. Moreover, for each company, all manufacturing processes of an oil refinery are conducted within one large plant. The division of labour with other companies is not well developed. Therefore, the direct ripple effect on the regional economy through employment and business transactions can be regarded as limited.

NIC-24: basic metals

The share of basic metals to the total industry is 6.6% in terms of employment, which is lower than that of its output: 12.4% in FY 2015. The steel industry, a typical component of the basic metals division, is divided into two categories: integrated steel plants (ISP) and mini steel plants (MSP). The former has large-scale blast furnaces for mass-producing steel products. Based on industrial location theory, ISPs tend to be set up in coalfields or in iron mining areas. India has abundant coal resources, especially in its eastern states. Chhattisgarh, Jharkhand, and Odisha account for more than 60% of the total coal production in India. Odisha, Karnataka, and Chhattisgarh are the top iron ore producers. Before liberalisation, ISPs were established in the eastern Indian states by the public sector, except for the Tata Iron and Steel Company. Subsequently, private companies such as Essar Steel and JSW Steel entered the market and have recently established ISPs in Gujarat, Maharashtra, and Karnataka.

In India, MSPs have also played an important role. They account for one-third of the total crude steel production. Whereas ISPs produce only low-carbon steel, MSPs produce both low-carbon steel and alloy steel using induction furnaces. MSPs are small and are run by the private sector. They tend to be located in metropolitan areas to meet local demand. Overall, the basic metals division displays a more scattered location pattern (Map 1.5(b)) than that of coke and refined petroleum products.

NIC-29: motor vehicles, trailers, and semi-trailers

The employment scale, 947,944 persons, for this division is 6.9% of total employment, which is a bit smaller than its share of output (7.6%) in FY 2015.

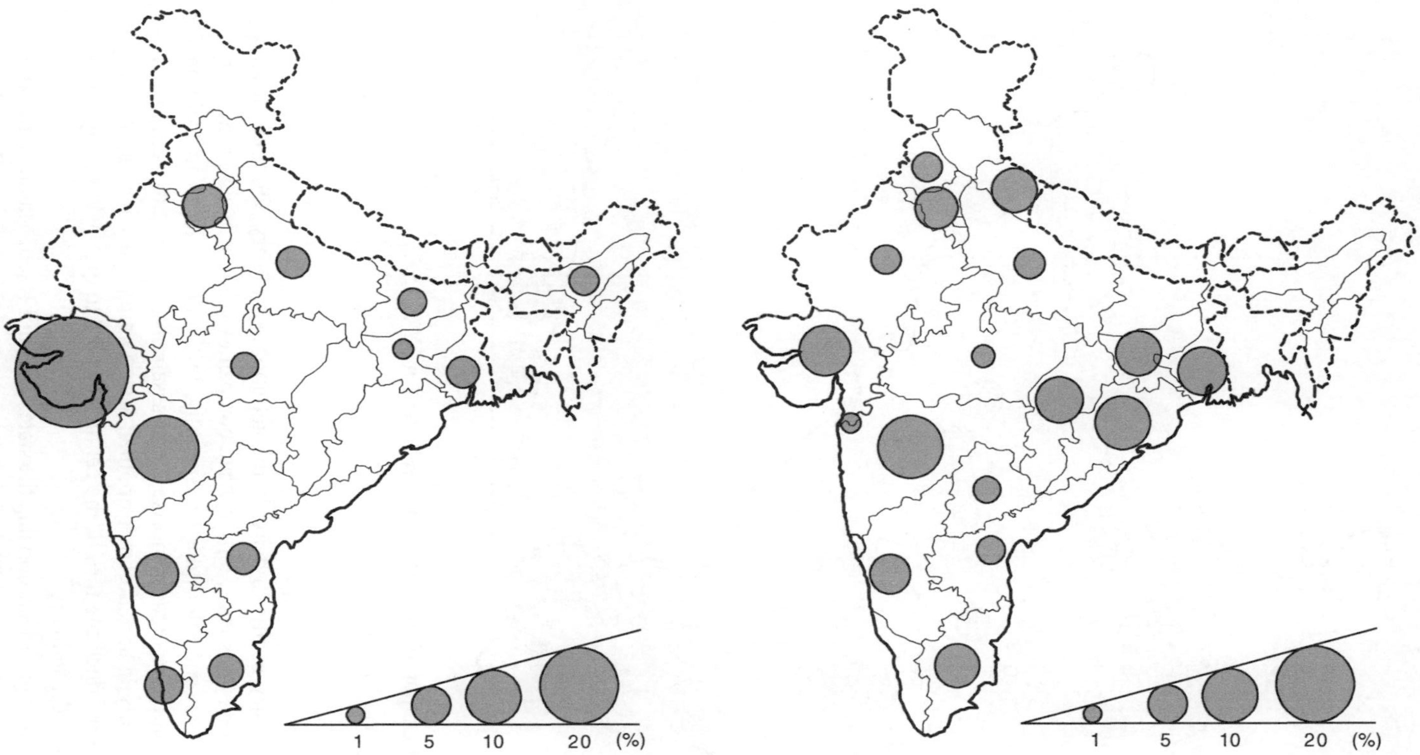

(a) Coal and refined petroleum products

(b) Basic metals

MAP 1.5 Total Output of NIC-19 (Coal and Refined Petroleum Products) and NIC-24 (Basic Metals) in FY 2015

Note: Values less than 1% are not displayed.

Source: See Table 1.2.

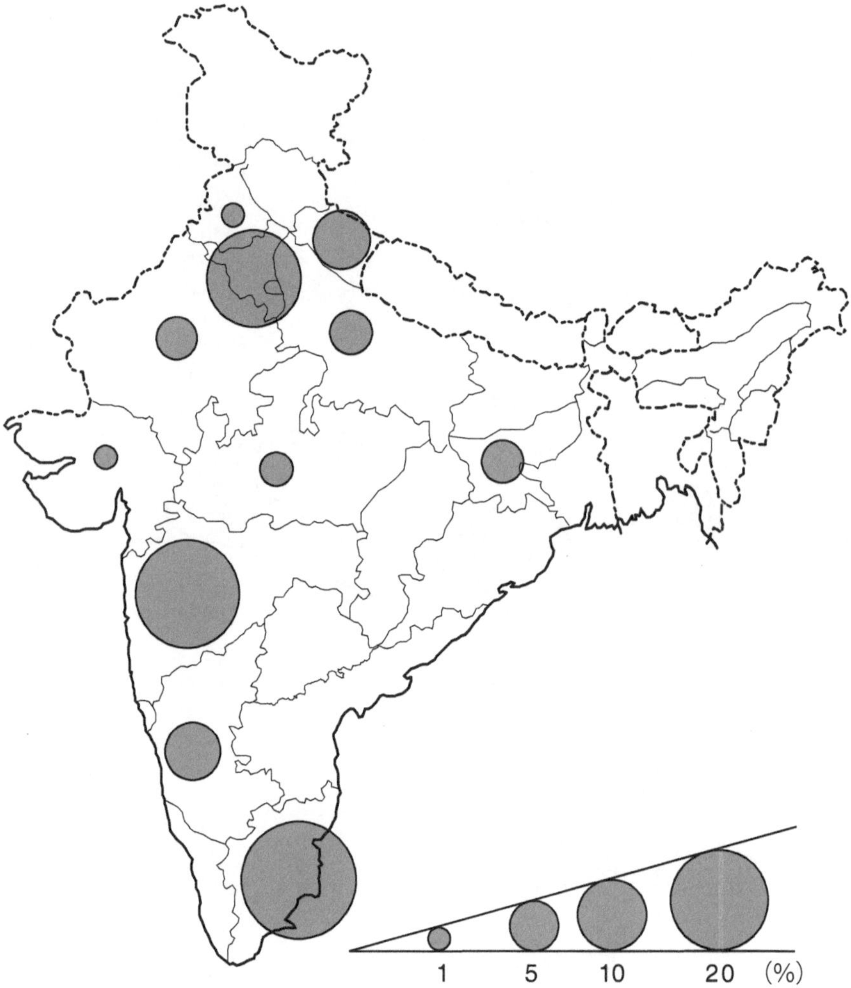

MAP 1.6 Total Output of NIC-29 (Motor Vehicles) in FY 2015

Note: Values less than 1% are not displayed.

Source: See Table 1.2.

The typical industry in this division is the automobile industry. Different from the other two main industries, only private companies are practising production activities in the automobile industry. Spatially, this industry tends to form an industrial agglomeration that comprises a car assembly plant and its component suppliers, generally in a market metropolitan area. Dramatically increased automobile production since the turn of the century has led to expansion of agglomeration related to the industry.

In India, the first group, comprising the states of Tamil Nadu, Maharashtra, and Haryana, contributes nearly 70% to the total output of this division (Map 1.6).

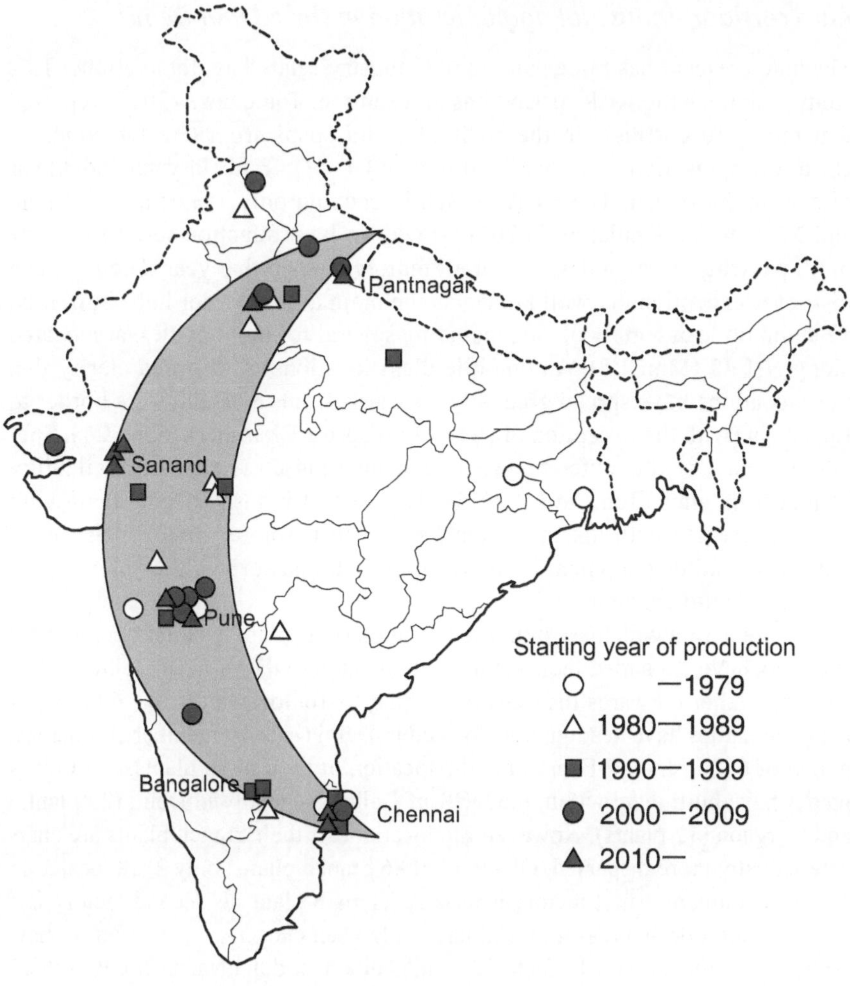

MAP 1.7 Locations of Automobile Assembly Plants Along the 'Auto Crescent'

Furthermore, Karnataka and Uttarakhand each constitute 6% or more of the total. Together they comprise the second group. These five states alone account for more than 80% of total production. Therefore, industrial production for this industry is spatially biased. More specifically, India has three major automobile production centres: NCR of Delhi, Mumbai–Pune, and Chennai–Bangalore (Map 1.7). Overall, most vehicle assemblers and component suppliers are located in the 'auto crescent': a belt that includes these three production centres (Tomozawa, 2016).

The location patterns for the first two industries discussed (coke and refined petroleum and basic metals) do not fit into 'India's Banana': only the auto crescent fits within the pattern. Therefore, this study explores spatial features of the automobile industry.

Auto corridor: Industrial agglomeration in the NCR of Delhi

The auto crescent has three automobile industry-related agglomerations. This study examines the NCR of Delhi as an example. Tomozawa (2015) reported that the 'auto corridor' in the NCR of Delhi spans from Greater Noida in UP to the areas along with national highway (NH) 48 in Haryana and Alwar district in Rajasthan. The NCR of Delhi occupied only 1% of national land and 3.8% of the population in 2011. However, its production supplied 37.9% of all passenger cars and 45.1% of all motorcycles in that year. The Gurgaon district is exceptionally well known as the main auto corridor hub. Currently, 12 automobile assembly plants, including several for motorcycles, are located along NH 48 (Map 1.8). Automobile plant locations in this area clarify that their locations have spread gradually outwards from the Delhi state border to Rajasthan (with the exception of Hero MotoCorp's Dharuhera plant, C1). Specific reasons for this outcome are land acquisition costs and the availability of industrial sites (Tomozawa, 2015). The cost of industrial land along with NH48 decreases with distance from Delhi. Furthermore, suburbanisation of industrial land development in the NCR of Delhi has driven the outer expansion of the auto corridor.

In conjunction with these trends in the automobile plant locations, component suppliers have expanded their plant locations along NH 48 from Delhi to Gurgaon and other outwards districts. According to Tomozawa (2016), 67 component companies have headquarters located in Delhi (ACMA member companies, a total of 610 in India). Examining the location of their main plants, most companies have built them within the NCR of Delhi, especially in Delhi (22 plants) and Gurgaon (12 plants). However, the locations of their branch plants are characteristically more dispersed. Of a total of 86 branch plants, only 2 are located in Delhi. A company's first factory is usually its main plant; its second factory is a branch plant. For that reason, Delhi has rarely been chosen as a location for new factories. Gurgaon, with 17 factories, and Gautam Buddha Nagar in UP, with 11 factories, are the main locations for branch plants. A strong tendency exists for the dispersion of main plants and branch plants in the suburbs. Comparing the NCR of Delhi with other locations reveals that the numbers of branch plants are approximately equal, with NCR of Delhi hosting 46 branch plants and other locations hosting 41. The major locations for branch plants outside the NCR are Pune with seven plants, and Haridwar, in the state of Uttarakhand, with five plants. Moreover, other branch plant locations are mostly confined to the auto crescent. The same spatial trend is apparent in the case of branch plant locations for companies with headquarters in Gurgaon. Consequently, two branch plant location patterns become apparent: dispersion within the NCR of Delhi and dispersion outside the NCR, that is, other agglomerations of the automobile industry in the auto crescent. This represents the dynamism of the formation of the auto crescent and the auto corridor.

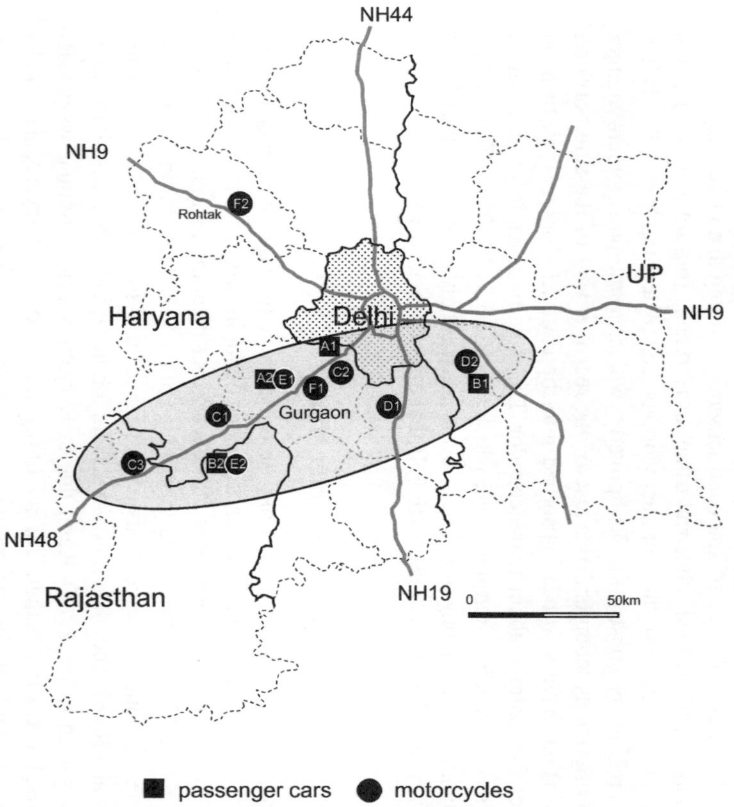

Company	Code	Start of operation
Maruti Suzuki	A1	1983
	A2	2006
Honda Cars	B1	1997
	B2	2008
Hero MotoCorp	C1	1985
	C2	1997
	C3	2014
India Yamaha	D1	
	D2	Succession from Escorts
Honda Motorcycles and Scooters	E1	2001
	E2	2011
Suzuki Motorcycle	F1	2006
	F2	2016

MAP 1.8 Locations of Automobile Assembly Plants Along the Auto Corridor

Source: Tomozawa (2015: 16).

4 Third layer: automobile industry labour market

Contract workers' belt

Moving from a discussion of plant locations, the automobile industry labour market is considered next. Tomozawa (2017) pointed out that the automobile industry in Haryana is deeply dependent on contract workers as the primary labour source for their production line. The contract ratio reached 67% in FY 2013, which was the highest in India. Two reasons can be given for the use of contract workers: coping with labour difficulties and reducing labour costs. Contract workers have no right to form labour unions, which has been recognised as an effective countermeasure for labour difficulties in Haryana, where labour disputes have frequently occurred. In addition, payments for contract workers are generally based on the state's minimum wage, which means they are compensated at a lower level than regular, permanent workers. Therefore, companies using contract workers can benefit from reduced labour costs. In Haryana, the maximum tenure for a contract worker is legally six months. That person must be given regular worker status if a company intends to use a person's labour for more than six months. However, this rule includes some loopholes: for example, some workers continue to work after six months at the same company using methods such as registration with another contractor.

Based on a 2014 survey of 254 contract workers living in a village adjacent to IMT Manesar, the largest industrial estate in Haryana, Tomozawa (2017) found that most had come from the 'contract workers' belt' extending from UP to Bihar. In this area, many households face poverty, which, in the past, forced younger men to migrate as labourers. Because of the recent advent of the auto corridor, UP and Bihar have also been absorbed into the contract workers' belt to meet demands for contract labour in the corridor. The monthly wage level for contract workers is the state's minimum wage, which was Rs. 5,342 in 2014. Their actual monthly income, including overtime allowances, was only Rs. 6,500 at the time of the survey, which remained less than half that of permanent workers.

Proactive aspects of labour market entry

Consequently, Tomozawa (2017) has described how the contract labour market entailed a negative meaning for participants stemming from its low wages and lack of job security. A survey of contract workers (including temporary workers) for the automobile industry living in a village in the IMT Manesar in 2016 found the same fundamental perceptions as described in a study reported by Tomozawa et al. (2018). They face low wages and job instability. Their actual monthly income gained to Rs. 8,000–9,500 due to Haryana states' minimum wage rise. However, it was still less than half that of regular workers. In Haryana, six months is the maximum limit for non-regular employment, which causes a high turnover of workers over a short period of time. Spatially, most of them originated from the

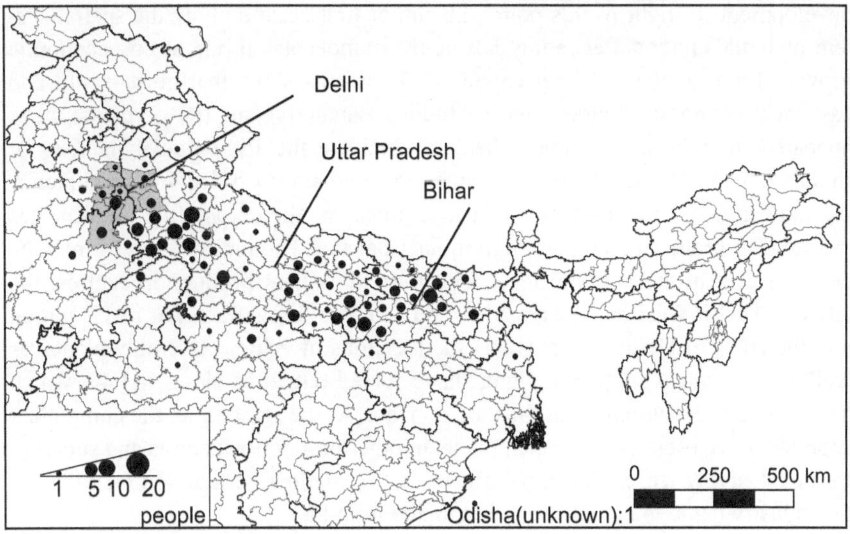

MAP 1.9 Worker Origins (2016 Survey)

Source: Tomozawa et al. (2018: 7).

areas (Map 1.9) in concordance with the contract workers' belt, which was found in the 2014 survey.

It is apparent that the workers are proactive about their economic life. They retain funds for their own expenses for the reproduction of labour power to a minimum and remit the balance to their families (parents, wives, and children) in their respective home towns. An examination of 147 workers who shared room rent (which means they are single migrant workers) reveals that 127 remit funds. The average remittance amount per month was Rs. 3,874 (median Rs. 4,000), about 40% of average take-home pay, which indicates a strong bond with workers' families back home. What are the remittances used for? The remittances are allocated to daily living expenses (selected by 116 workers), but they are also used to pay their children's and younger siblings' educational expenses (54) and for durable consumer goods (31). Other uses (42) include various investments for agriculture, medical expenses, and the purchase of medical supplies. These are regarded as expenditures that contribute to the economic and social development of their families. Entering into this industrial labour market can be regarded as a path to securing better living conditions and maximising returns from their limited income. In other words, by entering into the labour market, they are striving to derive benefits from Indian industrialisation.

5 Conclusion

The starting point of this paper describes what economic geographers can do to enhance the understanding of India's economic growth in terms of inclusive development. In light of this point, the author first clarified how the spatial system of India's national economy has evolved under its current strong economic growth. From analyses of per capita NSDP, results show that north–south and east–west economic divides, that is, India's Banana versus the northeast, have appeared in India as a whole. Then, to elucidate the formation dynamism of India's Banana, the author examined the location patterns of leading manufacturing industries. Of the top three industrial divisions, the automobile industry has the most harmonic spatial pattern in India's Banana. The industry has formed the auto crescent at the national level with three dominant production centres: the NCR of Delhi, Western Maharashtra, and Chennai–Bangalore. An investigation into the NCR of Delhi indicates that the locations of vehicle assembly plants, as well as component suppliers' plants, have spread outwards along NH 48, which has led to the development of the auto corridor. At the same time, the component suppliers have established branch plants in other production centres and sub-centres, exclusively within the auto crescent. In this manner, production facilities for the industry came to be unevenly distributed in India.

The procurement of workers by the industry has yielded quite different spatial patterns. Contract workers, who face unstable working conditions and low wages, have become dominant in the workforce. The automobile industry has created not only a middle class, which comprises permanent staff and workers, but also a working poor class consisting of contract-based labourers. Moreover, contract workers have mostly originated from one specific region, that is, the contract workers' belt extending from UP to Bihar. Younger men who live in economically weaker regions are involved in the auto crescent as a socio-economically vulnerable working class. The current supply zone of the workforce is quite distant from the auto corridor, which means the automobile industry in the NCR of Delhi has two industrial spaces: one for production and the other for labour supply. This is a typical spatial consequence of India's industrialisation. The relation between the auto crescent and the contract workers' belt seems to present possibilities of affecting the north–south, east–west divided spatial structure of India's national economy.

Regarding the formation of such a spatial structure, the centre-periphery approach provides an effective illustration: The labour market for the automobile industry uses the excessive population from low-income areas as its main working force while maintaining poor working conditions. Formation of the auto corridor is a fundamental cause of the economic prosperity in the NCR of Delhi. In contrast, the contract workers' belt is in a subordinate position to the auto corridor through the labour demand and supply system developed by industrialisation. It is noteworthy that contract workers seek to derive benefits from Indian industrialisation by entering the industrial labour market. However, this uneven inter-regional relation is regarded as a challenge that must be resolved as long as this labour system continues.

Lastly, one must devote attention to the lack of a growth pole in the northeast. For this discussion, it is necessary to confirm the current situation of Kolkata, one of the four largest cities in India, and the state of West Bengal as the city's hinterland. Regarding the automobile industry, no factory is located in West Bengal. Hindustan Motors, the oldest car company in India, had produced passenger cars in Uttarpara, near Kolkata. However, because of severe market competition after the turn of the century, the company lowered its production volume and eventually closed its factory in 2014. Tata Motors strove to establish a dedicated factory in the area for its *Nano* low-priced mini car. However, it was changed to Gujarat because of strong protests by local farmers against its construction. Moreover, according to Une (2017), who analysed foreign direct investment (FDIs) during 2000–2015 in India, West Bengal acquired only 1.4% of the total FDI. In terms of the locations of Japanese-owned companies, Une (2017) also pointed out that Kolkata accounted for only 3.9% of the total, which indicates that marked gaps exist between this city and India's other three metropolises. Kolkata and West Bengal are lagging in industrialisation and in FDI acquisition, which is closely related. The area has failed to become an engine for globalisation. In other words, the absence of a growth pole in the northeast is apparently a cause of its economic depression. Therefore, exploration of the main reason for the absence of a growth pole in the northeast is a major research topic necessitating further discussion.

Acknowledgement

The research of this chapter was realised by JSPS (Japan Society for the Promotion of Science) project fund [26257012 and 19H01384].

References

Barnes, T. (2015). *Informal Labour in Urban India: Three Cities, Three Journeys*, London: Routledge.

Barnes, T. (2018). *Making Cars in the New India: Industry, Precarity and Informality*, Cambridge: Cambridge University Press.

Chaubey, P. K. (2008). "Contractual Employment in Formal Sector: Concepts and Contemporary Structure in India," in Verma, N. M. P. and I. C. Awasthi eds., *Contractual Employment in Indian Labour Market*, New Delhi: Concept: 3–15.

Himanshu (2011). "Employment Trends in India: A Re-examination," *Economic and Political Weekly*, vol. 46(37), 43–59.

Johnson, B. L. C. (1983). *India: Resources and Development*, 2nd edition, London: Heinemann Educational Books.

Neethi, P. (2008). "Contract Work in the Organized Manufacturing Sector: A Disaggregated Analysis of Trends and Their Implications," *Indian Journal of Labour Economics*, vol. 51, 559–573.

Sato, T. (2017). "Indo sangyo hatten no kiseki to tenbou (in Japanese: Trajectory and Prospects for Industrialization in India)," in Sato, T. ed., *Indo Sangyo Hatten to Nikkeikigyo (Industrialization and Japanese Multinational Companies in India)*, Kobe: Research Institute for Economics and Business Administration, Kobe University: 3–56.

Tomozawa, K. (2015). "The Frontier of the Expanding Industrial Agglomeration in the National Capital Region of Delhi: Industrial Development of Alwar District, Rajasthan,

Especially Particularly Addressing the Japanese-exclusive Industrial Estate of Neemrana," *Journal of Urban and Regional Studies on Contemporary India*, vol. 2(1), 13–25.

Tomozawa, K. (2016). "Development and Spatial Dynamism of the Automobile Component Industry in India," *Journal of Urban and Regional Studies on Contemporary India*, vol. 3(1), 11–27.

Tomozawa, K. (2017). " 'Inclusive Development' of Employment in the Indian Automobile Industry: Have Contract-Based Workers in the State of Haryana Achieved it?" in Mio, M., K. Fujita, K. Tomozawa, and T. Awaya eds., *Structural Transformation in Globalizing South Asia: Comprehensive Area Studies for Sustainable, Inclusive and Peaceful Development (Senri Ethnological Studies 96)*, Osaka: National Museum of Ethnology: 81–95.

Tomozawa, K., L. Chen, T. Furuya, and I. Nury (2018). "Industrial Labor Market and Workers' Economic Life in the National Capital Region of Delhi: Comparative Study on the Automobile and Light Industries," *Journal of Urban and Regional Studies on Contemporary India*, vol. 5(1), 1–16.

Une, Y. (2017). "Indo niokeru nikkeikigyo no ritti tokusei (in Japanese: Location Characteristics of Japanese-owned Companies in India)," in Sato, T. ed., *Indo Sangyo Hatten to Nikkeikigyo (Industrialization and Japanese Multinational Companies in India)*, Kobe: Research Institute for Economics and Business Administration, Kobe University: 95–124.

Verma, N. M. and I. C. Awasthi eds. (2010). *Contractual Employment in India Labour Market*, New Delhi: Concept.

2

REGIONAL DIVERSITY OF WORK OPPORTUNITIES AND NEW ECONOMIC SPACE IN INDIA

Kentaro Kuwatsuka

1 Introduction

This chapter maps the spatial structure of contemporary India by mainly analysing data from the B-series of the 2011 Census of India. The selected 34 variables were aggregated to four dimensions using principal component analysis (PCA) and cluster analysis (CA) to reveal five regional types of work opportunities. This map also underscores the regional disparities of work opportunities in India, highlighting a spatial division of labour: some regions are integrated into a mega-region providing more diverse work opportunities; other regions have remained excluded from those chances. Nevertheless, the diversification of regional work opportunities suggests inclusive development with economic growth and emergence into a new economic space in India.

The following sections describe the background of this study (Section 2) and the analytical methods for extracting the spatial structure of India based on the census data (Section 3). Then the results of the PCA will be interpreted (Section 4). Districts, the spatial units for analysis and administrative division of Indian state or territory, will be classified into five types according to the CA (Section 5). The spatial structure of India as calculated using the methodology is compared to the 'regional structure of Indian economy' reported by Sato (1994). Finally, in Section 6, the spatial structure will be discussed in terms of developing a theoretical framework to describe and evaluate the formation and transformation of economic regions and their spatial divisions of labour.

2 India's economic growth and the new economic space

In light of the spatial structure of contemporary India, analyses must consider not only the regional reproduction structure that has formed historically based

DOI: 10.4324/9781003304760-4

on initial conditions such as geography, society, and culture; one must also consider the new economic space that is rapidly placing increasing pressure on regional reproduction structures. Particularly in relation to the latter, critical factors forming the spatially circular flow of the economy must be elucidated: industrial location, agglomeration, and regional economies (Okahashi, 2015a).

Regarding industrial location and agglomeration since economic liberalisation in India in the 1990s, the automotive industry has led to industrialisation processes (Tomozawa, 2008, 2016). Moreover, the country's ICT service industry, which has achieved global competitiveness (Kuwatsuka and Kitagawa, 2008; Kuwatsuka, 2013), has been used in case studies. These studies based on fieldwork have clarified the spatial division of labour and location strategies of companies aiming at securing low operational costs. Moreover, the influence of foreign capital from economically developed countries cannot be ignored; therefore, location strategies of FDI have been discussed (Une, 2018).

In addition, Chakravorty and Lall (2007) used spatial statistics methods to clarify changes that occurred in the geographical distribution of the manufacturing industry. They discussed the relation between policy externalities and industrial location. Policy effects must be considered when discussing the new economic space. For example, regional policies aimed at solving regional disparities and regional problems can define and regulate industrial locations and construction of the built environment (Okahashi, 2015a). In some cases (e.g., Kuwatsuka, 2013, 2017; Tomozawa, 2015, 2016), the location behaviour of private enterprises, including foreign capital, since India's economic liberalisation led to active expansion of their business and setting up of new locations. Simultaneously, state governments increasingly pursued policies for industrial development and job opportunity creation in their own jurisdictions. These movements can be understood from large-scale development of Special Economic Zones by state governments (Sato, 2017).

As described earlier, studies particularly addressing the location and agglomeration process of different industries have revealed that a new economic space has been appearing because of the combined actions of the government seeking to attract industry and because of the behaviour of corporations evaluating their regional policies.

However, research conducted to date has not considered the regional reproduction structure as opposed to the new economic space. Of course, the fact that the transformation of rural society and agricultural production systems has not progressed uniformly even after the 'green revolution' has been demonstrated by economic development, labour migration, and rural markets (Yanagisawa and Mizushima, 2014). Differences between types of agricultural economies and the existence of linkages with non-agricultural sectors can lead to differences in economic development among rural areas. Regarding these types, Usami et al. (2015) examined differences in the development patterns of Punjab, Tamil Nadu, and

Bihar. However, it seems that reformation of the regional reproduction structures, a process strongly affected by the expansion of the new economic space, has not been fully explored.

Regarding this issue, Sato (1994) describes the ‘regional structure of the Indian economy’ using three opposing spatial axes: inland and coastal India, eastern and western India, and southern and northern India. He then emphasised the importance of Delhi as an industrial hub occupying a strategic location for newly developed industries. Okahashi (2015a, 2015b) emphasises these spatial axes by regarding them as representative of the spatial structure of India. He assumed a ‘mega-region’ extending from Delhi to Haryana and Punjab as a core region serving as one growth pole for developing the national economy, the situation he argued would deeply intensify India’s problems with regional disparities. In light of these perspectives, the emerging of mega-region can be argued as the most important issue for understanding the causality of regional disparities and regional problems. Additionally, it can also be considered the historically organising regional reproduction structures which have been reconfigured by the strongly emerging new economic space. This process underlies India’s spatial structure transformation from the rural–urban nexus to core–periphery structure in which the mega-region plays an important role.

It is impossible to address such a broad issue in this chapter alone. This study is intended not as an exploration of the causal mechanism but rather as an exploration of the spatial structure of India grounded on a concept of the homogeneous region[1] using quantitative data. General and inclusive understanding of India’s spatial structure is necessary to extend the findings beyond those earlier studies that have examined individual industries to assess their industrial and regional development.

Spatial analyses of India based on quantitative data have already been conducted. Kurosaki and Wada (2014) explain the regional growth patterns of agricultural production systems and land-use patterns using district-level statistical data. Chakravorty and Lall (2007) clarify the location and agglomeration tendencies of the manufacturing industry not only throughout India but also specifically within metropolises such as Mumbai, Kolkata, and Chennai. However, consideration of industry on an individual basis makes it impossible to understand India’s spatial structure comprehensively because a single-industry approach ignores linkages among industries. In order to understand the spatial structure, it is necessary to get the overall picture of the industrial structure. Accordingly, Takahashi and Mizushima (2015: 69–78) strove to identify regional patterns of economic activities using cluster analysis with sub-district-wise agricultural and non-agricultural statistical data. However, they used only three variables from non-agricultural data: household industry workers, other workers, and non-workers. To clarify the transformation of the regional reproduction structure’s composition, the leading industries of the new economic space must be identified. In other words, industry data of more kinds are needed.

3 Data and analytical methods

The census data for analyses

Some limitations of using only statistical data aggregated individually exist for each industry. However, statistics related to a primary and a secondary sector regarding the three-sector model have long been accumulated and maintained. Nonetheless, a tertiary sector is the residual category of the primary and the secondary sectors. It includes non-classified industries. For this reason, statistics for the tertiary sector are limited despite their importance for elucidating the spatial structure of India. The tertiary sector contributes more to GDP than other sectors do. Moreover, the share of the services sector is increasing. Because of increasing growth and the share of the urban population in India, work opportunities related to service activities cannot be ignored when considering the inclusive growth of India's economy.

In this regard, one cannot overlook the benefits of using Indian census data for understanding the spatial structure of India: it represents the overall industrial structure. The census is compiled as several series. Of these, the B-series includes general economic tables, including the economic activity status of the population. Although it includes estimated values, it specifically presents the geographical distribution of work opportunities according to industrial classification, which includes all industries from primary through tertiary.

Spatial units and analytical methods

Using data from the Census of India, one can not only grasp work opportunities within all industries but also map their spatial distribution by industrial classification with higher spatial resolution than the state level. This higher resolution allows consideration not only of interstate problems of regional disparities but also of internal state issues.

Spatial data from the 2011 Census of India were tabulated in terms of a range of spatial units: 28 states, 7 union territories, 640 districts, and about 6,000 sub-districts. A district comprises sub-districts, which in turn are divided into rural and urban areas. In all, 601 districts can be analysed separately for rural and urban areas. Because no data exist for the remaining districts, the analysis will use spatial data aggregated by the district.

Urbanisation has led some districts to expand their built-up areas beyond their administrative borders. The National Capital Territory of Delhi (NCT), which comprises nine districts, is important, particularly. The districts of NCT are integrated into one district for data analysis. Metropolitan areas such as Mumbai and Kolkata have also spread beyond their administrative boundaries. However, compared to NCT, some districts have many rural areas in these metropolitan areas. Therefore, if contiguous districts that are developing as suburban areas were integrated into a city's district, the characteristics of these metropolitan areas would be diluted. With this point in mind and given the integration of nine districts of NCT to one district, 632 districts are used as spatial units for data analysis.

This study followed the analytical procedure adopted by Okahashi (1986) to extract the 'peripheral region' of Japan. This procedure involves two analytical steps. First, the principal dimensions of the employment structure are interpreted using the PCA. Second, the districts which have a principal component score (PC or factor score) are classified using the CA.[2] Although not a new method, it can spur novel insights related to the spatial structure of India when used with quantitative data and the concept of homogeneous regions.

Selected variables from B-series economic table of the 2011 Census of India

For the PCA, 34 variables related to work opportunities were selected. These variables can be classified roughly into four categories (Table 2.1). For the first category, two variables related to population were chosen: population density and the share of the population aged 5 years old and older among the total population.

TABLE 2.1 List of Variables for Principal Component Analysis

Variable of ID and name		*Denominator*
Population		
01	Population density (per km^2)[1]	Total population/Total area (sq km)
02	Population aged 5 or above[2]	Total population
Labour force status		
03	Workers (= Main workers + Marginal workers)	Total population
04	Main workers	Workers
05	Marginal workers	Workers
06	Female workers (= Female main workers + Female marginal workers)	Age 5 and above population
07	Female main workers	Female workers
08	Female marginal workers	Female workers
09	Marginal workers seeking or available for work	Marginal workers
10	Non-workers seeking or available for work	Non-workers
11	Non-workers	Age 5 and above population
Industrial classification[3,4]		
12	Cultivators	Main workers
13	Agricultural labourers	Main workers
14	Plantation, livestock, forestry, fishing, hunting, and allied activities	Main workers
15	Mining and quarrying	Main workers

(*Continued*)

TABLE 2.1 Continued

Variable of ID and name		*Denominator*
16	Manufacturing (HHI)	Main workers
17	Manufacturing (non-HHI)	Main workers
18	Electricity, gas, and water supply	Main workers
19	Construction	Main workers
20	Wholesale and retail trade (HHI)	Main workers
21	Wholesale and retail trade (non-HHI)	Main workers
22	Transportation and storage	Main workers
23	Accommodation and food service activities	Main workers
24	Information and communication (HHI)[5]	Main workers
25	Information and communication (non-HHI)	Main workers
26	FIRE services[6]	Main workers
27	Public administration and defence	Main workers
28	Education, human health, and social work activities	Main workers
29	Other service activities (HHI)	Main workers
30	Other service activities (non-HHI)	Main workers
Class of workers		
31	Employer	Employer/Main workers*
32	Employee	Employee/Main workers*
33	Single worker	Single worker/Main workers*
34	Family worker	Family worker/Main workers*

Note: 1) Except for population density, a numerical value of variable is percentage with a denominator defined in this table. A value is calculated by a district.
2) Each value of the industrial classification and the class of workers is based on the estimated number of the Census of India.
3) The variable of industrial classification is percentage of the number of main workers of the industry to total main workers of ID 12 to 30.
4) Values of the Class of Main Workers* are percentage of the number of main workers of the class to total number of main workers excepting cultivators (ID 12), agricultural labourers (ID 13), plantation and allied activities (ID 14), and industries classified to HHI (ID 16, 20, 24, 29).
5) HHI is short for Household Industry which is defined as an industry conducted by one or more members of the household at home or within the village in rural areas and only within the precincts of the house where the household lives in urban areas.
6) FIRE services include K—Financial and Insurance activities, L—Real Estate activities, and M—Professional, Scientific, and Technical activities.

Source: 2011 Census of India.

The second category includes nine variables pertaining to the labour force status listed in table B-1 of the census. Labour force status was distinguished between workers and non-workers depending on participation or non-participation in any economically productive activity for any length of time during the reference period, which was one-year preceding data collection. Workers who worked for more than six months during the reference period are designated as main workers. Workers who worked for fewer than six months during the period are termed as marginal workers. The number of women and total numbers for these variables were collected. The census also categorises individuals as 'non-workers' and as 'workers seeking/available for work' instead of designating them simply as unemployed.

To elucidate various industries more accurately, the third category includes 19 variables selected from table B-4, which tabulated main workers according to the National Industrial classification 2008.[3] Variables of the census included household industry[4] as well as a non-household industry. In addition, only main workers were selected. Therefore, the category of marginal workers includes persons who have returned to their home town or village from their workplace. Isolating work opportunities that arose within the district where the survey was administered is difficult. For this study, the variables are ratios of the number of main workers in one industry to the total number of main workers.

The fourth category includes four variables related to the class of employment listed in table B-21: employer, employee, single worker, and family worker. Therefore, the class of employment was aggregated to main workers in a non-household industry, with the exception of cultivators and agricultural labourers. Moreover, the variables are defined as a ratio to the number of total main workers excluding cultivators, agricultural labourers, and household industry employees. All 34 variables selected for this study are presented in Table 2.1. Except for population density, variables are converted to ratios reflecting the amount of a variable to the total number in each district.

Based on the 2011 Primary Census Abstract, the total number of main and marginal workers in India is 488 million, accounting for about 40% of the total population. Of these, 75% (363 million) are main workers. These main workers include 108 million people working in non-agricultural sectors, excluding cultivators and agricultural labourers. In addition, 93% of main workers are employed in a non-household sector, which accounts for a large share of India's work opportunities.

4 Principal dimensions of work opportunities in 2011

A geographical data matrix comprising the 632 districts as rows and the 34 variables as columns was created from tables of the 2011 Census of India. The eigenvalue, value of proportion, and cumulative proportion were obtained from the correlation coefficient matrix, which was generated from the variance–covariance matrix. Nine PCs having eigenvalues greater than 1.0 by application of the Kaiser–Guttman rule were retained. Table 2.2 presents the eigenvalues, value of proportion, and PC loading (factor loading) generated from the eigenvectors.

Plotting the eigenvalues in descending order with the scree test revealed knick-points at the fourth and the sixth principal components. The cumulative proportion of variances from the first to fourth principal components explains 59.2% of the total variation of the 34 selected variables. That from the first to sixth principal components explains 68.8% of the total variation. To classify the regional types of work opportunities using cluster analysis, the first to fourth principal components

TABLE 2.2 Distribution of Principal Component Loading

	Variable of ID and name	*Average of value*	*PC1*	*PC2*	*PC3*	*PC4*	*PC5*	*PC6*	*PC7*	*PC8*	*PC9*
01	Population density (per km2)	722.34	0.45				0.27		0.53	−0.36	
02	Population aged 5 or above	90.42	0.46	0.42	0.28	0.26		−0.27	−0.23		
03	Workers	45.65	-0.61	0.69			0.27				
04	Main workers	33.33		0.71	0.57						
05	Marginal workers	12.31	−0.50		−0.58		0.56				
06	Female workers	31.55	−0.70	0.61			0.29				
07	Female main workers	18.11	−0.42	0.71	0.39			−0.21			
08	Female marginal workers	13.45	−0.60		−0.46		0.53			−0.21	
09	Marginal workers seeking or available for work	43.59		−0.35	−0.55	0.35	0.22	−0.23			−0.28
10	Non−workers seeking or available for work	8.27	0.38		−0.61	0.28		−0.45			
11	Non−workers	58.71	0.54	−0.73			−0.26				
12	Cultivators	32.78	−0.77			−0.34				−0.25	
13	Agricultural labourers	21.16	−0.38	−0.38	0.38	0.38			0.26	0.32	−0.21
14	Plantation, livestock, forestry, fishing, hunting, and allied activities	2.76	0.22			0.25	−0.43			−0.23	0.43
15	Mining and quarrying	0.58				0.29	0.26	0.49		0.32	
16	Manufacturing (HHI)	2.27		−0.29		0.20	0.26	−0.39	−0.27	0.23	0.46
17	Manufacturing (non−HHI)	6.19	0.57		0.34						0.23
18	Electricity, gas, and water supply	0.72		0.41	−0.43	−0.28	−0.21				
19	Construction	5.30	0.65	0.25	−0.24						
20	Wholesale and retail trade (HHI)	0.02	0.50				0.29		−0.59		−0.22

21	Wholesale and retail trade (non–HHI)	6.71	0.86							−0.22	
22	Transportation and storage	3.44	0.83			0.24					
23	Accommodation and food service activities	0.88	0.63	0.39		0.28					
24	Information and communication (HHI)	0.01	0.56			−0.25	0.40	−0.20	−0.27		−0.23
25	Information and communication (non–HHI)	0.43	0.67	0.29			0.29		0.24		
26	FIRE services	1.11	0.87				0.24				
27	Public administration and defence	5.27	0.38	0.29	−0.47	−0.39					
28	Education, human health, and social work activities	5.01	0.43	0.35	−0.66						
29	Other service activities (HHI)	0.73		−0.63		−0.45		−0.25		0.24	0.28
30	Other service activities (non–HHI)	4.62	0.71	−0.25		−0.24	0.22				
31	Employer	7.50		−0.36	0.55	−0.20		0.35			
32	Employee	60.49	0.22	0.77		−0.28				0.36	
33	Single worker	24.97		−0.63		0.54				−0.31	
34	Family worker	7.04	−0.38	−0.55		−0.27				−0.29	0.26
Eigenvalue			8.82	5.65	3.56	2.10	1.91	1.35	1.22	1.14	1.03
Contribution ratio (%)			26.0	16.6	10.5	6.2	5.6	4.0	3.6	3.4	3.0
Cumulative contribution ratio (%)			26.0	42.6	53.0	59.2	64.8	68.8	72.4	75.8	78.8

Note: Printed value of principal component loading is 0.20 and above. The procomp function of R is applied.

Source: 2011 Census of India, Tables A–1, B–1, B–4, B–21, and C–14.

were selected because the effects of PCs having a small eigenvalue were excluded from the results of the analysis. This is also to avoid evaluating the major components' PC scores to be equivalent to the minor components' PC scores when classifying the regional types. Furthermore, the PC scores of 632 districts were standardised (mean = 0, standard deviation = 1), interpreted, and mapped.

The four principal components derived from the previously described procedures were (1) diverse work opportunities in metropolitan regions, (2) government-related work opportunities, (3) stable work opportunities in the agricultural and manufacturing sectors, and (4) fewer optional and unstable work opportunities in rural areas. The following subsection presents an interpretation of the features of four PCs based on certain variables that had large absolute values of the PC loading and spatial distribution of the PC score.

First Principal Component: diverse work opportunities in metropolitan regions

This PC explains 26.0% of the total variation among the selected 34 variables. Focusing on the PC loading, the value of *Finance and insurance, real estate, and professional, scientific, and technical* (hereinafter called *FIRE*) services is the greatest among the 34 variables, followed by the *Wholesale and Retail Trade* (*non-HHI*) and *Transportation and Storage*. Loading values of *Other Service Activities* (*non-HHI*), including unclassifiable activities, and the *Information and Communication* (*non-HHI*), including IT services, which lead India's 'service exports,' are also large. The first PC also includes an intermediate positive correlation with population density as well as a strong negative correlation with *Cultivators*, who are individuals engaged in cultivation of land, whether owned or held, and a weak negative correlation with *Agricultural labourers*, who work on another person's land for money wages. These findings indicate that the first PC represents work opportunities in industries located in cities.

The first PC reveals distinctive features of work opportunities only established in metropolises rather than in cities in general. However, this PC indicates employment opportunities in industries established in large cities, rather than characteristics commonly found in urban areas, because strong or weak positive correlations are found not only with *FIRE Service*s and *Information and Communication* (*non-HHI*) but also with *Wholesale and Retail Trade* (*non-HHI*) and *Accommodation and Food Service Activities*, which are established according to population size.

The Gini index is useful for considering the regional disparity of work opportunities. It is based on the difference between the Lorenz curve of each industry and the observed cumulative total population distribution. The *Wholesale and Retail Trade* (*non-HHI*) has a Gini index value of 0.12. *Accommodation and Food Service Activities* has a Gini value of 0.09. These lower values indicate that it is distributed according to population. In contrast, the higher Gini index values for *FIRE Services* (0.21) and *Information and Communication* Services (*non-HHI*)

TABLE 2.3 Gini Index by Industry

Variable of ID and industry		*Gini index*[1]
12	Cultivators	0.15
13	Agricultural labourers	0.01
14	Plantation, livestock, forestry, fishing, hunting, and allied activities	0.21
15	Mining and quarrying	0.17
16	Manufacturing (HHI)	0.09
17	Manufacturing (non-HHI)	0.21
18	Electricity, gas, and water supply	0.06
19	Construction	0.05
20	Wholesale and retail trade (HHI)	0.07
21	Wholesale and retail trade (non-HHI)	0.12
22	Transportation and storage	0.11
23	Accommodation and food service activities	0.09
24	Information and communication (HHI)	0.22
25	Information and communication (non-HHI)	0.38
26	FIRE services[2]	0.21
27	Public administration and defence	0.11
28	Education, human health, and social work activities	0.01
29	Other service activities (HHI)	0.08
30	Other service activities (non-HHI)	0.11
Main workers (Total from ID 12 to ID 30)[3]		0.01

Note: 1) The Gini index of each variable is calculated with geographical distribution of total population as referential standard.
2) FIRE services are Financial and insurance, Real estate, and Professional, scientific, and technical.
3) Gini index of 'Main Workers' is the total number of industries from ID 12 to ID 30.

Source: 2011 Census of India, Tables A-1 and B4.

(0.38) show that these industries have regional disparities and concentrations (Table 2.3).

In other words, the *Wholesale and Retail Trade* industry is located not only in large cities but also in small- and medium-sized cities. However, because of their tendency of employing higher-education graduates, the *FIRE Services* and *Information and Communication Services* are generally located within cities having a sufficient labour pool of graduates, that is, metropolises. In addition, this PC has a positive correlation with *Manufacturing* (*non-HHI*) *and Construction.* Therefore, the first PC is interpreted as having diverse work opportunities in India's metropolises.

Some interesting variables are related to unemployment, such as ID 9 and ID 10 in Table 2.2, denoting persons seeking work or who are available for work. Regarding these variables, no correlation was found with *Marginal Workers Seeking or Available for Work*, but a weak positive correlation was found with *Non-Workers Seeking or Available for Work.* Consequently, the first PC suggests that non-workers tend to seek new employment opportunities in the metropolises,

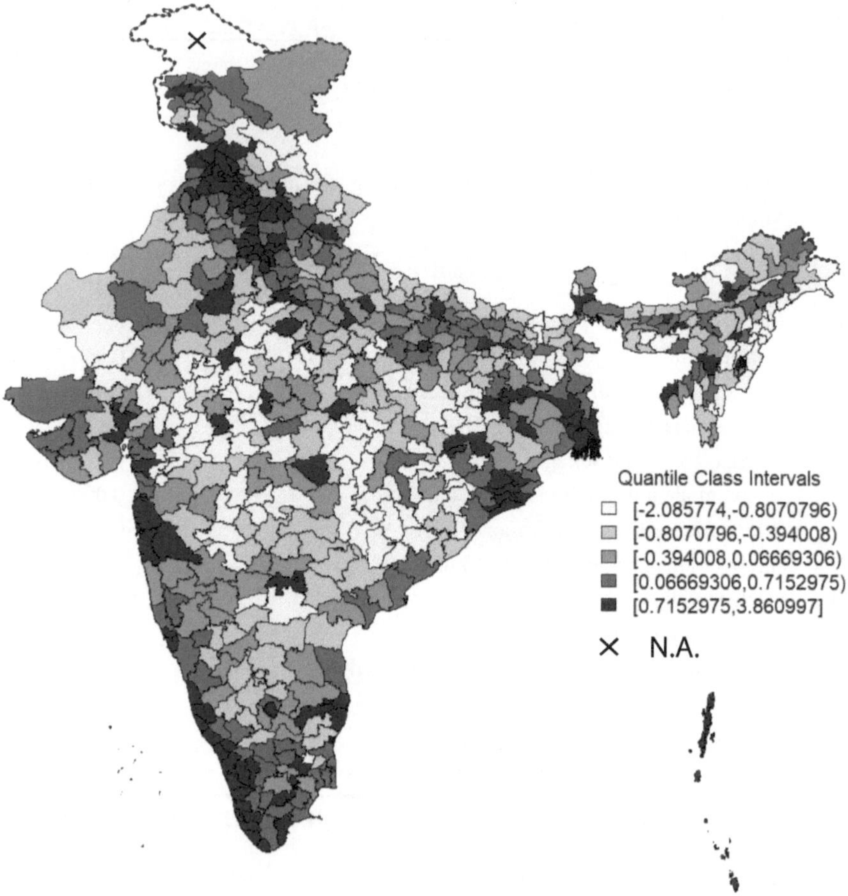

MAP 2.1 Distribution of the First PC Score

Source: 2011 Census of India, Tables A-1, B-1, B-4, B-21, and C-14 (Kuwatsuka, 2018: 101).

which offer diverse work opportunities. Non-workers include women and children who have never worked in the past year. This finding suggests that many young people seeking work opportunities do so in the metropolises.

Map 2.1 presents the district-wise distribution of the PC score. The districts with high scores are not only metropolises such as Kolkata, Hyderabad, Bangalore, and Chennai but also state capitals and cities equivalent to a capital. Aside from this, it is apparent that the mass of districts having higher scores is located in northern India, where Okahashi (2015a) assumed the emergence of a mega-region spreading from Delhi to Haryana and Punjab.

Second Principal Component: government-related work opportunities

This PC explains 16.6% of the total variation. It has a strong positive correlation with *Main Workers*, especially *Female Main Workers*. Looking at the class of workers, a strong positive correlation with *Employee* is also apparent. The second PC has an intermediate negative correlation with *Single Workers* and *Family Workers* and a weak negative correlation with *Marginal Workers Seeking or Available for Work*. Because the *Employee* in this analysis is *Main Workers*, it can be inferred that the second PC represents stable work opportunities.

Specifically examining main workers by industrial classification, the second PC has positive correlation with several industries. It is noteworthy that these are not the industries oriented to metropolises in the first PC. Positive correlations having PC loading of 0.30 and greater values are shown by three industrial sectors: (1) *Electricity, Gas, and Water Supply*, (2) *Accommodation and Food Service Activities*, and (3) *Education, Human Health, and Social Work Activities*. These industries tend to locate according to population size. The Gini index of *Electricity, Gas, and Water Supply* is 0.06, which indicates that its spread is proportional to the population distribution. Except for *Accommodation and Food Service Activities*, these sectors have had strong relations with governments. For that reason, work opportunities in them are created through the public sector. In addition, an intermediate negative correlation exists with *Other Service Activities (HHI)*, including miscellaneous and small service industries, along with weaker negative correlations with *Agricultural Labourers* and *Manufacturing (HHI)*. These findings indicate that the public sector compensates for poor work opportunities in agriculture and household industries. Therefore, the second PC represents government-related work opportunities.

Incidentally, *Non-Workers* has a strong negative correlation with this PC. At first glance, this also seems to indicate that good work opportunities are being created in the public sector. However, considering the distribution of the PC score shown in Map 2.2, it can in fact be regarded as reflecting the influence of out-migration. For this reason, high-scoring districts have a notable outflow of migrant workers, particularly from mountain regions such as Himachal Pradesh, Uttarakhand in northern India, and the states in northeastern India to India's metropolises and from southern India such as Kerala to oil-producing Middle Eastern countries. The population growth ratio of districts having a higher score was examined further by the aggregating ratio of natural and social increases during 2001–2011 based on Table A-2 of the Census of India. The results indicated that many districts have a lower ratio than the Indian average, a finding partly attributable to the declining population in those areas.

The weak negative correlation with *Marginal Workers Seeking or Available for Work* as well as *Non-Workers* indicates that international outflow migration for work opportunities is occurring actively. In contrast, where work opportunities are limited, and outward migration is absent, marginal workers seek opportunities within their district or become non-workers who opt to remain in the district. In these cases, these two variables will have a positive correlation with this PC. Therefore, the variables were found to be negative. One can conclude that marginal workers and non-workers do not remain in their districts but that they instead move to other districts for work opportunities.

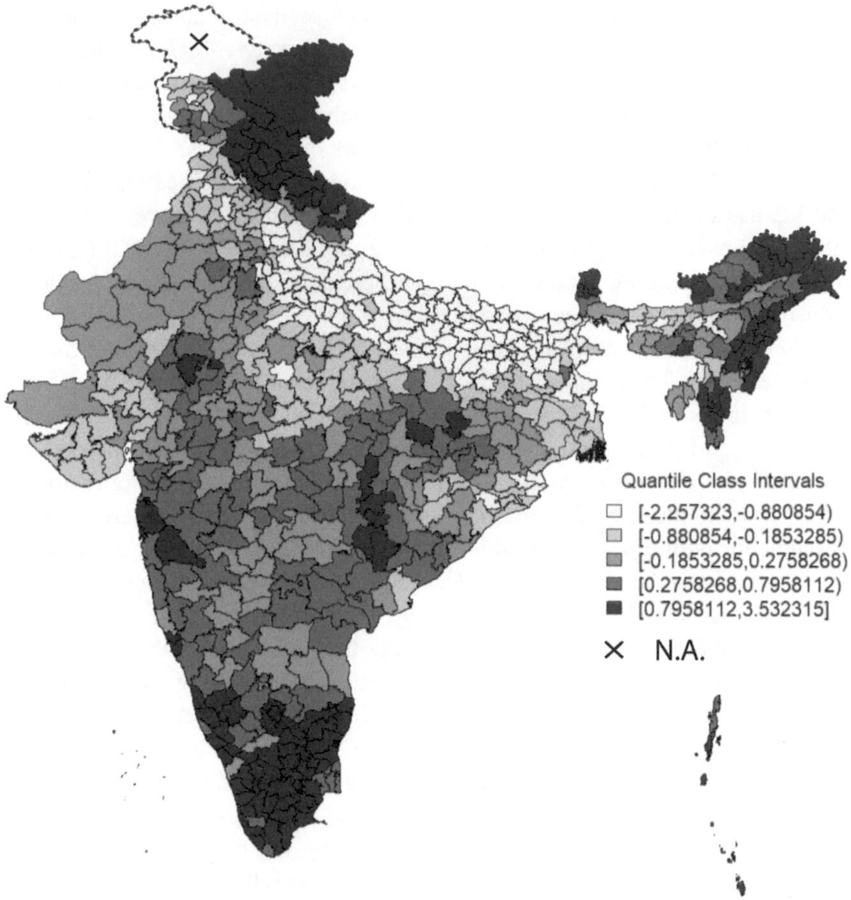

MAP 2.2 Distribution of the Second PC Score

Source: 2011 Census of India, Tables A-1, B-1, B-4, B-21, and C-14 (Kuwatsuka, 2018: 102).

Districts having a low principal component score are distributed from Bihar to the western part of Uttar Pradesh. These areas tend to be densely populated and exhibit high illiteracy rates, reflecting regional difficulties (Sato, 1994). Although work opportunities exist in agricultural and household industries, these districts' low principal component score reflects limited work opportunities and a high unemployment rate that has not been sufficiently alleviated by public sector employment or other opportunities.

In terms of these regional difficulties, Usami (2014) discussed limited work opportunities in non-agricultural sectors of rural areas and described how active outflow migration of the labour force to other states could be inferred. However, he also points out that migrant workers would return to their home villages or towns if they failed to find employment at their destination. As a result, a large 'reserve army of migrant workers' formed in these areas. These districts' low PC scores are closely related to such economic difficulties.

Third Principal Component: stable work opportunities in the agricultural and manufacturing sectors

This PC explains 10.5% of the total variation. Intermediate positive correlations are found with *Main Workers* and *Employer* and weak positive correlations with *Female Main Workers*. The PC strongly reflects the existence of self-employed persons and company organisations. In addition, intermediate negative correlations were found with *Marginal Workers* and *Non-Workers* of *Seeking or Available for Work*. These results indicate that the third PC represents good work opportunities in an organised sector.

Specifically emphasising main workers by industrial classification, this PC has a weak positive correlation with *Agricultural Labourers* and *Manufacturing* (*non-HHI*). These industries contribute to creating stable work opportunities.

Negative correlations were found with *Education, Human Health, and Social Work Activities* and *Electricity, Gas, and Water Supply*. The Gini index values of these industries are low, especially that of *Education, Human Health, and Social Work Activities*, which is 0.01. This low score reflects the fact that this industry provides basic services and is therefore distributed evenly along with the population. Given this situation, lower employment rates in other industries make the employment rate in this industry higher by comparison. In contrast, if an industry that is distributed unevenly has a high value of Gini index, then evenly distributed industries with a Gini index value will get a small share of a district's employment rate. This scenario indicates that basic service industries have less interpretability, but agriculture and manufacturing industries serve an important role in the third PC.

At first glance, the third PC appears to have symmetry with the second PC. That is to say, if the PC score of the third PC is low, then the public sector compensates by offering work opportunities outside the leading industries. However, it is premised that no correlation or symmetrical features exist between PCs within the procedure of PCA. Accordingly, a dimensional difference exists between the PCs.

It is important that the variable *Non-Workers Seeking or Available for Work* shows an intermediate negative correlation with this PC. If the principal component score is low, then the greater the importance of basic services becomes and the larger the value of the variable becomes. Those characteristics indicate that non-workers remain in their districts to look for work without outflow of migrants even when leading industries are not developed, and work opportunities are limited. In contrast, a smaller value of the variable is associated with a larger value of the variables of *Agriculture Labour* and *Manufacturing*. This case varies greatly from the second PC in that leading industries such as agriculture and

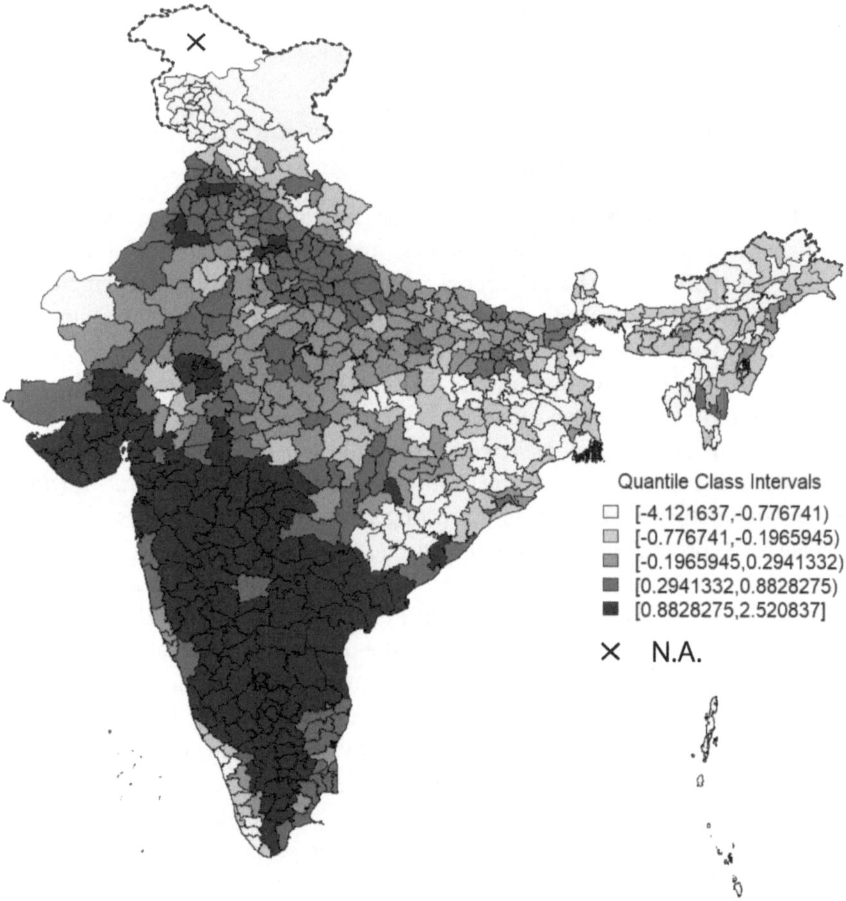

MAP 2.3 Distribution of the Third PC Score

Source: 2011 Census of India, Tables A-1, B-1, B-4, B-21, and C-14 (Kuwatsuka, 2018: 103).

manufacturing are present. Therefore, the third PC reflects stable work opportunities in the agricultural and manufacturing sectors.

Map 2.3 presents a distribution of this principal component score. High-scoring districts are spread across Gujarat and Maharashtra in western India and three states excluding Kerala in southern India. Low-scoring districts offering limited work opportunities are distributed in the mountain regions of northern India, northeastern India, West Bengal, Jharkhand, and Odisha.

It is worth noting that districts having high scores can be found around the Delhi metropolitan area and Ludhiana in Punjab. As Okahashi (2015a) indicated that Punjab is home to manufacturing industries related to agricultural production. Sugimoto (2004) discussed farming in Punjab using agricultural machineries such as tractors and harvesters. The positive correlation between the third PC and

Agricultural Labour and *Manufacturing* industry might indicate the development of mutual inter-industrial linkages.

Fourth Principal Component: less optional and unstable work opportunities in rural areas

This PC explains 6.2% of the total variation. The variable with the highest value is *Single Worker*. This type of worker is not integrated into an organised sector and has an intermediate positive correlation. From this, the fourth PC seems to indicate a situation in which limited work opportunities are available in the corporate organisation and public sectors. In addition, the fourth PC has a weak positive correlation with the variable *Marginal Workers Seeking or Available for Work*. Consequently, this PC shows limited work opportunities for marginal workers seeking work.

Regarding industrial classification, although a weak positive correlation was found with *Agricultural Labours* who provide only their own labour force, a weak negative correlation was found with *Cultivators* who cultivated land irrespective of whether leased or owned personally. This PC shows the contrast between these two types of workers. Furthermore, *Mining and Quarrying* has a weak positive correlation with the PC. However, this variable differs from the third PC and shows features that make it difficult to infer inter-industrial linkages between agricultural and other industries. *Other Service Activities* (*HHI*) has an intermediate negative correlation and *Public Administration and Defence* has a weak negative correlation. Based on these indications, the fourth PC can be interpreted as indicating the feature of rural areas that have work opportunities only in agriculture.

A map of this PC score (Map 2.4) shows that high-scoring districts are distributed in West Bengal, Odisha, Andhra Pradesh, and Kerala. These districts also have a high value of the rate of *Marginal Workers Seeking or Available for Work*. It can be concluded that the fourth PC shows fewer optional and unstable work opportunities in rural areas.

5 Classification and five types of work opportunities

Work opportunities of five types are classified using CA based on the PC score with the PCA for 632 districts. In the CA, four PCs that explain the cumulative proportion of 59.2% of the total variation are selected; PCs that have a small eigenvalue are not selected. This choice reflects the fact that if the CA is processed using the PCs, it will treat PCs with small and large eigenvalues identically. In that case, the principal component score of a PC having a small eigenvalue will be overvalued.

The procedure for the CA is the following. First, for hierarchical clustering computation, the standardised PC scores are converted into a distance matrix

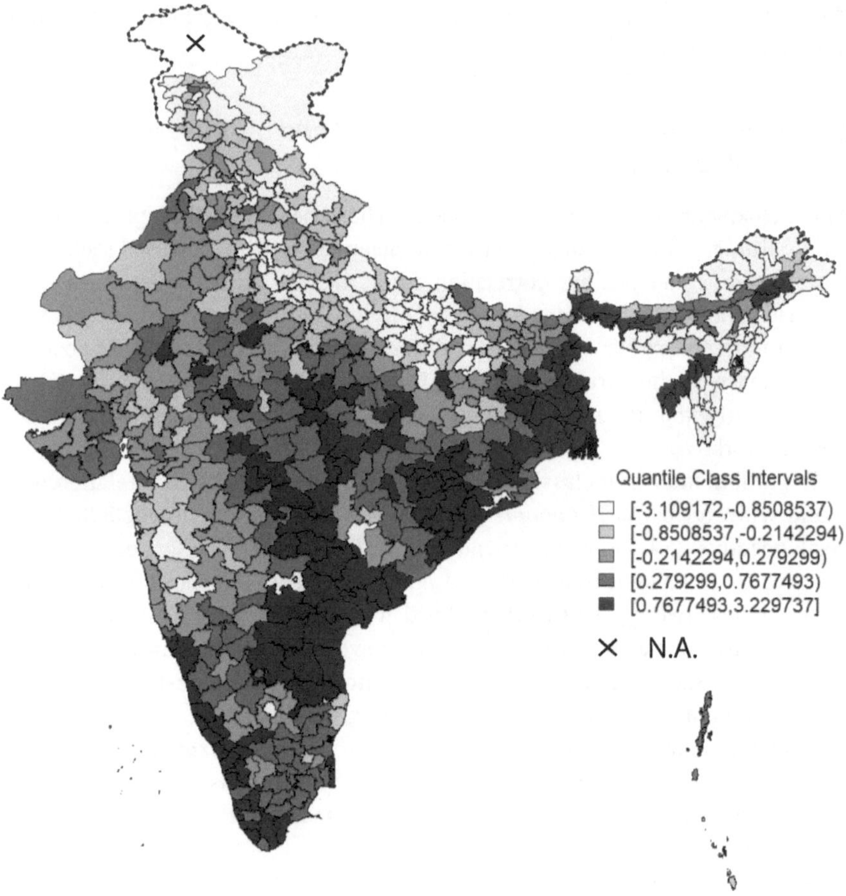

MAP 2.4 Distribution of the Fourth PC Score

Source: 2011 Census of India, Tables A-1, B-1, B-4, B-21, and C-14 (Kuwatsuka, 2018: 104).

based on the Euclidean distance. Then, to obtain the dendrogram depicted in Figure 2.1, a Cophenetic matrix was calculated using Ward's method or minimum variance method for hierarchical clustering. As the figure shows, the largest gap was found between the heights classifying 632 districts into five types. Because of this gap, the five classified types were selected and were designated, respectively, as Type I through Type V. Type I is most different from the other four types. Type III makes a cluster at the earliest stage, with a height of 9.6. It is similar to Type II and Type V.

Figure 2.2 presents PC scores recalculated for each type as a result of the CA and displays them as boxplots. The heavy line in the boxplots denotes the median PC score value. The first quartile score is on the lower side of the boxes. The third quartile score is on the upper side. For consideration of the features of

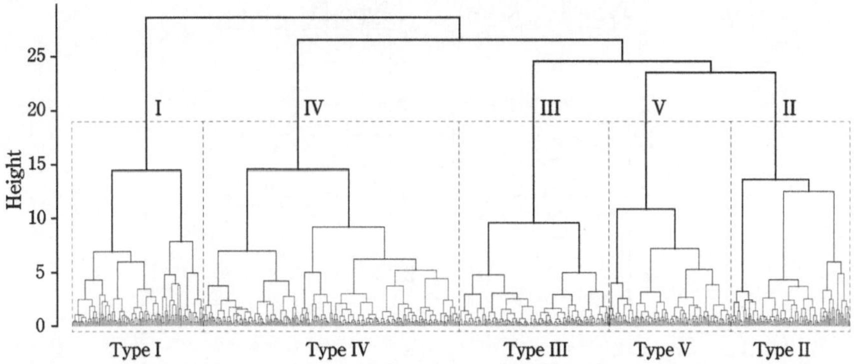

FIGURE 2.1 Dendrogram of Districts Classified Into Five Types of Work Opportunities Through Cluster Analysis Based on the Standardised PC Scores

Note: Applied Cluster Analysis with Ward's method based on the Euclidean distance. The dotted frames in the figure show the range of five types.

Source: 2011 Census of India, Tables A-1, B-1, B-4, B-21, and C-14 (Kuwatsuka, 2018: 106).

the respective types, the distribution of the score in the boxplots is examined as explained from Type I to Type V.

First, 106 districts were classified as Type I, which is the most distinct from the other types. Looking at the score distribution of each PC, the second PC, which shows government-related work opportunities, has higher scores. In contrast, the levels of the third PC, which indicates 'stable work opportunities in the agricultural and manufacturing sectors,' and the fourth PC, which indicates 'fewer optional and unstable work opportunities in rural areas,' are lower than the first PC score. Districts classified as Type I are distributed unevenly in geographic terms within the mountain region of northern India and border regions in northeastern India (Map 2.5). These districts are characterised by a lack of key industries and underlying support for creating work opportunities in the public sector.

Second, 98 districts are classified as Type II, but here, the level of the first PC, which indicates 'diverse work opportunities in metropolitan regions,' is high and prominent. These districts are distributed through the Delhi metropolitan area to Punjab in northern India, overlapping with the extent of the mega-region. Additionally, it can be recognised that districts classified as Type II are located in the plains and foothill areas of Uttarakhand, not so far from Delhi. This state has developed its economy since the 2000s. Large-scale manufacturing companies have received central and state government subsidies and sited plants in industrial parks developed by the state government. This state's mountain region is also becoming a tourist destination and is attracting the urban middle class from the Delhi metropolitan area (Okahashi, 2016; Nakajo, 2017).

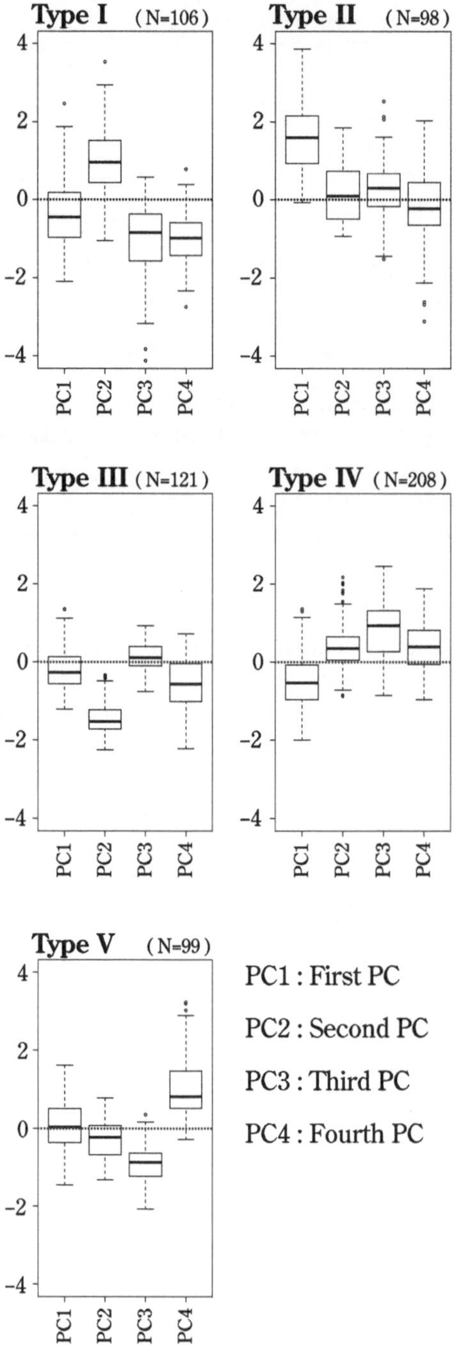

FIGURE 2.2 PC Score of Districts by Classification of Work Opportunities

Source: 2011 Census of India, Tables A-1, B-1, B-4, B-21, and C-14 (Kuwatsuka, 2018: 107).

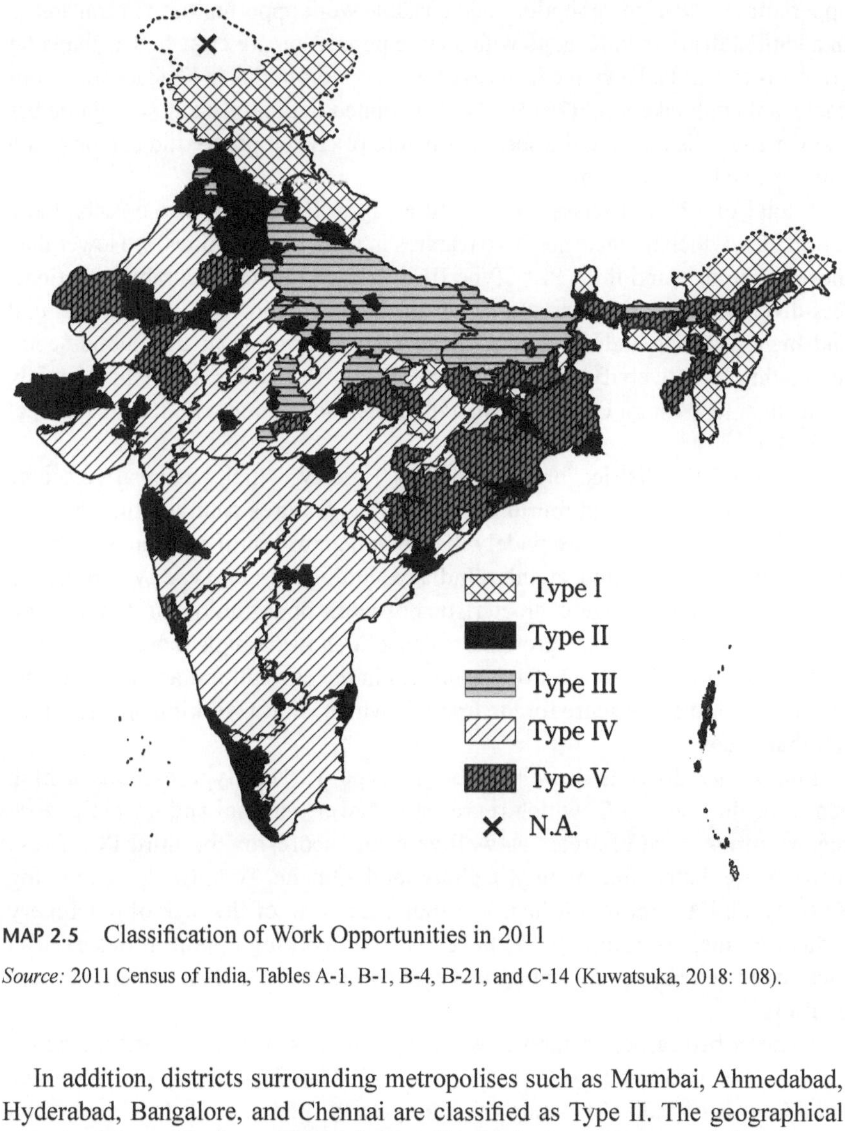

MAP 2.5 Classification of Work Opportunities in 2011

Source: 2011 Census of India, Tables A-1, B-1, B-4, B-21, and C-14 (Kuwatsuka, 2018: 108).

In addition, districts surrounding metropolises such as Mumbai, Ahmedabad, Hyderabad, Bangalore, and Chennai are classified as Type II. The geographical ranges of these districts exhibit similar distributions as the metropolitan areas. Furthermore, Type II includes state capitals and second-tier cities such as Lucknow and Kanpur in Uttar Pradesh and Bhopal and Indore in Madhya Pradesh.

As described earlier, especially in northern India, Type II areas tend to be core areas which are home to high-density agglomerations of various industries. However, as shown in the dendrogram (Figure 2.1), Type II includes districts of two kinds. Considering the two groups of PC scores, the first and third PCs have a high level in one group. In the other group, the first, second, and fourth PCs are high. The former group has the same characteristics as Type II, whereas the latter has negative features applicable to Kerala, such as 'government-related work opportunities,' and 'fewer options and unstable work opportunities in rural areas.' In addition, districts in Kolkata with a large population are classified as the latter group, as is Kerala. Negative features of work opportunities in Kolkata are identifiable, although Okahashi (2015b: 34–35) pointed out that Kolkata is regarded as a key metropolis forming the spatial structure of contemporary India, along with Mumbai, Delhi, and Chennai.

A total of 121 districts are classified as Type III. Scores of the second and fourth PCs, which indicate negative features in work opportunities, are lower than those of the first and third PCs. Type III districts show unfavourable situations, less-diversified industrial structures, unstable work opportunities in agricultural and manufacturing industries, and weak contributions from the public sector in creating and diversifying opportunities. Type III districts, distributed mainly from Bihar to Western Uttar Pradesh, reflect a close relation with India's regional difficulties.

A total of 208 districts are classified as Type IV, which has positive scores for the second, third, and fourth PCs, but it has features contradicting those of Type III. These districts are widely distributed across rural areas in Maharashtra, Madhya Pradesh, and southern India excluding Kerala. Type IV is regarded as indicating the average characteristics of work opportunities in Indian rural areas when economies are growing because it shows a high score or the third PC representing 'stable work opportunities in the agricultural and manufacturing sectors' but a low score for the first PC, which shows working opportunities in urban areas.

Finally, 99 districts are classified as Type V. This type exhibits a high score for the fourth PC, which represents 'fewer optional and unstable work opportunities in rural areas' as well as a low score for the third PC. These districts are distributed mainly in Jharkhand, Odisha, West Bengal excluding Kolkata, and Assam in northeastern India. Because of the lack of machinery industries such as automobiles, fewer diverse working opportunities exist in these districts. However, mining and related industries are prominent in these districts.

As described earlier, features of work opportunities in these respective districts are classified into five types and are mapped in Map 2.5 using CA based on the 2011 Census of India. This map does not portray differences between rural and urban areas' work opportunities. Rather, the map can represent work opportunities created in non-agricultural industries and their uneven distributions. According to the identified patterns, the spatial structure of India in 2011 demonstrates the difficulty of comprehending a country's true structure and dynamics using only the 'rural–urban nexus' framework.

6 Conclusion

The spatial structure of contemporary India has been examined using statistical analyses conducted based on the 2011 Census of India. The 34 variables were reduced to four principal components using PCA. The PCs explaining the greatest number of variables were interpreted as indicating 'diverse work opportunities in metropolitan regions.'

The importance of agricultural workers when considering work opportunities in India might be readily apparent. All workers account for about 40% of India's total population of 1.2 billion. Furthermore, agricultural workers, which include both agricultural labourers and cultivators, predominate, constituting 38% of all workers. If marginal workers in the agricultural sector are included, then 55% of all workers are engaged in agriculture. Nevertheless, only the third and fourth principal components were found to have a positive correlation with agricultural workers. Even considering the influence of input variables for the PCA, that is, main workers by industrial classification, it is readily apparent that non-agricultural sectors are important for explaining the spatial structure of India under a growing economy.

Among these non-agricultural sectors, industries classified as being of the tertiary sector have a considerably strong effect on the geographical distribution of work opportunities in 2011. This sector should not be regarded as an industry that becomes a target of industrial policy for economic development, unlike agriculture and manufacturing. For a desirable statistical solution, the tertiary sector is a compilation of indiscriminate and diverse activities that cannot be classified as belonging to primary or secondary sectors. The distinctive feature of these sectors is the ability of 'diverse industries' to offer greater insight into work opportunities and inclusive development in contemporary India than the agriculture and manufacturing industry.

In this study, districts were classified into five types using CA based on the PC scores, following the procedure for PCA to consider the basic dimensions of work opportunities. The results of these analyses confirmed that the spatial structure of India in 2011 could not be explained completely by the three opposing spatial axes described by Sato (1994): inland and coastal India, eastern and western India, and southern and northern India. Particularly for consideration of the spatial structure of India, a comprehensive analysis must use a classification reflecting the features of work opportunities in the metropolises. The geographical distribution of the districts classified by type of work opportunities revealed a shape almost identical to 'mega-regions' extracted from 'night lights' satellite data (Florida et al., 2008). This is a crucially important research result derived from the analyses conducted in this study. However, determining the internal structure of the mega-region will require more detailed analyses using the concept of urban and industrial agglomerations. The rise of the 'new economic space' is deeply related to the 'mega-region,' which seems to exert effects on the regional reproduction structure that had been formed historically based on initial conditions such as geography, society, and culture.

In addition, a distinctive feature that earlier studies were unable to extract through analysis is the most distant relations between districts classified as Type I to those classified as other types in the dendrogram. Based on the results of geographical studies of Uttarakhand in northern India (Okahashi, 2014, 2016; Tomozawa, 2015; Yui, 2015; Kuwatsuka, 2017; Nakajo, 2017) overlapping in the spatial extent of Type I, new industries in Uttarakhand such as tourism and manufacturing have been developed with inflowing investment from outside the region. In other words, this region has become integrated into the agglomeration economy in the Delhi metropolitan region. This outcome suggests that general decentralisation should be replaced by the process of 'concentrated decentralisation,' encouraging the expansion of urban regions on the periphery (Friedmann, 1968). This process thus implies a mechanism by which features of each type of district are mutually related. These results call for more discussion for reforming the regional reproduction structure and doing so in the context of inclusive development.

This process also affects the inland states in northern India known as the 'Hindi Belt.' They are experiencing economic difficulties. However, this region cannot be regarded as homogeneous according to the classification of districts used for this study. Most districts in Bihar and Uttar Pradesh are classified as Type II; they exhibit negative features in terms of work opportunities. In Madhya Pradesh and Rajasthan, however, several districts are classified as Type IV and have positive features. These districts also have average characteristics of work opportunities in India's rural areas. It is particularly interesting that several districts classified as Type II, the same classification as the Delhi metropolitan area, are located in these states. Consequently, the inland states in northern India are differentiated into a region that offers positive and negative work opportunities. As a result, southern India, which comprises districts classified as Type II and Type IV, has a simpler structure, whereas northern India has a more complicated spatial structure. Further studies are needed on the complicated spatial structure inherited via the historically determined regional reproduction structure. It should be examined whether or not this is a result of the newly forming process of the spatial structure of contemporary India, which has a 'mega-region' as the core region.

Acknowledgement

This is a revised version of a paper presented at the 10th INDAS International Conference, at Tokyo University of Foreign Studies, Japan, 15–16 December 2018. This work was supported by JSPS KAKENHI Grant Number JP19H01384.

Notes

1 Additionally called a uniform or formal region, which is an area defined by one or more of the features that occur within them (Gregory et al., 2009: 631).
2 The PCA is a method for extracting correlated information from a complicated data set and reducing it to a lower dimension to reveal simplified structures that are readily comprehensible. Therefore, PCA was adopted to identify PCs as synthesised variables and to interpret general characteristics for considering the spatial structure.

3 Central Statistical Organisation, 'National Industrial Classification [All Economic Activities],' http://mospi.nic.in/sites/default/files/main_menu/national_industrial_classification/nic_2008_17apr09.pdf (accessed 28 June 2019).

4 The HHI is short for household industry, which is defined as an industry conducted by one or more household members at home or within a village in rural areas and only within the precincts of the house where the household members live in urban areas. Census Office of the Registrar General & Census Commissioner, India, 'Census Data 2001/Metadata,' http://censusindia.gov.in/Metadata/Metada.htm#2o (accessed 14 February 2019).

References

Chakravorty, S. and S. V. Lall (2007). *Made in India: The Economic Geography and Political Economy of Industrialization*, New Delhi: Oxford University Press.

Florida, R., T. Gulden, and C. Mellander (2008). "The Rise of the Mega-region," *Cambridge Journal of Regions*, vol. 1(3), 459–476.

Friedmann, J. (1968). "The Strategy of Deliberate Urbanization," *Journal of the American Institute of Planners*, vol. 34(6), 364–373.

Gregory, D., R. Johnston, G. Pratt, M. Watts, and S. Whatmore eds. (2009). *The Dictionary of Human Geography*, 5th edition, West Sussex: Wiley-Blackwell.

Kurosaki, T. and K. Wada (2014). "Ken-deita de mita Nougyo-seisan no Choki-hendo to sono Kuukan-teki Tokucho (Long-term Fluctuation and Spatial Distribution of Agricultural Production by District-Wise Data)," in Yanagisawa, H. and T. Mizushima eds., *Nogyo to Noson* (*Agriculture and Rural Area*), *Gekido no Indo* (*A rapidly changing India*), Tokyo: Nihon Keizai Hyouronsha: 73–123. (in Japanese)

Kuwatsuka, K. (2013). "Spatial Expansion of ICT Service Industries to Non-Metropolitan Areas in India," *The Journal of Business Studies*, *Ryukoku University*, vol. 53(1), 16–31.

Kuwatsuka, K. (2017). "Regional Initiatives and Operations of ICT Service Companies in Dehradun, the Capital City of Uttarakhand," *Journal of Urban and Regional Studies on Contemporary India*, vol. 4(1), 13–23.

Kuwatsuka, K. (2018). "Indo no kukan-kozo ni kansuru deita bunseki (Data Analysis for Spatial Structure of Contemporary India: Classification of Work Opportunities Using the 2011 Census of India)," *Geographical Sciences*, vol. 73, 93–113. (in Japanese)

Kuwatsuka, K. and H. Kitagawa (2008). "Growth of the Software Industry and Agglomeration in Large Cities," in Okahashi, H. ed., *Emerging New Industrial Spaces and Regional Development in India*, New Delhi: Manohar: 35–48.

Nakajo, A. (2017). "Development of Tourism and the Tourist Industry in India: A Case Study of Uttarakhand," *Journal of Urban and Regional Studies on Contemporary India*, vol. 3(2), 1–12.

Okahashi, H. (1986). "Waga-kuni niokeru Sanson-Mondai no Genjyo to sono Chiiki-teki Seikaku (Rural Deprivation in Mountainous Areas of Japan: A Preliminary Assessment)," *Japanese Journal of Human Geography*, vol. 38, 461–479. (in Japanese)

Okahashi, H. (2014). "Transformation of India's Underdeveloped Regions during Economic Growth Period Focusing on Uttarakhand," *Journal of Urban and Regional Studies on Contemporary India*, vol. 1(1), 13–23.

Okahashi, H. (2015a). "Keizai Hatten to Atarashii Keizai Kukan (Economic Development and New Economic Space)," in Okahashi, H. and K. Tomozawa eds., *Taito suru Shin Keizai Kuukan (The Emergence of New Economic Space) Gendai Indo (Contemporary India) 4*, Tokyo: University of Tokyo Press: 3–25. (in Japanese)

Okahashi, H. (2015b). "Kuukan Kozo no Keisei to Hendou (Formation and Transformation of Spatial Structure)," in Okahashi, H. and K. Tomozawa eds., *Taito suru Shin Keizai Kuukan (The Emergence of New Economic Space) Gendai Indo (Contemporary India) 4*, Tokyo: University of Tokyo Press: 29–51. (in Japanese)

Okahashi, H. (2016). "The Transformation of a Himalayan Mountain Village under the Rapid Economic Growth in India: A Case Study of the State of Uttarakhand," *Journal of Urban and Regional Studies on Contemporary India*, vol. 2(2), 11–24.

Sato, H. (1994). *Indo Keizai no Chiiki Bunseki (Regional Analysis of India's Economy)*, Tokyo: Kokon Shoin. (in Japanese)

Sato, Y. (2017). "Indo niokeru Keizai-Tokubetsu-ku (SEZ) Kaihatsu to sono Chiriteki-Bunpu ni kansuru Yosatsuteki-Kosatsu (A Note on Development of Special Economic Zones (SEZs) and Their Location Pattern in India)," *Shimonoseki City University Review*, vol. 60(3), 91–103. (in Japanese)

Sugimoto, D. (2004). "Indo Panjabu Syuu niokeru Rodou Setsuyaku-teki Gijyutsu no Fukyu to Nougyou-Rodou koyou (Diffusion of Labour-saving Technology and its Effect on Agricultural Employment: A Case of Indian Punjab)," *Journal of Economics*, vol. 105(1), 102–127. (in Japanese)

Takahashi, A. and T. Mizushima (2015). "Nouson-Jinko Douko to Chiiki Ruikei (Population Changes in Villages and Regional Classification)," in Mizushima, T. and H. Yanagisawa eds., *Youyu suru Tosi/Nouson (Urban-rural Nexus in Transition), Gendai Indo (Contemporary India) 2*, Tokyo: University of Tokyo Press: 59–78. (in Japanese)

Tomozawa, K. (2008). "Growth of the Automobile Industry," in Okahashi, H. ed., *Emerging New Industrial Spaces and Regional Development in India*, New Delhi: Manohar: 23–34.

Tomozawa, K. (2015). "Industrialization and the Development of Regional Economies in the State of Uttarakhand," *Journal of Urban and Regional Studies on Contemporary India*, vol. 1(2), 9–20.

Tomozawa, K. (2016). "Development and Spatial Dynamism of the Automobile Component Industry in India," *Journal of Urban and Regional Studies on Contemporary India*, vol. 3(1), 11–27.

Une, Y. (2018). "Indo niokeru Nikkei-Kigyou no Richi-Tokusei (Location Patterns of Japanese Companies in India)," in Sato, T. ed., *Indo no Sangyou Hatten to Nikkei Kigyou (Industrial Development and Japanese Companies in India)*, Kobe: Research Institute for Economics and Business Administration, Kobe University: 95–124. (in Japanese)

Usami, Y. (2014). "Rodou-Ryoku Ido to Nouson Syakai (Labour Migration and Rural Society)," in Yanagisawa, H. and T. Mizushima eds., *Nougyou to Nouson (Agriculture and Rural Area), Gekido no Indo (A Rapidly Changing India) 4*, Tokyo: Nihon Keizai Hyouronsha: 339–371. (in Japanese)

Usami, Y., H. Yanagisawa, and F. Oshikawa (2015). "Nouson Hatten no Ruikei Ron (Typology of Rural Development)," in Mizushima, T. and H. Yanagisawa eds., *Youyu suru Tosi/Nouson (Urban-rural Nexus in Transition), Gendai Indo (Contemporary India) 2*, Tokyo: University of Tokyo Press: 79–124. (in Japanese)

Yanagisawa, H. and T. Mizushima eds. (2014). *Nougyo to Nouson (Agriculture and Rural Area), Gekidou no Indo (A Rapidly Changing India) 4*, Tokyo: Nihon Keizai Hyouronsha. (in Japanese)

Yui, Y. (2015). "Urban Development in Newly Industrial Regions in Peripheral India: A Case Study of Rudrapur," *Journal of Urban and Regional Studies on Contemporary India*, vol. 2(2), 1–9.

3

THE BURGEONING SMALL TOWNS OF INDIA

Lessons for Inclusive Development

Eric Denis

1 Introduction

Over the past ten years, we have defined subaltern urbanisation as vibrant smaller settlements and spaces outside the metropolitan shadow that support a dispersed pattern of urbanisation to help improve understanding of urban challenges, notably in the case of India (Denis et al., 2012; Denis and Zérah, 2017). Thus, we developed new arguments to focus on urban policy choices and more specifically, inclusive approaches. Within that frame, what is the significance of small towns' invisibility? How could an inclusive agenda (if it exists in practice in India) materialise in a truncated conception of the urban domain? We re-examine the link between urbanisation and inclusive development by widening our conceptualisation of the Indian system of cities. A noteworthy fact is that since the idea of inclusion made its way into the corridors of Indian ministries, including the Ministry of Housing and Urban Poverty Alleviation and Ministry of Urban Development,[1] it has evolved into 'inclusive growth.' This denotes a significant semantic shift; the economy is thus expected to generate inclusion.

Although studies have achieved complexity and widened our understanding of the urban transition, the current urban policies remain driven by a conceptualisation that reflects the dominant turn-of-the-century theories related to the New Economic Geography (NEG)[2] dogma and its apology of the metropolitan concentration (Moriconi-Ebrard et al., 2010). On the ground, public efforts and private investments have together helped to push for improved infrastructures and business-friendly major metropolitan cities. They conjugate Harris' mantra that 'cities are motor engines of economic growth.' The trade-off between spatial justice and polarisation for productivity gain is driven by the growth coalition towards the concentration of investments in major cities and avenues of development.

DOI: 10.4324/9781003304760-5

Because our research is conducted using mixed methods combining quantitative, statistical, and land-use data as well as approximately 20 ethnographies,[3] it is able to construct an understanding of this layer of urban structure (Zérah and Denis, 2017: 9–12). Our research focuses on settlements with lower than 100,000 people, where 41.1% of the urban population lives in India in 2011, which has increased since 2001 and has continued to grow. Our results show that the Indian system of cities is characterised by its dispersion.

This leads us to coin the notion of subaltern urbanisation, which is elaborated in Section 2. The quantitative results are presented in Section 3, wherein they demonstrate that the logic of agglomeration is insufficient for mapping shifts in the Indian system of cities. The constant relative weight of small towns and a process of in situ urbanisation serve to highlight the reality of urbanisation of 'morphing places' and bleeding urban–rural frontiers. Based on our ethnographic studies, the diversity of pathways and forms of subaltern urbanisation are analysed in Section 4. A typology of settlements is first proposed based on the nature of socio-economic transitions of these localities, considering various factors (land, employment, agency and innovation, history and the nature of capital, and shifts in rural–urban relations). The intersection of these shifts with the unique official definition of Indian urbanisation is discussed in Section 5. We argue that the performative role of the existing rural–urban nomenclature calls for closer attention to the methods through which government regimes influence the process of (dispersed) urbanisation—administrative classification matters. Based on the importance of the emergence of small towns supporting a horizontal urbanisation process in India, in Section 6, we propose the analysis of recent urban policies and their inclusive ambition in socio-spatial terms. To what extent do they consider, benefit from, or interact incidentally with the growing importance of the small-town stratum? Finally, we demonstrate that diffuse urbanisation, which characterises India in addition to its major metropolitan areas, provides an opportunity for spatial justice in India. Small towns constitute various bases for increasingly inclusive development and access to rural margins as well to limit migration towards major cities in the context of rapid economic transition.

2 Subaltern urbanisation and urban theory

We first proposed (Denis et al., 2012) the notion of subaltern urbanisation to qualify the observed trends as well as a heuristic tool to engage a collective in research.

We begin by considering the autonomous growth of settlement agglomerations—large and dense clusters of people, higher than 10,000 and lower than 100,000 inhabitants, regardless of their administrative status as urban or not. We attempted to investigate the growth of these settlements and focused on the self-determining capabilities of each settlement (through the agency of its inhabitants). This individual and collective ability reflects and is mediated by social and governance structures.

Our second claim is that subaltern urbanisation refers to a commitment to restore visibility to an unseen and often unspoken process of myriad forms affected by local actors. Most invisible settlements are far from the major metropolitan areas and are not necessarily covered by public urban schemes. Some are located in the shadow of major cities; these are also included in our framework. We posit that the transformations these towns are undergoing are not only subject to the influence or spread of metropolitan growth as well as the extension and deconcentration of banal and polluting activities. The trajectories and configurations of these small towns are also dependent on their own historical capital and their local and long-distance linkages.

Our focus on the historicity, ordinariness, and local agency of urban sites located off the map anchors our perspective of urbanisation from the critical and postcolonial perspective (Robinson, 2006; Roy, 2011a, 2011b). We also aim to pursue, debate, and extend the ontological and topological frame delineating the 'ordinary city' (Robinson, 2002; Amin and Graham, 1997).

Consequently, the centrality we assign to small settlements is central to subaltern urbanisation. This represents one of the key differences between our idea of subaltern urbanisation and the subaltern urbanism posited by Roy (2009), despite the common insistence on the notion of agency. We partly resituate the idea of 'subaltern urbanism' (Roy, 2009) outside the metropolis. Another difference between the two ideas is that we do not associate agency solely with spaces of poverty and vulnerability, and instead include innovative actors, local entrepreneurs, and the practices of the local elites in an extended link between agency and subaltern urbanisation.

Furthermore, the idea of subaltern urbanisation confronts the theses on planetary urbanisation (Brenner, 2014; Brenner and Schmid, 2011); in particular, this involves the acknowledgement of the unbounded process of urbanisation, as well as determining whether the rural/urban frontier is being blurred. There is strong proximity between the subaltern and recent works in planetary urbanisation research, due to the attention provided to the intersection of morphological changes, legal framework, and the practices of grounded local actors (Schmid, 2018). However, although planetary urbanisation acknowledges the role of small towns, our research features two differences when compared with this framework: first, subaltern urbanisation does not analyse small towns in a classical dependence relationship with large agglomerations, similar to the method used in central place theory (Christaller, 1933); second, subaltern urbanisation provides nuances to the ontology of the urban in planetary urbanisation, which continues to be perceived through the lens of large cities, their 'endless' peripheries, and small towns on the edge of rurality that are only being transformed due to a trickle-down effect and the diffusion of banal activities and extractivism. To some extent, it remains similar to the framework featured in the NEG, in terms of its adherence to the idea of universal history and teleological trajectory towards modernity. This is common among both neoclassical as well as Marxian conceptualisations, wherein cities are ordered vis-à-vis the stylised European system of cities since the European pre-industrial and industrial movements, which were dominated by nation states and colonial relations. We argue that this order may be insufficient to map the nature of inter-linkages and exchanges in an open and globalised postcolonial world, wherein horizontal as well as direct long-distance relations matter.

However, before focusing on subaltern urbanisation, we wish to clarify two important points. First, our intent is not to propose a claim in opposition to major cities. The idea of subaltern urbanisation is featured while discussing other approaches to urbanisation, and we perceive it as a bridge to think across agency and scale. In this study, we agree with other commentators that what is 'lost as a consequence of the bias toward large cities is a full picture of urban form and function: the urban world is not made up of a handful of global metropolises, but characterised by heterogeneity. Studying small cities enables us to see the full extent of this' (Bell and Jayne, 2009: 683). Smaller settlements must be examined not in contrast to large cities, but by themselves as sites of urbanity, economic activity, and social transformation and to understand their place as rural–urban links and as part of the global economy in the process of urbanisation (Zérah and Denis, 2017). Second, by restoring visibility to smaller settlements, subaltern urbanisation does not reinforce the perspective of subordinate settlements, but instead aims to underscore the multi-layered and trans-local material and immaterial flows that shape a non-hierarchical urban landscape.

3 Beyond the metropolis: the weight of small urban settlements in the Indian system of cities

This section analyses the long-term evolution of the system of cities, one of the first urbanised regions of the world, by a network of cities, as early as 2500 BC, and shows its resilience. The official Indian urbanisation rate is low (and underestimated, see Denis et al., 2012) at 31.2%. However, in 2011, 377 million urban residents in India represented a population larger than all the inhabitants of North America (Canada and the United States). The yearly increase in the urban population is equivalent to that of a megacity (more than 9 million people). The data analysis results show that policies favouring the logics of agglomeration have limited impact on the long-term restructuring of an urban system, wherein small towns continue to play a crucial role.

India serves as yet another example of Asian urbanisation, characterised by the coexistence of gigantic megalopolises and a rural environment, with many villages becoming towns at the bottom of a system of cities, and fast-expanding metropolises at the apex. Ancient and complex forms of irrigated agriculture, powerful rivers, and wide deltas have resulted in large basins with high human densities. Through natural growth associated with a diversification of activities, these ancient systems of settlements set an environment wherein many settlements emerge as urban candidates. Therefore, a significant share of urban growth is caused by the natural population growth in existing cities and the formation of new urban units, usually by reclassification and/or mergers of existing villages (Heitzman, 2008; Denis and Marius-Gnanou, 2010).

We posit that Indian urbanisation is focused on morphing places, instead of moving people, and is thus partly characterised by the urbanisation of its countryside (Mukhopadhyay, 2012). Structurally, and contrary to the dominant perception of the migrant influx, since 1971, residential migration from rural areas to urban localities has remained limited. Using census data, Chandrasekhar and Sharma (2014) showed that this occurrence did not contribute to more than one-fourth of urban growth. From 2001 to 2011, among the 90.9 million new members of the urban population, 38.5 million were attributed to the natural growth and expansion of the area, 20.6 million were attributed to net migration or moving to other areas,[4] and the remaining 31.8 million were attributed to the reclassification from rural to urban areas. This reclassification acknowledges the morphing of places into census towns, which are large, dense villages with urban characteristics, and without an administrative status.

From 2001 to 2011, the percentage of the urban population in census towns nearly doubled from 7.4% to 14.6%, and their number rose from 1,362 to 3,894 (Pradhan, 2013), whereas the percentage of small towns with urban administrative status (called statutory towns) fell from 32.9% to 26.5%. This indicates that as of 2011, 41.1% of the urban population lived in small towns with a population lower than 100,000—an increase from 40.3% in 2001. However, these statistics do not fully reflect the ongoing process of change. Another 23.5% of the rural population, which comprises 47.4% of the total population (including the population officially classified as urban), lived in settlement agglomerations of more than 5,000 people. This configuration leads to questions about the definition of 'what is urban' and underscores the rapid urbanisation of the Indian countryside.

Although a top-heavy urban structure has prevailed in many Indian states, the national urban system remains dispersed and balanced (Swerts et al., 2014, 2018). Overall, the growth of cities, regardless of size, has tended to decrease and converge over the past 20 years. As seen in Table 3.1 (including all cities classified as urban in the 2011 Census), the annual population growth rate of the urban sector is currently closer to the national figure, compared with that of 1971–1981. With an annualised urban growth rate of 3.9%, the urban differential was +1.7% during 1971–1981. During 2001–2011, with an annualised urban growth rate of 2.4%, the differential was at +0.9% only. A detailed study of the system of cities subdivided based on population size classes of urban units since 1971 demonstrated that cities, regardless of size, have had similar opportunities for growth. Currently, no significant differential is noted in terms of growth for the largest cities.

The output of this structural trend is an almost constant percentage of the urban population being distributed based on city class sizes. The differential growth of major cities is a limited phenomenon, and the growth of cities is not based on their size. Large metropolises do not grow at the expense of smaller towns, which continue to multiply, as an increasing number of villages become towns. Therefore, the evolution of the Indian system of cities questions the canonical trends

TABLE 3.1 Annual Population Growth Rate (%) by Size Class of Urban Unites (Cities)

	Gross increase (including intercensal class changes)				*Constant classes of 2011 (without reclassification effects)*		
	1971–81	1981–91	1991–2001	2001–11	1971–81	1981–91	1991–2001
Cities*	4.4	3.7	3.5	2.7	3.7	3.2	2.9
Metropolises	4.2	4.9	4.2	3.5	2.8	3.8	2.9
Class IA	5.5	4.3	4.8	3.3	2.7	3.4	2.8
Class IB	2.7	5.7	3.5	3.8	3.4	4.0	3.1
Class IC	4.5	2.6	2.6	1.7	4.2	3.1	3.3
Towns	2.7	2.4	1.5	1.6	3.4	3.2	2.3
Class II	4.1	2.8	1.6	1.6	4.8	3.7	2.5
Class III	2.4	3.0	1.9	1.6	2.7	3.4	2.3
Others	1.9	1.3	1.0	1.6	2.3	2.4	2.2
Memo: Population growth							
Urban	3.9	3.2	2.8	2.4			
Rural	1.8	1.8	1.7	1.2			
Total	2.2	2.1	2	1.5			

Note: Class IA is above 5 million inhabitants, IB between 1 and 5 million, IC between 100,000 and 1 million, Class II towns between 50,000 and 100,000, and Class III between 20,000 and 50,000.
* Official cities and towns comprising the urban sector of the 2011 Census.

currently associated with urban transition, particularly in terms of a hierarchical and spatial reorganisation of the population, as well as in terms of the polarisation of economic growth among the largest urban areas (Table 3.1).

This diffused urbanisation is resilient to urban policies and focuses on significant agglomerations since economic liberalisation. After independence, during the first phase, Indian policies focused on rural areas. In 1979, a scheme was developed for the benefit of small- and medium-sized towns. The fifth Five-Year Plan promoted smaller towns, whereas the sixth one focused on connecting towns with their hinterland. A turning point was noted during the mid-1980s, with the introduction of economic liberalisation. The National Commission on Urbanisation was launched in 1985 and recommended the strengthening of existing larger metropolises, which led to a paradigm shift and shaped the discourse on cities as engines of growth sustained by numerous policies and schemes that favoured the largest cities (Sivaramakrishnan, 2011). This focus on the economy of agglomeration contrasts with the first phase, wherein industrial policies supported small-scale and cottage industries connected to local resources and the creation of employment opportunities without migration. Due to this shift, smaller towns have been side-lined in the public policy debate, even though they continue to play a significant role in India's economy.

If we observe the modality and temporality of the Indian insertion into the global value chain, recent studies have shown that industries tend to be located away from the urban environment (Ghani et al., 2012) and non-farm activities are expanded outside municipal boundaries (Vishwanath et al., 2013). Reducing costs through a less unionised and low-cost workforce, lower environmental regulations, and cheaper land prices are among the potential motivations for this structural trend. Furthermore, significantly improved road connectivity and low employment rates in villages serve as evidence to support the emergence of large settlements and small towns as pivotal places, as well as the clustering of villages around manufacturing activities.

Consequently, the configuration of the Indian system of cities leads to questions regarding the concept of agglomeration economy introduced by Marshall in 1890 (Henderson, 2003) and the universality of the hierarchical system of cities (Pumain and Moriconi-Ebrard, 1997), dominated by large, innovative metropolises where talents converge. The New Economic Geography models (Krugman, 1998) led to the incorporation of this spatially differentiated approach into mainstream economics (Glaeser, 2010). The global city networks approach (Taylor, 2004) that attempted to parameterise the global city debates (Sassen, 2001) led to a quasi-exclusive focus on large metropolises, thereby blurring the extension of the urban domain beyond the megacity. This approach provides intellectual legitimacy for pro-metropolitan and urban mega-infrastructure policies that have become increasingly common. However, the metro-centricity of private and public investments disregards the diversity and diffuse urbanisation in India. In particular, by focusing on the mechanisms and agency of stakeholders in the 'non-metropolitan world,' we must adopt other analytical lenses and develop a new conceptualisation of the urban.

4 Subaltern urbanisation in India: diverse forms and processes

The primary methodological approach in subaltern urbanisation is to rely on a methodology that constantly shifts between quantitative and qualitative methodologies to capture the nature of the urbanisation process. As explained earlier, urbanisation in India primarily occurs by morphing places, thus blurring the urban–rural frontiers and underscoring the reality of unbounded processes. We posit that this overall unbounded process must be considered in terms of varied configurations that account for complex institutional and economic linkages (Mukhopadhyay et al., 2020).

This section highlights the first step towards qualifying the types of settlement by observing the multiple and complex economic processes playing out in small towns. We present four broad types that can be identified to summarise the diversity of local conditions (micropolises as well as influence, market, and census towns). Locally, it is noteworthy that these four ideal types are interlaced with each other. The aforementioned types of small towns do not exist in a pure configuration. Each one is the product of multiple influences supported by an increasingly diverse population, which is often well-connected with distant places. We are aware of the risk of creating an oversimplified typology, but this constitutes the first step towards qualifying the varied pathways of urbanisation to enlarge the recent debate regarding the forms of agrarian Asian urbanism (Roy, 2016).

A common factor prevalent in all types of settlements is the centrality of the land-based economy underpinning the financing of the urban transition, particularly in increasingly developed states, in the context of poor access to institutional banking and credit. The rapid and extensive conversion of fertile land into popular real estate, educational institutions, and factories, as well as for securing access to loans, supports the monetisation and diversification of local economies, thus blurring the frontiers of urban and rural environments and questioning the effectiveness of the present regulations.

5 Towards a type of settlements

The first category—**the Influenced Town**—corresponds to small towns incorporated into functional areas influenced by metropolitan and large cities. The diffusion, localisation, and re-localisation processes of economic activities in the extended peripheries of large cities radically transform peri-urban land use. The combination of economic liberalisation and foreign direct investment accelerates entrepreneurs' tendency to procure the privilege of such peripheral locations. Our ethnographies underline the simultaneous processes.

First, a diffusion process made with a heterogeneous amalgam of investments in infrastructure, real estate, commercial ventures, industrial parks, and educational institutions surrounds small towns, which, in turn, become central locations (i.e., nodes and sites of agglomeration). In this case, the agency of local actors is limited. The urban transformation of such localities is dependent on their perceived attractiveness, in terms of accessibility and location (new roads, mass transportation, etc.). Other factors determine the development of these peripheries, such as the lower cost of land, the local tolerance to pollution, and the availability of a labour force willing to accept difficult working conditions, characterised by low wages, daily contracts, and a weak level of unionisation. In most cases, the weak enforcement of regulations by the government has become an added advantage, in terms of attractiveness. Because there is limited availability of significant tracts of land within large cities, majority of the globalisation-related investment occurs in these peri-urban areas wherein megaprojects, such as special economic zones (SEZs), materialise. Banal and polluting activities are de-concentrated from the city centre to these peripheral small towns alongside industrial development parks. Over time, however, the physical planning of metropolitan regions, megaprojects, and SEZs as well as the appetite for new land opportunities among real estate promoters can serve as destabilising factors for existing flourishing clusters of activities that depend on the intensive workforce, inherited knowledge, and local capital. Examples of these instances can be seen in the cases of the Kartarpur furniture industry in the periphery of Ludhiana (Bercegol and Gowda, 2017) and the Malpe fishing industries in coastal Karnataka (Benjamin, 2017), wherein SEZ projects and large highways threaten to destabilise vibrant local economies.

The re-localisation process of commuters is the second component of effervescent small towns surrounding large cities. The circular migration of daily commuters[5] transforms small towns into new households, comprising primarily of young people who cannot find affordable housing in the core city. They stimulate the diversification of local economies and alter the local political equilibrium. Among the youth, those with access to technical colleges are also increasingly engaged in commuting. This daily circulation tends to adjust itself as major firms relocate their factories and offices to peripheral parks, thus ensuring that circular migration comes full circle as people from the core city begin commuting to the periphery.

The second category—**the Micropolis**—is comprised of entrepreneurial, resilient, and innovative small towns (Mukhopadhyay et al., 2018). Outside the direct influence of metropolitan cities, many such vibrant small towns exist due to a strong and often fast-growing network of interconnected and interdependent entrepreneurs as well as skilled workers who contribute to the development of industrial clusters. They are able to expand their market, adapt to changes, innovate, and eventually export products, thereby reaching markets far away.

Small- and medium-sized towns have proven to be attractive locations for establishing and developing productive activities, particularly in response to the immense demand constituted by the vast majority of Indian families that do not belong to the middle and upper urban classes. In these locations, entrepreneurs innovate to create low-cost products responding to the specificities of the non-metropolitan environment with solid and rustic equipment that is easy to operate and repair by using local skills. It is an environment of *jugaad* (low-tech innovations) and trans-local circuits of knowledge, skills, and capital that enable entrepreneurs to do more with less. Such innovative products, particularly vehicles adapted to bad roads and difficult weather, are not only limited to the Indian customer base because some small companies manage to export to other emerging low-cost markets.

Based on frugal innovations and retro-engineering focusing on the needs of end users, in many aspects, several of these types of settlements possess the qualities associated with large metropolises, such as innovation and global connectivity, albeit at significantly smaller scales. This can be observed in localities, such as Tiruchengode (Tastevin, 2017; Raman, 2017) in Tamil Nadu, which have been reinventing themselves over the course of decades, and adapting their entrepreneurial endeavours to suit the local demand as well as global market transformations. Tiruchengode excels in the drilling rig industry. Currently, companies from Tiruchengode are able to export their low-cost borewell drilling trucks to Africa, wherein their adaptability to local needs is appreciated, particularly the ease of repair and maintenance. These manufacturers developed the ability to satisfy the markets neglected by large European and American truck makers, who produce sophisticated vehicles that are too expensive for certain countries. Furthermore, these large firms are unable to provide customised vehicles. In all Indian states, such small- and medium-sized towns are flourishing due to their ancient crafting traditions, such as textile and furniture, as well as the ability to design and develop low-cost products, often based on reverse engineering. These products are adapted to fulfil the relatively frugal needs of a non-metropolitan population transitioning into an urban environment. This type of milieu is not limited to India, and global diffusion does occur.

In some places, these innovative environments extend beyond individual settlements, to specialised clusters of towns and villages with a long-standing tradition of manufacturing and trading. In Udupi, coastal Karnataka, an assemblage of towns and villages is known as far away as Japan for supplying fishnets, and for the quality of their fish products (Benjamin, 2017). These traditional activities have been able to cope with globalised trading. Since the beginning of the previous century, local private actors have been engaged in development initiatives to grow this strong and open regional economy. Starting from the 1930s, investments were geared to build an integrated and affordable bus network, and starting from the 1960s, banks were set up (such as the well-known Canara Bank that is now owned by the Government of India) to facilitate local investments. However, planners, consultants, and private corporations continue to perceive this coast as a tabula rasa, well-suited for SEZs, power plants, tourism, and real estate investments, ignoring its current economic global presence and its importance for employment.

Small **market and/or administrative towns as well as emerging census towns** constitute the third and fourth categories. Both categories can be subsumed under the image of an **Anyplace town** (locality with diverse economic and cultural identity). Market and administrative towns, which cater to the needs of the rural areas in their hinterland, constitute a notable proportion of small towns. Many such towns have historically been market towns or administrative centres. Depending on their administrative functions (whether they are home to a block office or a police station, etc.), and the dynamism of the local agriculture (such as the nature of production and volume of cash crops), they can be more or less dynamic. They are primarily categorised as statutory towns and are governed by an urban local body. Emerging census towns are large, urbanised or rapidly urbanised, and villages expand and grow, including a workforce moving away from the farm sector.

These types of settlements fulfil a more ordinary, but necessary function. Although these are often not sites of production, with the exception of construction, they are service towns with markets, private health and education, and local transit hubs. They are spaces of change, wherein people drift in and out of non-farm and farm work. The density of India as a country enables the spread and depth of this phenomenon, which is further accentuated by the rapidly improving rural transportation networks. In these small urban settlements, the nature of economic transformation can be grouped into three categories: i) an everyday economy; ii) settlement-specific activities, which may reflect their historical functions; and iii) new activities. Almost all of these are primarily financed through non-formal sources. It is crucial to highlight that these ordinary but necessary functions can often provide incomes notably higher than those of traditional agricultural activities.

The everyday economy, which is geared towards servicing the demands of surrounding areas, benefits from higher levels of connectivity, and improved transport possibilities. Local markets or bazaars are at the centre of this everyday economy. However, despite its resilience in providing employment and trade in the surrounding villages, its scale of activity is typically insufficient for generating surplus capital. Some settlements also benefit from external investment in their area, such as the road to the Dhamra port project in Erein, Odisha, or the public hospital and college in Bishnugarh, Jharkhand (Mukhopadhyay et al., 2016). The bazaar economy benefits from the rising incomes of the rural areas, and their demand for diverse consumer goods, which are supplied through an intricate locally specific logistics chain. Few consumer goods are produced locally; however, the logistics chain generates local employment.

Activities specific to settlements can differ considerably; however, they tend to be small-scale and often linked to traditional caste occupations, such as the yoghurt industry in Gopalpur, West Bengal, and small-scale foundries in Cherra, Jharkhand. The ability of such specific activities to scale up and provide increased income and employment opportunities improves with enhanced connectivity, because transport networks increase the market for such products. The markets for these goods can be quite far-flung, particularly for handloom and handicrafts or bidi manufacturing, which have well-developed supply chains. These settlement-specific economic activities may also be linked to local natural resources, such as stone crushing in Domchanch, Jharkhand (entrepreneurs adjusting to the loss of traditional mica mining) or cold storage for potato farmers in Garbeta, West Bengal, as highlighted by Sircar (2017).

Identifying the specific characteristics of emerging census towns is a crucial task. With a decline in farm employment, people must generate incomes with access to minimal resources. This is how mandi towns as well as large villages become increasingly diverse. A significant number of the labour force open petty shops or become daily workers in the construction sector or at brick kilns, either locally or in other towns through seasonal migrations. In turn, their remittances stimulate the morphing of their place of origin. This morphing, which occurs in villages, leads to increased growth in the number of census towns, as the workforce shifts away from non-farm work. The local economy tends to move away from agricultural activities, as noted in the aforementioned settlements. However, there is no previous history of urban-like activity, such as administration or regional markets. Therefore, the emergence of these census towns is not supported by the presence of a local elite related to the presence of a market, educational, or administrative functions, but markets do emerge. These emerging urban areas consolidate and diversify because of the need for their population to create new activities and access resources through self-employment and mobility. Therefore, these settlements often serve as local transport hubs, assisted by improved rural roads and growing access to vehicle finance from formal banks.

In these emerging census towns, the presence of five new activities can be observed. Two such activities, which are considered significant in terms of employment and/or local impact, are construction and paratransit services. Construction is driven by the continuous shift to brick and mortar (*pucca*) housing that appears to be taking place in rural India, whereas the paratransit services for both freight and passengers lubricate the everyday economy. Growth in paratransit transport is driven by public investment in rural roads, and increased demand for travel (e.g., for education and general consumption, and manufacturers and/or banks providing financing to purchase vehicles). Those engaged in paratransit activity are often migrants returning from large cities, wherein they acquired finance and the skills required to drive vehicles, and they contribute to drastically transforming the connections between rural and urban settlements and the creation of increasingly integrated rural regions. In addition to these, three other common activities are smartphone-related services (sale and recharge of SIM cards, loading multimedia, sale and repair of instruments, etc.), private education, and private healthcare. The ubiquitous manifestation of these new activities is primarily driven by self-employment hint at a shift towards post-agrarian urbanism that is taking place in sites often disregarded by urban research and theory.

The multiplication of towns in India must be understood in terms of a social transition. In a subcontinent wherein the workforce is colossal, 487 million in 2011—second only after China—and sectoral transformation is underway; small towns constitute the privileged sites facilitating this adaptation; they accommodate people and ensure access to jobs and resources. This occurs through diversification of sources of income or occupational pluralism around areas where people already live.

A key factor shaping this urban system of cities as well as supporting the dispersion and importance of small towns is related to types of employment and methods through which people access resources. Despite the rapid fall of the farm sector in the GDP, the destruction of jobs in agriculture has only recently started to become noticeable. Although farmers continue to account for approximately half of the workforce (48.9% in 2011–2012[6]), a rising number of people are slowly dropping out of the agriculture sector (the percentage of farm employment decreased by approximately 1% per year); however, residential migration to large cities remains limited. In addition, instead of leading to a boom in job creation outside of agriculture, the acceleration of economic growth after liberalisation and in the 2000s has been termed a 'jobless growth' decade because most of the job creation, primarily in construction and services, barely compensates the loss of employment opportunities in agriculture and industry (Himanshu et al., 2011). The service sector, which contributed to more than 60% of the GDP in 2013, employs only 27% of the workforce, whereas the celebrated IT sector employs only 3 million people (0.6% of the total workforce). These figures help to comprehend the limited attraction of large cities in a context wherein most jobseekers have limited skills (Kundu and Saraswati, 2012). Once we recognise that the job situation in India is characterised by precariousness, we can determine that the scale of the challenge to include the workforce in the context of rapid economic transition is tremendous and includes additional stress on urban environments.

In this context, small towns are at the forefront of the transition. They are places that accommodate a higher share of non-regular workers, compared with larger cities. They usually constitute settlements wherein people access or self-generate non-farm activities and access resources, notably through commuting and temporary migration. Therefore, the multiplication of small towns and the urban transformation of villages constitute the material expression of the current socio-economic transition in India, which is characterised by a notable reduction of jobs in the farm sector and low creation of employment in the industrial sector, associated with a limited level of residential migration towards large cities. Many emerging small urban centres are places where people struggle to access resources; however, most of them prefer to live in a known environment wherein solidarity from their extended family can provide support and the cost of living remains lower.

6 Subaltern urbanisation and the politics of classification

By engaging with the notion of agency and innovation, we posit that the system of cities is created through multi-layered connections that are not necessarily going through large towns. We observe the urbanisation of the countryside and of the peripheries (of metropolitan and non-metropolitan cities) that reshaped urban–rural relationships in a notably less hierarchical perspective, compared with the one hinted at in planetary urbanisation. In this section, another nuance of this framework is highlighted through our focus on the impact of governance regimes, particularly through the manner in which essential services expand in these liminal territories.

First, the unique and complex definition of 'urban' in India as well as its related institutional structure complicates the reading of the dissipating urban–rural frontier. This definition has consequences for the economic, social, and demographic development of a settlement because it determines how it is governed as well as its access to funds. It is essential to recall that the definition of the urban population in India includes two primary categories of settlements: statutory and census towns. Statutory towns are settlements that are administratively designated as such by the state government and are of different types, with their corresponding urban local bodies. The functions, budgets, and responsibilities of these local governments differ based on their size and the power delegated to them by the provincial legislature. Furthermore, each regional government defines its rules and thresholds for designating statutory towns that can be different, flexible, and arbitrary.

In contrast, the second type of urban unit—the census town—is defined on the basis of statistical specifications that are identical throughout the country. A locality is classified as a census town when it crosses three thresholds simultaneously: a population of more than 5,000, a density higher than 400 inhabitants per square kilometre, and over 75% of the primarily male workforce working in non-farm occupations.[7] Census towns are settlements that are designated to be urban, but do not have statutory urban status.

This dual definition of urbanisation, based on administrative (statutory towns) and functional criteria (census towns) poses several problems of harmonisation. The inter-state variability of statutory town status is accentuated by regional political interests and relations between local and regional powers that determine urban classification. The list of statutory towns is strongly influenced by the state government's decisions, thus signifying a lack of homogeneity within the statutory category. Thus, a significant variation is noted in the size of statutory towns and some census towns have significantly larger populations, compared with many statutory towns.

From a governance and public policy perspective, the distinction between the two different types of settlements is crucial. Statutory towns are full-fledged urban local bodies, whereas census towns remain governed, similar to a village. This has major consequences for the delegation of responsibilities and access to government schemes. For instance, census towns can access rural government schemes, whereas small statutory towns can benefit from urban-oriented schemes that provide increased funding for basic infrastructure.

Determining whether a census town must remain a village or become a small town is a matter of vigorous discussion at the local level. Our qualitative inquiries show that on the ground, proposals for alternative administrative formations (developed at different scales, such as the redefinition of boundaries, demand for urban status, or reversion to rural status) can be traced, in varying degrees, to the four axes of contestation: the first axes of contestation is service provision (Mukhopadhyay et al., 2016); the second is related to the nature of non-farm activity and related land-use changes; the third is related to benefits from public housing schemes, such as *Indira Awas Yojana*[8] and employment guaranteed schemes; and the costs of new taxes and local sociopolitical formations comprise the fourth subject of contestation.

In particular, social grouping and local conflicts in the area influence the debate on governance in a 'politics of classification.' In some areas, aspirations for urban status appear to be driven by local elites and resisted by poorer groups, thus reflecting an economic divide between the bazaar (market, including traders and members of the local elites) and *basti* (residential area). In contrast, aspirations for urban status among others appear to be driven by poorer groups and resisted by local elites, because the landed elites perceive the rural status as offering increased freedom to monetise land. The increase in taxes and the enforcement of building by-laws associated with the urban status are perceived as constraints on local development. In states wherein access to welfare schemes is low, such programmes do not by themselves offer a strong argument to remain rural. Social elements, such as caste, can feature prominently within political coalitions resisting or advocating the transition from rural to urban status. In more developed states, the monetisation of land, inter alia, plays an increasingly crucial role and can lead to the appearance of a capital surplus, which can be invested in productive activities in the same or a different place, immediately or at a later date.

In census towns, service provision remains a major axis of mobilisation related to the applicable form of public policy (rural versus urban). These complex modalities of governance regimes have a deep impact and can accentuate regional disparities, particularly in states with a high number of census towns, which are not recognised as statutorily urban. A form of denied urbanisation has emerged in terms of a lack of public infrastructure and financial resources (Denis et al., 2012: 56; Samanta, 2017: 52). Therefore, a complicated relationship is noted between the governance of small towns and service provision. Although there are variations in the service delivery, depending on the effectiveness of local governance mechanisms and controlling for size, there is little measurable difference in the service provision between small-sized census and statutory towns (Mukhopadhyay, 2017).

Based on multiple trajectories of small towns and quantitative and geographical analyses, our research provided results that helped us to learn about the complexity of the urban transformation process and the biases induced by analytical oversimplification into dichotomous, supposedly universal categories. The spatial pattern of development and relationships across settlements are presented in various hues, instead of distinct colours, and one must have equivalent focus on the similarities and differences. However, if dichotomous categories pose problems, claims about the disappearing boundaries between the urban and rural also pose problems, and the concept of a city no longer makes sense.

The recent 'planetary urbanisation' trope (Brenner and Schmid, 2015) can also be perceived as a reflection on the morphing of places or the blurring of rural–urban boundaries; however, our more grounded approach leads us to articulate two primary reservations:

First, legislation and public policies that maintain a clear distinction between rural and urban affect the actions of governments, corporations, and individuals. Although our results demonstrate a shift in rural–urban relationships, the nature of the difference is not undermined. On the contrary, in India, the structure of governance and public policies effectively reinforce this divide.

Second, the nature of the subaltern urbanisation process deeply interrogates the nature of economic transformation. Although Brenner and Schmid (2015) argued that emerging urban forms must be understood based on their dependence on large cities and primarily vertical relationships, we consider that subaltern urbanisation is imbued with agency. This agency provides an opportunity for a socio-spatially more inclusive development if it is supported by the appropriate public policies. These emerging forms are not necessarily linked to a metropolitan hierarchy, and both local and external factors, which are often distant, are at play. In a recent publication, Schmid (2018) agreed to the same and pledged in favour of a decentred and open-ended vision of urbanisation.

7 A growth coalition more favourable than ever to the polarisation of territorial development

Despite the reality of the Indian system of cities, prioritised investment locations are determined based on the opportunity of returns and the maximisation of profit, instead of a socio-spatial fair distribution of (public) services, means, and wealth.

However, profit maximisation in the context of present-day India is also fuelling the expansion of disperse and in situ urbanisation, thus supporting the economic emergence of small towns. Investors of different origins: local, regional, and foreigners meet in small towns. Local and external investments are focused on locations where workers will accept low wages, pools of resilient skills, and local agrarian capital. Small towns constitute places wherein land is less expensive, polluted, and controlled. These conditions underpin horizontal interconnections between sites of production and the redistribution of workforce-intensive activities along a chain of values.

Therefore, the attractiveness of these small cities goes hand-in-hand with their lack of territorial and social inclusion as well as the lack of governance that characterises them. It is primarily because they remain, from an administrative perspective, villages that they attract industrial investments. Investors encounter little resistance that can easily be circumvented. Land assemblies for small, medium, and intermediate projects are easily negotiated with the local dominant castes. To a certain extent, their invisibility in territorial policies serves the small towns. Greater inclusion would indicate higher costs for industrial plants, more taxes, more environmental standards to be respected, and unions and authorities with whom it becomes crucial to negotiate.

It is regrettable that small towns were underleveraged in their ability to deliver widespread improvements in both prosperity and liveability. They are places where people cope with poverty and experience inequalities. However, these conditions of injustice are also the factors that make them attractive in the globalised environment wherein India is integrating. Its attractiveness as a country entering the global market outside IT services late[9] depends on its advantage in terms of low labour costs, flexibility, and the right to pollute.

The observation of the business fabrics of these small towns also indicates that they are the focus of a dynamic of low-cost innovations. They are the places of *Jugaad*. Their status as places of *jugaad* involves seeking exporting opportunities in major emerging markets. There are manufactured products that are easy to repair under difficult conditions. They fulfil the modest needs of a mass of poor people in India, but also in other countries in Asia and Africa.

The urban official framework is Malthusian, with the exception of a myriad of large villages that can be recognised as small towns. This reflects a neglected/ignored bottom of the urban hierarchy, small towns; however, in a certain extension, it serves their economic growth and the creation of wealth in general. This can be perceived as an opportunity for the development of those localities. This is not a simple mechanism of invisibility or neglect but also a local strategy stimulated by local dominant actors, and works with a local agency. People in small towns are not passive but are instead actors of this position. Local politicians and entrepreneurs actively refuse opportunities to become part of the urban frame and convert the locality where they live in to an official town belonging to the urban framework.

For instance, unrecognised small towns and large villages benefit from the rural connectivity programme, notably the *Pradhan Mantri Gram Sadak Yojana* scheme launched in 2000. With good roads, distance from national highways and metropolises is no longer an issue in most regions. Small towns benefit from India's infrastructure-driven development paradigm, which was promoted in the turn of the millennium universal access, not only in terms of roads but also for sanitation and electricity. In that sense, they are favoured due to their rurality.

In addition, in the trade-off between sharing wealth and alleviating poverty or stimulating economic growth, urban policies clearly support the motor engine of growth—in other words, the large cities. In the urban context, inclusive policies are limited to poverty reduction schemes and slum rehabilitation, essentially focusing on large cities. As explained in the following paragraph, public expenditure is focused on only the largest metropolitan areas.

The first consistent urban policy in terms of means invested (INR 1,205–360 million—USD 26.7 billion) began from 2005 onwards.[10] The Jawaharlal Nehru National Urban Renewal Mission (JNNURM; 2005–2014) concentrated its means on the 67 largest cities in India. It signified infrastructure improvement driven by compulsory city governance reforms (Kundu, 2014). An inclusion approach was embedded in; it focuses on urban poverty reduction and integrated slum rehabilitation through the Basic Services to Urban Poor (BSUP) scheme and the flagship of the UPA government—the *Rajiv Awas Yojana* mission or Slum-Free City scheme. They were all centred on large cities and their results were limited in terms of inclusion. Only the sub-mission for Urban Infrastructure Development Scheme for Small and Medium Towns (UIDSSMT) administered by the Ministry of Urban Development and the Integrated Housing and Slum Development Programme (IHSDP) component targeted smaller towns, but it focused on water supply and their means were limited (Khan, 2017).[11]

After the shift in the central government and the victory of the National Democratic Alliance, urban policy aligns itself with the pro-business agenda of the dominant growth coalition. A new scheme called the Atal Mission for Rejuvenation and Urban Transformation (AMRUT) was launched in June 2015, with an outlay of INR 500,000 million (USD 11.06 billion) for five years from 2015–2016 to 2019–2020. AMRUT constitutes a remodelled and less-funded version of JNNURM, which primarily relies on earlier infrastructure-centred JNNURM components, such as augmentation of water supply, collection and treatment of sewage and garbage, and building roads and flyovers. The new additions that are being introduced include digitisation and Wi-Fi zones in cities. The incomplete projects under JNNURM will be covered under the AMRUT. In addition to AMRUT, the Smart City Mission flagship programme promotes 100 cities across the country, thus 'making them citizen-friendly and sustainable.' If participation and inclusiveness are claimed, smart cities are in fact, a new declination of spatial concentration of investments for economic growth and innovation. 'The vision about smart cities in India being about symbols instead of enabling the power of citizens to find the financial and intellectual resources to address their problems is unsmart,' stated Partha Mukhopadhyay (2016).

By connecting the largest metropolitan regions of India with their string of smart cities and SEZ, several industrial corridor projects are taking off. The largest project is the 1,500-kilometre-long Delhi–Mumbai Industrial Corridor Project (DMICDC), and another similar project will connect Chennai and Bangalore. Conceived in 2008, DMICDC reached an agreement for INR 1,000 crore (USD 139.1 million) between India and Japan. Corridors are conceived to articulate and expand the mega pole of growth.

The urban imagination is focused on the attractiveness of the largest metropolitan regions, and Make in India policy has contributed to this. Extreme heatwaves may soon render cities like Delhi unliveable (Im et al., 2017). Almost every year, Bangalore and Chennai experience an acute lack of water. Floods linked to cyclones affect all the coastal cities, notably Mumbai and Chennai, thus resulting in massive destruction.

In addition to metropolitan regions' further adaptation to rapid climate changes, the network of small towns could represent a complementary approach in terms of crisis mitigation. The post-disaster resilience of the diffuse clusters of small towns and their capacity to avoid it must be investigated vis-à-vis the large metropolis.

Delhi is, almost every day, the most polluted city in the world, and despite the investments in road and mass transportation, the average speed of traffic in the largest cities continues to slow down. In other words, without even considering the effects of climate change, the negative externalities of concentration far outweigh the benefits of concentration in large Indian cities. This is particularly true if we consider the social inequalities in the face of these constraints, that is, if we consider the daily commute time of the poorest workers from peripheral slums marked by extreme pollution and without access to drinking water.

The challenge then becomes to design new integrated, inclusive mega-regions that integrate the halo of dispersed small towns. Although meta-forms/configurations of a horizontal metropolis region start to be conceptualised (Vigano et al., 2018), it is no longer a polarised urban region but is instead a multi-polarised assemblage that shares relationships with distant localities, abroad, and their immediate hinterland. Here is the case for new modernity without a metropolitan bias. India, with its diffuse urbanisation characterised by the growing weight of small towns in its system of cities, can represent an emerging case of horizontal urbanism. This may be a method for the reconciliation of the entire urban system from an inclusive perspective. In the words of Vigano et al. (2018: 1), 'the horizontal metropolis as a radical project, is both an image and a conceptual device through which to criticise, apprehend and imagine the contemporary city. It refers to a specific spatial condition characterised by a horizontality of infrastructure, urbanity, relationships, and by closely interlinked, co-penetrating rural/urban realms, communication, transport, and economic systems.' It constitutes a pursuit of McGee *desakota* conceptualisation, *zwischenstadt* in Germany after Sieverts (2003), or *città diffusa* in Italy (Indovina et al., 1990). The horizontal metropolis adds a performative/programmatic agenda in favour of spatial justice and horizontal circulations. We are invited to apprehend Mega-Urban-Regions, which differ from those centred on a major metropolis, and are invited to conceive the possibility of the emergence of urban–rural/rurban concentrations without a core. Metropolitan areas are not necessarily created by big cities. They could be the product of a multipolar dynamics as well as an anisotropic development and may generate a 'non-centred' or de-centred urban region.[12] In the horizontal emergence, there is no place for a hierarchical structure, and the opportunities for more inclusive development are less constrained. It is, in that sense, an innovative territory.

The emerging multipolar Coimbatore-Tiruppur-Erode conurbation is emblematic of the horizontal metropolis paradigm, which is becoming a dominant functional landscape (Map 3.1). It gathers from Coimbatore to Erode a population

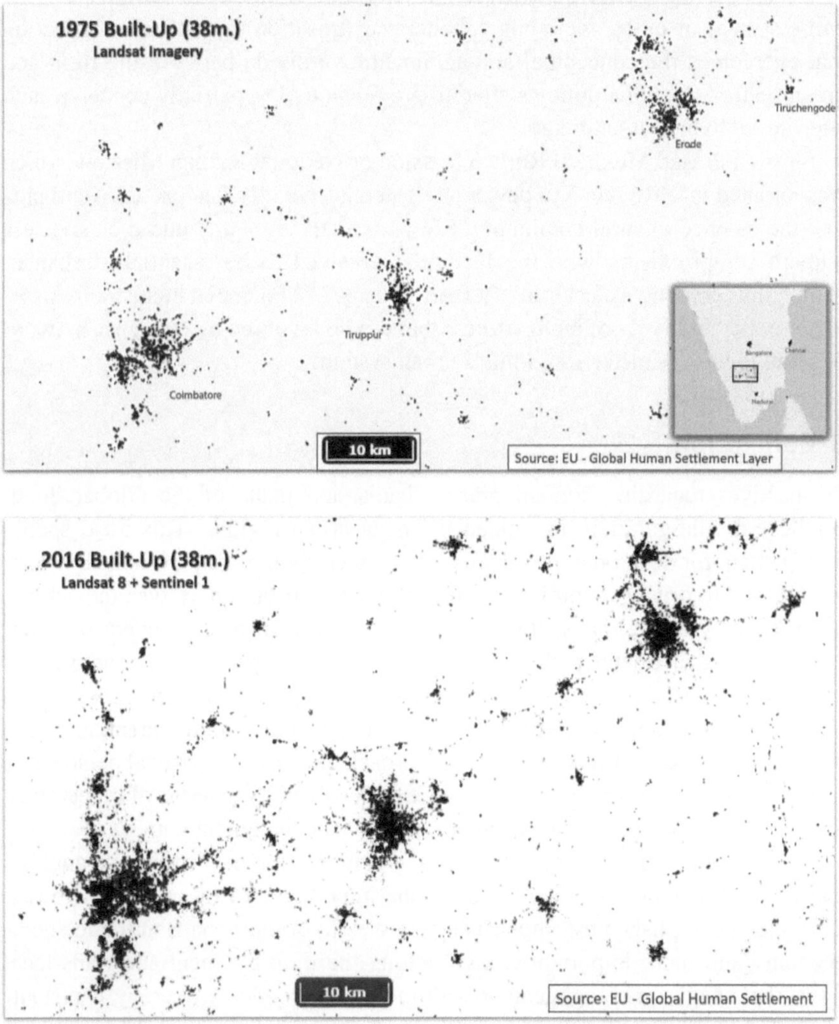

MAP 3.1 Example of an Emerging Horizontal Metropolis in South India (Tamil Nadu)

equivalent to the metropolitan region of Chennai: approximately 8.5 million inhabitants and major industrial clusters and a myriad of census towns. Coimbatore is known as the Manchester of the South for a long time. It is a major centre for machine factoring and in recent times, an emerging hub in the software industry (two SEZs have been implemented to support it). Along the National Highway, in small towns and villages, a string of technical colleges and private universities are fast expanding. The Tiruppur cluster for knitwear exportation is of national importance with 6,000 textile units. It is an assemblage of five villages that began to be recognised as a city corporation only since 2008. Tiruppur accounted for 90% of Indian knitwear exports (INR 200 billion—USD 2.8 billion in 2014–2015). Tiruchengode, with its truck industry, belongs to it too.

Observing these macro-territories, in addition to the consideration for the entire system of cities, including subaltern urbanisation, introduces a reflection that overcomes the conceptual and administrative divide between the rural and urban sectors. A public policy started to provide a tool to partially conceive such a territorial hybrid assemblage.

Shyama Prasad Mukherji Rurban Mission or National Rurban Mission, which was initiated in 2016, aims to develop 'clusters of villages that preserve and nurture the essence of rural community life with focus on equity and inclusiveness without compromising with the facilities perceived to be essentially urban in nature, thus creating a cluster of "Rurban Villages".'[13] Financial inclusion is also a major policy in favour of inclusiveness that can be favoured by the dense network of small towns characterising India's urban system.

8 Conclusion

Perspectives regarding contemporary urbanisation paths of the Global South privilege a configuration dominated by mega urban regions. This ideal spatial arrangement for development, including large metropolitan regions and corridors, is supposed to drive economic growth. Natural redistribution, or wealth trickling down socially as well as spatially, is the only mechanism conceived to ensure inclusion in that liberal path to prosperity. However, outside metropolises, an urban world exists with thousands of towns wherein people consume, make a living, create opportunities to access resources and generate employment, and connect with others on various scales. Our approach contributes a critical perspective that focuses attention on this other urban area, its diversity in terms of trajectories, and its significance for ensuring a more inclusive development path.

Through the current research, we used a combination of quantitative analysis and in-depth ethnographies to highlight the importance of these smaller towns. This was accomplished by emphasising the weight of their contribution to socio-economy and more importantly, highlighting the multiple local and trans-local flows that shape their engagement with the global economy, thereby contributing to (what can be mischievously called) subaltern globalisation. This attention to horizontal linkages, in addition to a vertical dependence framework, suggests a different perspective—more relational, open-ended, multi-layered, and multi-scalar approaches—of the urban transition.

This is a first step towards recoding our understanding of the Indian urban system as a whole, including the full variety of its components. It acknowledges the role of metropolitan areas, but questions their pre-eminence in fashioning the transition from agriculture (and the transition of agriculture) and the broader developmental process. It is instead the smaller settlements—the Anyplace towns—that have diverse and durable effects on their neighbourhood, thus making for a broader and more inclusive process of change. Concomitantly, the autonomous global connections of the Micropolis town (clusters of towns) bring into relief the manner with which global interconnections are rapidly becoming scale-free. Global cities are not the only hubs for regional and international interconnections.

The various forms of governance play a crucial role in the evolution of this urban system as well as the regional history of governing. The designation of settlements as 'urban' or 'rural' is performative because it affects the type of infrastructure that will be available to the settlement. Its physical connectivity will determine the settlement's ability to network with its neighbours, whereas the availability of electricity would determine the nature of economic activity. If it is selected as the site for the administrative offices, it automatically acquires a collection of consumers for a potential market. Although such infrastructure does not over-determine the path that the settlement will follow, it would be unwise to ignore the possibility that it exerts (substantial) influence on it.

This reality underlines the importance of the notion of Subaltern Urbanisation to think of a great diversity of connections and flows that can articulate scales in unexpected, complex, and myriad ways. Before the advent of agglomeration as a major urban analytical theme, small towns were largely perceived as counter-magnets to large towns, because the population sought to move away from rural life—similar to a buffer, but with an underdeveloped role of their own. Subaltern urbanisation moves away from this perspective and acknowledges the functionality of this layer of settlements as a stratum that is not subordinate, but is instead an integral and often parallel part of the manner in which cities are increasingly linked. We posit that it is important to go far beyond and to cease ignoring their agency and innovativeness, particularly in a world wherein in 2015, only 35 out of 115 countries had more than half of their urban population in large cities (agglomerations of more than a million in population).

Such a dispersed urban system may be increasingly future-ready as economic activities transform from large-scale Fordist manufacturing to increased mass customisation and localisation. Future studies must determine whether the contingent circumstances that support the emergence and stability of smaller towns in other geographies, such as Vietnam and China (Zhu, 2000), are similar to the process of subaltern urbanisation in India. Although the importance of smaller towns is not unique to India, the processes of subaltern urbanisation may well be. Small towns constitute a myriad of gates to an increasingly inclusive development path conceived in terms of socio-spatial justice.

Notes

1 In 2017, the UPA government merged the urban development and housing and urban poverty alleviation ministries to form the Ministry of Housing and Urban Affairs (MoHUA).

2 NEG refers to a major and influential trend in the neoclassical economy that has promoted the introduction of geographical space into economics since the 1990s, notably with the aim to explain concentration. This has led to policies promoting the concentration of investment in large metropolitan areas, thereby affirming that this polarisation is beneficial to growth through the redistribution of wealth to all territories and populations. It tends to justify the persistent and eventually increasing spatial inequalities.

3 This collective research was conducted by a group of 20 researchers as part of a French National Research Agency Grant. The ethnographies include small towns across different states in India and across different governance regimes. See Zérah and Denis (2017).

4 To be precise, 32.1 million people moved from rural to urban areas and another 11.5 million people moved from urban to rural areas, thus indicating a bidirectional flow of population.

5 Defined by a non-permanent movement to the city, but instead going back and forth from a place of residence towards jobs within the city.

6 Based on the usual status of the National Sample Survey data. Alternatively, cultivators and agricultural labourers constitute 54.6% of the total workforce in the 2011 Census data.

7 The classification is decided prior to each census enumeration because the urban and rural schedules differ on the basis of information collected during the previous census. For details, see http://censusindia.gov.in/2011-Circulars/Circulars/11-31-10-Circular-02.doc (accessed 10 January 2016). In short, the designation criteria for census towns are based on the data collected during the census conducted ten years prior to their designation. This led to a decadal underestimation of small towns.

8 Indira Awas Yojana (Indira Housing Scheme) was a subsidy programme for housing the poor in rural areas. This has since been replaced by the Prime Minister's Awas Yojana, which has included a large urban component.

9 We must not forget that although the IT sector is successful, it only employs 3 million persons and is not growing within an Indian workforce, which comprises 580 million people. It is a component of the exclusionary metropolitan growth of India and an illustration of the jobless growth that characterises India since the past 15 years of economic liberalisation. The IT sector is now being affected due to automation and cloud computing.

10 The Integrated Development of Small and Medium Towns (IDSMT), which was launched in 1979–1980, was a modest antecedent. The IDSMT was applicable to all towns/cities with a population of up to 0.5 million. The scheme continued until the middle of the 10th plan period and covered 1,854 towns until 2004–2005, after which it was subsumed into the Urban Infrastructure Development Scheme for Small and Medium Towns (UIDSSMT). Thereafter, the Megacity scheme was initiated in 1993–1994. The objective of the scheme was to undertake infrastructure development projects of city-wide/regional significance covering a wide range of components, such as water supply and sewerage, roads and bridges, city transport, and solid waste management. The Scheme was applicable to Mumbai, Kolkata, Chennai, Bangalore, and Hyderabad. This phase of urban policy was marked by an emphasis on mega-cities as being central to urban development. This bias has never been structurally corrected since then. During this period, the 74th Constitutional Amendment Act in 1992 that sought to make the third tier of governance increasingly autonomous and participatory was passed. However, the larger municipal corporations with adequate finances were able to benefit from this act, whereas the municipalities in smaller towns have not significantly benefitted from it.

11 After Khan (2017), we observed that in the ten major states, 71% of the central assistance has been committed to the big city UIG and BSUP schemes that account for 36% of the total urban population of India. Only 29% of the total central share has been committed to the remaining small- and medium-sized towns under the UIDSSMT and IHSDP, although these towns account for 43% of the total urban population. The scenario is similar in other states as well, wherein 65% of the central share has been committed to the big city UIG and BSUP schemes that account for 6% of the total urban population, whereas 35% of the total central share has been committed to the remaining small- and medium-sized towns under the UIDSSMT and IHSDP that account for 15% of the total urban population.

12 For an introduction to a classical perspective on the emergence of a 'meta-agglomeration' in India, see Perez et al. (2019).

13 http://rurban.gov.in/about.html

References

Amin, A. and S. Graham (1997). "The Ordinary City," *Transactions of the Institute of British Geographers*, vol. 22, 411–429.

Bell, D. and M. Jayne (2009). "Small Cities? Towards a Research Agenda," *International Journal of Urban and Regional Research*, vol. 33, 683–699.

Benjamin, S. (2017). "Multilayered Urbanisation of the South Canara Territory," in Denis, E. and M.-H. Zérah eds., *Subaltern Urbanisation in India: An Introduction to the Dynamics of Ordinary Towns*, New Delhi: Springer: 199–233.

Bercegol, R. D. and S. Gowda (2017). "Development on the Urban Fringe: The Prosperity of Kartarpur, a Small Town-Cluster in Punjab," in Denis, E. and M.-H. Zérah eds., *Subaltern Urbanisation in India: An Introduction to the Dynamics of Ordinary Towns*, New Delhi: Springer: 473–495.

Brenner, N. ed. (2014). *Implosions/Explosions. Towards a Study of Planetary Urbanization*, Berlin: Jovis.

Brenner, N. and C. Schmid (2011). "Planetary Urbanisation," in Gandy, M. ed., *Urban Constellations*, Berlin: Jovis: 10–13.

Brenner, N. and C. Schmid (2015). "Towards a New Epistemology of the Urban?" *City*, vol. 19(2–3), 151–182.

Chandrasekhar, S. and A. Sharma (2014). "On the Spatial Concentration of Employment in India," *Economic and Political Weekly*, vol. 49(21), 16–18.

Christaller, W. (1933). *Die zentralen Orte in Suddeutschland*, Jena: G. Fischer, (Translated in part), by Charlisle W. Baskin, as Central Places in Southern Germany. Prentice Hall 1966).

Denis, E. and K. Marius-Gnanou (2010). "Toward a Better Appraisal of Urbanization in India," *Cybergeo: European Journal of Geography*, vol. 569.

Denis, E., P. Mukhopadhyay, and M.-H. Zérah (2012). "Subaltern Urbanisation in India," *Economic and Political Weekly*, vol. 47(30), 52–62.

Denis, E. and M.-H. Zérah eds. (2017). *Subaltern Urbanisation in India: An Introduction to the Dynamics of Ordinary Towns*, New Delhi: Springer.

Ghani, E., A. G. Goswami, and W. R. Kerr (2012). *Is India's Manufacturing Sector Moving Away from Cities?* Cambridge, MA: NBER Working Paper Series, 17992.

Glaeser, E. L. (2010). *Agglomeration Economics*, Chicago: The University of Chicago Press.

Heitzman, J. (2008). *The City in South Asia*, London: Routledge.

Henderson, V. (2003). "The Urbanization Process and Economic Growth: The So-What Question," *Journal of Economic Growth*, vol. 8, 47–71.

Himanshu, P. L., A. Mukhopadhyay, and R. Murgai (2011). *Non-farm Diversification and Rural Poverty Decline: A Perspective from Indian Sample Survey and Village Study Data*, Working Paper 44, London: London School of Economics and Political Science.

Im, E. S., J. S. Pal, and E. A. Eltahir (2017). "Deadly Heat Waves Projected in the Densely Populated Agricultural Regions of South Asia," *Science Advances*, vol. 3(8), e1603322.

Indovina, F., F. Matassoni, M. Savino, M. Sernini, M. Torres, and L. Vettoretto (1990). *La città diffusa*, Venetia: Daest.

Khan, S. (2017). "The Other Jawaharlal Nehru National Urban Renewal Mission: What Does It Mean for Small Town India?" in Denis, E. and M.-H. Zérah eds., *Subaltern Urbanisation in India: An Introduction to the Dynamics of Ordinary Towns*, New Delhi: Springer: 337–370.

Krugman, P. (1998). "What's New About the New Economic Geography?" *Oxford Review of Economic Policy*, vol. 14(2), 7–17.

Kundu, A. and L. R. Saraswati (2012). "Migration and Exclusionary Urbanisation in India," *Economic and Political Weekly*, vol. 47(26–27), 219–227.

Kundu, D. (2014). "Urban Development Programmes in India: A Critique of JNNURM," *Social Change*, vol. 44(4), 615–632.

Moriconi-Ebrard, F., E. Denis, and K. Marius-Gnanou (2010). "Repenser la géographie économique. Les arrangements du rapport de la Banque Mondiale avec les sciences géographiques urbaines," *Cybergeo: European Journal of Geography*, 23144.

Mukhopadhyay, P. (2012). "Moving People and Morphing Places," *Mint*, 7. www.livemint.com/Opinion/b4AVxWTKCmduNCTNIgGUjO/Moving-people-and-morphing-places.html

Mukhopadhyay, P. (2016). "Unsmart City," *Mint*, www.livemint.com/Politics/yUF-GJqOznzhziuolmt7v9O/Unsmart-cities.html

Mukhopadhyay, P. (2017). "Does Administrative Status Matter for Small Towns in India?" in Denis, E. and M.-H. Zérah eds., *Subaltern Urbanisation in India: An Introduction to the Dynamics of Ordinary Towns*, New Delhi: Springer: 443–469.

Mukhopadhyay, P., M.-H. Zérah, and E. Denis (2018). "Subaltern Urbanization Revisited," in Patel, S. and O. Goyal eds., *India's Contemporary Urban Conundrum*, London: Routledge: 54–66.

Mukhopadhyay, P., M. H. Zérah, and E. Denis (2020). "Subaltern Urbanization: Indian Insights for Urban Theory," *International Journal of Urban and Regional Research*, vol. 44(4), 582–598.

Mukhopadhyay, P., M.-H. Zérah, G. Samanta, and A. Maria (2016). *Understanding India's Urban Frontier. What Is Behind the Emergence of Census Towns in India?* Policy Research Working Paper 7923, Washington: The World Bank Group.

Perez, J., G. Fusco, and F. Moriconi-Ebrard (2019). "Identification and Quantification of Urban Space in India: Defining Urban Macro-Structures," *Urban Studies*, vol. 56(10), 1988–2004.

Pradhan, K. C. (2013). "Unacknowledged Urbanisation: The New Census Towns in India," *Economic and Political Weekly*, vol. 48(36), 43–51.

Pumain, D. and F. Moriconi-Ebrard (1997). "City Size Distributions and Metropolisation," *GeoJournal*, vol. 43, 307–314.

Raman, B. (2017). "Practices of Territory in Small and Medium Cities of South India," in Denis, E. and M.-H. Zérah eds., *Subaltern Urbanisation in India: An Introduction to the Dynamics of Ordinary Towns*, New Delhi: Springer: 235–260.

Robinson, J. (2002). "Global and World Cities: A View from off the Map," *International Journal of Urban and Regional Research*, vol. 26, 531–554.

Robinson, J. (2006). *Ordinary Cities: Between Modernity and Development*, London: Routledge.

Roy, A. (2009). "Strangely Familiar: Planning and the Worlds of Insurgence and Informality," *Planning Theory*, vol. 8, 7–11.

Roy, A. (2011a). "Postcolonial Urbanism: Speed, Hysteria, Mass Dreams," in Roy, A. and A. Ong eds., *Worlding Cities: Asian Experiments and the Art of Being Global*, Wiley-Blackwell: 307–335.

Roy, A. (2011b). "Slumdog Cities: Rethinking Subaltern Urbanism," *International Journal of Urban and Regional Research*, vol. 35, 223–238.

Roy, A. (2016). "What is Urban about Critical Urban Theory?" *Urban Geography*, vol. 37, 810–823.

Samanta, G. (2017). "Beyond Metropolitan Shadow: Growth and Governance of Small Town in Eastern India," *Jindal Journal of Public Policy*, vol. 3(1), 51–70.

Sassen, S. (2001). *The Global City: New York, London, Tokyo*, Princeton, NJ: Princeton University Press.

Schmid, C. (2018). "Journeys through Planetary Urbanization: Decentering Perspectives on the Urban," *Environment and Planning D: Society and Space*, vol. 36(3), 591–610.

Sieverts, T. (2003). *Cities without Cities: An Interpretation of the Zwischenstadt*, London: Routledge.

Sircar, S. (2017). " 'Census Towns' in India and What it Means to be 'Urban': Competing Epistemologies and Potential New Approaches," *Singapore Journal of Tropical Geography*, vol. 38, 229–244.

Sivaramakrishnan, K. C. (2011). *Re-visioning Indian Cities: The Urban Renewal Mission*, New Delhi: Sage.

Swerts, E., D. Pumain, and E. Denis (2014). "The Future of India's Urbanization," *Futures*, vol. 56, 43–52.

Swerts, E., E. Denis, and P. Mukhopadhyay (2018). "Diffuse Urbanization and Mega-Urban Regions in India: Between Reluctant and Restrictive Urbanism?" in Rozenblat, C. ed., *International and Transnational Perspectives on Urban Systems*, Singapore: Springer: 237–262.

Tastevin, Y. P. (2017). "From Ox-Carts to Borewell Rigs: Maintenance, Manufacture and Innovation in Tiruchengode," in Denis, E. and M.-H. Zérah eds., *Subaltern Urbanisation in India: An Introduction to the Dynamics of Ordinary Towns*, New Delhi: Springer: 497–525.

Taylor, P. J. (2004). "Regionality in the World City Network," *International Social Science Journal*, vol. 56(181), 361–372.

Vigano, P., C. Cavalieri, and M. B. Corte eds. (2018). *The Horizontal Metropolis Between Urbanism and Urbanization*, Switzerland: Springer.

Vishwanath, T., S. V. Lall, D. Dowall, N. Lozano-Gracia, S. Sharma, and H. G. Wang (2013). *Urbanization beyond Municipal Boundaries: Nurturing Metropolitan Economies and Connecting Peri-Urban Areas in India*, Washington, DC: World Bank.

Zérah, M.-H. and E. Denis (2017). "Introduction: Reclaiming Small Towns," in Denis, E. and M.-H. Zérah eds., *Subaltern Urbanisation in India: An Introduction to the Dynamics of Ordinary Towns*, New Delhi: Springer: 1–35.

Zhu, Y. (2000). "In Situ Urbanization in Rural China: Case Studies from Fujian Province," *Development and Change*, vol. 31, 413–434.

4

EDUCATION SYSTEM AND ECONOMIC DEVELOPMENT IN RURAL BANGLADESH

A Comparative Study Between Remote and Suburban Rural Villages

Tatsuya Kusakabe

1 Introduction

Study background

This chapter is conducted as a comparative case study of two rural areas to elucidate how rural people in Bangladesh used their school careers or certificates throughout their life and ascertain what educational development outcomes were derived from them. For discussion, it is necessary to describe how Bangladesh established its workable education system and how it was intended to function in the country in this research area. The education system can be divided roughly into two driving forces: the education policy arrangement and the movement of people as a component element towards education systems.

The rise in Bangladesh of Education for All

'Education for All' (EFA), an education-based political movement, can be cited as the first of the driving forces. The educational development of Bangladesh at the policy level was accelerated by the EFA declaration given at the World Conference on Education for All (WCEFA) in Jomtien, Thailand, in 1990, known as the World Educational Development Campaign (WCEFA, 1990). The WCEFA asked developing countries for commitment and action to universalise access to basic and primary education by 2000. The global tide of educational development took to the World Education Forum in Dakar, Senegal (UNESCO, 2000), which reaffirmed the vision set out in the World Declaration of EFA and, furthermore, was embraced at the World Education Forum, Incheon, South Korea (UNESCO et al., 2015). The latter adopted the Education 2030-Incheon Declaration

DOI: 10.4324/9781003304760-6

TABLE 4.1 EFA Policies in Bangladesh

1990	Compulsory Education Act
	- Primary education schooling became **free and compulsory** as a basic human right.
1992	Food for Education Programme (FFEP)
	- To provide households with **10–12 kg wheat or paddy** when a child's school attendance exceeds 85% in a month.
1994	Female Secondary Education Project (FSEP)
	- Girls can obtain **free lower secondary education** when they meet these requirements: a higher than 75% school attendance rate and a better than 45% academic record.
2002	Stipend for Education Project (SFEP)
	- The government provision changed to **100 tk cash** in place of 10–12 kg wheat or paddy of FFEP.

Source: (Kusakabe, 2008).

and Framework for Action in affiliation with Sustainable Development Goals 4 (SDG4), which aims to disseminate quality education for all people.

Bangladesh responded to the declaration through legislation and policymaking for educational development as an exemplary model, as seen in Table 4.1. This study analyses the period of quantitative expansion until the early 2000s, meaning the EFA period.

These incentive policies brought children into the education system even in remote rural areas unfamiliar with it. Nonetheless, such progress has led to the deterioration of education quality as a logical consequence. Concretely, from the independence of Bangladesh from 1971 to 2017, the number of primary schools (28,731 → 83,498), the enrolment number of students (5,040,000 thousand → 1,7251,350 thousand), and the number of teachers (117,275 thousand → 623,964 thousand) gradually increased, despite the education sector being rapidly bloated (BBS, 1985; BANBEIS, 1991, 1992; PMED, 2001; PMED, 2002; BANBEIS, 2010, 2018). The employment of untrained teachers to improve the teacher–student ratio triggered the quality deterioration. Quality control by the government could not keep pace with the increasing number of students and the diversification of children. Despite quality deterioration, the number of students continued to rise until the 2010s. As neo-institutionalists have pointed out (Meyer et al., 1997; Meyer and Ramirez, 2000), people in Bangladesh also experienced standardised subjects, as was the case in other developed or developing countries during the EFA period.

Some education statistics indicate that these increasing tendencies of rapid growth at the primary level have influenced secondary education, although such rapidity is not apparent. Some educational statistics published by the Bangladesh Bureau of Educational Information and Statistics (BANBEIS) indicate that the number of secondary school students has also increased. The number of secondary schools (6,162 → 20,467), the enrolment number of students (1,261,000 thousand → 10,330,695 thousand), and the number of teachers (117,275 thousand → 623,964 thousand) from 1971 to 2017 also show that secondary education has bloated as well as primary level (BBS, 1985; BANBEIS, 1991, 1992; PMED, 2002; BANBEIS, 2010, 2018). In-kind policies, such as Food for Education Programme (FFEP), Female Secondary Assistant Programme (FSAP), and Stipend for Education Project (SFEP), contributed to the increased access to school education. The contribution was not as greatly needed in urban areas, which originally had sufficient awareness of the value of education, but has been felt more strongly in rural areas where impoverished people live, who need more help to overcome poverty. It suggests that the EFA policy had greater and more varied effects on rural areas than urban areas.

The educational development described earlier has introduced rural people to school systems and has given them, particularly the poor ones, some perspective on the fact that their children can use educational certificates to gain economic or employment opportunities.

Education demands from the popular side in rural Bangladesh

When the EFA period started in the 1990s, the economic development of rural people in Bangladesh reached a tipping point. Statistical figures show that the rapid growth of the Bangladeshi economy since the 1990s correlates with school education development.

Much media, studies, and reports have indicated the increasing economic growth in today's Bangladesh. *The Daily Star*, a well-known Bangladeshi newspaper, often carries topics on the bright economic prospects of the nation. In December 2017, *The Daily Star* carried 'The World Economic Situation and Prospects 2018,' edited by the United Nations. An article reported that 'the Bangladesh economy is set to continue expanding at a rapid pace, underpinned by strong domestic demand, especially large infrastructure projects and new initiatives in the energy sector.' (*The Daily Star* 2017) In March 2018, the paper discussed 'Graduation from Low Developing Countries' (LDCs). The associated article stated that Bangladesh had upgraded to the World Bank's 'lower-middle-income' category by increasing its gross national income and that it must prepare for 'preference erosion,' whereby it loses duty-free access to foreign markets as a privilege, mainly in garment exports, after graduating from LDCs (*The Daily Star*, 2018). Basu, a non-resident senior fellow of the Asian Development Bank, pointed out, 'Bangladesh's annual GDP growth has exceeded Pakistan's by roughly 2.5 percentage points per year. Furthermore, this year, its growth rate is likely to surpass India. Moreover, at 1.1 percent per year, Bangladesh's population growth is well below Pakistan's 2 percent rate, which means that its per capita income is growing faster than Pakistan's by approximately 3.3 percentage points per year. By extrapolation, Bangladesh will overtake Pakistan in terms of per capita GDP in 2020, even with a correction for purchasing power parity' (Basu, 2018).

Today, there are numerous discussions about the economic boom in Bangladesh. Nevertheless, few reports in the relevant literature describe studies on how it has affected the general population of Bangladesh. According to accepted notions and many studies, this vibrant economic development of Bangladesh began in the 1990s because of garment industry development, increasing overseas remittances, and rapid urbanisation (Suda, 2010; JICA, 2017). Suda (2010) analysed how the rural economy in Bangladesh has become connected to the global economy through micro-level case studies of two villages. This study explains that the global and domestic effects of the garment industry, overseas remittances, and rapid urbanisation have increased the income of villagers. Increased income has economic effects that boost positive cash circulation within rural areas. For example, some richer agricultural landholders can now send family members to work in foreign countries or maintain their income through stable wage jobs. Normally, richer households have no desire for agricultural management, except for growing food for their own consumption. For that reason, their agricultural lands will be lent to landless households as a mortgage through an informal financial system known as *bondok*. It leads to some economic or employment opportunities for agricultural labourers or landless farmers and even for poor households (Suda, 2010: 19–20). It has undoubtedly improved the income of rural Bangladeshi residents. However, most poor households remain agricultural landowners, even given the increase in cash circulation. Consequently, if poor households hope to realise social mobility by obtaining salaried jobs or working abroad, then obtaining education, particularly secondary-level education and its certification, would become an absolute requirement.

2 Research questions

The stage of discussion has come to investigate whether poor people can use secondary educational certificates to obtain an upper level of education and work nowadays. The general discussion about Bangladesh's education is no longer at the stage of considering whether to provide schooling to poor people from the viewpoint of social welfare, except for some ethnic minorities, language minorities, and disabled children. Moreover, a study must elucidate whether some merits of educational development have already reached poor people in rural areas. One must ask whether poor people in rural Bangladesh are included in the education system and whether they are able to use their education and certification.

For that reason, this study attempts to examine and evaluate evidence of the inclusiveness of poor people in the education system through the following research questions used to analyse case studies: **1.** Is social mobility based on meritocracy through an education system designed to guarantee a degree or educational career acquisition possible for people, particularly poor people, in rural Bangladesh? **2.** Is it possible to develop human resources as an inclusive educational system that works on its own beyond social welfare through the current Bangladeshi education system? **3.** Is there any difference in the inclusiveness of the national education system between poor people in a remote rural setting and suburban rural setting?

3 Methodology

As described earlier, this study attempts to identify whether the current education system in Bangladesh is working for meritocratic social mobility. To achieve this goal, this study employs a comparative method between two target villages and an examination of decadal transitions to analyse the acceptance of the education system, the utilisation status of education certification, and whether a rise in the meritocratic hierarchy has been realised through educational development. The research period was divided into baseline and endline research for a comparative study of decadal transitions. Baseline studies were conducted during September–October 1999 for K village, as the remote rural setting, and during August–October 2002 for B village, as the suburban rural setting (Map 4.1). Endline studies were conducted from August to September 2009 for K village and in September 2011 for B village.

To identify factors that contribute to greater socio-economic change in one area than in another, two villages with different geographic and socio-economic backgrounds were chosen and compared. In both cases, rural rather than urban areas were selected for this study because, as described, tremendous growth in school participation has been observed mainly in rural areas. Second, the distance from the village to the closest city was considered because the village location is directly related to the penetration of the industrial economy, which induces school attendance. For instance, people residing far from industrial areas are more likely

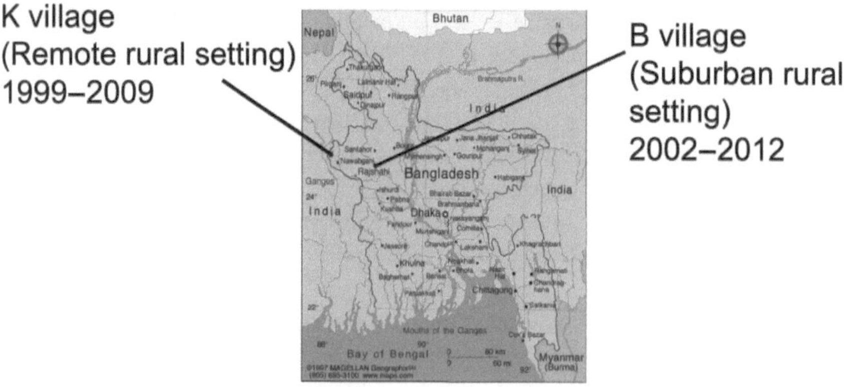

MAP 4.1 Target Villages: Locations of B Village and K Village

to remain engaged in traditional agrarian labour because of their limited access to *chakri* (salaried work), which requires formal education. The development of the industrial economy is positively correlated with degree-issuing schools, even in a rural context. Given these conditions, the two chosen target villages were from a remote rural area and a suburban rural area.

The author classified the collected household and education data in each village, through specific criteria, into upper, middle, and lower classes. There are two criteria. The first is the income of each household. The study identified the boundary between the upper and middle classes at 25,000 tk per year in terms of household income, which comes from the householders and other earners in each household, and that between the middle class and the lower class at 8,000 tk per year. The second is whether a household holds sustainable wage jobs, such as white-collar jobs or factory work.

This comparative study was designed to identify commonalities and differences in factors affecting life transformations, including socio-economic and educational changes, and ascertain signs of social mobility between the two villages.

Aside from the main approach, the study used two research methods. First, a school visit survey to obtain data on educational development. Second, an education administrative organisation survey. The author interviewed county education officers (Thana education officer, TEO) and several officers of the Ministry of Education of the central government about the present education condition in the counties.

B village: suburban rural village

B village is in Putia county, Rajshahi district, in western Bangladesh. For this study, we selected 54 sample households for a scheduled census.

From the 1980s to the 1990s, economic development progressed gradually in this area, in accordance with the rising economic influence from outside of the village, particularly Rajshahi City, where the light industry is situated. For this reason, almost all villagers could receive multiple incomes, both from agriculture and as *chakri* (salaried workers). Rajshahi City, the fifth largest metropolis in Bangladesh, has about 450,000 residents and is a central location in the western part of the country. It is host to the garment industry, silk factories, food processing factories, and related industries. In addition, the city is a distribution base for these products. Hence, the related industries and companies offer services such as logistics and transportation. Therefore, Rajshahi City has an economic impact on peripheral areas.

Many people commute daily from areas surrounding the city. B village supplies labour to these industries because of its proximity to Rajshahi City, a 30-to-40-minute bus ride away. Obtaining a salaried job, such as white-collar, factory work rather than unskilled labour, requires, at least, a secondary school certificate. Village residents are encouraged to pursue education in or outside the village.

K village: remote rural village

K village, Gangni county of Meherpur district, is in the westernmost region of Bangladesh. From this village, 50 samples were selected for the scheduled census.

The village is near the national border with West Bengal state, India. Therefore, many villagers cross the border to visit relatives in West Bengal. Until recently, many of them were engaged in small-scale, cross-border businesses. However, with the deterioration of bilateral relations between India and Bangladesh, the border has closed. From Dhaka, the capital city of Bangladesh, K village takes seven to eight hours by bus. Most farmers are peasants called *bhumihin*, possessing little or no land to support themselves. Consequently, some are obliged to travel to other districts as labourers during harvesting periods because of the lack of agrarian labour opportunities inside their villages. What is worse, they have a little opportunity to work in factories, mills, or other industries. This study specifically examines *bhumihin* and poor households to see whether their children have recently cultivated their educational placement or career access through educational development.

4 Modalities of socio-economic development in both villages

Decadal transitions of household economies in the respective villages

With regard to economic development, income levels have increased in the villages during the last decade (Table 4.2). Of course, this is not to say that the villagers' lives have improved since the household economy itself is invariably influenced by rising prices. Although this economic situation is a commonality in the chosen villages, their main occupations are different. In B village, according to the 2002 research, the villagers' main jobs were agriculture, fisheries, furniture, or fruit businesses, or as labourers, rickshaw drivers (*ricshaw-wara*), teachers, and bankers. In 2011, the study revealed that the variety of main occupations had increased, including positions such as company employees, IT assistants, homoeopathy workers, and drivers. However, in the case of K village in 1999, sample households included those working in agriculture, in the army, or as teachers, agriculture workers, labourers, rickshaw drivers, agricultural business workers, husking mill owners, tailors, those working abroad, etc. In the 2009 survey, the variety of main occupations included only argamon drivers (drivers of rickshaws with an engine). On the other hand, the villagers were trying to improve their household economy through a change in planting, from grains, such as paddy or wheat, to some commercial crops, such as tobacco and vegetables.

According to the earlier comparison between the two villages, occupations in B village are more diversified than those in K village.

TABLE 4.2 Decadal Transitions of Household Economy in the Respective Villages

Suburban rural setting: B village	Remote rural setting: K village
Transition of household economy from 2002 to 2011	Transition of household economy from 1999 to 2009
The 54 sample households	The 50 sample households
(population 257→231) 10 households migrated	(population 343→373) 2 households migrated
Total yearly cash income per capita	Total yearly cash income per capita
698,660tk→1,384,992tk(1.98 fold)	204,716tk→604,015tk(2.95 fold)
Monthly living expenses	Monthly living expenses
158,600tk→361,700tk(2.28 fold)	96,714tk→300,733tk(3.11 fold)
Total yearly borrowing money	Total yearly borrowing money
621,800tk→696,000tk(1.1 fold)	112,400tk→459,000tk(4.08 fold)
Borrowed for: Daughters' marriage, investing in agriculture or business, living expenses, land or home acquisition	Borrowed for: Agriculture, tobacco planting business, agricultural running costs

Source: Fieldwork results in K village (1999/2009) and B village (2002/2011).

Examining why income increased in the villages shows that different revenue growth structures exist between the two study villages. Since the economic environment in a suburban rural setting has provided salaried job opportunities for villagers, their job types have increased. However, the remote rural setting residents have no way to access salaried job opportunities because the remoteness of their environment cannot provide it. Nevertheless, agricultural innovations, such as tobacco planting in K village, have provided new income opportunities. It was noted that B village, as a suburban rural setting, used and accessed its surrounding urban economy by getting salaried jobs. However, K village, as a remote rural setting, used its agricultural resources to increase income.

Acceptance of the education system in rural Bangladesh

In this subsection, I present a comparison of the acceptance of Bangladeshi education systems in the respective villages. As the chronological table of B village shows (Table 4.3), the education system was accepted by villagers before the start of the EFA period. The establishment of schools in Bangladesh is often undertaken on residents' initiative rather than that of the government. Initially, the residents themselves operated schools for several years, and in many cases, they applied for government subsidies. Thus, Table 4.3 shows that the acceptance of the education system in B village started before the EFA policies.

The K village chronological table shows that the villagers started to accept the education system after the EFA policy (Table 4.4). Prior to the EFA, K village had a minimum number of schools, but it was not large enough to accommodate all the children. After the EFA period, the education policy stimulated their educational

TABLE 4.3 Chronological Table of School Establishment in B Village

1865	Puthia P.N. High School
1878	Kandela Government Primary School
1910	Shuresory Government Primary School
1968	Gondgohari Government Primary School
	Puthia Girls' High School
1969	Firigasa Government Primary School
1973	Laskulpur Degree College
1974	B Government Primary School
1990	Beginning of Education for All
	Nirfa Sunna Madrasa (Unrecognised)
1995	Puthia Girls' Degree College
	Puthia Dhakil Madrasa
1996	Baptist Aid Kindergarten
2010	Oxford Child Academy (KG to P2)

Source: Author fieldwork 2002, 2011.

TABLE 4.4 Chronological Table of School Establishment in K Village

1920	K Government Primary School
1970	Japani Primary School
1973	K Jr. High and High school
1974	K Aliya Madrasa
1990	Beginning of Education for All
1991	K No. 4 School
1994	Satellite School
1999	K KG School
2000	K College (for HSC)
	K Konranpur Jr. Secondary Girl's College
	Mathpara K Registered Primary School
2007	Two BRAC (NGO) Schools
2010	Progoti Primary School

Note: Accessible secondary schools did not increase.
Source: Author fieldwork 1999, 2009.

development because the government started providing food to householders who sent their children to primary schools. On the school side, the school establishments were stimulated by the possibility that teachers could obtain a monthly salary if the school is promoted as a monthly payment order (MPO) school. Some youths from villages with academic backgrounds were inspired to establish schools based on the increasing need of children for schooling. One can readily understand that the villagers recognised education as a new type of business; however, it is difficult to say that the people recognised the importance of the education system. Accessing salaried jobs is difficult because of the remote rural setting. The relationship between obtaining an education certificate and job placement was more tenuous here than in the suburban rural setting.

In that sense, it can be said that educational development in K village was stimulated by some EFA policies. However, B village had developed school education autonomously because of the need for academic background and certificates.

5 Finding

Finally, the results of the two longitudinal studies comparing the two villages are as follows. The following tables show the research results of whether the children receiving education in the first research realised their ideal placement, such as further education or obtaining a job, or dropped out of school after a decade.

Decadal transition in the upper classes of the respective villages

Upper-class households in the respective villages consist of large-scale landowners, salaried workers, business and factory owners, and civil servants (Tables 4.5 and 4.6). Therefore, they can invest in their children's education to a higher level than the other classes. In the suburban rural setting, 7 of 20 children continued their education to the secondary level or obtained salaried jobs such as professor, IT serviceman, and multi-level marketing. In the remote rural setting, 10 of 19 children were successful cases, meaning they obtained further education or a salaried job. The study revealed that the remote rural setting had a better percentage of successful cases in the upper class. The study found that all female children married early if they dropped out of the school track.

Decadal transition in the upper-middle classes of the respective villages

The upper-middle-class households in the respective villages consist of salaried workers such as teachers, vehicle drivers, business owners, and farmers (Tables 4.7 and 4.8). There has been an explosive growth in job opportunities for people in this class. Nowadays, they can invest in their children's education to a high level. In the suburban rural setting, 29 out of 47 children continued their school education or obtained salaried jobs. In the remote rural setting, only 3 out of 13 children were successful cases. The data show that the suburban rural setting has a better percentage of successful cases in this class. A correlation exists between economic improvement in the household economy and education-career improvement. Successful cases in remote rural settings suddenly became few in contrast to the suburban rural setting, probably because a family's investment in their children's education can be more effective in the semi-urban rural setting. The mechanism is as described earlier; increasing the variety of salaried jobs expanded the placement choices of educated children in B village. However, finding salaried job opportunities in remote rural settings is difficult. Consequently, people in remote rural settings had to engage in agricultural innovations, such

TABLE 4.5 Decadal Transition of Upper-Class Educated Children in B Village

	No.	*Main occupation*	*Subsidiary occupation*	*Yearly income*	*Income growth*	*No. of children*	*Son*	*Daughter*
Upper *7 households*	48	Farmer	Service in movie theatre	345000	↓	3	—	M(14–24) M(8–18) *(1–10)
	48	Farmer	Electrician	119750				
	50	Farmer, Labour	None	256000	↓	2	D(17–27) *(15–25)	—
	50	Farmer	Operator	128125				
	53	College teacher	Farmer	204800	↑	2	*(24–33)	*(18–28)
	53	Professor (Degree college)	Farmer	382400				
	16	Farmer	Shopkeeper	312000	↓	3	—	M(20–30) M(15–25) *(4–14)
	16	Farmer	None	9200				
	52	Architecture, Teacher	None	195800	↑	3	*(18–27)	M(16–25) M(12–21)
	52	Service (Bridge construction, IT assistant), English teacher, Service (IT)	None	434400				
	38	Teacher (High school)	Farmer	96000	↑	3	—	—
	38	None	None	156000				
	6	Farmer	Service, Business	183000	↓	4	? D(12–22) D(8–18) *(2–12)	
	6	Service (Gov.), Business (vegetables), Business (electrical work), Army veteran	MLM (Multi-Level Marketing)	101800				

Upper: Researched in 2002
Lower: Researched in 2011
M (Ages between 2002 and 2011): Married
D (Ages between 2002 and 2011): Dropped out from a school course
*: Found work or continued education
Note: Main occupations and subsidiary occupations reflect the positions held by all earners in a household.

TABLE 4.6 Decadal Transition of Upper-Class Educated Children in K Village

	No.	*Main occupation*	*Subsidiary occupation*	*Yearly income*	*Income growth*	*No. of children*	*Son*	*Daughter*
Upper 9	131	Army	Border security	207600	↓	3	*(9–19)	M(13–23)
	131	Border security	Farmer	172000			*(7–16)	
	106	Farmer	Border trade	127400	↑	4	D(13–22)	M(14–23)
	106	Farmer	Rice business/Border trade	406000			*(6–15)	M(8–18)
	24	Farmer	None	60000	↑	3	D(18–28)	*(4–13)
	24	Farmer	Labour	184000				*(1–10)
	109	Husking mill	Farmer	35950	↑	2	*(17–26)	M(12–22)
	109	Husking mill	Farmer	179800				
	142	High school officer	Teacher	44250	↑	2	*(25–35)	*(2–12)
	142	High school officer	Garment worker	171200				
	20	Farmer	None	70000	↑	1	D(19–29)	–
	20	Farmer	Garment shopkeeper	210000				
	110	Tea store	Work abroad in Malaysia	25350	↑	0	–	–
	110	Tea store	Farmer	232000				
	101	Farmer	Mustard oil business	40330	↑	3	*(14–24)	M(11–21)
	101	Farmer	Mustard oil business	65600				M(8–18)
	71	Tailor	Farmer/Border trade	24000	↑	1	*(5–16)	–
	71	Tailor	Farmer	104900				

Upper: Researched in 1999
Lower: Researched in 2009
M (Ages between 1999 and 2009): Married
D (Ages between 1999 and 2009): Dropped out from a school course
*: Found work or continued education
Note: Main occupations and subsidiary occupations reflect the positions held by all earners in a household.

TABLE 4.7 Decadal Transition of Upper-Middle-Class Educated Children in B Village

	No.	*Main occupation*	*Subsidiary occupation*	*Yearly income*	*Income growth*	*No. of children*	*Son*	*Daughter*
Upper-Middle 2	55	Truck driver	None	96000	→	3	*(25–35)	M(18–28)
	55	None	None	96000			*(22–33)	
	28	Rikshaw driver	Farmer	56000	→	1	?(6–16)	–
	28	None	None	56000				
	1	High school teacher	None	87600	↓	2	?(23–33)	*(20–30)
	1	None	Farmer	66000				
	9	Service	None	85000	↓	2	*(25–35)	–
	9	Farmer, Officer, Teacher of PS	Farmer	78000			*(22–32)	
	11	Madrasa teacher	Farmer	60000	↑	2	*(15–25)	M(17–27)
	11	Madrasa teacher	Farmer	85100				
	54	Service	Farmer	60000	↑	2	*(17–27)	–
	54	Service	None	136000			*(13–23)	
	39	Steel furniture seller	None	60000	↑	2	*(4–13)	M(7–16)
	39	Motor cycle driver	None	360000				
	7	Bank service	Farmer	72000	→	2	*(18–27)	–
	7	Bank service	None	72000			*(13–22)	
	22	Service	None	66000	↑	3	*(22–32)	*(5–15)
	22	None	Record room	135250			*(22–32)	
	45	Coconut seller	Farmer	63400	→	3	*(10–19)	M(12–22)
	45	Coconut seller	None	63400			*(0–9)	
	30	Farmer	None	74800	↑	2	D(15–25)	–
	30	Farmer	Bus business	202900			D(10–20)	

14	Farmer	None	37000	↑	1	D(22–32)	–
14	Farmer	Land register	233800				
23	Jeweller, Fisherman	None	49000	↓	1	–	M(15–25)
23	Jeweller, Driver	None	192000				
10	Pharmacist	Farmer	60500	↑	3	*(9–19)	M(23–33) *(21–31)
10	Homeopathy	Land rent	120000				
25	Fisherman	None	60000	↑	3	D(11–18) *(7–17)	*(4–14)
25	Business	None	114000				
37	Imam	Private teacher	42000	↑	2	*(9–18)	D(13–22)
37	Imam	Service	117600				
35	Labour	Truck driver	48600	→	3	?	??
35	None	None	48600				
32	Farmer	None	28200	→	1	–	–
32	None	None	28200				
26	Fisherman	None	36000	↑	2	*(11–21)	M(13–23)
26	Fisherman, Business	Shopkeeper	108000				
51	Farmer	Service	62400	↑	4	*(15–24) *(8–17) *(6–15)	*(13–22)
51	Business	Farmer	615000				
34	Farmer, Vegetable seller	Farmer	89000	↑	4	*(16–26) ?(12–22)	*(4–14) *(0–10)
34	Farmer	Agriculture labour	96000				

Note: See Table 4.5.

TABLE 4.8 Decadal Transition of Upper-Middle-Class Educated Children in K Village

	No.	*Main occupation*	*Subsidiary occupation*	*Yearly income*	*Income growth*	*No. of children*	*Son*	*Daughter*
Upper-Middle 10	15	Curd business	Ice business	36000	↓	2	D(17–27)	M(14–24)
	15	Silver dish business	Tea shopkeeper	3500				
	17	Banana selling	Labour	19200	↑	1	*(2–12)	–
	17	Interior decoration	Farmer	66000				
	92	Silver dish business	Farmer Labour/Farmer	18700	↑	0	–	–
	92	Silver dish business	Farmer/Labour	30000				
	66	Farmer	None	30590	↓	0	–	–
	66	Farmer	None	12000				
	136	Farmer	None	41875	↑	3	*(15–25)	M(11–21) M(5–15)
	136	Farmer	Work abroad in Malaysia	186800				
	160	Lumber labour	Farmer	17440	↑	1	D(7–17)	–
	160	Lumber business	Farmer/Labour	18000				
	77	Wheat mill	Border trade	55000	↓	3	D(11–21) D(5–15) *(2–12)	–
	77	Labour/Business	Work abroad in Dubai	50000				
	134	Labour/Farmer	Work abroad in Dhaka	31000	↓	1	D(14–24)	–
	134	Labour/Farmer	Work abroad in Dhaka	9000				
	140	Farmer	None	17650	↑	2	D(19–29	M(9–19)
	140	Farmer	None	93700				
	23	Labour	None	13050	↑	0	–	–
	23	Farmer/Labour	None	24000				

Note: See Table 4.6.

as tobacco planting or working abroad. Moreover, working in a foreign country entails large commissions paid to an agent. In the case of girls, those who dropped out of school married early.

Decadal transition in the lower-middle class of the respective villages

Lower-middle-class households in the respective villages consist of farmers, fishermen, tailors, teachers, and labourers (Tables 4.9 and 4.10). Economic growth in terms of income remained the same as before. Therefore, because of price increases, living costs have fundamentally increased. For the most part, their jobs are not salaried. Hence, it is also difficult to invest in the education of children so that they might become salaried workers. In the suburban rural setting, 7 out of 19 children could be regarded as successful cases. In the remote rural setting, 9 out of 16 children were successful, fewer than those from the upper-middle class in the suburban rural setting. One can infer that recent price increases have cancelled out economic gains, even though their income levels have increased considerably.

There is an exceptional example in this class in terms of awareness of the importance of education. Three children in Household No. 16 in K village succeeded in remaining on the school education track. After completing school, the eldest son entered the military in Dhaka. The other two sons also succeeded in continuing education through secondary schools. Their father was killed in 1999 during a traffic accident. Therefore, the household was in an economic crisis during the 2009 survey. The child who became employed in the army could not send remittances. The mother maintained the family by working as a domestic. However, the two sons continued their education despite the economic crisis because their dead father had invested in the children's education, as earlier research conducted in 1999 showed. The deceased father engaged in vegetable sales as his main occupation. His income from the sale of vegetables was insufficient for daily life. Nevertheless, he employed a home tutor for his son and aspired to continue their education. The parents' understanding of the importance of education was instrumental in their son finding employment in the army. In contrast to this special case, other households were increasing their income, but they were often unable to continue their children's education.

Decadal transition in the lower classes of the respective villages

The social mobility of lower-class people is a key point in this study. An important question is whether children from the lower classes at school reached the next stage of education or economic and employment opportunities through the educational system. Has the education or certification obtained contributed to their recent economic growth?

TABLE 4.9 Decadal Transition of Lower-Middle-Class Educated Children in B Village

	No.	*Main occupation*	*Subsidiary occupation*	*Yearly income*	*Income growth*	*No. of children*	*Son*	*Daughter*
Lower-Middle 12	41	Teacher	None	25300	→	1	?(2–12)	–
	41	None	None	25300				
	21	Clothes tailor	None	24000	↑	1	*(3–12)	–
	21	Farmer	None	70200				
	3	Farmer	None	23600	↓	1	D(22–28)	–
	3	Farmer	MLM (Multi-Level Marketing)	22750				
	18	Farmer	Service	42500	→	2	–	?(19–28) ?(17–26)
	18	None	None	42500				
	27	Fisherman	None	48000	↑	2	D(13–23) D(11–21)	–
	27	Furniture seller, Fisherman	None	2E+05				
	13	Farmer	Homeopathy	20000	→	1	–	*(4–14)
	13	Farmer	None	20000				
	24	Fisherman	None	20000	→	1	–	–
	24	Fisherman	None	20000				
	49	Farmer, Service	None	30700	↑	1	*(15–25)	–
	49	Self-employment, Farmer	None	33875				
	42	Labour	None	24000	→	2	*(3–13)	D(4–14)
	42	Truck driver	Agriculture labour	24000				
	46	Labour	None	24000	↑	2	–	*(6–15) *(1–10)
	46	Labour	None	30000				
	47	Labour	None	24000	→	2	?(12–22)	?(7–17)
	47	None	None	24000				
	19	Farmer	Tractor driver, Shopkeeper	31800	↑	3	*(12–22) D(0–9)	M(10–20)
	19	Farmer	None	37100				

Note: See Table 4.5.

TABLE 4.10 Decadal Transition of Lower-Middle-Class Educated Children in K Village

	No.	*Main occupation*	*Subsidiary occupation*	*Yearly income*	*Income growth*	*No. of children*	*Son*	*Daughter*
Lower-Middle 10	16	Vegetable seller	None	24000	↓	3	*(14–24) *(8–17) *(4–13)	–
	16	Army	Work abroad	4000				
	30	Labour	None	7200	↑	0	–	–
	30	Labour	None	36000				
	103	Farmer	None	14080	↑	2	D(10–22)	M(13–25?)
	103	Farmer	None	87400				
	31	Labour	None	9200	↑	1	–	*(3–12)
	31	Farmer	Labour	29000				
	43	Nuts seller	Labour	14775	↑	1	–	*(8–18)
	43	Cloth business	Farmer	86200				
	91	Labour/Farmer	Work abroad in Saudi	19900	↑	2	*(3–13)	M(5–15)
	91	Farmer, Labour	Work abroad in Saudi	44200				
	45	Labour	Bag seller	14200	↑	2	D(11–22)	*(2–13)
	45	Farmer	Garment business	420600				
	113	Farmer	Oil business	15900	↑	4	D(9–20) *(7–15)	M(14–30) M(11–22)
	113	Farmer	Argamon driver	215800				
	69	Farmer	Private tutor	7500	↑	1	*(11–21)	–
	69	Part time (Land registry office)	None	36500				
	137	Grain business	Farmer	8660	↑	0	–	–
	137	Farmer	Some business	30300				

Note: See Table 4.6.

The main occupations of the lower-class residents of the respective villages are agricultural labourers, farmers, drivers, fishery workers, and agricultural business holders (Tables 4.11 and 4.12). The economic situation in the lower classes has improved similarly to the other classes, but price increases have meant that their living costs have also fundamentally increased. Their jobs are not salaried, as they are in the lower-middle class. Moreover, the households consist of landless farmers or labourers who must be economically subordinate to some upper classes. For this reason, realising better job placement or getting more education is difficult as a result of educational investment in children. In the suburban rural setting, 15 of 26 children could be regarded as successful cases. In the remote rural setting, only 9 of 26 children were successful.

In B village, unexpectedly, 50% of the children had continued their education (14 cases) or obtained salaried jobs (2 cases). However, the two households became excellent proof of the value of the education system and achieved post-agrarian life. This study shows that lower-class households recently felt the increased pressure of insufficient income due to rising prices. Furthermore, those who witnessed the expansion of occupational possibilities were probably impatient to obtain salaried jobs. In terms of protecting their livelihood, lower-class households needed to have their children receive a school education.

In contrast, K village showed no relation between further education and job placement. As this study has shown, improvement of the household economy is caused by agricultural ingenuity, such as tobacco or vegetable planting. The villagers understood that engaging in agriculture is an action that improves the economic aspect of the household better than getting jobs that use education. Therefore, dropping out of school had no adverse effects on households. In other words, in the remote rural setting, it can be understood that the value of the educational system is on the social welfare that it brings to vulnerable people who have their children in school. It does not provide the same benefits as the educational system in less remote areas.

However, two special cases were examined in the lower class. Two sons of Household No. 35 in K village continued their education. First, the elderly son obtained a secondary school certificate (SSC) in 2009. Second, the younger son, who had dropped out of school in the fourth grade of elementary school, began studying again after seeing his brother's SSC acquisition. These cases are special because they show the villagers' awareness of the value of education, even though No. 35 belongs to the lower class in K village. Due to difficulties in their daily lives in the lower classes of this village, there are few cases where they leave their jobs and return to school to complete their education. However, this was made possible in the decade following 1999 because of the declining cost of education, improved household economies, and increased awareness of the importance of education among household members, including children.

However, it is necessary to wait 20 years for follow-up research to ascertain whether the children in this household could use their degree or certificate.

TABLE 4.11 Decadal Transition of Lower-Class Educated Children in B Village

	No.	*Main occupation*	*Subsidiary occupation*	*Yearly income*	*Income growth*	*No. of children*	*Son*	*Daughter*
Lower	8	Farmer	None	17200	↓	1	D(18–28)	-
14	8	Farmer	Farmer	9200				
	4	Tractor driver	Farmer	16400	↑	1	-	*(4–14)
	4	Power cultivator driver	Farmer	39700				
	36	Farmer	Fruits seller	21800	↑	2	-	*(3–12)
	36	Fruit business	Farmer	80000				*(1–10)
	20	Fisherman	Farmer	19620	↑	2	*(11–21)	M(14–24)
	20	Farmer	Business (fish)	120900				
	43	Labour	None	18000	↑	2	*(5–14)	-
	43	Rikshaw wara (ban)	Agriculture labour	102000			*(1–10)	
	15	Labour	None	12000	?	1	-	?
	15	None	None	None				
	17	Labour	None	10800	↓	1	D(12–22)	-
	17	Farmer	Agriculture labour, Electrician	9900				
	40	Labour	None	10000	↑	1	D(15–24)	-
	40	Labour	None	36000				
	33	Labour	Truck driver	15900	↑	3	*(10–20)	-
	33	Farmer	Labour	134150			*(5–15)	
							*(2–12)	
	44	Labour	None	12000	↑	3	-	*(8–18)
	44	Labour	None	42000				*(3–13)
								*(2–12)
	5	Farmer	None	16500	↓	2	D(13–23)	-
	5	Farmer	Power tyrral lending	7700			D(11–21)	
	2	Labour	None	12000	↑	2	D(12–22)	-
	2	Agriculture labour, Tailor	Rikshaw driver (ban)	90000			*(5–15)	
	12	Labour	None	2900	↑	3	D(16–26)	-
	12	Agriculture labour	Agriculture labour	78480			D(8–18)	
							D(5–15)	
	31	Farmer	None	17000	↑	2	*(23–33)	-
	31	Farmer, Pharmacist	Veterinary surgeon	92300			*(7–17)	

Note: See Table 4.5.

TABLE 4.12 Decadal Transition of Lower-Class Educated Children in K Village

	No.	*Main occupation*	*Subsidiary occupation*	*Yearly income*	*Income growth*	*No. of children*	*Son*	*Daughter*
Lower 1	121	Labour	None	7000	↑	1	-	M(7–18)
	121	Labour	None	24000				
	126	Labour	Blanket maker/House worker	10825	↓	2	-	M(7–20)
	126	Labour	Blanket maker	18000				*(5–17)
	35	Farmer	Labour	12960	↑	3	*(10–19)	*(1–11)
	35	Farmer	Labour	31000			*(7–17)	
	81	Farmer/Labour	Labour	8200	↑	2	D(6–16)	-
	81	Farmer	Wood carpenter/Shopkeeper	27400			D(2–12)	
	67	Border trader	Farmer	8000	↑	2	D(9–19)	*(1–12)
	67	Sugar business	Farmer/Labour	37200				
	28	Labour	Farmer	11920	↑	4	D(14–24)	*(1–12)
	28	Farmer	Labour	78000			D(12–22) *(6–16)	
	22	Labour	None	7900	↑	2	D(11–22)	M(9–20)
	22	Farmer/Labour	Argamon driver	24000				
	34	Labour	Accessory business/Blanket maker	7650	↑	1	-	M(9–20)
	34	Farmer/Labour	Blanket maker	13000				
	148	Farmer	None	20850	↑	4	D(6–15)	M(12–22)
	148	Farmer	Painter	26700				M(10–20) *(2–12)
	143	Farmer	None	7940	↑	1	-	D(7–14?)
	143	Farmer	College clerk	82000				
	80	Farmer/Labour	Farmer	5800	↑	2	*(3–13)	M(8–18)
	80	Sugar and nuts business	Farmer	30000				
	36	House worker	None	720	↑	1	D(8–24)	-
	36	Labour	None	7000				
	29	Cleaner	Blanket maker	?	?	1	-	M(10–20)
	29	Labour	Cleaner	2000				

Note: See Table 4.6.

6 Conclusion

This study raises three research questions. First, is meritocratic social mobility through the education system for a guaranteed degree or education history acquisition possible for people, particularly poor people, in rural Bangladesh? The results of the comparative analysis show that the education system in suburban rural settings provides a new pathway to salaried employment because of the increasing variety of such jobs. Even children in the lower class achieved more education than they had earlier. The remote rural setting has space for development in terms of educational institutionalisation. Lower-class people must wait for fruitful educational advancement. Despite the harsh reality, some special cases were found in which the children in the lower-middle and lower classes continued along the school track despite being poor. Although these special cases are certainly very few, they can be regarded as instances where employment and social mobility were obtained using the degree and certificate of completion. Moreover, one son of a lower-class family was inspired to return to education after dropping out of primary school. In other words, these cases can be interpreted as signs that social mobility is possible through the current educational system in Bangladesh if the household and the children themselves are motivated. With sufficient motivation, they attempted a reliable approach. Of course, they must wait for the maturation of the socio-economic environment in remote rural areas. When the environment has improved, job opportunities and human resource demands will widen. Thus, the few special cases in this study would become more general.

Second, is it possible to develop human resources as an inclusive educational system beyond the meaning of social welfare? As described, it is possible, at least in suburban rural settings. However, the lower class in remote rural settings requires more time to develop a pathway to salaried jobs and other economic structural innovations related to the education system. However, it is even more problematic to realise and overcome the disadvantages of rural areas. Perhaps it is necessary to wait until the synergies between economic development and educational development are apparent in remote rural areas.

Third, is there any difference in the inclusiveness of poor people when comparing a remote rural setting and a suburban rural setting? The research results revealed that the salaried job-hunting environment developed in the suburbs rather than in the remote rural, as the study showed increasing salaried jobs on the suburban side. Furthermore, the connection between the job-hunting environment and education system growth has strengthened on the suburban side. However, such a linkage is not unheard of on the remote rural side. Still, it is questionable to fill the gap between the job-hunting environment and the growth of the education system in a remote rural setting. However, the study found a rise in meritocratic social mobility for poor people through the education system as a new phenomenon in the lower-class suburban rural setting. Several special cases showing successful perseverance on the education track were found in poor households in remote rural areas. It will be necessary to continuously observe whether these cases will become universal in future studies.

References

BANBEIS (1991). *Bangladesh Education Statistics*. BANBEIS, Dhaka, Bangladesh.

BANBEIS (1992). *Bangladesh Education Statistics*. BANBEIS, Dhaka, Bangladesh.

Bangladesh Bureau of Education Information and Statistics (BANBEIS) (2009, 2010). *Bangladesh Education Statistics*. BANBEIS, Dhaka, Bangladesh.

BANBEIS (2017, 2018). *Bangladesh Education Statistics*. BANBEIS, Dhaka Bangladesh.

Bangladesh Bureau of Statistics (BBS) (1985). *Bangladesh Education in Statistics*. BANBEIS, Dhaka, Bangladesh.

Basu, K. (2018). "Why Is Bangladesh Booming?" www.project-syndicate.org/commentary/bangladesh-sources-of-economic-growth-by-kaushik-basu-2018-04?barrier=accesspaylog (accessed November 23, 2020)

The Daily Star (2017). "Economic Prospects Bright in 2018-Policy Reforms Can Only Help Growth," www.thedailystar.net/editorial/economic-prospects-bright-2018-1505464 (accessed November 16, 2018)

The Daily Star (2018). "LDC Graduation: What it Means for Bangladesh," www.thedailystar.net/opinion/macro-mirror/ldc-graduation-what-it-means-bangladesh-1550542 (accessed November 16, 2018)

JICA (2017). *Gekidō suru gurōbaru keizai to Bangladesh-Naze nihon kigyō no sōsharu bijinesu ga motome rarerunoka? (The Turbulent Global Economy and Bangladesh—Why Are Japanese Companies in Need of the Social Business?)*. Banglandesh website, industry report. (in Japanese) www.jica.go.jp/bangladesh/bangland/reports/report28.html (accessed November 17, 2018).

Kusakabe, T. (2008). *Banguradeshu noson no shoto kyoiku seido jyuyo (The Acceptance of Primary Education in Bangladesh)*, Tokyo: Toshindo. (in Japanese)

Meyer, J. W., J. Boli, G. Thomas, and F. Ramirez (1997). "World Society and the Nation-State," *American Journal of Sociology*, vol. 103, 144–181.

Meyer, J. W. and F. O. Ramirez (2000). "The World Institutionalization of Education," in Schriewer, J. ed., *Discourse and Comparative Education*, Peter Lang, Frankfurt, Germany: 111–132.

Primary and Mass Education Division (PMED) (2001). *Primary Education Statistics in Bangladesh*. PMED, Dhaka, Bangladesh.

Primary and Mass Education Division (PMED) (2002). *Primary Education Statistics in Bangladesh*. PMED, Dhaka, Bangladesh.

Suda, T. (2010). "Grōbaruka suru Bangladesh nouson keizai-Keizai kouzou henka no mekanizumu to hinkon heno eikyou (Globalizing Rural Economy of Bangladesh: Mechanism of Structural Change of Rural Economy and its Impact on the Poor)," *Ajia Keizai*, vol. 51(11), Tokyo, Japan, 2–43. (in Japanese)

UNESCO (2000). *The Dakar Framework for Action*, Paris, France.

UNESCO, UNDP, UNFPA, UNHCR, UNICEF, UNWOMEN, World Bank and ILO (2015). *Education 2030: Incheon Declaration and Framework for Action for the implementation of Sustainable Development Goal 4*, Incheon, Republic of Korea.

WCEFA Inter Agency Commission (1990). *Final Report of the World Conference of Education for All*, Jomtien Thailand, 1–70.

5

MOBILITY BETWEEN FORMAL AND INFORMAL SECTORS AND INCLUSIVENESS

A Study of Ahmedabad

Junko Kiso

1 Introduction

The concept of the 'informal sector' has been discussed in India since the 1980s as an employment field for the large number of working poor. The upward mobility of workers in the informal sector and improvement in their socio-economic conditions are significant aspects of the inclusive growth pursued in India. However, although impressive economic growth has been achieved, especially since the inception of economic reform, it has also been called 'jobless growth' because of the sluggish growth in employment in the organised sector compared to the sharp increase in the total number of workers. In contrast, employment in the informal sector and the number of informal workers have increased. Simultaneously, various studies have revealed progress in terms of poverty alleviation, improved access to education and health services, and so on.

Given this context, this chapter explores the background and realities of 'jobless inclusiveness.' As the term suggests, it is an insufficient inclusive growth which has not been accompanied by a sufficient increase in employment with 'decent work' conditions. As such, the reality of the exclusion and inclusion that working people and their households have experienced, which is difficult to ascertain solely from macro-level data, is examined here based on long-term field surveys.

The chapter is organised as follows. Section 2 touches upon macro-structural changes in the Indian labour market and briefly describes changes in the labour market of the survey area, namely Gujarat state and Ahmedabad. Section 3 discusses what has occurred over the long term, both inter-generationally and intra-generationally with respect to factory workers—those employed in the organised sector of the manufacturing industry—to ascertain the history of inclusion and exclusion in the labour market across economic reform. Section 4 deals with the

DOI: 10.4324/9781003304760-7

socio-economic mobility of informal sector workers to elucidate the situation of jobless inclusiveness. Finally, Section 5 summarises the main points of the paper and highlights the challenges.

2 Changing labour market and Ahmedabad

Changes in the Indian labour market

Figure 5.1 shows the changes in the number of employed persons in India over a long period, between 1977–1978 and 2017–2018. The number of employed persons increased from an estimated 271 million to 471 million during that period. However, notable in the labour market is the slow growth in the number of workers in the organised sector, in other words, jobless growth. Workers in the organised sector generally include those in all establishments in the public sector regardless of the number of employees, and non-agricultural establishments employing ten and more persons in the private sector. These have been covered by major provisions of labour and social security laws. Therefore, employment in the

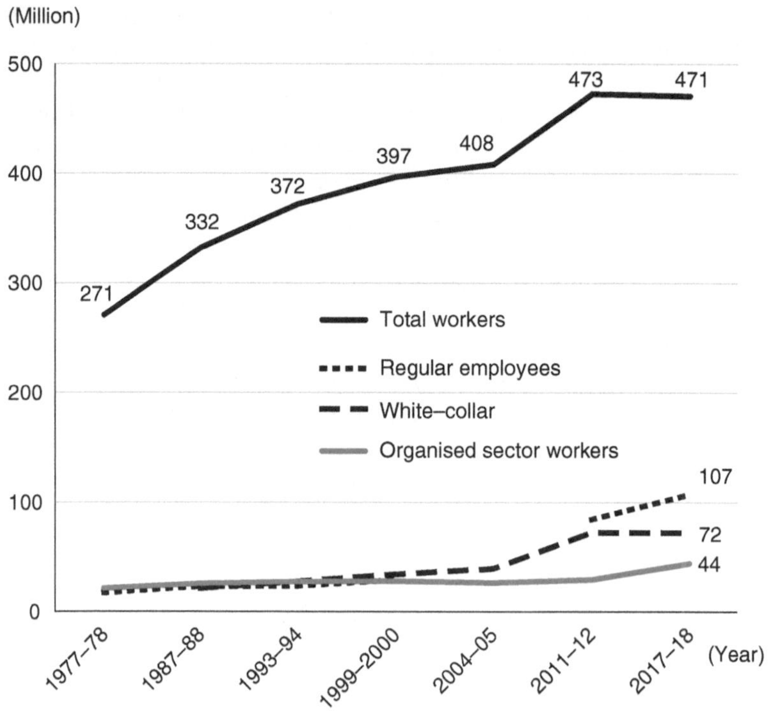

FIGURE 5.1 Number of Workers

Note: The data sources and sampling methods are different between 2017–2018 and earlier.

Source: IAMR (2009), NSSO (2013), Government of India (2016, 2020), NSO (2019).

organised sector is expected to expand sufficiently in terms of inclusive growth. However, after economic reform and even after realising high economic growth in the 2000s, employment in the organised sector remained slow. In 2017–2018, the number of workers in the organised sector was estimated as 90 million, of which formal employment was 44 million. This means that the remaining about 90% are workers in the agriculture and non-agricultural unorganised sector or non-regular employees[1] working in the organised sector. However, note that these workers also include self-employed professionals and technicians, and employees of micro or small enterprises with good standing.

Furthermore, slower than expected growth was also evident for regular employees classified by employment status and white-collar workers classified by occupation. In the 2000s, the number of regular and white-collar workers started to increase, but even in 2017–2018, they accounted for 23% and 15% of the total employed persons, respectively.

The employment structure by industry also changed significantly over the same period. The primary industry shrank from 72% in 1977–1978 to 44.1% in 2017–2018, conversely, the secondary and tertiary industries have expanded their employment share from 15.4% and 12.6% to 31.1% and 24.8%, respectively.[2] The major source of employment growth in the secondary industry was in construction, while that in the manufacturing industry has lagged. Based on these circumstances, the importance of employment-intensive industries was emphasised in the 'National Manufacturing Policy' in 2011 and the 'Make in India' campaign was launched in 2014.

Furthermore, as Table 5.1 shows, the proportion of tertiary industry workers has expanded in the organised sector between 1981 and 2012, while that of secondary industry workers has diminished. Here, the finance, real estate, and business service industries, which are relatively labour-saving, have contributed to increasing the share of employment in the tertiary industry, while that for

TABLE 5.1 Employment Structure by Industry in Organised Sector

	(%)				
	1981	*1991*	*1998*	*2006*	*2012*
Agriculture, hunting, etc.	5.8	5.4	5.1	5.6	4.8
Mining and quarrying	4.1	4.1	3.6	4.7	4.1
Manufacturing	26.4	23.7	24.3	21.2	22.5
Electricity, gas, and water	3.1	3.5	3.5	3.3	3.0
Construction	5.1	4.6	4.2	3.6	3.2
Wholesale and retail trade	1.7	1.7	1.7	2.1	2.6
Transport, storage, and communications	12.1	11.5	11.2	10.4	9.2
Finance, insurance, real estate, etc.	4.1	5.4	5.8	7.7	11.2
Community, social, and personal services	37.5	40.1	40.5	41.5	39.2
Total	100.0	100.0	100.0	100.0	100.0

Source: Govt. of India (2002, 2018).

manufacturing and construction in the secondary industry has decreased. Notable is that this structural change has progressed along with changes in technology and business characteristics, which seems to have altered the quality and type of labour demand. In addition, the shift to non-regular employment has progressed in the manufacturing industry. The proportion of contract workers in factories was 11.2% in 1992–1993, increasing to 36.0% in 2016–2017.[3]

Changes in Ahmedabad, Gujarat state

Gujarat state

Ahmedabad, the site of the field surveys, is located in Gujarat, one of India's leading developed states. The real yearly growth rate of the gross state domestic product (GSDP) was 6.5% from 1994–1995 to 2004–2005, and 10.1% from 2004–2005 to 2011–2012. The high growth of 9.8% was maintained from 2011–2012 to 2015–2016.[4] It has been recently debated whether this development was inclusive or not, especially in terms of addressing changes in poverty rates, the employment situation, human development index, policies and budget allocation for the social sector, etc.[5] The fact that economic growth has not markedly increased employment with decent work conditions has also been a key aspect of the argument.

The number of workers in Gujarat state has risen from 16.62 million (1991) to 21.26 million (2001) and 24.77 million (2011), an increase of around 50% over 20 years.[6] However, the slow growth of employment in the organised sector was also evident in Gujarat, where the annual growth rate decreased from 2.1% in the 1980s to less than 0.5% in the 1990s. Although increasing to around 2% from 2000 to 2011, employment remained at 2.1 million in 2011,[7] accounting for only 8.5% of all workers in Gujarat. Furthermore, using data from the *National Sample Survey* (*NSS*), Unni and Naik (2014) estimated that employment in the informal sector increased by 4% per year between 2000 and 2010, but only 0.3% in the formal sector. The respective shares of workers in the formal and informal sectors in non-agricultural employment were estimated as 17.2% and 82.8% in 2009–2010.[8]

Since Gujarat state was established in 1960, the state government has promoted industrial development preferentially and adopted more aggressive industrial measures including various incentive schemes after the start of economic reform.[9] In Gujarat, agriculture accounted for 48.8% of employment, construction 4.8%, and manufacturing 19.7% in 2010–2011. Thinking that the corresponding all-India figures were 48.9%, 10.6%, and 12.6%, respectively, the percentage of manufacturing employment was relatively high in Gujarat state. However, given that the manufacturing sector contributed 35% (provisional) of the gross state value added (GSVA) in 2015–2016,[10] the imbalanced contribution of its growth to production and employment is clear.

In the early 1990s, labour reform movements and labour union resistance emerged, and in the process, factory closures and various employment restructuring initiatives including retrenchment and voluntary retirement schemes were implemented. Gujarat state was no exception. Figure 5.2 shows the changes in the number of working registered factories and their workers. Both figures remained stagnant until the early 2000s, with data of some years suggesting a declining trend. Traversing this situation in the 1990s, the employment numbers nearly doubled during the 16 years since 2000. However, it has been pointed out that compared to the large growth in gross production and fixed capital in the factories, employment growth has been poor because of capital-intensive industrialisation, which has contributed to jobless growth in Gujarat.[11] Furthermore, the quality of employment has changed. According to the *Annual Survey of Industries* (*ASI*), the proportion of contract workers among factory workers has increased from 16.4% (1992–1993) to 31.0% (2001–2002), 36.1% (2010–2011), and 36.0% (2016–2017), which represents the progress in the shift to non-regular employment. The corresponding all-India figures were 11.2%, 21.5%, 33.9%, and 36.0%, indicating that Gujarat has been ahead of the increase in non-regular employment.[12]

Next, Table 5.2 shows changes in the employment status of the workers. Clearly, the percentage of regular employees has increased in both urban and rural areas, as well as for men and women. Particularly in urban areas, 52% of men and 37% of women were regular employees in 2011–2012. Furthermore, while this share for men is quite large compared to the whole of India (urban), small for women.

Ahmedabad

According to the 2011 census, Ahmedabad city had a population of about 5.6 million. It was the largest city in Gujarat state and fifth largest in India. Influenced by the expansion of the city area, the population has grown at 4.6% per year over the past ten years. Population ratios by religion are Hindu (81.4%), Muslim (13.6%), and others (5.0%). The scheduled caste (SC) population accounts for 10.7% and the scheduled tribe (ST) population for 1.2%.[13]

The city developed as an industrial centre based on its cotton textile industry under colonial rule and has acquired a position as the most important industrial centre in the state. However, with the decline in India's large-scale cotton textile industry, the retrenchment of workers and closure of mills began in the mid-1980s through the 1990s. As a result, the number of cotton mill workers, which was almost 160,000 in the late 1970s including temporary workers and contract workers, was estimated to have decreased to 25,000 in 1996.[14]

Factory closures and employment restructuring were extensively implemented, not only in the textile industry but also in various others. As Figure 5.2 indicates, the number of workers in working registered factories also considerably decreased in Ahmedabad city. Then, after bottoming in 2000, it continued to increase until 2006 (provisional). Although changes after that could not be statistically confirmed, many special economic zones and industrial parks were

TABLE 5.2 Changes in Employment Structure in Gujarat State, 1993–1994 to 2011–2012

	Male			*Female*		*(%)*
	Self-employed	*Regular wage/salaried*	*Casual labour*	*Self-employed*	*Regular wage/salaried*	*Casual labour*
Gujarat state (Rural)						
1993–94	46.9	9.9	43.2	55.4	1.5	43.1
1999–2000	50.9	9.6	39.5	59.1	1.6	39.3
2004–05	49.6	10.2	40.2	59.5	2.6	37.9
2011–12	56.6	12.5	31.1	58.6	5	36.7
India (Rural)						
2011–12	54.5	10	35.5	59.3	5.6	35.1
Gujarat state (Urban)						
1993–94	37.3	44.9	17.8	42.6	24.1	33.3
1999–2000	40.8	35.9	23.3	41.9	26.4	31.7
2004–05	41.4	48.2	10.4	42.9	30.3	26.8
2011–12	40.3	51.9	7.8	48.1	36.8	15.0
India (Urban)						
2011–12	41.7	43.4	14.9	42.8	42.8	14.3

Source: NSSO (1997, 2001, 2006, 2014).

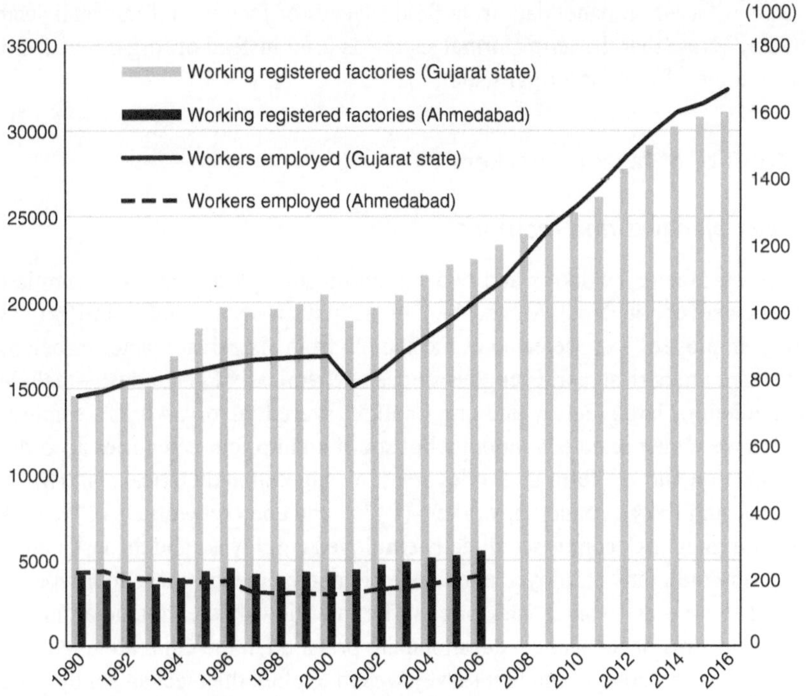

FIGURE 5.2 Working Registered Factories and Workers Employed

Source: AMC (2008), Government of Gujarat (2017).

quickly constructed outside the city accompanied by changes in industrial structure, which has also contributed to increasing the number of factories and their employees in Gujarat. Further considering that 24.2% of factories operating in Gujarat and 20.6% of their workers were concentrated in Ahmedabad district in 2016 (provisional),[15] Ahmedabad city and its surroundings have continued to rapidly progress as an important growth centre.

The number of workers in Ahmedabad city in 2011 exceeded 1.95 million, accounting for 75% of the total workers in Ahmedabad district.[16] According to NSS data, the percentage of self-employed in 2010–2011 was 48% for men and 64% for women,[17] noticeably higher than the figures for urban Gujarat around the same period (Table 5.2). Many of these are considered workers in the informal sector. It is also pointed out that the proportions of informal non-agricultural sector workers and informal employment have increased from 73.3% to 84.8% and from 83.5% to 86.8%, respectively, between 1999–2000 and 2004–2005 in Ahmedabad city.[18]

In the following, bearing aspects of exclusivity and inclusiveness in mind, the author explores ways in which economic growth has affected the work and life of 'ordinary people' in Gujarat, an economically advanced state. The following analysis is based on panel data from field surveys of factory and informal sector workers.[19] Note that the term 'formal sector' is used instead of 'organised sector' as an antonym for the informal sector.

3 Mobility of factory workers

Survey objectives and methods

A survey of factory workers and two follow-up surveys on the same sample of workers were conducted in Ahmedabad. In the first survey conducted in 1991, 233 factory employees were selected as the sample from six private factories belonging to three industries: textile, engineering, and chemical.[20] Each industry included one medium or large factory and one small registered factory. All 233 employee samples were men selected randomly but stratified into four categories according to occupation and the form of employment: managerial and clerical staff (MCS), technical staff (TS), production workers (PWs), and contract workers (CWs). The first three categories comprised directly employed employees and the last, namely CWs, were indirectly employed employees. For convenience, these four types are referred to here as 'worker categories.' The interviews were conducted in each respondent's residence using a questionnaire prepared in the Gujarati language.[21]

The main objective of the first survey was to explore the mechanism by which workers enter the formal sector, including the recruitment and job access process, in the context in which the number of workers in the informal sector continued to increase. This was to better understand who is unable to enter the formal sector and thus forced to enter the informal sector, and why. This paper summarises only personal characteristics and job changes until the 1991 survey.

The second survey was conducted in 1998 after the storm of closure of factories and employment restructuring such as the enforcement of voluntary retirement and replacement of directly employed workers by contract workers in Ahmedabad. By then, two medium/large factories of the six surveyed in 1991 had been closed down. We traced the initial 233 workers in the sample and obtained 168 valid responses. The objective of the second survey was to ascertain the effects of job loss on their job mobility and life through a comparative analysis of the workers forced into unemployment and those who were not. It was observed for many workers that labour market flexibility at that time meant one-way mobility with an exit from but without re-entry into factories or the formal sector.

The third survey was conducted in 2006. By then, factory closures and employment restructuring had further progressed, meaning that most employees of the five factories, except those at one small factory, had lost their jobs during the 15 years since 1991. In the third survey, we obtained 130 valid responses from the previous 168 samples. Furthermore, in the same year, a survey of their working children was conducted separately. In this paper, the results of the first and third surveys, and the survey of their children are summarised with a focus on labour market mobility.[22]

Characteristics and mobility of factory workers in 1991

Social group and education level

Persons of various social groups worked in the sample factories. However, the religious and caste composition[23] varies across worker categories. As Figure 5.3 shows, whereas upper castes are strongly represented in white-collar such as MCS and TS, SCs and STs are predominantly represented in CWs. PWs are between these two extreme patterns and are composed of various social groups.

Education level (Figure 5.4)[24] also differs distinctly between worker categories. MCS and TS are highly educated people overall, and many are college graduates. In contrast, many CWs were educated up to primary level or are illiterate. Although each education level includes both those who have completed that

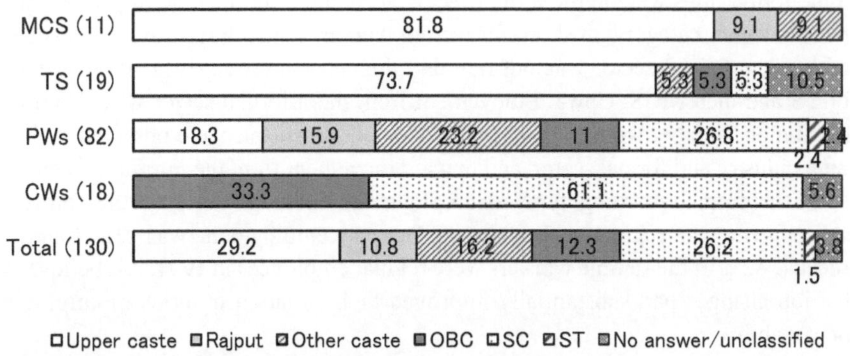

FIGURE 5.3 Caste Composition by Worker Category (%)

Note: Figures in parentheses show the number of respondents.

Source: The author's survey (1991).

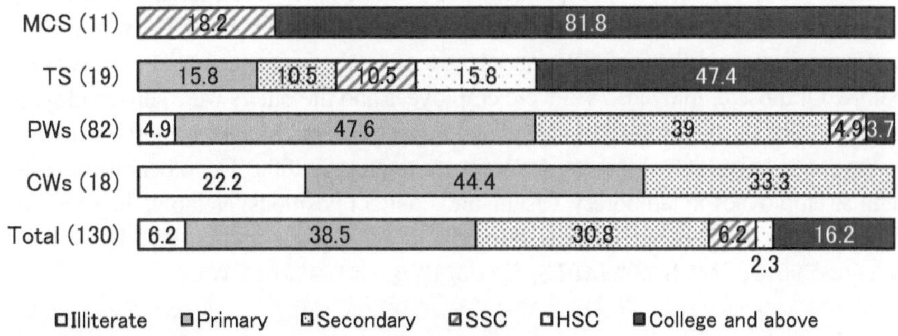

FIGURE 5.4 Education Level by Worker Category (%)

Note: See Figure 5.3.

Source: See Figure 5.3.

education level and dropouts, PWs' education levels are distributed similarly to those of CWs, but more broadly. There was a clear relation between social group and education level.

Therefore, although blue-collar and white-collar workers differed in terms of social group and education level, recruitment methods—that is, the mechanisms of inclusion in factory work—also differed. In other words, unlike white-collar workers, where formal recruitment procedures are undertaken to screen academic background and specific skills, blue-collar workers were mainly selected through personal connections regardless of education background.

Mobility through job change

Of the sample workers, 60% had experienced a job change at least once before working at the then factories. The total number of job changes was 212 times. Half of the former jobs were in the formal sector, accounting for the highest percentage in each worker category. In short, for factory workers at the time, moving between units in the formal sector was not rare and this tendency was particularly strong for TS and then MCS. Upward movement from the informal sector was also not uncommon. In other words, considerable parallel movements were observed in the same industry and formal sector, and upward movement from the informal sector.

Furthermore, regarding type of employment, although 40% of the former employment was regular, temporary and casual employment was also found. Because 82% of the sample workers were regular employees in 1991, it is believed that job changes had substantially improved their situation in terms of employment stability.

Job loss, job change, and mobility of factory workers by 2006

Employment situation

In the third survey, of the 130 respondents, 109 were employed. Regarding their occupations in 2006 based on worker category, 90% of MCS and 60% of TS were white-collar workers, and 95% of PWs and 100% of CWs were blue-collar workers, as before. Of those employed, 78% were employees and the others were self-employed or employers. Furthermore, although all employees except CWs were regular employees in 1991, only 38% of the employees were regular in 2006. The others were non-regular employees in temporary, casual, and contract positions. Notably, the share of formal sector workers had decreased to 55% of all workers and differed by worker category: 90% of MCS, 60% of TS, 52% of PWs, and 44% of CWs.

Job changes

Mainly because of the aforementioned circumstances, 85% of the respondents had experienced job changes at least once in the 15 years following the first survey in

TABLE 5.3 Job Changes 1998–2006

	(%)				
	Total	*MCS*	*TS*	*PWs*	*CWs*
Occupation	(110)	(8)	(15)	(67)	(20)
White collar	12.7	87.5	33.3		5.0
Blue collar	86.4	12.5	66.7	98.5	95.0
Unknown	0.9			1.5	
Sector					
Formal	41.8	62.5	53.3	35.8	45.0
Informal	53.6	37.5	46.7	58.2	50.0
Agriculture	2.7			3.0	5.0
Unknown	1.8			3.0	
Sector change					
Informal→Informal	26.4	37.5	13.3	26.9	30.0
Formal→Formal	22.7	62.5	40.0	17.9	10.0
Informal→Formal	18.2		13.3	16.4	35.0
Formal→Informal	23.6		20.0	29.9	15.0
Others	4.5			4.5	10.0
Unknown	4.5		13.3	4.5	
Income change					
Up	43.6	50.0	46.7	40.3	50.0
Down	40.9	25.0	26.7	47.8	35.0
No change	11.8	12.5	20.0	9.0	15.0
Unknown	3.6	12.5	6.7	3.0	
Employment security of employee	(86)	(6)	(10)	(52)	(18)
Regular	20.9	50.0	50.0	13.5	16.7
Temporary	18.6	0.0	10.0	25.0	11.1
Casual	32.6	50.0	40.0	23.1	50.0
Contract	27.9	0.0	0.0	38.5	22.2

Note: Figures in parentheses show the number of changes. 'Others' in sector change includes shifts between agriculture and formal sector or informal sector.
Source: The author's surveys (1998, 2006).

1991. During the eight years between the second and third surveys, around 60% of the respondents experienced job changes: 110 times in total. These 110 job changes are elaborated below.

First, there were 115 responses regarding the reasons for the job changes, including multiple responses. As expected, the main reasons were factory closure, voluntary retirement, and organised dismissal. These reasons were attributed to the management side.

As Table 5.3 shows, the share of formal sector units in former jobs increased compared to that in the second survey in 1998. Although downward mobility from the formal sector or parallel movement within the informal sector were found more often than upward mobility from the informal sector and movement within the formal sector in the third survey as well, downward mobility decreased compared to that found in the second survey. The main reason is that many respondents had already lost their jobs in the factories and were working in the informal sector at the time of the second survey. Also noteworthy is that more job changes came with an increased income. (Salary or wage including bonus, if any, in cases of employees; and profit: sales minus expenses, in cases of those who are employers or self-employed. The definition of income is the same below.) Furthermore, regarding employment status, only one-fifth of the former jobs were as regular employees, indicating that once regular status was lost, it was difficult to re-attain. Factory workers had moved from one unstable job to another. Thus, many former factory employees who were rendered unemployed after factory closures or employment restructuring had not been able to re-enter the formal sector including registered factories, and remained in the informal sector and/or non-regular jobs. However, some had secured an increased income through a job change.

However, job experiences after losing employment differed significantly between worker categories. Whereas the situation of MCS and TS tended to improve afterwards, this was not the case for most CWs and PWs, who found upward movement difficult. Furthermore, as mentioned, the MCS who demonstrated the most remarkable recovery were mostly from the upper castes and had a high level of education. In addition, for TS, those with a higher level of education demonstrated upward mobility. In contrast, CWs were from the lower castes and mostly not educated. PWs were from various social groups and generally had a lower level of education.[25]

Children of former factory workers: mobility across four generations

Survey method

The sample consists of children of the respondents in the 2006 survey who were working in factories in 1991. In total, 96 working children (79 sons and 17 daughters) of 80 fathers[26] (former factory employees) are referred to as the respondents here.[27] Regarding age, most respondents were in their 20s (50%) and 30s (42%), and the rest were aged less than 20 (6%) or more than 40 (2%) years. Because the respondents are of different age groups, the analysis here should be considered a summary of the changes from great-grandfather–grandfather–father–respondent rather than inter-generational mobility.

Reduction and continuity of disparities

The most noteworthy change for this generation is a marked improvement in education level. This is clarified in Table 5.4 (data of married daughters who completed education are included), where the figures in the shaded sections indicate respondents with the same level of education as that of their fathers'. The figures in the upper right show respondents with a higher level of education than their

TABLE 5.4 Changes in Education Level

Father \ *Child*	*Illiterate*	*Primary*	*Secondary*	*SSC*	*HSC*	*College and above*
Illiterate	1	1	3	4	1	
Primary	2	17	22	6	4	7
Secondary		1	8	2	5	11
SSC	1		2	0	2	3
HSC					2	
College and above				1	1	3

Note: One hundred and ten respondents. Figures in shaded parts are numbers of respondents whose education level is almost the same as the fathers'.
Source: The author's surveys (1991, 2006).

fathers, and those in the lower left have a lower level of education than their fathers. The high concentration in the upper right indicates that many respondents obtained a similar or higher level of education than their fathers. Overall, 22% of respondents obtained a college or higher education compared to 6% of fathers. In contrast, very few respondents were illiterate, and more than one-third had undertaken vocational training.

Noteworthy is that regardless of the overall improvement in education level, the disparity between worker categories for the fathers' generation was broadly mirrored in the children's generation. Although there is an analytical limit because of the limited sample, except for PWs, most respondents whose father was a TS or MCS had obtained a college-level education or Higher Secondary Certificate (HSC); however, most of the children of CWs had obtained lower secondary education.

Also important is that although some improvements were observed in the level of education and vocational training overall, improvement in their employment was not evident. Figure 5.5 depicts the changing employment structure by industry over four generations. Respondents exhibit two patterns: sons only, and sons and daughters. With respondents' generation as the base, approximately half of their great-grandfathers were engaged in agriculture and about 20% worked in the manufacturing industry. More than half of the grandfathers and 100% of the fathers were employed in the manufacturing industry. These great-grandfathers and grandfathers included many pioneers who supported India's industrialisation. Furthermore, the respondents' fathers inherited these jobs when traditional industries were still an important foundation for economic growth and job creation. However, the proportion of workers in the manufacturing industry dwindled to two-thirds during the respondents' generation, while the proportion in the tertiary industry grew. Consequently, three-quarters of the respondents were working in the informal sector as self-employed workers or employees.

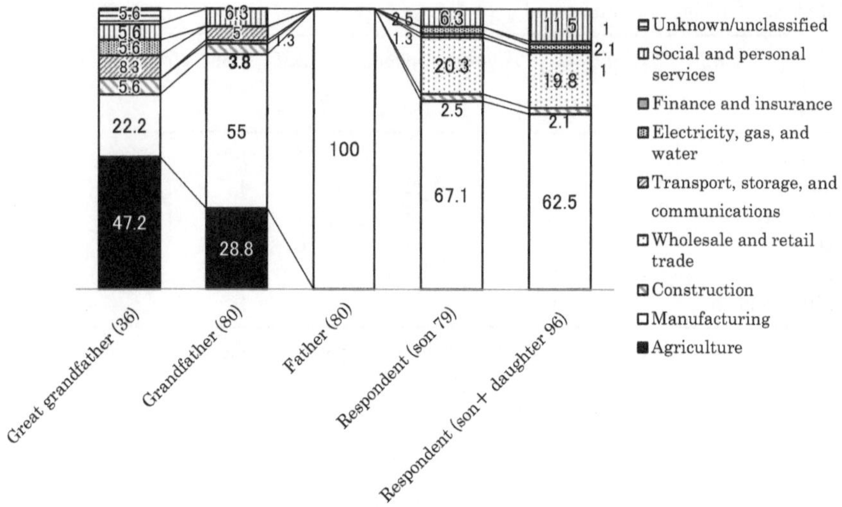

FIGURE 5.5 Changes of Industry Among Generations (%)

Source: See Table 5.4.

Respondents whose fathers were white-collar MCS or TS were more engaged in white-collar occupations. In contrast, no respondents whose fathers were CWs were engaged in white-collar occupations. In addition, the number of non-regular employees increased in their generation for all worker categories except TS.

However, the occupations of children of PWs were more diversified, possibly because of the large number of respondents. Of the 78 respondents, 18% were white-collar workers and most had a college degree. Almost half of the white-collar workers were from the upper castes and the rest from other social groups except SCs. Therefore, it is believed that their higher level of education secured inter-generational mobility from blue to white-collar work, regardless of their origin. However, there were no white-collar workers in SCs (*N*=17), which was exceptional.

Next, the informal sector and mobility of its workers and households are examined.

4 Mobility of informal sector workers

Survey objectives and methods

The first survey of workers in the informal sector was conducted in 2010–2011 to explore the reality of their socio-economic mobility in the context of the slow employment growth in the formal sector.[28]

The sample of workers in the informal sector was selected from residents of the slums listed in Ahmedabad's slum list in 2000–2001.[29] These were selected because many residents in the slum areas work in the informal sector and thus, we expected to pick up workers engaged in several of these types of jobs. Therefore, first, we selected ten slums all over Ahmedabad. Thereafter, 2,016 households living in those slums were listed, and their basic information was collected. Based on the results of this 'household census survey,' a sample list of informal sector workers in each of the slums was formulated. Our sample list was structured to include only households whose heads were working in the informal sector engaged in any of the five types of job: sales, service, manufacturing or repairing, transportation, and construction or odd jobs. These categories were almost evenly represented. We then began interviewing the heads of the sample households in each of the ten slums, with the target of interviewing 200 households. Ultimately, 215 workers were interviewed, but the sample size was reduced to 189 because some respondents were found to be working in the formal sector. All respondents were men. The interviews were mostly conducted in 2010 and some in 2011.

The objective of the second survey was to identify economic and living-related changes among informal sector workers and their families during the seven years of continuous economic growth, and to elucidate the factors leading to these changes. In other words, we attempted to clarify the reality of inclusiveness for the working poor. To this end, 53 samples were selected from the ten slums and traced in 2017 and 2018. Of these, we could interview 45 people. These included two formal sector workers (one was a manhole sweeper regularly employed by the Ahmedabad Municipal Corporation (AMC) and another a casual driver for a large factory, that is, an informal worker, at the time of the first survey), and five sons who had become heads of their households because of the death or illness of the previous respondent. These 45 people are referred to as the respondents in Section 4–3.

Characteristics and mobility of informal sector workers in 2010–2011

Characteristics

As Table 5.5 shows, many respondents belonged to either SCs (36.0%) or Other Backward Classes (OBCs, 32.8%), and STs accounted for 3.7%. These proportions were much higher than the aforementioned percentages for Ahmedabad city: SCs (10.7%) and STs (1.2%). Regarding age, more than 60% of respondents were aged 30–49 years and the rest were aged 50 and above or in their 20s.

Education levels were generally low: 15.3% were not literate, combined with the ratio of primary level of education, it stood at nearly 70%. Even respondents with Secondary School Certificate (SSC) were rare.

Income was also generally low. Around only one-third of respondents earned Rs. 5,000 or more a month. Although a few were earning more than Rs. 10,000, around a quarter were not earning even Rs. 3,000. Average monthly income varied between regular employees, casual workers, and those self-employed: Rs. 3,294, Rs. 4,194, and Rs. 5,105, respectively.[30]

Note that income by other household members such as wives also contributed towards increasing the average household income: 84% of households indicated having 'other income sources.' Nearly 50% of households reported earnings by wives and 70% by other family members such as brothers, sisters, parents, and children. As a result, around 70% of the households had a total monthly household income of Rs. 5,000 and more. This increased the average monthly household income to Rs. 7,617, 70% more than the average monthly income of individual respondents.

TABLE 5.5 Comparison of 45 Sample Workers With the 2017–2018 Samples

		2010–2011		*2017–2018*	
		Number	*%*	*Number*	*%*
Total		189	100.0	45	100.0
Religion/Caste	SC	68	36.0	18	40.0
	ST	7	3.7	4	8.9
	OBC	62	32.8	16	35.6
	Other Hindus	24	12.7	2	4.4
	Muslim	22	11.6	5	11.1
	Other religion	23	12.1		
	Unknown/Unclassified	5	1.7		
Education level	Illiterate	29	15.3	9	20.0
	Primary	101	53.4	22	48.9
	Secondary	35	18.5	9	20.0
	SSC	13	6.9	4	8.9
	HSC (dropout)	5	2.6		
	HSC (pass)	3	1.6		
	College and above	3	1.6	1	2.2
Occupation	Sales	53	28.0	10	22.2
	Service	33	17.5	7	15.6
	Manufacturing and repairing	39	20.6	9	20.0
	Transportation	28	14.8	8	17.8
	Construction and odd jobs	36	19.0	7	15.6
	Not working			4	8.9
Employment status	Regular employee	44	23.3	6	13.3
	Casual labour	40	21.2	11	24.4
	Self-employed	105	55.6	24	53.3
	Not working			4	8.9

Note: This shows the detail of 189 respondents of informal sector workers in 2010–2011 and 45 respondents traced in 2017–2018.

Source: The author's surveys (2010–2011, 2017–2018).

Job changes

Of the 189 respondents, 162 had experienced 358 job changes overall: 2.2 times on average, as shown in Table 5.6. First, although many former jobs were in the formal sector such as in large-scale cotton mills, most were in the informal sector, meaning that they had mostly moved within the informal sector (62.3%). However, comparing the monthly income just before and after the job change showed that most job changes (75.4%) came with an increased income. Thus, they had changed jobs in the direction they wanted, mostly by realising a higher income, and sometimes by becoming self-employed.[31] Self-employed was their most favourite employment status to which they want to shift. However, note that the increased income often resulted from a job change from child to adult work, because many informal sector workers had started working in childhood.

Inter-generational mobility

Inter-generational mobility in terms of education level and jobs is analysed next. More accurately, this is a summary of the changes from grandfather–father–respondent–working son rather than inter-generational mobility, because the respondents are in different age groups. In addition, there are a considerable

TABLE 5.6 Job Changes of the Informal Sector Workers

	Number	*%*		*Number*	*%*
Total	358	100.0	*Sector*		
Occupation			Informal sector	260	72.6
Clerical	6	1.7	Formal sector	80	22.3
Sales	58	16.2	Agriculture	17	4.7
Service	68	19.0	Unclassified	1	0.3
Agricultural	17	4.7	*Sector change*		
Manufacturing and repairing	117	32.7	Informal→Formal	33	9.2
Transportation	23	6.4	Formal→Informal	60	16.8
			Informal→Informal	223	62.3
Construction and odd jobs	68	19.0	Formal→Formal	15	4.2
Unknown/Unclassified	1	0.3	Informal sector or Formal sector ←→Agriculture	23	6.4
Employment status					
Employed (directly)	215	60.1	Unclassified	4	1.1
Employed (indirectly)	63	17.6	*Change in monthly income*		
Employer	1	0.3			
			Up	270	75.4
Self-employed	64	17.9	Down	67	18.7
Home workers	3	0.8	No change	13	3.6
Unpaid family workers	12	3.4	Unclassified	8	2.2

Source: The author's survey (2010–2011).

number of grandfathers whose education, occupation and work sector were not known and the number of working sons was small at 73.

The level of education greatly improved (Figure 5.6), especially between fathers and the respondents, and the proportion of the respondents who were illiterate was much lower. Furthermore, a conspicuous change in sector (Figure 5.7) was evident between grandfathers, fathers, and respondents, but was limited between respondents and sons. Also noteworthy is that 30% of the fathers worked in the formal sector and 9% in large textile mills. Moreover, two-thirds of these were regular employees of the textile mills.

Therefore, it is apparent that the structural changes observed between grandfathers, fathers, and respondents became marginal in the sons' generation. As such, this mobility partly reflects the industrial structural change in Ahmedabad. However, the data is limited for sons, and as most are still young, their employment situation is likely to further change.

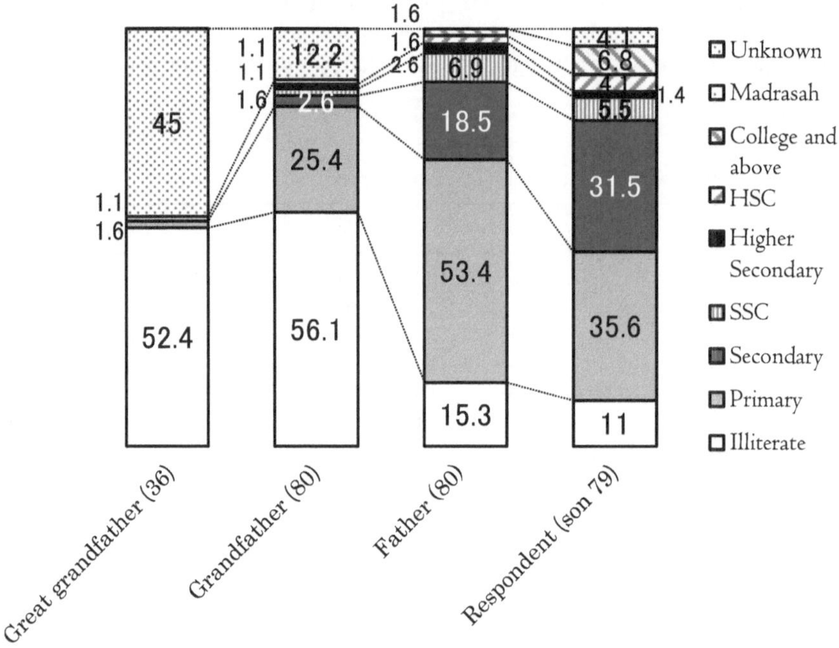

FIGURE 5.6 Changes in Education Level

Note: Figures in parentheses are numbers; figures in graphs are percentages (%).

Source: See Table 5.6.

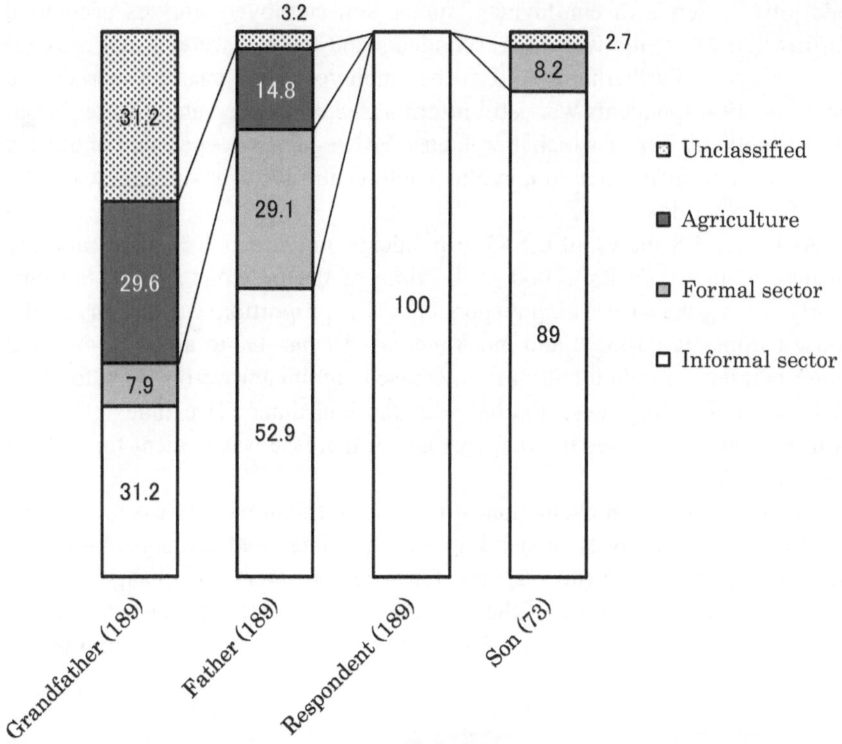

FIGURE 5.7 Changes in Sector

Note: See Figure 5.6.

Source: See Table 5.6.

Seven to eight years for informal sector workers: 45 cases

As Table 5.5 shows, both samples have similar features, although in the 2017–2018 samples, the proportions of SCs, STs, and OBCs are slightly larger and the proportion of other Hindus is smaller instead. In addition, the proportion of those illiterate is somewhat larger, and that of those with a primary level of education is lower.

Work and earnings

Of the 45 respondents, 41 were working, 3 had retired, and 1 was unemployed at the time of the follow-up survey. Their occupations ranged in the order of sales, manufacturing or repairing, transportation, services, and construction or odd jobs. In terms of employment status, self-employed workers accounted for nearly 60% of the working respondents and the rest were casual or regular employees. Furthermore, half of the employees were contract workers. In addition, 39 respondents were still informal sector workers and 2 were formal sector workers, but of which 1 was an AMC regular sweeper, and another a security guard dispatched to a public health centre through an agency, that is, an informal worker.

As Figure 5.8 shows, of the 45 respondents, more than 30% had a monthly income of less than Rs. 3,000 at the time of the previous survey, but currently, among the 41 working respondents, this proportion was 0. Conversely, those earning Rs. 10,000 and more increased from 4% to around 24%, and those earning Rs. 5,000 and more increased significantly from 33% to 80%. Even after deflating these figures with the consumer price index (CPI) of Ahmedabad city[32] to see the real change, an increase was evident for 63% of the respondents.

However, their own evaluation of the improvement of business or working conditions was not always consistent with their increased earnings. Asking 24 self-employed workers (no response for 1 person) about the change in business compared to the time of the previous survey, 54% indicated that it was 'fairly worse' or 'slightly worse,' 33% indicated that it had 'slightly improved,'

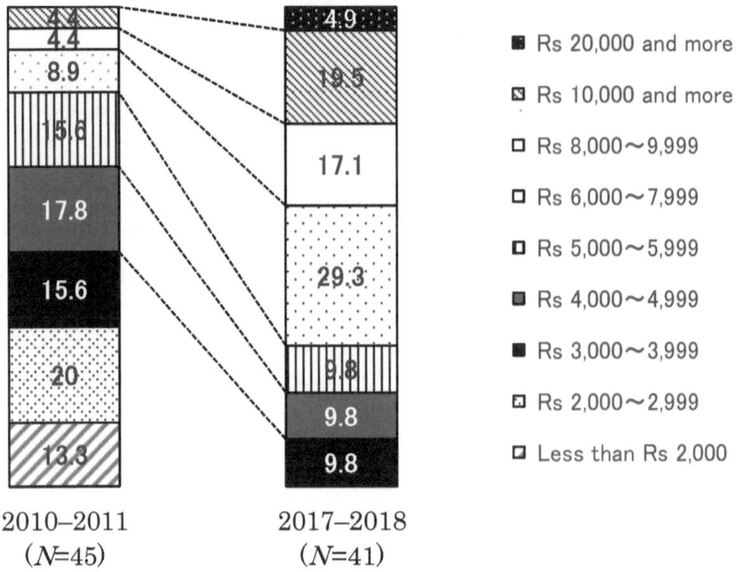

FIGURE 5.8 Monthly Income

Note: Four retired respondents were removed in 2017–2018.

Source: The author's survey (2017–2018).

and 13% indicated 'no change.' The reasons (multiple answers) provided for it being 'worse' were 'loss of customers,' 'competition with others in business,' and 'loss in sales,' among others. The reasons for 'improved' were reportedly the 'expansion of business,' 'investment,' 'good reputation among customers,' 'good relationships with customers,' and others. Furthermore, employees were asked about changes in working conditions. Of the 16 responses, half indicated 'no change,' 38% said they had 'deteriorated,' and 12% said that they had 'improved.'

In addition, the monthly income of more than half of the self-employed workers who responded 'worse' or 'no change,' and two-thirds of the employees who responded 'deteriorated' or 'no change' had increased virtually and nominally. This gap between the actual increase in monthly income and their evaluation could be because the degree of the income increase is too low or that greater earnings alone is insufficient for them to perceive improved business or working conditions. In addition, to the question about the requirements for improving business conditions (multiple answers), about two-thirds of the self-employed indicated 'money,' nearly half 'a good location,' and nearly a quarter 'public loan' or 'customer acquisition.' Only one answered 'knowledge,' and none mentioned 'training and skills' and/or 'information.'

Household income and debt

In total, 37 respondents had income sources other than their own earnings from their main job. Their contribution to household income is large, so the household group with more earners has a higher average household income. The average household income is Rs. 9,202 in the group of households with 1 earner, Rs. 12,826 for 2 earners, Rs. 16,469 for 3 earners, Rs. 19,550 for 4 earners, and Rs. 29,513 for 5 earners. Consequently, household income has also increased considerably as a whole from the time of the previous survey (Figure 5.9). The share of households with an income of Rs. 10,000 and more, which was only 13% previously, was 67% this time. Around 27% of households earned Rs. 20,000 and more. Calculating with the CPI, household income had also increased in real terms for nearly 80% of households. Although one reason for the rise is the income increase of the respondent himself mentioned earlier, the increase in the number of earning members and in their earnings also seems to have contributed. However, the rise in household income because of the addition of earning members does not necessarily increase per capita income when family size including dependents is expanded and/or the increased earnings are inefficient.

Debt was also examined. Most respondents reported having no savings, although it is difficult to ascertain whether that response is correct. However, more than half (25 respondents) indicated having debt and provided details. More than half of the debts exceeded Rs. 100,000, and the highest amount was more than Rs. 300,000. Lenders (multiple answers) were mainly relatives or friends

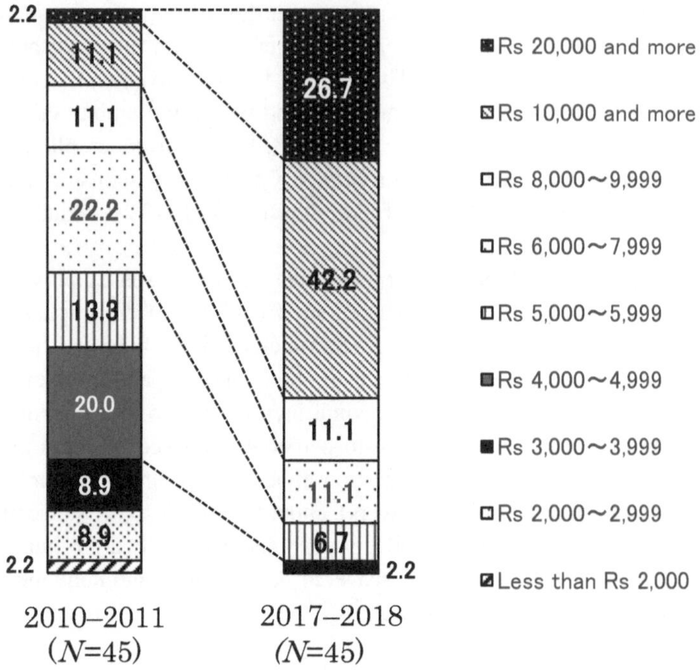

FIGURE 5.9 Monthly Household Income

Source: See Figure 5.8.

(58.3%) and money lenders (21%). Only two (8.3%) had borrowed from a bank. The purpose of the debt (multiple answers) was for family members' medical treatment (33.3%), weddings of children or other family members (25.0%), and house renovations (16.7%). Few had debt for business purposes (4.2%), suggesting that financial services for running businesses may not have been sufficiently extended to these respondents.

Changes in the living environment

Most respondents lived in the same slums as before.[33] Three-quarters of the families live in a small house with up to two rooms including cooking space; for example, one room including cooking space and one room + kitchen. Although this is far from sufficient in terms of space and quality, some houses had been visibly improved through renovations. Around half of the respondents own the land on which they live, and more than 80% own the house.

Table 5.7 details their basic living conditions. The status of not only informal sector workers' households in 2010–2011 and 2017–2018 but also that of factory workers' households in 2006 according to blue and white-collar are shown. In 2010–2011, the status of ownership of all items other than mobile phones was inferior to that of blue-collar factory workers four or five years ago. Clearly, the situation in 2017–2018 had changed significantly.

Of the 45 households, those with a water tap, latrine, and bathing space within their premises increased during the seven to eight years from 30 to 40, 28 to 41, and 22 to 39 households, respectively,[34] meaning that most of the houses came to have all these three amenities. The Government of India named it a 'Clean India' and has promoted the spread of toilets as a priority, which may have influenced the spread of basic infrastructure in Ahmedabad[35] and in respondents' houses. However, half of the 39 bathing spaces had no water taps and were just small spaces for bathing covered with a cloth or plastic sheet. Regarding the possession of household goods, ownership rates for colour TVs, ceiling fans, and mobile phones are particularly high, and the ownership rate of expensive refrigerators has risen considerably.[36]

Self-assessment of changes

How do they assess the change in their own living standards? Nearly half of the respondents feel that their living standard improved from the time of the previous survey. Furthermore, combining responses of 'considerably improved' and 'improved to some extent,' two-thirds of respondents thought their situation had bettered compared to their childhood. However, the reasons they thought 'improved' differed between when compared to seven or eight years ago and when compared to their childhood. In the former case, 'increase in income,' 'decrease in expenditure,' 'income increase because of children's growth and work,' and 'improvement of living conditions' were provided as the reasons. They seem to have expressed these reasons based on their evaluation of the present situation. On the other hand, in the latter case, they often gave reasons such as 'too poor in childhood' or 'no water, toilet, electricity, or nothing in childhood.' Thus, more difficult lives in the past led them to choose 'improved' as a response to this question.

5 Summary and concluding remarks

As the 1991 survey of factory workers showed, numerous persons of lower social groups and with lower education levels were hired in the manufacturing industry. Including them, factory employees then had mostly moved from other formal sector units or the agriculture sector, or experienced upward mobility from the informal sector in the process of industrialisation. This can be considered one aspect of the history of inclusive development. However, thereafter, it became difficult for the workers in the sample to remain in their original factories and obtain other regular jobs in other formal sector units, because of the wave of industrial

TABLE 5.7 Ownership of Various Household Goods and Basic Amenities

					(%)
	White-collar of factories	*Blue-collar of factories*	*Informal sector workers*		*Ahmedabad district (Urban) 2011*
	2006 N=30	*2006 N=82*	*2010–2011 N=45*	*2017–2018 N=45*	
Television (colour)	100.0	65.9	64.4	84.4	82.7
Television (black&white)	0.0	20.7	13.3	8.9	
Refrigerator	80.0	28.0	22.2	51.1	
Washing machine	20.0	3.7	2.2	2.2	
Telephone (landline)	–	–	–	–	
Telephone (mobile)	60.0	31.7	68.9	84.4	77.8(1)
Computer	–	–	–	–	21.0
Scooter/motorcycle	80.0	34.1	17.8	28.9	51.4
Car	10.0	4.9	2.2	2.2(2)	13.4
Ceiling fan	100.0	97.6	88.9	97.8	
Air conditioner	10.0	0.0	0.0	9.1(3)	
Water tap within the premises	100.0	82.9	66.6	88.9	
Latrine within the premises	100.0	79.3	62.2	91.1	92.1
Bathing space(4) within the premises	100.0	81.7	48.9	86.7	

Note: Distinction between 'white-collar' and 'blue-collar' are based on the occupations at the time of 1991 survey. –: No question (1) Households with both mobile and landline are included (2) 'Auto' for the business is also included (3) Air cooler (4) Bathing space without water tap is included.

Source: The author's surveys and Govt. of Gujarat (2017).

restructuring that became a turning point in the economy. Eventually, most of them moved into the informal sector and only some people could exit from that situation afterwards. Thus, a history of exclusion in the labour market was embodied in their experience.

However, the next generation of former factory workers included the children who entered the formal sector, even if not a factory. They were highly educated, their fathers were often white-collar workers such as MCS and TS, and they were from upper social groups. In addition, some children of PWs also had achieved a degree of inter-generational upward job mobility with higher education. However, the number of non-regular employees was increasing.

A survey on workers in the informal sector clarified that job changes had occurred mostly within the informal sector but to some extent in the desired direction, and that many job changes were accompanied by increased income. In addition, the education level increased, and vocational mobility was remarkable through generations: from grandfather to father and from father to respondent. However, fewer vocational changes were evident between respondents and their sons. Furthermore, as quite a few fathers once worked in the formal sector such as large-scale textile mills, it can be said that their inter-generational mobility also partly reflects the history of exclusion of factory workers in Ahmedabad.

However, the obvious improvement (= inclusiveness) in the households of informal sector workers was noteworthy, even in the short period of seven to eight years. Important is that upward mobility in these households was realised through changes such as an increase in income and job change intra- or inter-generationally, and through other changes at the household level, such as in housing conditions, ownership of household goods and basic amenities, and self-assessment of changes. However, compared with rapid economic growth and the abundance, more affluent people with better opportunities have reaped from it, the changes described earlier are modest. The major reasons for this are the lack of opportunities for improvement and development in the informal sector, poor working conditions including exceedingly low wages, non-regular employment, and poor employment growth in the organised sector.

Furthermore, a 'demographic dividend' at the household level, namely an increase in the number or ratio of productive population or earning members in the household, strongly affected changes in household income. However, conversely, this means that the situation can be easily aggravated over generations when the dependent population or number of non-earning members increase when productive employment opportunities with better working conditions do not sufficiently increase. In other words, this will be the limit of jobless inclusiveness.

Efforts to increase productive employment and decent work, and to improve the education and skills of human resources are required more than ever to effectively use the demographic dividend and realise *sufficiently inclusive growth in India.*

Notes

1 The terms regular and non-regular employment refer to the status or security of employment. Employees outside regular employment, such as casual and contract workers, are included among non-regular employees.
2 IAMR (2009), NSO (2019).
3 Govt. of India, *Annual Survey of Industries*, various issues. See note 12. Kapoor (2015) also points out the increasing share of contract workers compared with 2000–2001 and 2010–2011. That study analyses the background of capital-intensive and technology-intensive development in the organised manufacturing sector.
4 The growth rates of 1994–1995 to 2004–2005 and 2004–2005 to 2011–2012 (in 2004–2005 price) are from Joshi (2015: 134). From 2011–2012 to 2015–2016 (provisional), the author calculated figures from Government of Gujarat (2018: 9) at the 2011–2012 price.
5 For example, see Hirway et al. (2014), Kannan (2015), Baxi (2019), etc.
6 Government of Gujarat (2017: 14).
7 Government of Gujarat (2006: S-107, 2012: S-77). There, the 'organised sector' includes data for all public sector and private sector establishments employing 25 or more persons, and data are collected on a voluntary basis from non-agricultural establishments engaging 10–24 persons.
8 Unni and Naik (2014: 282–283). Reportedly, the figures are computed from unit-level records of various NSS data. In addition, according to the estimation of NSSO (2012: 103), the proportion of informal sector workers in Gujarat state then was 81.3%.
9 See Hirway et al. (2014) and Dash and Kumar (2015).
10 Government of Gujarat (2018: S-59).
11 Rao (2015: 117).
12 Government of India, Labour Bureau (1998, 2004, 2014), Government of India, Industrial Statistics Wing (2019). Note that the 2010–2011 and 2016–2017 figures are for the entire factory sector and the other figures are for the census sector only.
13 Government of Gujarat (2016: 32, 34, 35).
14 Breman (2004: 143–145).
15 Government of Gujarat (2017: 280, Table 25.3).
16 Government of Gujarat (2016: 159).
17 NSSO (2015). The small sample size in Ahmedabad city might also have affected the difference.
18 Unni and Naik (2014: 288–289). Figures are based on 55th NSS and 61st NSS. However, it notes that the small rise in the number of total informal workers in the formal sector is not reliable.
19 The criterion of informal sector units used here is 20 or fewer employees including self-employed workers. However, the workers in construction are fundamentally regarded as informal sector workers, more precisely 'informal workers', irrespective of the employment size of the prime contractor or construction site and the size of the group to which they belong, considering that most are contract casual workers employed indirectly through contractors.
20 The employment scale of surveyed factories including contract workers is a minimum of 58 and maximum of 1,260.

21 All personal interview surveys discussed here, except the last one in 2017–2018, were conducted with the help of local investigators. The author herself also interviewed numerous respondents with the sincere cooperation of one assistant and interpreter for all field surveys including one in 2017–2018. The author would like to thank them again for their cooperation.

22 For a detailed analysis based on the first survey data, see Kiso (2002), and for the analysis based on the second and third surveys except the survey of children, see Kiso (2008). Regarding the effects on the workers experiencing voluntary retirement or factory closures at that time, the following studies, although not focusing on Gujarat, might be helpful: Delhi Janwadi Adikar Manch (1998), Bhagat et al. (2000), Gupta et al. (1994), Guha (1996), and Khasnabis and Banerjea (1996).

23 Of 233 respondents, 218 were Hindus and the rest were of other religions. All respondents were asked about their caste and classified by their responses into six social groups, including non-Hindus. Respondents who did not respond regarding their caste were classified as 'unclassified/no answer.'

24 Education levels up to the Higher Secondary Certificate (HSC) were classified as follows according to Gujarat's education system at that time: seven years of primary (four years of pre-primary + three years of middle), three years of secondary, and two years of higher secondary including drop-out rate at each level. It is labelled Secondary School Certificate (SSC) or HSC if each exam is passed.

25 The characteristics of caste and education level by worker category were very similar to the original samples, even though the number of samples decreased to less than 60% of the initial survey.

26 In some cases, more than one child such as two sons or a son and daughter were surveyed if they lived separately.

27 Interviews were conducted on different days from the interview with their fathers to avoid confusion if they lived together in the same house.

28 As related studies at that time, the following are useful: Mitra (2006) and Jodhka (2010). Both are interesting for their description of the dynamism of the informal sector.

29 A list prepared by SEWA, SAATH, and CEPT University, which contains 710 slums.

30 Why are income levels of regular employees lower? They are paid regularly on a monthly basis, which means they receive a fixed amount of salary stably. They obtain such income security in exchange for low pay, and might earn more than casual workers on an annual basis.

31 Whereas 56% of respondents were self-employed, self-employed workers accounted for only 18% of former jobs.

32 Calculated using the CPI for industrial workers: Government of India, Labour Bureau (2018).

33 Of the six respondents who left, four moved because of slum resettlement. Two of these four had relocated to rehabilitation apartments.

34 In Ahmedabad city, 8% of households had no toilet facilities and 20% had no access to tap water (from treated source) within the premises in 2010: Government of India, Ministry of Housing and Urban Affairs (2018).

35 Cf. Bhatkal et al. (2015). The Clean India Mission (called SBM) was launched in October 2014. The spread of toilets has been planned and promoted in rural and urban areas.

36 In some respondents' houses, a second-hand refrigerator was used as storage without being plugged in. They sometimes get a second-hand refrigerator from a worksite when employed as a housemaid, etc., which reflects the increasing replacement of such durable goods in middle-income households.

References

Ahmedabad Municipal Corporation (AMC) (2008). "Statistical Outline for 2006–07," https://ahmedabadcity.gov.in/portal/jsp/Static_pages/amc_statistical_outline.jsp (accessed December 24, 2009)

Baxi, H. (2019). "Social Expenditure and Human Development in Gujarat," *Economic and Political Weekly*, vol. 54(14), 58–64.

Bhagat, M., R. Dixit, and B. R. Sharma (2000). *The Rehabilitation of Workers Affected by Closure/Relocation of Hazardous Industrial Units in Delhi*, New Delhi: Shri Ram Centre for Industrial Relations & Human Resources.

Bhatkal, T., W. Avis, and S. Nicolai (2015). *Towards A Better Life? A Cautionary Tale of Progress in Ahmedabad*, Overseas Development Institute. https://cdn.odi.org/media/documents/9664.pdf (accessed January 5, 2019)

Breman, J. (2004). *The Making and Unmaking of an Industrial Working Class: Sliding Down the Labour Hierarchy in Ahmedabad, India*, Amsterdam: Amsterdam University Press.

Dash, N. R., and S. Kumar (2015). "Economic Geography of Gujarat: Regional Development Perspectives," in Rao, A. S. and A. Nanavati eds., *Gujarat Economy: Structure and Performance*, Delhi: Wisdom Publications: 1–34.

Delhi Janwadi Adikar Manch (1998). "Living on the Edge: Human Cost of Closure of Industries," *Economic and Political Weekly*, vol. 33(15), 817–820.

Government of Gujarat (2006). *Socio-Economic Review 2005–06: Gujarat State*, Gandhinagar: Government of Gujarat.

Government of Gujarat (2012). *Socio-Economic Review 2011–12: Gujarat State*, Gandhinagar: Government of Gujarat.

Government of Gujarat (2016). *District Human Development Report, Ahmedabad 2016*, Gandhinagar: Government of Gujarat. www.undp.org/content/dam/india/docs/human-development/District%20HDRs/9.%20Ahmedabad_DHDR_2016.pdf (accessed November 26, 2018).

Government of Gujarat (2017). *Statistical Abstract of Gujarat State 2017*, Gandhinagar: Government of Gujarat.

Government of Gujarat (2018). *Socio-Economic Review 2017–18*, Gandhinagar: Government of Gujarat.

Government of India (2002). *Economic Survey 2001–02*, New Delhi: Government of India.

Government of India (2016). *Economic Survey 2015–16*, New Delhi: Government of India.

Government of India (2018). *Economic Survey 2017-18*, New Delhi: Government of India.

Government of India (2020). *Economic Survey 2019–20*, New Delhi. www.indiabudget.gov.in/economicsurvey/ (accessed August 13, 2020).

Government of India, Industrial Statistics Wing (2019). *Annual Survey of Industries 2016-17*, Vol. I, http://www.csoisw.gov.in/CMS/UploadedFiles/VolumeI_2016_2017.pdf (accessed January 22, 2022).

Government of India, Labour Bureau (1998). *Annual Survey of Industries 1992-93, Summary Report on Absenteeism, Labour Turnover, Employment and Labour Cost in the Census Sector*, Calcutta: Government of India.

Government of India, Labour Bureau (2004). *Annual Survey of Industries 2001-02, Vol. II, Summary Report on Absenteeism, Labour Turnover, Employment and Labour Cost in the Census Sector*, Kolkata: Government of India.

Government of India, Labour Bureau (2014). *Annual Survey of Industries 2010-11, Vol. I, Statistics on Employment and Labour Cost*, Chandigarh/Shimla: Government of India.

Government of India, Labour Bureau (2018). http://labourbureaunew.gov.in/LBO-indtab_new_Dec_2018.pdf (accessed January 5, 2019).

Government of India, Ministry of Housing and Urban Affairs (2018). "India Smart City Profile: Ahmedabad," http://smartcities.gov.in/content/innerpage/cities-profile-of-20-smart-cities.php (accessed December 30, 2018).

Guha, B. P. (1996). *Problems and Prospects of Rehabilitation after Voluntary Retirement*, New Deli: Friedrich Ebert Stiftung and Shri Ram Centre for Industrial Relations and Human Resources.

Gupta, V., A. Shrouti, and Nandkumar (1994). *Voluntary Retirement Schemes and Workers' Response*, New Delhi: Friedrich Evert Stiftung.

Hirway, I., N. Shah, and R. Sharma (2014). "Political Economy of Subsidies and Incentives to Industries in Gujarat," in Hirway, I., A. Shah and G. Shah eds., *Growth or Development: Which Way is Gujarat Going?* New Delhi: Oxford University Press: 139–192.

Institute of Applied Manpower Research (IAMR) (2009). *India Yearbook 2009: Manpower Profile*, New Delhi: Institute of Applied Manpower Research.

Jodhka, S. (2010). "Dalits in Business: Self-employed Scheduled Castes in North-West India," *Economic and Political Weekly*, vol. 45(11), 41–48.

Joshi, S. (2015). "Gujarat Economy: A Review of its Economic Performance," in Rao, A. S. and A. Nanavati eds., *Gujarat Economy: Structure and Performance*, New Delhi: Wisdom Publications: 131–141.

Kannan, K. P. (2015). "Growth without Inclusion: The Gujarat 'Model' for India's Development Exposed," *Indian Journal of Labour Economics*, vol. 58(4), 653–676.

Kapoor, R. (2015). "Creating Jobs in India's Organised Manufacturing Sector," *Indian Journal of Labour Economics*, vol. 58(3), 349–375.

Khasnabis, R. and S. Banerjea (1996). "Political Economy of Voluntary Retirement: Study of Rationalised Workers in Durgapur," *Economic and Political Weekly*, vol. 31(52), L64–L72.

Kiso, J. (2002). "Factory Workers and Their Mobility in Ahmedabad City," in Shinoda, T. ed., *The Other Gujarat: Social Transformations among Weaker Sections*, Mumbai: Popular Prakashan: 221–259.

Kiso, J. (2008). "Job Loss and Job Opportunities of Factory Workers in Ahmedabad: Flexible Labour Rethink," in Sato, H. and M. Murayama eds., *Globalization, Employment and Mobility*, IDE-JETRO Series, Hampshire: Palgrave Macmillan: 31–61.

Mitra, A. (2006). "Labour Market Mobility of Low Income Households," *Economic and Political Weekly*, vol. 41(21), 2123–2130.

NSO (National Statistical Office), Government of India (2019). "Annual Report: Periodic Labour Force Survey (PLFS) 2017–18," www.mospi.gov.in (accessed June 15, 2020)

NSSO (National Sample Survey Organisation) (1997). *Employment and Unemployment in India, 1993-94*, Report No. 409, New Delhi: Government of India.

NSSO (National Sample Survey Organisation) (2001). *Employment and Unemployment Situation in India, 1999-2000*, Report No. 458, New Delhi: Government of India.

NSSO (National Sample Survey Organisation) (2006). *Employment and Unemployment Situation in India, 2004-05*, Report No. 515, New Delhi: Government of India.

NSSO (National Sample Survey Office) (2014). *Employment and Unemployment Situation in India, 2011-12*, Report No. 554, New Delhi: Government of India.

Rao, A. S. (2015). "Growth and Structural Change in Gujarat Economy," in Rao, A. S. and A. Nanavati eds., *Gujarat Economy: Structure and Performance*, Delhi: Wisdom Publications: 75–120.

Unni, J. and R. Naik (2014). "Gujarat's Employment Story: Growth with Informality," in Hirway, I., A. Shah, and G. Shah eds., *Growth or Development: Which Way is Gujarat Going?* New Delhi: Oxford University Press: 270–300.

6

INDIAN MIGRATION AND LABOUR MARKETS

Shuji Uchikawa

1 Introduction

In India, domestic and international migration started long before independence. Urban areas have long absorbed surplus labourers from rural areas. Economic theory explains that rural–urban migration continues as long as the expected urban real income at the margin exceeds the real agricultural product (Harris and Todaro, 1970). The theory relies on the assumption that a politically determined minimum urban wage in the formal sector is higher than agricultural earnings, which suggests that benefits of economic growth might be enjoyed mainly by the urban formal sector.

In India, the rural area situation changed during the 2000s. The workforce engaged in agriculture has declined since 2004–2005. Agriculture cannot absorb more labourers in rural areas in spite of constant growth of food grain production. The total workforce in all industries increased, which might have encouraged migration from rural area to urban area or movement to non-farm employment in rural areas. The manufacturing workforce in urban areas increased, although the global financial crisis affected it temporarily. In official statistics, the manufacturing sector consists of both organised and unorganised sectors. For the former, working hours and well-being of workers in factories are regulated by the Factories Act.[1] Wages and labour productivity are high in the sector, which can benefit from economies of scale. The latter has advantages of employing workers at low wages because they need not bear the costs of social security for workers. In the second half of the 2000s, employment in the organised sector increased, introducing more contract labourers.

This chapter represents an attempt to investigate who is migrating from rural to urban areas and why and how that migration is progressing. Migration might exert effects not only on urban labour markets but also on rural economies. Migration

DOI: 10.4324/9781003304760-8

has caused tightening in local labour markets and rising wages of agricultural labourers.[2] Many migrants from low-income groups have difficulty obtaining permanent non-agriculture employment because of inadequate educational backgrounds. For that reason, they usually join contract work in organised or unorganised sectors.[3] They might compare wages of the informal sector in urban area with those of agricultural labourers to judge migration.

The second section estimates trends of employment in agriculture. The third section presents a description of the features of migration. The fourth section investigates the relation between remittances and household incomes in rural areas and the effects of migration on the local economy. The fifth section analyses employment conditions during short-term migration and migration. The sixth section presents the labour markets in organised and unorganised manufacturing sectors.

2 Decline of employment in agriculture

The situation of rural areas at the national level has changed. Employment in agriculture has declined since 2004–2005 despite increased food grain production. Agricultural production has increased since the mid-1960s. After food grain production stagnated during 1999–2000 through 2005–2006, it increased from 208.6 million tonnes in 2005–2006 to 275.7 million tonnes in 2016–2017 because of rising yields. The number of workers in agriculture between 1993–1994 and 2011–2012 is estimated as explained in the following steps. First, the mid-year population for the four segments of population (rural men, rural women, urban men, and urban women) is calculated using compound growth rates based on data of Population Census in 1991, 2001, and 2011. Second, the estimated population of the four segments of the population is multiplied by the worker population ratio of each segment in its usual status, taking Principal status (PS) and Subsidiary status (SS) to arrive at the total number of workers. PS is the activity status on which a person spent longer time during 365 days preceding the date of the survey. SS is the activity status on which a person spent a shorter time but not less than 30 days. The worker population ratio of rural women shows a long-term declining trend but it rose rapidly in 2004–2005 (Table 6.1). Stagnation of agricultural production during 1999–2000 through

TABLE 6.1 Worker Population Ratios in Rural and Urban Areas (%)

		1993–1994	*1999–2000*	*2004–2005*	*2009–2010*	*2011–2012*
Rural	Men	55.3	53.1	54.6	54.7	54.3
	Women	32.8	29.9	32.7	26.1	24.8
Urban	Men	52.1	51.8	54.9	54.3	54.6
	Women	15.5	13.9	16.6	13.8	14.7

Source: National Sample Survey Office (NSSO) (2014). *Employment and Unemployment Situation in India*, National Sample Survey 68th Round, New Delhi: NSSO. p. 99.

TABLE 6.2 Numbers of Workers in Agriculture, Manufacturing, and Construction (Thousands)

		1993–1994	*1999–2000*	*2004–2005*	*2009–2010*	*2011–2012*
Agriculture		233,530	234,727	243,662	232,681	219,951
Rural	Men	135,440	138,678	141,891	142,065	136,511
	Women	88,625	88,441	92,279	81,733	75,040
Urban	Men	5,308	4,507	5,098	5,649	5,538
	Women	4,156	3,102	4,395	3,234	2,862
Manufacturing		39,106	43,074	54,247	52,318	60,293
Organised sector		7,549	7,824	8,178	11,198	12,852
Unorganised Sector		31,557	35,250	46,069	41,120	47,441
Construction		5,668	17,258	25,500	43,834	49,290
Rural		5,132	9,974	16,339	31,224	36,852
Urban		537	7,284	9,161	12,610	12,439

Source: Author calculations based on Population Census, Employment–Unemployment Survey of NSS, and Annual Survey of Industries (various numbers).

2004–2005 pushed women from households into self-employment to supplement household income (Himanshu, 2011). Figures in 2004–2005 are apparently outliers. Therefore, figures of the worker population ratio of rural women in 1999–2000 were taken as figures in 2004–2005. Third, the number of workers in agriculture, manufacturing, and construction were obtained from their respective shares among usually working persons given by the Employment Unemployment Survey of National Sample Survey (NSS). Table 6.2 shows that the number of female workers in agriculture in rural and urban areas decreased from 97 million in 2004–2005 to 78 million in 2011–2012. The number of male workers in agriculture in rural and urban areas also decreased slightly, from 147 million in 2009–2010 to 142 million in 2011–2012. As a result, total workers in agriculture decreased from 244 million in 2004–2005 to 220 million in 2011–2012 during the same period. The decrease in agricultural employment, particularly female employment, continued during 2013–2014 through 2015–2016 (Abraham, 2017).

Structural factors are impelling the withdrawal of women from the labour force. Two contrasting arguments can be made to explain this change. On one hand, Rangarajan et al. (2011) report the possibility that female workers moved out of low-paying, self-employment activities, choosing instead either to study or devote themselves to domestic duties with increasing rural affluence. On the other hand, Kannan and Raveendar (2012) point out that 72% of women who dropped out of the labour force were 25 years or older. They emphasise that an overwhelming proportion of women who dropped out of the labour force were from rural areas belonging to poor households. Men lost their self-employment activities because of the marginalisation of land possession. Then numerous women also lost their status as unpaid family labour to assist these men.

Table 6.3 expresses status-based employment in agriculture and construction during 2004–2005 through 2011–2012. The worker population ratio in PS and SS and the share of agriculture and construction in PS and SS are available from the Employment–Unemployment Survey of NSS. Although rural female employment in agriculture in PS declined dramatically, that in construction in SS increased rapidly, which suggests that women lost the status of unpaid family labour and joined construction in rural area as casual workers. Government programmes, such as the National Rural Employment Guarantee Programme, might have encouraged women to participate in construction. Rural male employment in construction in the PS grew rapidly, which means that private and public construction projects have absorbed the rural surplus labour force.

Mehrotra and Sinha (2017) ascribed the reduction of female employment to the effects of mechanisation in agriculture and the decline in household-level animal husbandry. Rising male and female participation in education, male migration, and female withdrawal from labour force because of the rise in household income tended to reduce the labour supply in rural areas. The rise in wages of agricultural labourers and technological changes led to mechanisation of agriculture. The mechanisation process reduced demand for labour, affecting female employment. The progress of mechanisation and the rising wages of agricultural labourers made agriculture more capital-intensive. The decline not only of female workers but also of male workers in agriculture is important. Progress of mechanisation reduced employment. Naturally, it affects conditions in labour markets in rural areas in addition to the marginalisation of land possession. Consequently, a surplus labour force was compelled to seek employment in the non-agricultural sector in rural and urban areas. Although rural male and female employment in PS and SS increased by 5.5 million during 2004–2005 through 2011–2012, those in urban areas did so by 19.6 million during the same period. Apparently, many people migrated from rural to urban areas seeking employment.

3 Features of migration

In the 64th round of NSS in 2007–2008, migrants are defined as 'those for whom the last usual place of residence is different from the present place of enumeration' (NSSO, 2010: 22). The usual place of residence is a place where the person has resided continuously for six months or more. Short-term migrants are defined as persons who stayed away from the village or town for one month or more but fewer than six months during the last 365 days for employment or in search of employment.

The NSS elicits reasons for migration in the survey. Marriage accounted for 83.6% of all reasons for the migration of women. Therefore, this study specifically examines the migration of men. Migration within India is classified into four types: rural-to-rural, rural-to-urban, urban-to-rural, and urban-to-urban. For male migrants, the rural-to-urban migration stream was the most dominant one, accounting for 39%. Rural-to-urban and urban-to-urban streams were fundamentally

TABLE 6.3 Numbers of Workers in Agriculture and Construction of Principal and Subsidiary Statuses (Thousands)

			2004–2005		*2009–2010*		*2011–2012*	
			Principal status	*Subsidiary status*	*Principal status*	*Subsidiary status*	*Principal status*	*Subsidiary status*
Agriculture	Rural	Men	138,398	3,492	138,794	3,271	134,065	2,446
		Women	69,739	22,540	62,937	18,796	52,898	22,142
	Urban	Men	4,935	162	5,508	142	5,391	147
		Women	2,509	1,171	2,382	852	1,929	934
	Total		215,582	27,366	209,620	23,061	194,282	25,669
Construction	Rural	Men	14,579	84	25,603	248	29,922	308
		Women	1,467	208	3,359	2,014	3,615	3,006
	Urban	Men	8,196	32	11,516	–15	11,324	62
		Women	899	34	1,038	71	984	69
	Total		25,141	359	41,515	2,318	45,845	3,446

Note: Principal status is the activity status on which a person spent longer time during 365 days preceding the date of the survey. Subsidiary status is the activity status on which a person spent a shorter time but not less than 30 days.

Source: Author calculations based on Employment–Unemployment Survey of NSS (various numbers).

TABLE 6.4 Male Migration and Short-term Migration Rates (%)

MPCE decile class	*Migration*		*Short-term migration*	
	Rural	*Urban*	*Rural*	*Urban*
0–10	2.6	9.6	4.5	1.0
10–20	3.1	14.2	3.9	1.1
20–30	3.4	16.0	3.7	0.9
30–40	3.4	17.5	3.2	0.6
40–50	3.7	23.8	3.2	0.5
50–60	4.5	26.7	2.6	0.4
60–70	4.1	30.1	2.1	0.6
70–80	5.3	34.7	2.2	0.6
80–90	7.0	37.3	1.6	0.5
90–100	16.6	46.2	1.4	0.3

Source: NSSO (2010: 25, 93).

Note: NSS defines short-term as a period of one month or more but less than six months.

driven by employment-related reasons. The reasons accounted for 60.9% and 48.2% of all reasons, respectively, in rural-to-urban and urban-to-urban streams. Other reasons for migration were movement of parents, studies, and other reasons. In rural-to-rural and urban-to-rural streams, employment-related reasons were, respectively, 29.1% and 28.8%.

The migration rate is estimated by NSS as the number of migrants among all men in the same categories. Table 6.4 presents a difference between migration and short-term migration. An increasing trend in the migration rate was found to occur along with the increase in monthly per capita consumer expenditure (MPCE) decile class. Conversely, persons with lower MPCE undertook short-term migration as one livelihood strategy in higher degrees compared to those who had higher MPCE (NSSO, 2010). Short-term migration rates were less than 5% for all classes of rural men. Of all rural male short-term migrant workers, 42.9% and 17.2% were engaged, respectively, in construction and agriculture. Construction and manufacturing, respectively, employed 27.8% and 26.1% of urban male short-term migrant workers.

Out-migration differs from migration in the definition of NSS. Any former member of a household who left the household, at any time in the past, for a stay outside the village or town was regarded as out-migrant. Information about the out-migration of the erstwhile household members is collected. The information related to out-migration cannot be collected if all members of a household migrate from village or town. When some members migrate from a household to take up residence in another country, they are regarded as out-migration but not migrants in India. Table 6.5 presents the percent distribution of out-migrants by their status of engagement in economic activity and sending remittance during the last 365 days to their former households. Only 58.8% engaged in economic activity in India and another country and were sending remittances to their former

TABLE 6.5 Out-migrant Distribution by Status of Engagement in Economic Activity and Sending Remittance for Respective Places of Residence (%)

	India				*Another country*			
	Engaged in economic activity		*Not engaged in economic activity*		*Engaged in economic activity*		*Not engaged in economic activity*	
	Making remittance	*Not making remittance*	*Making remittance*	*Not making remittance*	*Making remittance*	*Not making remittance*	*Making remittance*	*Not making remittance*
Rural men	53.0	20.8	0.3	17.5	5.8	1.0	0.1	0.3
Urban men	33.9	27.0	0.3	21.6	10.9	3.8	0.0	1.1

Source: NSSO (2010: 106).

households. Although 21.8% engaged in economic activity, they were not sending remittances. Out-migration does not guarantee employment and income sufficient to send remittances. The average amounts of remittances sent, respectively, by male out-migrants from rural and urban areas in India during the last 365 days were Rs. 13,400 and Rs. 27,700. Remittances sent by male out-migrants residing abroad were Rs. 57,800.

The remittance amounts vary depending on the migrant origin and out-migration destination. It can be assumed that economic conditions of migrant workers after migration and their remittance depend on the income of the original households before migration. Family in high-income groups can provide better education. Household members are likely to have better skills. Migrants from high-income groups can find higher-income jobs than those from low-income groups. The latter are apt to undertake short-term migration because they cannot find stable job opportunities. Furthermore, migrants must accept the risk of not finding jobs and must bear travel and living costs at the destination. Particularly, out-migration abroad takes more costs and higher risk. Therefore, the incidence of out-migration to another country is seen to be increasing with the increase in MPCE.

Both migration and short-term migration are undertaken as one livelihood strategy. Usami and Yanagisawa (2015) analysed the relation between migrants and educational background, using unit-level data of the 64th round of NSS. At the all-India level, different compositions of educational levels cannot be found for migrants and residents. However, a clear difference was apparent in Punjab. Whereas the share of illiterate and primary school educated persons among inter-state in-migrants was 58.0% in 2007–2008, that of residents was 28.1%. They find that although persons with low educational background have no move, migrants from Bihar and Uttar Pradesh are exceptions. The shares of illiterate and primary school educated persons among inter-state migrants from Bihar and Uttar Pradesh were, respectively, 8.8% and 5.7%. The share in all-India was 3.0%. The reason for migration with low educational background is ascribed to lack of good employment opportunities in Bihar and Uttar Pradesh. They compare the employment of migrants out of Bihar and persons residing in Bihar. Of illiterate persons residing in Bihar, 12.7% and 57.4% worked, respectively, as agriculture self-employed and agricultural labourers. Of illiterate migrants, 32.7% and 34.5% worked, respectively, as non-agriculture regular and casual employees. They were able to obtain some non-agriculture employment after migration out of Bihar. In other words, inter-state migration might provide opportunities for non-agriculture regular and casual employment to persons with low educational background. Therefore, they chose to migrate to Delhi, Haryana, and Punjab.

Migrants are following networks of relatives and regional communities. Once a person finds a good opportunity to earn income, other people follow him. Finally, an out-migration route is established. Destinations of out-migration in selected states are presented in Table 6.6. Three groups exist. In Gujarat and Maharashtra, out-migration occurs within the state. These states have industrialised areas

TABLE 6.6 Rural Male Out-migrant Distributions by Present Residence for Selected States

	Same state	*Outside the state in India*	*Another country*
Gujarat	906	63	30
Maharashtra	895	91	14
Bihar	122	852	23
Uttar Pradesh	264	700	32
Punjab	265	249	485
Kerala	362	212	421

Source: NSSO (2010: 118).

within states. In Bihar and Uttar Pradesh, out-migration mainly occurs to other states. In these states, the manufacturing sector has not developed sufficiently to absorb migrants from rural area within states. Inter-state migration flows from backward states to industrialised areas in other states such as Gujarat, and Maharashtra. In Kerala and Punjab, out-migration occurs mainly with people moving abroad. Kerala has an international linkage with the Middle East. Punjab has an international linkage with Europe and North America.

Remittances play important role in shrinking the gaps of expenditures between industrialised states and less-developed states. Since economic reforms from 1991, growth rates of manufacturing have risen faster. Industrialised areas where labour demand is increasing absorb migrants from less-developed areas where the average income is much lower than the national average. Migrants send remittances home in less-developed areas to bolster household incomes. Table 6.7 shows the index of per capita net state domestic product (NSDP) and state average MPCE data for rural areas in 2011–2012. The base of the index is the all-India average. Deviation of per capita MPCE is smaller than that of per capita NSDP. In states with per capita NSDP lower than the average, such as Bihar, Uttar Pradesh, and Madhya Pradesh, the index of MPCE is higher than that of per capita NSDP. In states with per capita NSDP higher than the average such as Tamil Nadu, Maharashtra, and Haryana, the index of per capita MPCE is lower than that of per capita NSDP. Apparently, remittances of migrants increased consumption in less-developed states and reduced consumption in more-developed states. Punjab and Kerala are noteworthy exceptions. Although per capita NSDP is higher than the average in each state, the index of MPCE is higher than that of per capita NSDP. Many migrants have gone abroad from these states; subsequently, families have received remittances from abroad. Remittances compensate for some disparity at a macro-regional level.

4 Remittance and household income

Remittances by migrants might affect the original households and local economy. The 64th round of NSS has data on the number of households reporting the use of remittances for each MPCE decile class in rural areas (Table 6.8). A decreasing

TABLE 6.7 Per Capita NSDP and Average Monthly Per Capita Expenditure by State in Rural Areas in 2011–2012 (Base: All-India average = 100)

	Per-capita net state domestic production	*Average monthly per-capita expenditures in rural areas*
Bihar	34.3	78.8
Uttar Pradesh	50.4	80.8
Madhya Pradesh	60.7	80.6
Manipur	62.7	105.0
Assam	64.8	85.2
Jharkhand	65.0	70.3
Tripura	74.2	93.3
Odisha	76.2	70.1
Nagaland	83.5	144.0
Jammu & Kashmir	83.8	121.9
Chhattisgarh	86.9	71.8
Rajasthan	90.1	111.7
Mizoram	90.8	115.0
Meghalaya	94.6	103.1
All-India average	100.0	100.0
Andhra Pradesh	108.7	122.7
Arunachal Pradesh	115.1	124.6
Punjab	134.8	164.0
Gujarat	137.8	107.4
Himachal Pradesh	138.2	142.2
Karnataka	142.2	109.2
Tamil Nadu	146.5	118.4
Kerala	154.3	186.6
Maharashtra	156.3	113.2
Uttarakhand	158.1	120.7
Haryana	167.2	152.2
Sikkim	250.0	109.4
Goa	408.8	168.4

Source: Author calculations based on NSSO (2013). *Key Indicators of Household Consumer Expenditure in India*, National Sample Survey 68th Round, New Delhi: NSSO and website of Ministry of Statistics and Programme Implementation (www.mospi.gov.in/data).

trend was apparent in expenditures for food and education expenditure with the increase in MPCE decile class. Higher MPCE decile classes are apt to allot remittances for saving. Although the data clarify that remittances contribute to the improvement of living conditions of households in rural area, the role of remittances in local economy cannot be judged from the data.

The Institute of Human Development and A N Sinha Institute of Social Studies conducted surveys of Bihar in 1981–1983, 1998–2000, and 2009–2011 (Sharma and Rodgers, 2015). On one hand, sharecropping by agricultural labourers attached to an employer declined during the period. The share of attached labourers in all households decreased dramatically from 16.1% in 1981–1983 to 1.6%

TABLE 6.8 Number of Households Reporting Use of Remittances Per 1,000 Households Receiving Remittances for Respective MPCE Decile Classes in Rural Areas (%)

MPCE decile class	*Food items*	*Education of household member*	*Healthcare*	*Saving*
0–10	78.2	31.8	35.4	1.8
10–20	79.9	35.1	38.2	4.4
20–30	80.0	32.4	37.2	3.4
30–40	78.8	34.1	35.1	2.6
40–50	77.2	31.5	39.1	2.3
50–60	76.8	31.7	37.7	3.8
60–70	76.5	30.2	39.9	4.8
70–80	75.0	29.7	37.4	6.1
80–90	73.7	27.9	35.3	6.9
90–100	70.6	27.9	39.9	9.7
All groups	75.6	30.5	37.7	5.4

Source: NSSO (2010: A-1).

in 2009–2011. On the other hand, the proportion of casual agricultural labourers, who do not own land and small peasants, who neither hire in nor hire out labour, has increased. Even in 2009–2011, a strong relation between caste and land holding is observed. Agricultural labourers are dominated by scheduled castes and some parts of other backward classes, whereas big peasants, who hire in labour and landlords, who rent out land and at most supervise agricultural work, derive from upper castes. Disappearance of old relationships between landlords and agricultural labourers has not necessarily changed the economic and social hierarchy (Rodgers and Rodgers, 2011; Sharma and Rodgers, 2015).

Migration changed the local economy in rural Bihar. In 1981–1983, 80% of principal occupations were agriculture in the villages surveyed by the two institutes. However, the share decreased to 39% in 2009–2011. Of men aged 15–59, 40% migrated for some or all the year in 2009–2011. Moreover, migration caused tightening in the local labour market and the rise in wages of agricultural labourers. It has narrowed the wage gap separating Bihar and other parts of India. Agricultural labourers can compare wages in Bihar and those in rural and urban areas in Punjab and Haryana.

The survey in 1998–2000 and 2009–2011 examined 904 households in 12 villages in 7 districts (Datta, 2016). The survey results reveal three points. First, the most striking increase in migration was experienced by agricultural labourer households, and by scheduled castes. However, migration is used by all castes and size of land ownership. As Kundu and Sarangi (2007) argue, the duration of migration and the nature of work undertaken by migrants at the destination are heterogeneous. Migrants among scheduled castes and Muslims are more likely to be in short-term, casual employment. Migrants from higher castes tend to migrate for longer durations and are generally found working in regular and salaried jobs.

Second, the share of income from agriculture is less than 40% in all income quintiles in 2009–2011. In other words, households in all income quintiles depend on non-agriculture income more than on agriculture income, even in rural Bihar. Cultivation becomes less profitable because of the rise in wages of agricultural labourers and marginalisation of land possession. In the highest income quintile, remittances accounted for 33.2% of the total income in households with migrants, and income from salary for 31.6% of total income of households without migrants. Because high-income groups can access high education, they have a chance to obtain stable regular employment at the destination of migration and local place. Low-income groups are proportionally more dependent on agriculture. The share of income from agriculture in all incomes was 37.3% and 21.8%, respectively, in the lowest quintile and highest income quintile. The incidence of migration was lowest in the lowest income quintile. They cannot secure the initial costs of migration and assume the risk of not finding jobs.

Third, remittances are a major source of income for households with migrants. The mean of the annual income of the household with migrant members was Rs. 73,108. That of households without migrant members was Rs. 62,235. In the lowest, second lowest, middle, second highest, and highest income quintiles of households with migrants, remittances accounted, respectively, for 58.7%, 58.0%, 54.3%, 46.5%, and 33.2% of household income. This phenomenon is paradoxical. Although migration is a pathway out of poverty, not all households in the bottom-income quintile can benefit from it. Higher-income households among economically and socially weak sections of society such as scheduled castes and Muslims can send migrants to industrialised areas.

Deshingkar et al. (2006) surveyed residents of six districts in Bihar, finding that although 'the poorest of the poor' cannot migrate, scheduled castes and other backward castes with low education as well as landless or nearly landless households are engaged in migration, but usually in the lowest-paid jobs. Agricultural labour work, casual labour work in construction, work in brick kilns, and rickshaw pulling are the four most important categories of work for these migrants. Factory work is more remunerative than those other four jobs. They argue that 'in general, poor and marginal farmers migrated seasonally or commuted and the rich migrated permanently' (p. 11). Practices such as borrowing food grain from high-income groups to subsist during lean seasons and borrowing at very high interest rates have virtually disappeared because of migration in several places in Bihar. Deshingkar et al. (2006) estimate that roughly 5–10% of migrating households have accumulated assets through migration.

Migration is driven fundamentally by employment-related considerations. Some migrants have settled down at a destination permanently. Then employment conditions of short-term migrants and migrants are investigated separately.

5 Employment conditions after migration

The putative relation between poverty and short-term migration has long been debated. On one hand, Keshri and Bhagat (2012) use unit-level data from the 64th round of NSS to analyse the relation between short-term migration and MPCE. The short-term migration rates in the lowest and second-lowest MPCE quintile in rural areas were, respectively, 44.8% and 32.1%. They point out that rural areas have much higher migration rates than urban areas. Binary logistic models are fitted to assess the effects of socio-economic characteristics on a person's likelihood of being a seasonal migrant. They reveal a statistically significant negative relation between short-term migration in rural areas and household income, land possession, and educational attainment. Results show that 'temporary mobility is higher among the poorer sections of Indian society irrespective of the level of economic development of the states concerned' (p. 87). On the other hand, Kundu and Sarangi (2007) report that the bottom 40% of the urban population accounted for only 29% of all short-term migrants. Not only are low-income groups struggling for survival, high-income groups constitute short-term migrants. Short-term migrants have socially and economically heterogeneous backgrounds. The short-duration movements include the periodic transfer of regular workers and temporary posting of marketing and extension workers. The nature of jobs sought by poor and rich households differs. It can be concluded from the aforementioned argument that low-income groups undertake short-term migration as a livelihood strategy.

Migration provides opportunities to improve household incomes in rural areas through remittance. However, migrants work very hard for long hours to send remittances. Pais and Usami (2014) conducted a survey on 469 migrant industrial workers in Ludhiana during May–June 2012. Among 469 sample workers, 47.5% and 47.3% came, respectively, from Bihar and Uttar Pradesh. 438 workers were men. Five industries have developed in Ludhiana, including apparel and textile, iron and steel, bicycle, machinery, and auto component industries. In the five industries, 442 workers were engaged. Among 469 sample workers, whereas 370 workers were sending remittances to their dependents regularly, 74 workers did not send them. As described previously, not all migrants can obtain employment after migration. Most of the workers were not short-term migrants. Only 20% of the workers spent over two months away from Ludhiana. Most of them work in Ludhiana for 10 or 11 months. They are employed directly by factories or through contractors. Because employment is casual in both cases, no job security is guaranteed. Estimated average monthly earnings of male workers were Rs. 7,391. Considering working hours, the eight-hourly wage received by production workers among sample workers was Rs. 4,988. The statutory monthly minimum wage for an unskilled worker on an eight-hour shift in urban Punjab between March and September 2012 was Rs. 4,568, which suggests that some sample workers could not receive less than minimum wage because other workers received more than Rs. 4,988.

Migrant workers were able to find employment, but they had to work for long hours to get sufficient income to send remittances to their homes.

Kundu and Sarangi (2007) argue that permanent migration emerges as a clear instrument for adults to improve their economic well-being and escape from poverty. They estimate the effects of factors including the level of education, migration status, occupation, nature of employment, and city size on the probability of a person falling below the poverty line, using data from the 55th round of the NSS. Effective and negative coefficients are found between rural to urban migration and the probability of living in poverty. They deny the hypothesis that urban poverty is a spillover of rural poverty because rural migrants into urban area have a lower probability of being poor than the local population. It is estimated that the high-income rural residents can migrate to urban centres because relocation of residence to cities requires some initial self-supporting capacity and a certain skill level.

Unskilled migrants from rural areas can join only the informal sector. Can experience in the informal sector improve their standards of living? Jegadeesan and Fujita (2014) examine the conditions of migrants who have settled down in Tiruppur in Tamil Nadu. They surveyed 90 Tamil migrants in four residential areas in Tiruppur and 25 from northern India. Migration improved the migrants' standards of living, but their livelihoods depend on the timing of their migration. The main motivation for migration was inter-caste violence before 1999, agricultural distress between 2000 and 2004, and indebtedness after 2005. The survey uncovered a large gap in income between Tamil workers who had migrated before 1999 and those who migrated after 2005. Per-worker monthly income was Rs. 10,314 among the former and Rs. 7,289 among the latter. That of North Indian migrants after 2005 was Rs. 5,456. Migrants before 1999 became self-employed packing agents, labour contractors, or managers. They improved their standard of living during the export boom, whereas Tamil migrants after 2005 faced difficult industry conditions such as intense competition in the export market. Although some factories faced temporary labour shortages, constant inflows of migrants suppressed wages, which suggests that whether migrants can improve their standard of living depends on the economic conditions of the area and period. However, the analysis result requires caution. Workers who had migrated before 1999 remained in Tiruppur longer than other workers. Their age is higher than that of other workers.

Mitra (2006) conducted a survey of 802 households in 30 slum clusters in Delhi in 1999–2000, and of 200 households in 2004–2005. That study finds inter-occupational and intra-occupational change within the informal sector makes upward income mobility possible. At the same time, the study results indicate that upward mobility was confined mainly to very low levels of past income, whereas some of those in higher income brackets in the past experienced a decline.

6 Labour markets in manufacturing

The labour market in manufacturing also changed. As described earlier, the manufacturing sector consists of organised and unorganised sectors. Data of the organised sector were obtained from the Annual Survey of Industries (ASI) during 1973–1974 through 2011–2012.[4] In the ASI, workers are defined as including all persons employed directly or through any agency, whether for wages or not, and engaged in any manufacturing process, in cleaning any part of the machinery or premises used for manufacturing processes, or any other kind of work incidental to or connected with a manufacturing process or the subject of a manufacturing process. The number of workers in the organised sector fluctuated around 6 million in 1994–1995 and 2004–2005, although the gross value added (GVA) in 2004–2005 prices increased by 4.5% per annum. Growth without creation of employment was clear during the period. However, the situation changed in the mid-2000s. Rapid economic growth expanded the domestic market. The annual growth rate of GVA was 8.5% during 2004–2005 through 2011–2012. The rapid growth of production induced employment creation. The total number of workers in the organised manufacturing sector increased by 6.3% per annum during 2004–2005 through 2011–2012. This important phenomenon signalled the end of growth without creation of employment.

Along with the fast growth of employment, informalisation of employment progressed during 2004–2005 through 2011–2012. The share of contract workers among workers in all manufacturing industries rose from 26.4% in 2004–2005 to 34.6% in 2011–2012. In all 22 industries at two-digit classification, the share increased. Competition led factories in the organised sector to reduce labour costs by replacing permanent workers with contract workers. At the same time, factories strove to prevent labour conflict. The share of wages to workers in all inputs in all manufacturing industries fell from 2.5% in 2004–2005 to 2.1% in 2011–2012.

Informalisation of employment started before 2004–2005. The National Commission for Enterprises in the Unorganised Sector (NCEUS) (2009: 12) defines informal employment as 'unorganised workers consist of those working in the unorganised enterprises or households, excluding regular workers with social security benefits, and the workers in the formal sector without any employment/social security benefits provided by the employers.' The NCEUS estimated the formal and informal workers in the organised and unorganised sectors in the entire Indian economy, including agricultural and non-agricultural sectors. The study clarifies an important point of employment growth between 1999–2000 and 2004–2005. Whereas formal employment grew slowly from 33.6 million to 35.0 million, employment in the organised sector increased rapidly from 54.9 million to 62.6 million.[5] This slow growth suggests that 'the entire increase in the employment in the organised sector over this period has largely been informal in nature' (NCEUS, 2009: 14). Informal employment spread not only in the manufacturing sector but also in the service sector. Uchikawa (2011) found through field surveys conducted between April and June 2010 in the National Capital Region that many small and medium enterprises in auto component industry that had been set up from the 1990s onwards tend to depend on contract workers. They replace workers after termination of their contracts and retain only skilled workers as permanent workers.

The workforce in the unorganised sector grew during 2004–2005 through 2011–2012, although it dropped because of the global financial crisis in 2009–2010. It was calculated by deducing the workforce provided by ASI from the estimated workforce in manufacturing (Table 6.2). Factories of the unorganised sector were located not only in urban areas but also in rural areas. The unorganised sector consists of own-account manufacturing enterprises that employ no hired workers on a fair basis and establishments that do so. The share of urban establishments in all employment of unorganised sector rose from 17.8%, 21.1%, 22.2%, and 26.5%, respectively, in 1994–1995, 2000–2001, 2005–2006, and 2010–2011. Urban establishments in the unorganised sector have expanded. Migrants from low-income households engaged in manufacturing work mainly as contract workers in the organised sector or urban establishments in the unorganised sector. In such places, minimum wages are not always guaranteed.

An enterprise survey of NSS has data on annual emoluments per hired worker. The amount is deflated by the wholesale price index of food articles. Annual emoluments per hired worker in 2004–2005 prices increased from Rs. 24,148 in 2000–2001 to Rs. 29,704 in 2005–006. However, it decreased to Rs. 27,149 in 2010–2011 because of a sharp hike in food articles. Decreases in real wages in the unorganised manufacturing sector deflated by food prices, the rise of agricultural labourers, and the expansion of rural employment by construction have all discouraged migration from rural to urban area. Mechanisation of agriculture reduced employment in agriculture. Also, marginalisation of land possession forced farmers to give up cultivation. Surplus labourers were therefore compelled to seek employment in the non-agricultural sector in rural and urban areas. On the other hand, the wage gap separating workers in the unorganised manufacturing sector and agricultural labourers shrank. In the second half of the 2000s, the sharp hike in food articles raised living costs in urban areas. Furthermore, rural male labour has been absorbed by private and public construction projects in rural and urban areas. Migration and short-term migration depend on many factors in rural and urban areas.

7 Conclusion

For poor households, particularly in rural areas, migration provides a pathway to escape poverty. Even an unskilled migrant with no opportunity for higher education can gain employment in the urban informal sector. Migrant workers engaged in the informal sector must work for long periods at low wages. Some are receiving less than minimum wages. However, not all households in the lowest-income quintile can take advantage of it. Migration does not guarantee employment or income sufficient to send remittances. Migrants must bear initial costs and the risk of being unable to find a job. Higher-income households among economically and socially weak sections of society such as scheduled castes and Muslims can send migrants to industrialised areas.

The duration of migration and the nature of work undertaken by migrants at destinations are heterogeneous. Migrants among weak sections of society are more likely to be in short-term, casual employment. Migrants from high-income groups tend to migrate for longer durations; they are generally found in regular and salaried jobs because family in high-income groups can provide better education. Household members are likely to have better skills. Migrants from high-income groups can find higher-income jobs than migrants from low-income groups. Therefore, amounts of remittances by migrants from high-income group are higher than that by migrants from low-income groups. Although remittances improve living conditions of low-income groups, they have not changed the structure of income distribution in villages.

Labour markets in rural area have changed. Migration has caused tightening in the local labour market and has raised wages of agricultural labourers. The rise in wages of labourers and technological change have led to the mechanisation of agriculture. Progress of mechanisation has subsequently reduced employment of agricultural labourers. Furthermore, marginalisation of land possession has forced farmers to give up cultivation. Whereas male rural employment in agriculture has decreased since the mid-2000s, construction has absorbed it. The total number of workers in the organised manufacturing sector has increased since the mid-2000s, replacing permanent workers with contract workers. Migrants from low-income households engaged in manufacturing mainly work as contract workers in the organised sector or in urban establishments in the unorganised sector. They compare the expected urban real income in informal employment with the expected income from agriculture or construction in rural areas to judge migration, considering gaps in living costs between rural and urban areas. Sharp hikes in food prices during the second half of the 2000s pushed up living costs in urban areas. As long as they remain in their villages, they can obtain food at cheaper prices through the public distribution system. Actually, migration and short-term migration depend on many factors in rural and urban areas.

Remittances of migrants contribute to the improvement of living conditions of rural poor households. However, migration opportunities are not shared equally among all households. Lower-income households among economically and socially weak sections of society cannot bear the initial costs and risks of migration. Highly educated migrants from high-income groups are actually experiencing greater income growth than those from low-income groups. Benefits of economic growth are enjoyed mainly by the urban formal sector. It can be argued that such situations are not conducive to a path of inclusive development. However, the argument overlooks the long-term gradual change of economic and rural structures of rural areas. 'Inclusive development' is the concept that expresses the goal of policies. Present conditions are not able to reach the goal for the short-term. In Bihar, where a strong relation between caste and land holding still prevails, the old relation between landlords and agricultural labourers disappeared over the last three decades. Migration has presented an alternative to sharecropping for them and has improved their bargaining power vis-à-vis landlords.

Notes

1 The Factories Act covers those factories employing 10 or more workers using power, and those employing 20 or more workers without it.
2 The 2001 Census defines an agricultural labourer as a person who works on another person's land for wages in money or payments in kind of shares. The labourer shoulders no risk from cultivation but merely works on another person's land for wages. An agricultural labourer has no right of lease or contract on the land that is worked.
3 Todaro (1969) includes in the informal sector those workers who are not regularly employed in the urban modern sector.
4 The industrial classification used for the ASI was the National Industrial Classification (NIC) 1970 version up to 1988–1989, NIC 1987 version up to 1997–1998, NIC 1998 version up to 2007–2008, and thereafter NIC 2008 version. All data were converted to NIC-98 using concordance at the 3-digit level. Estimates at the 2-digit level of industry classification from Division 15 to Division 36 were obtained by aggregating the relevant 3-digit level industries.
5 Total employment in the entire Indian economy including both the organised and unorganised sectors grew from 396.4 million to 455.7 million during 1999–2000 through 2004–2005. As a result, the share of formal employment in all employment declined from 8.5% to 7.7% during the period.

References

Abraham, V. (2017). "Last Three Years May Have Been the Worst Stagnant Employment Growth," *Economic and Political Weekly*, vol. 52(38), 13–17.

Datta, A. (2016). "Migration, Remittances and Changing Sources of Income in Rural Bihar (1999–2011)," *Economic and Political Weekly*, vol. 51(31), 85–93.

Deshingkar, P. et al. (2006). *The Role of Migration and Remittances in Promoting Livelihoods in Bihar*, London: Overseas Development Institute.

Harris, J. R. and M. P. Todaro (1970). "Migration, Unemployment and Development: A Two-Sector Analysis," *The American Economic Review*, vol. 60(1), 126–142.

Himanshu (2011). "Employment Trends in India: A Re-examination," *Economic and Political Weekly*, vol. 46(37), 43–59.

Jegadeesan, M. and K. Fujita, (2014). "Knitted Together: The Life of Migrants in Tiruppur Garment Cluster," in Uchikawa, S. ed., *Industrial Clusters, Migrant Workers, and Labour Markets in India*, London: Palgrave Macmillan: 62–88.

Kannan, K. P. and G. Raveendar (2012). "Counting and Profiling the Missing Labour Force," *Economic and Political Weekly*, vol. 47(6), 77–80.

Keshri, K. and R. B. Bhagat (2012). "Temporary and Seasonal Migration: Regional Pattern, Characteristics and Associated Factors," *Economic and Political Weekly*, vol. 47(4), 81–88.

Kundu, A. and N. Sarangi (2007). "Migration, Employment Status and Poverty: An Analysis across Urban Centres," *Economic and Political Weekly*, vol. 42(4), 299–306.

Mehrotra, S. and S. Sinha (2017). "Explaining Falling Female Employment during a High Growth Period," *Economic and Political Weekly*, vol. 52(39), 54–62.

Mitra, A. (2006). "Labour Market Mobility of Low Income Households," *Economic and Political Weekly*, vol. 41(21), 2123–2130.

National Commission for Enterprises in the Unorganised Sector (NCEUS) (2009). *The Challenge of Employment in India: An Informal Economy Perspective*, New Delhi: NCEUS, vol. I.

National Sample Survey Office (NSSO) (2010). *Migration in India 2007–08*, National Sample Survey 64th Round, New Delhi: NSSO.

National Sample Survey Office (NSSO) (2013). *Key Indicators of Household Consumer Expenditure in India*, National Sample Survey 68th Round, New Delhi: NSSO.

Pais, J. and Y. Usami (2014). "Migrant workers in Ludhiana," in Uchikawa, S. ed., *Industrial Clusters, Migrant Workers, and Labour Markets in India*, London: Palgrave Macmillan: 22–61.

Rangarajan, C., P. Iyer, and S. Kaul (2011). "Where Is the Missing Labour Force?" *Economic and Political Weekly*, vol. 46(39), 68–72.

Rodgers, G. and J. Rodgers (2011). "Inclusive Development? Migration, Governance and Social Change in Rural Bihar," *Economic and Political Weekly*, vol. 46(23), 43–50.

Sharma, A. N. and G. Rodgers (2015). "Structural Change in Bihar's Rural Economy," *Economic and Political Weekly*, vol. 50(52), 45–53.

Todaro, M. P. (1969). "A Model of Labor Migration and Urban Unemployment in Less Developed Countries," *The American Economic Review*, vol. 59(1), 138–148.

Uchikawa, S. (2011). "The Rise of Small and Medium Enterprises in Indian Auto Component Industry," *Economic and Political Weekly*, vol. 46(25), 51–59.

Usami, H. and H. Yanagisawa (2015). "Noson kara Toshi he (in Japanese: From Rural to Urban)," in Mizushima, T. and H. Yanagisawa eds., *Gendai Indo 2 (Contemporary India)*, Tokyo: University of Tokyo Press: 217–254.

7

INTERNATIONAL MIGRATION FROM INDIA AND THE GCM

Inclusion and Exclusion in South Asia?

Binod Khadria

1 Introduction: South Asian migration in the world

Over the last quarter of a century since 1990, there has been a steady rise in international migration to Asia (Khadria and Mishra, 2021a). The 2020 United Nations *International Migration Report* data of the United Nations show that as a destination for 86 million migrants, the continent hosted the second largest stock of the world's 281 million migrants, slightly below Europe. Although in 2019, as a proportion of population, it accounted for the lowest at 1.8% migrants in overpopulated Asia (equal to 1.8% in Latin America and the Caribbean too) as compared to 3.5% in the world, 2% in Africa, 11% in Europe, 16.0% in Northern America, and 21.2% in Oceania. Within Asia, by 2020, the sub-region of South Asia as a migration destination has, however, experienced a steady decline in numbers from 15 million in 1990 to 14 million in 2020 (Table 7.1). Despite this secular decline, the sub-region, comprising eight countries, viz., Afghanistan, Pakistan, India, Nepal, Bhutan, Bangladesh, Sri Lanka, and Maldives still hosted the second largest number of migrants after West Asia, as compared to the other sub-regions of Asia listed in Table 7.1. Intra-South-Asian migration among these countries; intra-Asian migration from other sub-regions of Asia comprising East Asia, Southeast Asia, Central Asia, and West Asia; and inter-regional migration from the rest of the world, including Africa, Latin America and the Caribbean, Europe, the Americas, and Oceania characterise this massive migration to South Asia as a destination.

Although the in-migrants comprise regular, irregular, low-skilled, high-skilled, and all kinds of migrants, six of the eight South Asian countries, viz., India, Bangladesh, Pakistan, Afghanistan, Nepal, and Sri Lanka are more well-known as the origin countries of migrants (Table 7.2). Table 7.2 shows a dramatic surge in the number of emigrants from South Asia between 2015 and 2017, mostly from India.

DOI: 10.4324/9781003304760-9

TABLE 7.1 Destination South Asia vis-à-vis Rest of the World: Stocks of Migrants in the World, Asia and Its Sub-regions, and in South Asian Countries, 1990–2020 (Mid-year Counts)

Number of immigrants in	*1990*	*2000*	*2010*	*2015*	*2017*	*2020*
World	152,542,373	172,604,257	220,019,266	247,585,744	257,715,425	280,598,105
Europe	49,232,191	56,314,416	70,747,947	74,501,508	77,895,217	86,706,068
North America	27,610,542	40,351,848	50,970,996	55,766,224	57,664,154	58 708 795
Africa	15,690,623	14,800,306	17,007,249	23,436,088	24,650,223	25,389,464
Latin America & the Caribbean	7,169,728	6,579,328	8,246,652	9,272,027	9,508,189	14,794,623
Oceania	4,730,858	5,360,027	7,124,634	8,051,745	8,410,933	9,380,653
Asia	48,108,431	49,198,332	65,921,788	76,558,152	79,586,709	85,618,502
West Asia (incl. Iran)	19,497,045	21,220,331	33,377,782	42,506,547	45,590,174	49,397,055
Southeast Asia	2,876,616	4,926,833	8,673,693	9,609,923	9,873,600	1,06,15,377
East Asia	3,959,345	5,393,081	7,061,814	7,600,768	7,776,716	89,75,729
Central Asia	6,630,683	5,183,872	5,262,414	5,393,504	5,462,972	55,64,042
South Asia (excl. Iran)	15,144,742	12,474,215	11,546,085	11,447,410	10,883,247	11,066,299
India	7,493,204	6,411,272	5,436,012	5,240,960	5,188,550	4,878,704
Pakistan	6,208,204	4,181,912	3,941,586	3,628,956	3,398,154	3,276,580
Bangladesh	881,617	987,853	1,345,546	1,422,805	1,500,921	2,115,408
Nepal	429,974	717,900	578,657	509,855	502,670	487,564
Afghanistan	57,686	75,917	102,246	489,749	133,612	144,098
Maldives	8,689	27,092	54,659	64,273	67,026	70,079
Bhutan	23,807	32,137	48,420	51,106	52,296	53,612
Sri Lanka	41,561	40,132	38,959	39,706	40,018	40,254

Source: UN, Department of Economic and Social Affairs, Population Division (2017). Trends in International Migrant Stock: The 2017 revision (United Nations database, POP/DB/MIG/Stock/Rev.2017) and Population Division (2020) International Migrant Stock 2020, (POP/DB/MIG/Stock/Rev.2020).

TABLE 7.2 Origin South Asia: Stocks of Migrants Worldwide, by South Asian Country of Origin: 1990–2020 (Mid-year Counts)

Number of emigrants from	*1990*	*2000*	*2010*	*2015*	*2017*	*2020*
South Asia	16,940,167	13,178,142	12,264,707	12,003,244	38,404,963	43,394,045
India	3,360,378	2,798,907	2,581,793	2,550,656	16,587,720	17,869,492
Bangladesh	4,377,309	3,885,119	3,318,585	3,209,010	7,499,919	7,401,763
Pakistan	1,942,747	1,390,626	1,226,379	1,485,399	5,978,635	6,328,400
Afghanistan	6,414,800	4,107,474	4,289,515	3,975,273	4,826,464	5,853,838
Nepal	528,220	677,773	597,478	583,065	1,738,442	2,599,701
Sri Lanka	286,991	198,247	168,556	162,624	1,726,900	1,960,025
Bhutan	27,895	119,383	80,721	35,619	43,970	51,998
Maldives	1,827	613	1,680	1,598	2,883	3,715

Source: See Table 7.1.

The emigrants comprise unskilled and/or semi-skilled labour to the high-income countries in West Asia (the Gulf Cooperation Countries of the Middle East), East Asia (Japan and South Korea), and Southeast Asia (Singapore and Malaysia). Whereas Bhutan sends very small numbers of semi-skilled and unskilled migrants to India and Nepal, and Maldives to India and Sri Lanka, India is known for sending large numbers of highly skilled professionals and tertiary level students to Western developed countries of Europe (the United Kingdom and Western Europe), North America (the United States and Canada), and Oceania (Australia and New Zealand).

Different sources of information and documents describe South Asian migration differently, in terms of focusing on one aspect or the other—low-skilled, irregular, high-skilled, and diasporic migration. The *World Migration Report 2018* of the International Organization for Migration (IOM, 2017), for example, highlighted the following features of migration in South Asia: First, intra-sub-regional migration, comprising movement of both regular and irregular migrant workers among countries. Major migration corridors in South Asia in 2019, as per *Statista 2020* data, were Bangladesh–India, Afghanistan–Pakistan, India–Pakistan, and Pakistan–India (Figure 7.1). Moreover, two corridors, viz., Bangladesh–India (Khadria, 2020) and Nepal–India (not among 11 leading intra-Asian corridors depicted in Figure 7.1) comprise millions of irregular labour migrants working in India, primarily in the informal sector as petty traders, rickshaw pullers, daily wagers, construction labourers, and domestic workers. While Nepali migrants do not need visas to come to India and hence cannot be called irregular, there are significant numbers of migrants from Sri Lanka too working in the informal labour markets in India. The Afghanistan–Pakistan corridor signifies the porous border between the two countries and their close ethnic, linguistic, religious, and economic ties. Pakistan has been the major host for Afghanis for decades, with most of its nearly

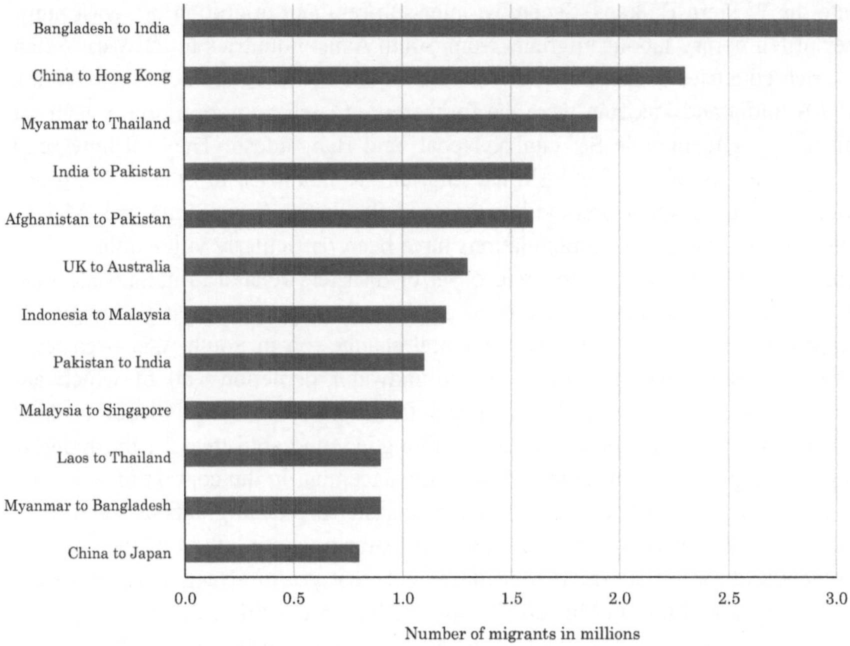

FIGURE 7.1 Eleven Leading Intra-Asian Corridors of Migration With Four Intra-South Asian, 2019

Note: These corridors represent an accumulation of migratory movements over time between two countries within the Global South. The United Kingdom to Australia corridor is for comparative reference to accumulated migration between two countries within the Global North.

Source: www.statista.com/statistics/1220365/apac-top-migration-corridors-by-number-of-migrants/

1.4 million refugees at the end of 2016 being exclusively Afghans. The year also saw a record 380,000 Afghan refugees returning from Pakistan, a 12-year high due to a number of drivers that include harassment and pressure by authorities, fears of arrest and deportation, economic hardship as the push, and perceptions of improvements in Afghanistan, return assistance packages, and a desire to reunite with family as the pull.

There have been many documented cases of migrants being exploited and abused by smugglers in South Asia, including rape and forced starvation, as was evident in the recent expulsion of the Rohingyas from Myanmar and their fleeing to refugee camps in Bangladesh and India. Other irregular migrants are smuggled through to Malaysia, Thailand, and Indonesia in Southeast Asia for work, or through these countries onwards to Australia. Australia and Europe both have been popular destinations for irregular migrants from South Asia, with the smuggling flow to Australia by the seas being stopped by the current Australian policies. For those heading to Europe, South Asian migrants are primarily smuggled through Central Asia and the Russian Federation, as well as through West Asia into the Western Balkans. Secondly, inter-sub-regional migration of a vast number of temporary labour migrants from South Asian countries to the West Asian oil-rich countries of the Gulf Cooperation Council (GCC) had built up since the 1970s. India and Pakistan were the forbearers of such migration origin, later on diversifying to include Sri Lanka, Nepal, and Bangladesh. They all now send a significant number of low-skilled migrants to countries in other sub-regions too, viz., East Asia (Korea and Japan) and Southeast Asia (Singapore, Malaysia). Thirdly, South Asian populations have been particularly vulnerable to slow onset of climate change and rapid onset of disasters related to natural hazards. Migration and mobility are said to be particularly important coping strategies in response to occurrences of environmental change too in South Asia—sea level rise, coastal erosion, flooding, and groundwater depletion—all of which are considerable in the region. Insufficient infrastructure, high dependency on land resources, and highly dense populations living in vulnerable areas are the underlying challenges that contribute to human displacement in the context of disasters. In 2016, there were about 3.6 million new disaster-driven migrants in South Asia, with India, Bangladesh, and Sri Lanka all featuring among the top 10 countries in the world for disaster-related displacements that year. In Bangladesh, disasters such as cyclone Mora in May 2017 displaced hundreds of thousands of people. In Nepal, disasters caused by the Gorkha and Udayapur earthquakes in 2015 led to immense displacement, while around half a million people were estimated to be displaced by severe flooding in Sri Lanka in May 2017.

Strikingly, none of these often talked-about features of South Asian migration has included the high-skill migration comprising professionals and tertiary-level students from the sub-region. In contrast, a few countries other than India in the region, viz., Pakistan, Bangladesh, and Sri Lanka too have been major origin countries of high- and medium-skilled labour, like IT professionals, teachers, doctors, and nurses to many developed countries of the world, many now generically categorised as the STEM professionals with expertise in the four generic fields of science, technology, engineering, and mathematics. These countries are in the same league as a few other Asian countries in other sub-regions, viz., China, the Philippines, South Korea, and Malaysia. These four South Asian countries have thus been predominantly known for large-scale emigration of their educated population to Western countries of the developed world, also called the Global North, viz., the United States, Canada, the United Kingdom, the EU countries of Western Europe, Australia, and New Zealand, leading to the so-called problem of 'brain drain' in the countries of origin. As an example, Figure 7.2 shows India-born migrants holding the top share of 21 % foreign-born (double of China's 10%), that is, one out of every five individuals (a total of over 1 million out of a total of 2 million Indian migrants), among the 5.1 million stock of college-educated foreign-born scientists and engineers employed in the United States as far back as in 2015 with their highest degree (bachelor's, master's, or doctorate) in S&E. Foreign-born individuals then accounted for 29% to 30% of all college-educated workers (foreign-born and native-born) employed in S&E occupations in the United States (NSF, 2018).

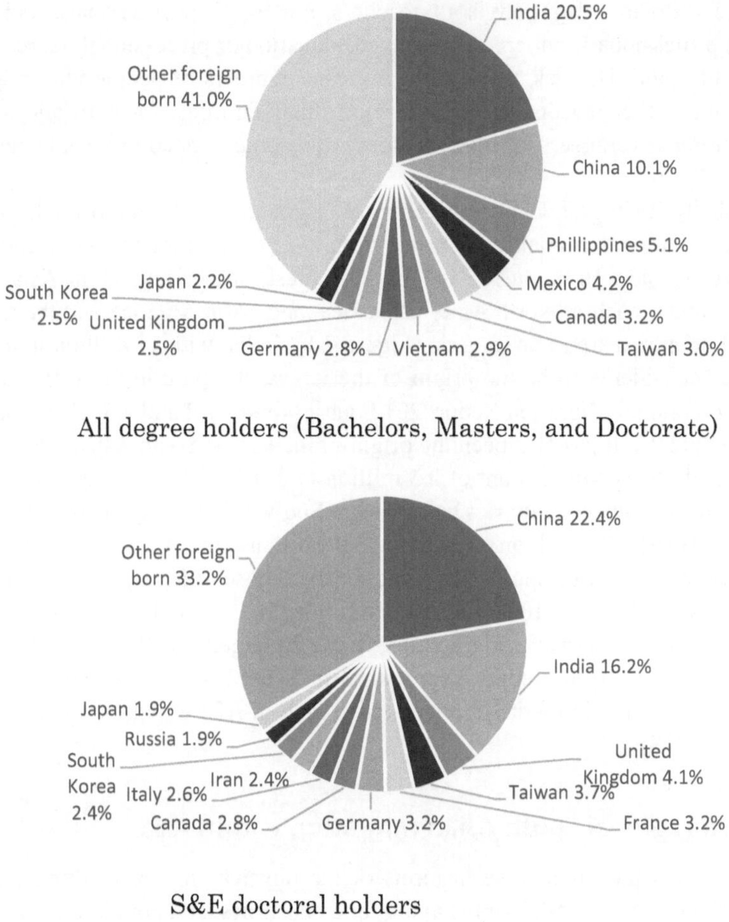

FIGURE 7.2 Foreign-Born Individuals With Highest Degree in S&E Living in the United States, by Place of Birth (2015)

Source: National Science Foundation, National Center for Science and Engineering Statistics, National Survey of College Graduates (2015), www.nsf.gov/statistics/srvygrads/.

Exclusively for doctorate degree holders in S&E field, Figure 7.2 shows them as having the second top share of 16 % (marginally below China's 22 %)—one out of every six among the 464,000 stock of foreign-born doctorates in S&E in the United States.

The South Asian region thus sends migrants belonging to all skill levels—ranging from unskilled and semi-skilled workers to medium- and highly skilled professionals and 'knowledge workers.' Migrants vary from those moving for economic reasons such as domestic workers, masons, construction workers, drivers, and caregivers who are considered to be in low-skilled occupations; to engineers, doctors, legal advisors, teachers, nurses, IT professionals, and now STEM professionals, who require college education or professional degrees and are highly paid. Besides, there are significant numbers of people who migrate for various other reasons such as to rejoin their families, for marriage, under persecution as refugees, for higher studies, and some trapped in illegal channels of trafficking.

Globally, 20 largest countries or areas of origin account for almost half (49 %) of all international migrants, while one-third (34 %) of all international migrants originate in only 10 countries. Of the 20 largest, comprising 11 in Asia, 6 in Europe, and 1 each in North America, Africa, and Latin America and the Caribbean, 4 countries are in South Asia (Figure 7.1). India, with 17 million individuals, was considered to be the origin of the largest diaspora in the world as the UN International Migration Report 2017 put it (Tables 7.2 and 7.3) (Khadria and Mishra, 2021b). It has also been the origin of the largest South Asian diaspora in the United States with a count of 2.3 million in 2017 (Table 7.3). In quantitative terms only, the other 3 countries belonging to South Asia among the top 20 origins are Bangladesh (7.5 million), Pakistan (6.0 million), and Afghanistan (4.8 million), although their diasporas were smaller than those of Mexico (13.0 million), the Russian Federation (10.6 million), and China (10.0 million). In the counterpart role of receiving international migrants, of the 20 largest countries of destination worldwide, 9 were located in Asia with 2 in South Asia (India and Pakistan), 7 in Europe, 2 in Northern America, and 1 each in Africa and Oceania (United Nations, 2018).

2 Intra-regional South Asian migration within Asia

South Asia, which is diverse in terms of the physical size of countries, some landlocked, some islands, some having long coastlines, and population size, history, societies, language, culture and political structures, have thus sent a higher number of migrants than it received in various skill categories. Still, South Asia was home to the second-largest number of migrant stocks after West Asia among the other Asian sub-regions (Table 7.1). However, cross-border or short-distance migration among the countries of South Asia has not been well-documented; rather it has been mired by contestable enumerations like the recent National Register of Citizens in India's northeast and Assam, and many a failed bilateral/multilateral negotiation by the SAARC member countries (Khadria and Kumar, 2015; Khadria, 2016b, 2016c). On the other hand, in the literature as well as public discourse, inter-regional migration across continents has overshadowed intra-regional migration within Asia. As a deviation from that, it is therefore a conscious effort to limit this chapter to the latter, that is, to address a regional migration system in and around South Asia, thereby leaving the former to the mass of existing literature on the so-called 'brain drain' to the Western developed countries and 'brawn drain' to the Middle East (Khadria, 1999; Lal et al., 2006; Potnuru and Khadria, 2018).

TABLE 7.3 Migration From South Asian Countries of Origin: 2017 (Mid-year) Stocks in Destination Countries

Migrant Origins *Migrant Destinations*	*India*	*Bangladesh*	*Pakistan*	*Afghanistan*	*Nepal*	*Sri Lanka*	*Bhutan*	*Maldives*
All countries of the world	16,587,720	7,499,919	5,978,635	4,826,464	1,738,442	1,726,900	43,970	2,883
More developed countries	4,723,840	708,357	1,459,298	497,551	244,515	752,426	8,804	1,106
Less developed countries	11,863,880	6,791,562	4,519,337	4,328,913	1,493,927	974,474	35,166	1,777
High-income countries	13,833,347	3,907,679	4,675,848	940,863	935,997	1,522,777	8,773	1,099
Middle-income countries	2,288,834	3,591,649	1,203,115	3,885,599	802,421	203,923	6,861	1,784
Low-income countries	465,329	591	99,672	2	24	200	28,336	-
United States of America	2,307,909	219,021	370,353	72,909	103,970	52,054	-	-
European countries	1,307,007	386,107	867,967	335,133	94,875	408,482	2,221	542
Countries in Oceania	482,282	42,211	50,961	41,904	36,093	127,988	4,014	564
African countries	103,992	14,521	24,213	721	409	5,962	2	157
Latin American & Caribbean countries	15,248	214	1,219	339	83	101	17	14
Other Asian countries	11,768,612	6,785,147	4,504,755	4,327,853	1,493,310	978,688	35,147	1,606
Other South Asian countries	2,419,636	3,178,887	1,220,723	3,848,759	578,582	161,324	35,147	1,606

Note: More Developed Regions comprise Europe, Northern America, Australia/New Zealand, and Japan; Less Developed Regions comprise Africa, Asia (except Japan), Latin America and the Caribbean plus Melanesia, Micronesia, and Polynesia. The classification as High/Medium/Low Income Level Countries is based on 2016 GNI per capita from the World Bank. See Source for details.

Source: See Table 7.1.

In 2019, just under 80% of the 14 million international migrants in South Asia originated from other countries in the sub-region (IOM, 2019: 77). The region has a long history of the intra-regional relationship of migration with other countries of Asia, but the patterns of its diversity and significance have not been analysed through any well-known definitive framework of analysis so far. Our thinking about intra-Asian high-skilled migration from/to South Asian countries is often characterised by stereotypical typologies based on criteria like developed versus developing countries of Asia (Japan, South Korea versus China, Malaysia), source versus destination countries (China, Philippines versus Singapore, Malaysia), adjacent versus long-distance destinations (Myanmar, Thailand versus Singapore, Brunei-Darussalam), and so on. The dimensions of these typologies are very specific and they tend to shed light on distinct aspects of migratory flows. However, since we do not have the required data sets to unpack all these dimensions, this paper uses what I have proposed as a generic model of 'hubs and hinterlands' of migration within Asia (Khadria, 2020), and thereby emphasises inclusion and exclusion through the simple distinction between immigration and emigration: Some countries in the region have emerged primarily as the destination hubs for inclusion of migrants from within the region while some others experience exclusion as hinterlands from where the migrants originate.

On the basis of this proposed hubs-hinterlands dichotomy, eight countries within the Asian region, top few with the highest stocks of immigrants in each sub-region, viz., Japan and South Korea in East Asia; Singapore, Malaysia, and Thailand in Southeast Asia; and China (Mainland), Hong Kong, and Taiwan in East Asia are identified to have emerged as the 'hubs' of inclusion through in-migration from some specific countries of South Asia that would define their respective 'hinterlands' of exclusion (Khadria, 2011b). Some of the hubs in South Asia themselves also belong to the hinterlands of some other hubs in Asia. For example, whereas India is an emerging destination, it is primarily a hinterland for the developed countries within Asia, like Singapore and fast-developing Malaysia because of its emergence as a country of origin for the migration of the so-called 'knowledge workers,' mainly IT professionals, teachers, health professionals including doctors and nurses, and a large number of STEM professionals and students in the twenty-first century.

3 Three divides of intra-regional migration in South Asia

Intra-regional migration to and from South Asia could be classified into different categories on various grounds. For example, international migration could be classified on the basis of (1) Motive (e.g., economic, family reunion, education, marriage), (2) Skill (e.g., high-skilled or low-skilled migration), (3) Distance (e.g., cross-border or overseas), (4) Legality (e.g., regular/authorised or irregular/unauthorised), (5) Trigger (e.g., induced by political instability, environmental disaster), etc. There are overlaps in these categories, which can be further enmeshed with the three 'Divides' of migration drivers:

The labour market divide

A significant amount of intra-regional migration involving South Asia occurs due to economic reasons arising from the labour market divides of supply of and demand for human capital. The demand for labour in the newly industrialised economies of East and Southeast Asian countries during the 1980s was responsible for attracting a growing volume of labour migration from the developing countries like Bangladesh, Sri Lanka, Nepal, and India. These migrants were mostly low-skilled and used to work in poorly paid jobs. Another group, which is much smaller in number but still significant, involves highly skilled professionals. These high-skilled migrants were attracted not only to fast-developing labour-short Newly Industrializing Countries (NICs) and near-NICs but also to labour surplus nations like Indonesia where a mismatch between the products of the education and training system and the skilled labour demands of a rapidly restructuring and growing economy was visible (Hugo, 2005; ESCAP, 2009). In 2006, about 90,000 high-skilled workers and professionals accounted for 13.4% of Singapore's total resident population of foreign origin. Apart from the Malaysians, the majority were from China and India. By 2012, their numbers rose to 240,000, accounting for 22.0% of Singapore's total foreign workforce (MPI, 2007, 2012). However, proximity to countries of origin with a large supply of labour, lax implementation of border control, and an active middleman system also results in large stocks of unauthorised intra-regional migrants in the region, but no data are available on them.

The education market divide

In the last four decades or so, transnational mobility for education has created a market for international education. South Asian countries, particularly those with colonial links, have become the major hinterland of the developed countries for the so-called 'recruitment' (implying enrolment!) of overseas students. There are 'education fairs' held in countries of South Asia, four times or more in a year in the metropolises, cities, and large towns to attract the students and their parents with limited number of scholarships, spot enrolment, and many other offers and awareness campaigns. The global stock of overseas students pursuing tertiary education outside their country of origin grew fourfold from 1.1 million in 1995 to 4.1 million in 2013 and further to 4.6 million in 2017 (UNESCO, 2017; IIE, 2017). By 2015, out of the total foreign or international students enrolled in tertiary institutions worldwide, more than 2 million students comprising 52.4 % were from Asian countries. In 2017, of the 4.6 million overseas students worldwide, 488.7 thousand or 10.6 % were South Asian students, their country-wise distribution being 278.4 thousand Indian, 60.4 thousand Bangladeshi, 51.9 thousand Pakistani, 44.3 thousand Nepali, 27.9 thousand Afghan, 18.5 thousand Sri Lankan, 4.4 thousand Bhutanese, and 2.9 thousand Maldivian. Of course, China alone had 847.3 thousand or 18.4 % of global students studying abroad (compiled from UNESCO, 2017).

Destination-wise, the South Asian students were present in the top six host countries of international students. As of 2016–2017, these were the United States (1.21 million); the United Kingdom (451 thousand); Australia (336 thousand); Germany (359 thousand); France (325 thousand); Russian Federation (244 thousand); Canada (190 thousand); China (138 thousand); and the Netherlands (112 thousand) (UNESCO, 2017). Of the South Asian countries as a destination for overseas students, India hosted 44.8 thousand international students in 2016 and Sri Lanka 1.3 thousand (there are no data for other countries). India, along with China, the two most populous countries of the world, have sent about one-fifth of all international students. However, both the origins and destinations of international students have become increasingly diverse in the last decade. Within Asia, China, Japan, Malaysia, and Singapore too have emerged as major destination hubs of foreign students from South Asia in the last decade.

The gendered divide

Gender-based segmentation of the global labour market has become distinctly visible through the migration of women. Women have constituted almost half of all the immigrants in Asia for long (IOM, 2005), and a substantial proportion of them are from South Asian countries. Other than trafficking (for prostitution and flesh trade), there are two main routes of female migration—women migrate as independent individuals to participate in the economic activities (nurses, housemaids, entertainers, caregivers); and by marrying a person in the destination country which allows spouses to live together. Intra-regional migration from and to South Asia for family reunification or marriage is a relatively new phenomenon, as compared to the East and Southeast Asian women. Sri Lanka figures among the world's top three suppliers of female domestic workers, with Indonesia and the Philippines being the other two largest hinterlands for the two hubs of domestic workers in Asia, that is, Singapore and Hong Kong. The large majority of women in the Asian region thus work in the domestic housemaid services or entertainment, and even in the flesh trade. Whereas all these areas of female migration are drawing increasing attention in South Asia, there is a gendered divide evident in the fact that there is very little research on high-skilled female migration worldwide, not to speak about intra-Asian (Thakur and Khadria, 2018).

4 Unwarranted dichotomies between high- and low-skilled migrants

Given the aforementioned dimensions of intra-regional migration in Asia, how does one assess whether high-skilled migration has changed societies in the hinterland countries in South Asia and whether it has adequately contributed to their social and economic development? In other words, what have been the socio-economic gains and losses to South Asian countries arising from high-skill migration within Asia (and elsewhere)? These questions have traditionally been raised in suggesting cost–benefit analysis at the micro-level for the individual migrant and the household, and at the macro-level for society and the economy as a whole (Khadria, 2009b, 2012b). But to what extent have those studies been undertaken, or have the data been generated and made available for pursuing are questions that have remained unaddressed.

Even if it is assumed that the psychic losses that separation of a family member entails for the household left behind in the hinterland countries would be intrinsic in the exclusion from the home country that takes place through emigration, there has not been many satisfactory surveys to document the evidence of this. Increase in temporary migration over permanent migration of even the high-skilled migrants has led to the creation of what I have elsewhere called 'nomadic families' on the one hand and a new kind of 'forced return,' on the other, of the high-skilled migrants, but these have not been assessed or analysed (Khadria, 2009a). Another related but unattended facet of high-skilled migration has been the gender issue (Thakur and Khadria, 2018). No comprehensive data are available on high-skilled women migrants as dependents or workers, not to consider in-depth analyses of the trend and impacts. Some receiving-country data are available, indicating the proportion of women among particular professional groups like the Indian nurses. Beyond this, analyses of the gender dimension of all Asian including South Asian migration have remained, by and large, either stereotypical or as case studies in most countries of the Global North, that is, outside the region. For example, one such neglected gender divide in high-skill emigration had been the proposal for denial of the right to work (i.e., work authorisation) of the dependent spouses accompanying the celebrated H-1B Visa holding highly qualified and skilled Indian male migrants in the United States. These spouses, residing in the United States under the H-4 Visa category, had no option but to lead a compulsory idle life outside the labour market despite being highly qualified and skilled themselves, leading to their being financially dependent on their husbands. Often, such measures lead to a 'semi-exclusion' through discrimination, exploitation, and sometimes mistreatment of the spouses, mostly women (Khadria, 2016a). When this proposal was withdrawn in 2015, inclusion and labour market participation of South Asian women in the US labour market had jumped, but the restriction was again proposed for being reintroduced in 2018 under the Trump regime, leading to a return of the exclusion psychosis among many high-skilled spouses in the American labour market. The talk itself of reintroducing the restriction thus has multiplier effects on people's expectations—leading to uncertainty and depression among not only the working skilled women but their families and children as well even if it was done away with in 2021 when the Biden regime took over. This kind of instability results in lower labour productivity through what is called the 'brain waste' among an important segment of the workforce and thereby lowering the overall feel-good factor all around—adversely affecting both 'human capital' and 'social capital' of the immigrants. There are other similar practices of semi-exclusion of migrant women in many other developed destination countries where qualified women are not given their due on one pretext of policy or the other.

In terms of the impact on migrant workers themselves in the hubs (and therefore on their families back in the hinterlands), there are commonalities and similarities of exclusion and semi-exclusion which had emerged among the unskilled and high-skilled migrants, respectively, to the Gulf and Southeast Asian countries (Khadria, 2016d; Khadria and Leclerc, 2006). Of course, there has been concern followed by diplomatic action at the plight of such migrant workers whenever a crisis has erupted, for example, the sudden arrests of Indian IT professionals in Malaysia over a decade ago, the incident being widely reported in the print media (*Hindustan Times*, *Times of India*, *Straight Times*, April–May 2006). However, hinterland countries in South Asia (or any other regions of the world) exert virtually no control over the inclusion of voluntary migration of the highly skilled categories. As a result, what has not been looked into is how the possibility of migration itself has created a sense of exclusion among the intra-Asian migrants, both high-skilled and low-skilled (Khadria, 2008). Similarly, there have been no studies of the impact of high-skilled migration on career choices and educational preferences in the hinterlands as well as the hubs, where there have been a lot of choice distortion and inter-generational conflict over educational choices (Khadria, 1989) due to inclusion and exclusion in migration that have taken place but remained unanalysed if not unnoticed.

At the macro level, the attempts have not progressed beyond the identification of three stereotypical indicators, viz., remittances, transfer of technology, and human capital embodied in returning migrants—what I have elsewhere termed as the three 'M's, respectively, for 'Money, Machines, and Man-hours' flowing back to the origin countries of the hinterland in South Asia (Khadria, 1999). Even in the case of macro-economic assessment of the much-talked-about remittances, there has been a 'silent backwash flow' that had begun from the hinterland countries of origin to destination hubs like Singapore, Japan, Malaysia, and so on in the form of 'overseas student' fees that the students and their parents in the former pay in the latter (Khadria, 2006b). In fact, this follows the pattern of international education boosting the profit-making investment for the private sector and marginalising the public sector in not only the destination hubs but also the hinterland countries in South Asia, viz., India, Bangladesh, Sri Lanka, and so on. The exclusion and inclusion created by this trend have remained unestimated and unanalysed so far, although a number of studies bear testimony to the following corroborating evidence (Zachariah et al., 2001; Rajan et al., 2018): The secular rise in disposable incomes of the households in the hinterland regions arising from remittances, for example, from the low-skilled emigrants in the state of Kerala in India, has had its effect on boosting conspicuous consumption but little on higher education for skill formation through investment in education. At the same time, remittances have led to the opening up of a large number of new schools and colleges on the one hand, and to enabling the youth to buy a costly private education on the other hand—both contributing to exclusion through unemployment amongst the current generations of Kerala youth who no longer want to work in traditional lines of occupations. Secondly, an equally important 'adverse' effect has been the emergence of internal 'replacement migration' of labour into Kerala from the other Indian states. Apart from the fact that wages have gone up to be the highest in India for local labour in Kerala due to shortage of unskilled and semi-skilled workers, labourers from other states now accept low wages and poor living conditions to work in Kerala, adding to the unemployment of the local generations of youth. Consumerism and house-building activities have drained the state of the development potential of its remittance receipts. It has resulted in exclusion through financial bankruptcy of many families leading to extreme effects like mental depression and suicide.

Notwithstanding this, whereas the volumes of remittances from low-skilled migrants have drawn much attention, say, in Bangladesh, the other two areas, viz., transfer of technology and return migration, have been thought of as the inclusive outcomes of high-skilled migration, even quantitative assessment have not been attempted. Most studies have not gone beyond talking about the need to assess the quantitative outcomes in terms of volumes of flows of technology collaborations and the numbers of returnees, and that too between the individual South Asian countries and the West. Collection and availability of data have been the main constraints of researchers in going beyond this in these two areas. In the case of transfer of technology, the 'reverse transfer of technology' (a term used by a number of UNCTAD studies in the 1970s) still seems to be continuing in the form of 'brain drain' of IT professionals and so on, leading to exclusion from sustainable global development (Khadria, 1989, 1990). Return migration has become topical, ironically as 'brain gain' in the context of 'outsourcing' of business processes to India picking up after the IT bubble burst in the United States, but here too there has been no systematic assessment in terms of the numbers and quality of the returnees arriving due to exclusion from the United States or Europe, not to speak of intra-Asian highly skilled returnees (Tejada et al., 2014). Some inclusive involvement of the circulating returnees has of course been noted in NGO activities for socio-economic development at the grassroots level, say in India, but that too from the Global North countries outside Asia (Khadria, 2002).

What possibly would be a useful policy tool, as I have often argued, is an 'adversary analysis' whereby the inclusion in social and economic development in the hinterland countries of South Asia would be assessed from the point of view of the stakeholders in the hubs in the Asia region and vice versa (Khadria, 2009a). To do this in a sub-regional Asian multilateral forum like the ASEAN or SAARC until there is a pan-Asian forum, the benefits of three 'M's (Money, Machines, and Man-hours) to hinterland countries of origin can be weighed and even pitted against the advantages of the three 'A's (embedded in 'Age, Wage, and Vintage') arising to the high-income hubs in Asia. The three 'A's are the advantages derived primarily through higher migrant turnover in-built in temporary and circulatory immigration, and operationalised by (a) bringing in younger migrants to correct the age-composition bias in their ageing population, for example, proactively in Singapore, (b) keeping the wage and pension commitments low by excluding older and long-term migrants and including younger and short-term migrants, for example, in Japan and South Korea, and (c) stockpiling latest vintage of knowledge embodied in younger cohorts of skilled workers, particularly higher-education students, for example, in Japan, South Korea, Malaysia, and lately increasingly in China (Khadria, 2006a, 2009a, 2009b). It remains to be judged and explored what are the inclusive and exclusive implications of these in the South Asian hinterland countries of origin like India, Pakistan, Bangladesh, Nepal, or Sri Lanka vis-à-vis those in the destination hubs like South Korea (Lee, 2003; Kong et al., 2010), Taiwan, Singapore, and so on within the region. Table 7.3 provides a global picture of the 2017 distribution of migrants originating from individual South Asian hinterland countries and hosted in destinations hubs worldwide by hubs in regions/countries belonging to different levels of development (more developed and less developed), income (high-, medium-, and low-income), and geographical entities of Europe, Americas, Oceania, Africa, Asia, and separately the United States, and other South Asian countries too.

The changed perceptions of the hubs, the countries in which the high-skilled migrants have settled to form a diaspora, might play a catalyst's role in this exercise. The changed values are now attributed to the South Asian diaspora itself that has defied the anticipated doom by rising to unforeseeable economic success in the destination countries of the Global North, leading to a paradigm shift in the societies and regions where they have settled. The reason lies also in the realisation of the host countries in the hubs of migration worldwide that, given the appropriate inclusion by providing resources and local support, one type of migrants—the suspected 'social parasite,' driving the so-called integration policies—can become the other, the social boon, generating inclusive employment, income, and stability for the local economy and society in turn (Khadria, 2007; ACOLA, 2015). This can equally apply to south–south cooperation between the hubs in the larger Asian region and the hinterlands of migration in South Asia, not only for the stereotypical 'homeland development' but also beyond for what I have called TCD—third-country-development through 'inter-diaspora cooperation' (Khadria, 2012a).

Presently, India has emerged as the most sought-after hinterland country of origin in South Asia for the supply of high-skilled knowledge workers in the developed countries of the Global North; and India, Bangladesh, Nepal, and even Sri Lanka for the low-skilled service workers in the Gulf countries of West Asia in the Global South. Other countries like Singapore and Malaysia in Southeast Asia have also emerged as recipients for an increasing number of these skilled and unskilled migrants from South Asia (Khadria and Leclerc, 2006). This has led to a significant paradigm shift in the first three South Asian origin countries and a gradual shift in Sri Lanka—to look at migration as a process leading to the formation of the 'Diaspora,' an option for turning the challenge of migration into an opportunity, and therefore *gainful* (Barré et al., 2003; Meyer ed., 2015). What remains for the origin and destination countries of migration in the emerging international relations paradigm is to judge where the loyalty of their respective diaspora would lie—with the country, with South Asia, with the Asian region, or somewhere else in the transnational global space. Whether migrants would no longer be excluded as the 'deserters of the motherland' by the origin country and as 'social parasites' by the destination countries? In other words, whether the diaspora would be really considered a great boon not only for the developed countries of the north but for South Asia too from within? For example, as a hinterland, India has gone through a paradigm shift in its stance towards its own diaspora, now the largest in the world, and come up with a number of diaspora-friendly policies since the turn of the century. However, it has a long way to go before ushering in a similar shift of stance as a hub towards the largest bilateral diaspora, that of Bangladesh, on its own soil.

The diaspora option, because it is holistic in identity, would also foster the emphasis that the Global Commission on International Migration (GCIM) report of 2005 had made in stating, 'the traditional distinction between skilled and unskilled workers is in certain respects an unhelpful one, as it fails to do justice to the complexity of international migration. . . . While they may have different levels of educational achievement, all of them could be legitimately described as *essential workers* (emphasis added).' (GCIM, 2005: 7). While India has drawn disproportionately high attention worldwide to the success stories of its highly skilled human resources doing remarkably well in the world labour markets abroad—the IT professionals, the biotechnologists, the financial managers, the scientists, the architects, the lawyers, the teachers, the nurses, and above all the STEM professionals—leading to an upsurge of demand to acquire the Indian talent potentially embodied in students as the future workers—the dichotomy between skilled and unskilled migrant workers is unwarranted.

5 Can there be a trans-South Asian diaspora policy of inclusive migration under the GCM?

What is required, however, is a long-term policy that is aimed at establishing the South Asian hinterland countries' links with their respective diasporas in the countries of migration hubs, whether within the Asian region or outside in the rest of the world. This would help attain Objective 19 of the Global Compact for Migration (GCM) towards sustainable socio-economic development in the forthcoming period of the United Nations' 2030-Sustainable Development Goals (SDGs). The 'GCM for making migration Safe, Orderly and Regular' was ratified by the UN member states at Marrakesh in Morocco on 18 December 2018 after multilateral negotiations over a period of three years since the launch of the SDGs in 2015. For the first time ever, GCM brought the 193 Member States together at the table to debate, agree, and even disagree (a few leading to withdrawal) on international migration, a subject so far kept cocooned on the pretext of the so-called individual sovereignty of nations. The GCM has 23 objectives, emanating from the Sustainable Development Goal no. 10 'to reduce inequalities within and between countries' and its Target no. 10.7 to facilitate orderly, safe, regular, and responsible migration and mobility of people, and 'leaving no one behind,' or in other words, to become inclusive globally. These objectives have been analysed for South Asia by Khadria et al. (2019). They conclude that not all 23 objectives are equally relevant to all South Asian countries. Objectives 3–14 are primarily meant to ensure the safety of migrants in the destination hubs. These measures are most relevant to low-skilled and unskilled migrant workers such as domestic workers, nurses, construction workers, taxi drivers, electricians, plumbers, and carpenters. Low-skilled and unskilled South Asian workers in the Middle East are more vulnerable to discrimination than highly skilled South Asian workers in North America or Europe or Australia–New Zealand. Objectives relating to labour migration and remittances are particularly relevant to South Asian countries, along with objectives that seek to ameliorate unemployment and poverty in the countries of origin. The following objectives are most relevant to South Asian countries: 2, 5, 6, 9, 10, 12, 13, 15, 18, 19, 20, and 22.

Objective 2 seeks to 'minimise the adverse drivers and structural factors that compel people to leave their country of origin.' Although all eight South Asian countries have developing economies, the countries vary in their levels of economic growth and development. These varying economic conditions determine the nature of migration flows in conjunction with social, political, and environmental factors such as caste, gender, and religion-based discrimination in India and other neighbouring countries.

Objective 6 stresses fair and ethical recruitment from countries of origin. This is relevant to South Asian countries that are sources of labour migration. Objectives 9 and 10 focus on smuggling and trafficking, particularly of women and children. This is relevant in South Asia, including the prevalence of fraudulent marriages in India.

Objectives 5 and 12 emphasise pathways for regular migration and stronger certainty and predictability in migration decision-making.

Objective 13 states that immigration detention should be a last resort. This provides migrants in India with a ray of hope for safety and security. Detention centres in India for irregular migrants are currently in the news, due to the dictates of the Supreme Court not to release the migrants. This follows the government of India's stated position on irregular immigration of Bangladeshis and Myanmar Rohingyas. In the last few years, these policies have created fears of detention and deportation among migrants.

Objective 15 states that destination countries should provide basic services to migrants in areas such as health, education, and sanitation.

Objective 18 emphasises skills development and mutual recognition, including learning-by-doing and on-the-job training, which are often without certification.

Objective 19 is to optimize the contribution of the migrants and diasporas in a sustained way for the development of both homelands and hostlands. Khadria (2021) has particularly addressed the relevance of this objective in the context of the pandemic Covid-19 and the challenge before the South Asian diasporas.

Objective 20 focuses on faster, cheaper and safer remittances. This is relevant to South Asia because India receives the highest volume of remittances at over

USD 80 billion per year. Bangladesh receives the highest proportion of remittances to gross-domestic-product.

Objective 22 seeks to establish the portability of social security contributions and earned benefits back to countries of origin.

To achieve these objectives in an optimal way by all the three stakeholders in migration—the hinterland country of origin, the migrants as part of its diaspora, and the destination hubs within the region—two specific conditions must be met: A 'necessary condition' of dominant or significant geo-economic presence of the South Asian migrants; and a 'sufficient condition' of the hinterland country of origin deriving *sustainable* benefits of inclusion from that presence. In terms of the large South Asian population in other parts of the world today, the first condition is more or less fulfilled (PEW Research Center, 2017). To satisfy the sufficient condition of the hinterland deriving significant gains of inclusion from the global presence of their migrants, the flows of remittances, transfer of technology, and return migration must all be directed not towards trade and business but towards the removal of two kinds of poverty which is rampant in South Asia. These are the 'poverty of education' and the 'poverty of health'—areas where migration has so far failed to change society in the hinterland countries of South Asia by contributing to their economic and social development. Large masses of the illiterate and uneducated population, excluded further by their poor health status, are the root causes of South Asian countries having the lowest levels of average productivity of labour, even lower than some African countries, and therefore lowest average wages in the world—a paradox when South Asian diaspora members, on the average, make up amongst the largest contributing ethnic communities in the Western global hubs of destination countries, even as per the latest 2017 estimates of the UN (United Nations, 2018; Khadria, 2022; Khadria et al., 2022). For example, it is indeed paradoxical that the average per-hour contribution of each employed worker within India to the production of India's gross domestic product (GDP) has been amongst the lowest in the world—a mere 2.2 purchasing power parity dollars (PPP$) as compared to the United States' 32.6 PPP$, that is, one-fifteenth of the latter in 1999 (Khadria, 2001, 2011a), and increasing insignificantly to 3.3 PPP$ as against the United States' 47.8 PPP$ in 2003, and further to a mere 4.8 PPP$ against the United States' 50.9 PPP$ in 2010 and then to 9 PPP$ against the US' 75 PPP$ in 2019 (Khadria, 2009b, 2012b, 2022). This is naturally ironical because the same average Indian employed worker abroad contributes a very high average share of the GDP of the country where he/she settles and works, as, for example, reflected in the US Community Survey data on average annual income of the population by their racial origin. The Trans-South Asian diaspora networks and associations could, therefore, play the catalyst's role—be it through economic, political or cultural inclusion—in raising the average productivity of their masses of workers at home by thinking health and education as areas of diaspora engagement, rather than focusing on immediate and short-term 'profit-making' ventures in industry and business.

6 Concluding remarks

There is a 'double challenge' of inclusive diaspora policy faced by a hinterland country in South Asia like India, Pakistan, Bangladesh, Nepal, Sri Lanka, Afghanistan, and so on: First, to convince one's own diaspora community to rethink the development process as a 'bottom-up' enhancement of sustainable productivities of labour through development of education and health rather than a 'top-down' engagement of business and industry—one comprehensive and inclusive, the other dispersed and exclusionary; one long-term, the other immediate. It is not just a matter of willingness; in many instances, it would entail long periods of struggle in patiently creating those decision-making and priority-setting discerning capabilities among the leaders of the migrant community in South Asia. Secondly, one must be able to convince the hub countries of destination (and the other hinterland countries of origin in the Asian region) as to where lies the distinction between most 'painfully exclusive' and most 'gainfully inclusive' impacts of migration on the socio-economics of its workers—both skilled and unskilled. The 'adversary analysis' through the proposed 'mini-multilateralism,' if made equitable, would help a South Asian superpower in the making, like India, to take leadership in pressing for a Trans-South Asian Diaspora so as to optimise the goals of the New York Declaration in the Global Compact for Migration (GCM) signed in Marrakesh, Morocco on 18 December 2018 to minimise the element of exclusion and maximise inclusion in South Asian migration. The vulnerability of the migrants and the instability of trends underlying the 'open-and-shut policy' of the destination hub countries, whether in the Global North or the Global South could be the two key aspects that the hinterland countries in South Asia must strive to negotiate out of international migration if their role of 'leaving no one behind' in the global agenda of inclusion set out in goal no. 10 of the Sustainable Development Goals (SDGs) is to be approached within a reasonable time horizon.

References

ACOLA (2015). *Smart Engagement with Asia: Leveraging Language, Research and Culture*, Final Report Vol. 3, Melbourne: Australian Council of Learned Academies.

Barré, R., V. Hernández, and J.-B. Meyer eds. (2003). *Diasporas Scientifiques*, France: IRD Editions.

ESCAP (2009). *Statistical Yearbook for Asia and the Pacific 2009*, Thailand: ESCAP, United Nations.

GCIM (2005). *Migration in an Interconnected World: New Directions for Action*, Geneva: Report of the Global Commission on International Migration.

Hugo, G. (2005). "Migration in the Asia-Pacific Region," Chapter prepared for the Policy Analysis and Research Programme of the Global Commission on International Migration, September.

IIE (2017). *Project Atlas Infographics*, Washington, DC: Institute of International Education. https://www.iie.org/en/Research-and-Insights/Project-Atlas/Explore-Data/Infographics/2017-Project-Atlas-Infographics

IOM (2005). *World Migration Report 2005*, Geneva: International Organisation for Migration.

IOM (2017). *World Migration Report 2018*, Geneva: International Organisation for Migration.

IOM (2019). *World Migration Report 2020*, Geneva: International Organisation for Migration.

Khadria, B. (1989). "Subsidies Question in Higher Education – Tight-Rope Walking for Public Policy Makers in Developing Countries," *Journal of Educational Planning & Administration*, vol. 3, 43–59.

Khadria, B. (1990). "Patents, Brain Drain and Higher Education: International Barriers to the Diffusion of Knowledge, Information and Technology," *Social Scientist*, vol. 18(5), 3–18.

Khadria, B. (1999). *The Migration of Knowledge Workers: Second-Generation Effects of India's Brain Drain*, New Delhi: Sage Publications.

Khadria, B. (2001). "Shifting Paradigms of Globalization: The Twenty-first Century Transition towards Generics in Skilled Migration from India," *International Migration*, vol. 39(5), 45–72.

Khadria, B. (2002). *Skilled Labour Migration from Developing Countries: Study on India*, International Migration Papers 49, Geneva: International Labour Office.

Khadria, B. (2006a). "Uncharted Contours of a Changing Paradigm: Skilled Migration and Brain Drain in India," *Harvard International Review*, vol. 28(1), Web-exclusive Symposium on featured topic: Immigration, www.hir.harvard.edu.

Khadria, B. (2006b). "Embodied and Disembodied Transfers of Knowledge: Geo-politics of Economic Development," in Carton, M. and J.-B. Meyer eds., *The Knowledge Society: Trompe-l'oel or Accurate Perspective?* Paris: l'Harmattan: 191–203.

Khadria, B. (2007). "Diasporas in Development: From 'Social Parasites' to 'Economic Boon'?" *Asian Population Studies*, vol. 3(2), 103–114.

Khadria, B. (2008). "India: Skilled Migration to the Developed Countries, Labour Migration to the Gulf," in Castles, S. and R. D. Wise eds., *Migration and Development: Perspectives from the South*, Geneva: International Organisation for Migration: 79–112.

Khadria, B. (2009a). "Adversary Analysis and the Quest for Global Development: Optimizing the Dynamic Conflict of Interest in Transnational Migration," *Social Analysis*, vol. 53(3), 106–122.

Khadria, B. ed. (2009b). *India Migration Report 2009: Past, Present and the Future Outlook*, New Delhi: International Migration and Diaspora Studies Project, Zakir Hussain Centre for Educational Studies, Jawaharlal Nehru University.

Khadria, B. (2011a). "Shifting Paradigms of Globalization: The Twenty-first Century Transition towards Generics in Skilled Migration from India," in Geddes, A. ed., *International Migration, Volume 2*, London: Sage: 1–24.

Khadria, B. (2011b). "Migration in Asia-Pacific through Hubs and Hinterland," *IMDS Working Paper Series* (International Migration and Diaspora Studies (IMDS) Project, Jawaharlal Nehru University), nos. 37/38/39, 1–17.

Khadria, B. (2012a). "Migration of Health Workers and Health of International Migrants: Framework for Bridging Some Knowledge Disjoints between Brain Drain and Brawn Drain," *International Journal of Public Policy*, vol. 8(4/5/6), 266–280.

Khadria, B. ed. (2012b). *India Migration Report 2010–11: The Americas*, Cambridge: Cambridge University Press.

Khadria, B. (2016a). "Gender-based Immigration Visa? On Rationality of a Legislative Innovation," in Rajan, I. ed., *India Migration Report 2015: Gender and Migration*, London: Routledge: 1–8.

Khadria, B. (2016b). "What after NRC Stocktaking? Fresh Thinking for India's Immigration Policy Innovation," *Research Journal of Contemporary Concerns*, Guwahati: Cotton College.

Khadria, B. (2016c). "Involuntary and Illegal Migration to India: The Case of Bangladesh," *Refugees, Displaced Persons and Education: New Challenges for Development and Policy, NORRAG News*, vol. 53, 118–119.

Khadria, B. (2016d). "Middle-east Country Policies," in Besharov, B. J. and M. H. Lopez eds., *Adjusting to a World in Motion: Trends in Global Migration and Migration Policy*, International Policy Exchange Series, Oxford: Oxford University Press: 291–307.

Khadria, B. (2020). "Between the 'Hubs' and 'Hinterlands' of Migration in South Asia: The Bangladesh-India Corridor," *Lead Article in International Journal of South Asian Studies, Japan*, vol. 10, 1–10. https://jasas.info/wp-content/uploads/2020/08/Article-1_Binod_vol-10_2020.pdf

Khadria, B. (2021). "COVID-19 and the GCM Objective-19: Trans-South Asian Diaspora Philanthropy for Internal and International Migrants in a Crisis," *Labour & Development*, vol. 28(2), December, 25–41.

Khadria, B. (2022). "Did catchy slogans and future commitments in the IMRF reflect poor implementation of the GCM?" International Workshop on *The Present and Future of the Global Compacts*, organized by Canada Excellence Research Centre (CERC), Toronto Metropolitan University, June 7, 2022.

Khadria, B. and P. Kumar (2015). "Immigrants and Immigration in India: A Fresh Approach," *Economic and Political Weekly*, vol. 50(8), 65–71.

Khadria, B. and E. Leclerc (2006). "Exode des emplois contre exode des cerveaux, les dau faces d'une meme piece?" Autrepart: Revue des sciences sociales au sud, No. 37, Special issue on La Migration des Emplois Vers le Sud, IRD Editions, France.

Khadria, B. and R. Mishra (2021a). "Migration in Asia and its subregions: Data challenges and coping strategies for 2021," *Migration Policy Practice*, vol. 11(1), 14–20, January–February, IOM-UN Migration & EurAsylum, Geneva. https://publications.iom.int/books/migration-policy-practice-vol-xi-number-1-january-february-2021

Khadria, B. and R. Mishra (2021b). "Mobility of tech professionals in the world economy: the case of Indian entrepreneurialism in the United States," Chapter 20, in McAuliffe, M., ed., *Research Handbook on International Migration and Digital Technology*, Edgar Handbooks in Migration Series, Edward Elgar, Cheltenham, UK.

Khadria, B., N. Thakur, and R. Mishra (2022). "Migration, Health and Development in India, South Asia and China: Perspectives in the COVID-19 Era," in D. E. Degila and V. M. Valle, eds. (2022). *Governing Migration for Development from the Global Souths*, International Development Policy|Revue internationale de politique de développement, 14, Graduate Institute, Geneva.

Khadria, B., N. Thakur, I. Nicolas, T. Lee, J. Yang, and Y. Jang (2019). "The UN Global Compact for Safe, Orderly and Regular Migration: Its Impact on Asia," *International Migration*, vol. 57(6), 286–302.

Kong, D., K. Yoon, and S. Yu (2010). "The Social Dimensions of Immigration in Korea," *Journal of Contemporary Asia*, vol. 40(2), 252–274.

Lal, B., P. Reeves, and R. Rai eds. (2006). *The Encyclopedia of the Indian Diaspora*, Singapore: Editions Didier Millet: 66–75, 80–81.

Lee, H. K. (2003). "Gender, Migration and Civil Activism in South Korea," *Asian and Pacific Migration Journal*, vol. 12(1–2), 127–153.

Meyer, J.-B. ed. (2015). *Diaspora: Towards the New Frontier*, France: Horizon/Pleins textes – IRD.

MPI (2007). "Singapore: Hungry for Foreign Workers at All Skill Levels," *Newsletter*, January 1, Migration Policy Institute, Washington, DC.

MPI (2012). "Rapid Growth in Singapore's Immigrant Population Brings Policy Challenges," *Newsletter*, April 3, Migration Policy Institute, Washington, DC.

NSF (2018). "Science and Engineering Indicators 2018," National Science Foundation, National Center for Science and Engineering Statistics, National Survey of College Graduates (NSCG) (2015), Table 3–25. www.nsf.gov/statistics/srvygrads/. www.nsf.gov/statistics/2018/nsb20181/report/sections/science-and-engineering-labor-force/immigration-and-the-s-e-workforce

PEW Research Center (2017). *FactTank: News in the Numbers*, Washington, DC, September 8. www.pewresearch.org/fact-tank/2017/09/08/key-facts-about-asian-americans/ (accessed August 30, 2018).

Potnuru, B. and B. Khadria (2018). "Have the 'London Dreams' of Indian Doctors Come to an End," in Rajan, I. S. ed., *India Migration Report 2018*, London: Routledge.

Rajan, I. S., P. Benoy, U. S. Mishra, and V. Narendran (2018). "Impact of Mortality and Fertility Transition on Migration and Its Implications for the State's Economy," Centre for Migration and Inclusive Development (CMID), and Centre for Development Studies (CDS), Kerala.

Tejada, G., U. Bhattacharya, B. Khadria, and C. Kuptch eds. (2014). *Indian Skilled Migration and Development: To Europe and Back*, New Delhi: Springer.

Thakur, N. and B. Khadria (2018). "Gender Differentials of Indian Knowledge and Service Workers in the US Labour Market: A Comparative Analysis in the Context of 'Age, Wage, and Vintage' Premia," in Pande, A. ed., *Women in the Indian Diaspora: Historical Narratives and Contemporary Challenges*, Singapore: Springer: 119–132.

UNESCO (2017). *Global Education Digest: Comparing Education Statistics Across the World*, Paris: UNESCO Institute for Statistics (UIS).

United Nations (2018). *International Migration Report 2017: Highlights*, New York: United Nations.

Zachariah, K. C., E. T. Mathew, and I. S. Rajan (2001). "Impact of Migration on Kerala's Economy and Society," *International Migration*, vol. 39(1), 63–87.

PART 2
Social Dimensions and Beyond Inclusion

8

HIGHER EDUCATION AND THE FUTURE OF SOCIAL INEQUALITY IN INDIA

Satish Deshpande

1 Introduction

Let me begin by acknowledging the obvious. First, the future of social inequality anywhere cannot depend on higher education alone, especially if we include all the various dimensions (economic, social, political) and sites (gender, caste, class, and community) that 'social inequality' usually invokes. Second, higher education, which is cast in the role of the independent variable here, is itself in flux globally, and both the historical and the contemporary claims about its social uses are undergoing fundamental revisions. Third, there are some specifically Indian uncertainties which ensure that the relationship between higher education and social inequality remains unpredictable. Finally, since I am engaging with this relationship from a standpoint within higher education itself, there is the unavoidable risk of bias and distortion however self-critical such a standpoint may claim to be.

Despite these formidable difficulties, in contexts such as contemporary India, an intuitively persuasive case can be made for viewing higher education (henceforth HE) as a critical factor in the struggle to reduce social inequality.[1] This case is based on the plausible claim that, in a large and poor country marked by sharp inequalities, HE is the only form of capital available for redistribution. Societies with large populations that are also burdened by massive poverty and enduring inequalities must somehow offer hope of social mobility to the mass of have-nots if social unrest is to be avoided. Access to HE and the mobility-enhancing credentials it provides seems to be the only feasible solution today. Historically, large-scale social mobility has been due to sustained economic booms (like the three decades following the end of World War II), or it has been triggered by programmes of massive redistribution. Both these routes have been blocked in

DOI: 10.4324/9781003304760-11

the neoliberal world, thus making HE perhaps the only socially feasible route to mobility.

Unfortunately, global experience in the twenty-first century suggests that the case for HE as an engine of social mobility be treated with scepticism despite its intuitive appeal. In an era that has seen the 'massification' of HE in a wide spectrum of societies, higher enrolment rates seem to be quite compatible with the reproduction of historical inequalities in modified forms.[2] This appears to be true both in the affluent countries as well as the poorer non-Western countries, thus setting up a new puzzle defined by the continuing presence of inequalities despite a significant widening of access to HE.[3]

It seems that there is essentially only one solution to this puzzle, though its forms of concrete appearance may differ according to context. This solution suggests that there is something illusory about the widening of access to HE that allows the older elites to maintain their lead—or 'social distance'—in HE despite the entry of non-elites. Empirical evidence from across the globe offers examples of the different ways in which this result is being achieved. One major strand of explanation is the quality dimension. Usually, massification can only be achieved at the cost of quality—that is, by directly or indirectly allowing institutions of poor quality to survive in HE. Another common explanation is a variant of the glass ceiling thesis, where informal barriers to full inclusion prevent the new (non-elite) social groups entering HE from reaping its full benefits. A third solution to the puzzle cites the fact that success in HE depends to a significant extent on other forms of social and economic capital to explain why, despite entry into HE, social groups who are poor in these forms of capital may be denied mobility.

The massification puzzle takes an especially bewildering form in India where HE has expanded at a rate not seen before in human history (except perhaps in China). Despite this, there is little sense today that the undeniable democratisation of HE has produced any significant or lasting changes. It is obvious that tackling this puzzle is a giant collective enterprise that will take time to produce results. This chapter sets itself the much more modest task of a detailed examination of the available statistical evidence on the 'great expansion' that Indian HE has experienced in the past quarter century. It aims to address the following questions: What are the structural features of this expansion? Has Indian HE offered access to hitherto excluded social groups and classes, including access to high-quality institutions? What are the forms of inequity that continue to exist, and have any new forms emerged?[4]

By focusing on these questions, this chapter deliberately sets aside others that are equally important. The most urgent question not considered here is that of the link between HE and employment in the time of neoliberalism. It has been amply clear for some time that simply being well-qualified is no guarantee of a good job, at least for the vast majority. When precarity is no longer reserved only for those with low skills, the instrumental-practical justifications for HE become unsustainable. Ironically, neoliberalism may end up forcing us to recognise afresh, and to value once more, the same virtues of HE as an end-in-itself that it worked so hard to discredit. However, these concerns are beyond the scope of this chapter.

The following discussion is divided into three parts: Section 2 is concerned with the recent history of the HE sector in India, particularly the transformations brought about in the twenty-first century. Section 3 examines whether, and to what extent, these recent changes have impacted historical inequalities and exclusions. Section 4 provides a brief speculative conclusion.

2 The transformation of Indian higher education in the twenty-first century

Indian higher education has changed so much in the first two decades of this century that it is almost unrecognisable. However, these changes were brought about within an institutional framework shaped by colonial and postcolonial history. There are certain specificities of higher education in the context of a poor and huge country like India, which was also a major site for the invention and practice of colonial governance. Before we go on to document the recent transformations, a summary of the historical context is needed.

Higher education in postcolonial India

Western-style higher education began in India with the decision to establish three universities in the Presidency cities of Calcutta, Bombay, and Madras in 1857. In the first quarter century of modern HE, from 1857–1882, there were three universities and the number of colleges increased from 27 to 72. The social character of the student body was predictably homogenous, as Philip Altbach points out,

> During this period, HE was almost exclusively limited to the sons of the very small Westernized middle and upper class and was largely confined to the cities. The student population remained numerically small and relatively homogeneous both in social class and caste. Most students hoped for careers in the civil service or the professions, particularly law and medicine.
>
> *(Altbach, 1968: 254–255)*

It is not surprising that after winning its independence, the postcolonial state worked to expand HE, especially its technical-professional disciplines. However, while this expansion naturally broadened access to HE, the social composition of its students and faculty remained relatively homogenous in terms of caste and did not extend much beyond the middle classes. But before outlining later changes, it may be helpful to reflect on some of the peculiarities of Indian HE.[5]

The early post-independence investment in higher and especially technical education enabled generations of first-time entrants to make the transition from the rural to the urban world, and from a pre-modern to a modern economy. This major transformation had a peculiar social dimension that remained largely unnoticed at the time. The vast majority of those who benefited from state-funded HE in the decades between the 1950s and the 1970s were from the so-called upper castes. Ironically, therefore, HE did function as the gateway to mobility, but because this gateway was utilised (or was available) only to those who were already at the topmost rungs of society, it did not change the social structure. Or rather, it changed things by cementing caste hierarchies and allowing the upper castes to convert their traditional caste capital into modern meritocratic capital. In other words, the kind of mobility that HE offered was mostly intra-class rather than across classes, though the latter did happen, particularly for the upper castes. As Jean Dreze and Amartya Sen put it,

> The Indian educational system . . . does seem to make sure, in line with the general division between 'the privileged and the rest' in Indian society, that a few young people, out of a huge pool, manage to get an excellent education. The picking is done not through any organized attempt to keep anyone out (indeed far from it), but through differentiations that are driven by economic and social inequality related to class, caste, gender, location and social privilege.
>
> *(Dreze and Amartya, 2013: 96)*

Like everywhere else, Indian HE too is affected by various kinds of 'resource discrimination.' The economic, cultural, and political resources required for success in HE are unequally distributed in society, and these inequalities are reproduced in educational outcomes. Another widespread feature of modern HE, often called 'credential inflation,' is also particularly virulent here. This is hardly surprising in a labour-surplus and job-scarce environment. But what is perhaps distinctive to India is the pervasive and permanent distortion of the HE market. There is a booming market for substandard technical and professional education that is sustained by collusion between three groups: parents willing to pay heavily for paper qualifications for their wards; politicians willing to procure state recognition for institutions that they control; and unscrupulous educational entrepreneurs willing to manage such institutions. First seen in medicine and engineering, this type of fraudulent institution has spread to every field where professional certification is legally required, such as school-teaching or nursing.

Twenty-first-century changes: expansion

Easily the most visible aspect of change is the phenomenal expansion that HE has undergone in the past two decades. Much of this growth has happened in the present century, as can be seen in Table 8.1.

TABLE 8.1 Growth in Higher Education, 1990–1991 to 2018–2019

Year	*Total number of universities*	*Percent change*	*Total enrolment (100,000s)*	*Percent change*	*Gross enrolment ratio (%)*	*Percent change*
1990–1991	184	–	49	–	10.9	–
2000–2001	254	*38.0*	86	*75.5*	13.8	*26.6*
2010–2011	621	*144.5*	275	*219.8*	19.4	*40.6*
2018–2019	993	*59.9*	374	*36.0*	26.3	*35.6*

Note: Enrolment is in all types of institutions.
Source: AISHE & MHRD.

Between 1990–1991 and 2018–2019, the number of universities has increased almost *five-and-a-half* times and total enrolment has shot up by *seven-and-a-half* times, while the Gross Enrolment Ratio (GER) has gone up by *two-and-a-half* times. This amounts to an astonishing average rate of growth of three-and-a-half new institutions *per month* and more than 4,000 new students *per day*, sustained over a period of *almost three decades!* With a total student enrolment of 37.4 million, the Indian HE sector would rank 40th in a list of countries ranked by population, about the same as Canada, and nearly one-and-half times the size of Australia.

If we look at decadal changes, the first decade of the new century is clearly when the major growth spurt happened. Comparing growth rates (rather than absolute increase), we see that rates in the 2000–2001 to 2010–2011 decade for both number of universities and total enrolment roughly tripled. However, the change in growth rates for the GER is more modest at roughly one-and-a-half, indicating that even these express rates of growth had to contend with the demographic drag of the rate of population growth. India is one of the youngest countries in the world, and much was expected from its 'demographic dividend' in the early years of the century. The realisation of this dividend obviously depended partly on higher education and partly on the economy. The performance of both these areas has not been such as to generate much enthusiasm about the demographic dividend.

It is therefore not surprising that growth rates have declined for the second decade of the century, indicating both a period of restructuring as the mushrooming of non-viable institutions had to be compensated for, and a phase of softening in growth of demand.

Table 8.2 shows the break-up of higher education into its broad institutional components. The table tells us that nearly three-quarters of total enrolment in 2018–2019 is in colleges (the rightmost column). University enrolment is roughly one-fifth of the total, and its share has declined over the decade. Stand-alone institutions—which grant diplomas and certificates usually below the undergraduate level—have declined in absolute number, and their share of total enrolment has also shrunk from about 9% to about 6%. In other words, the college sector has

TABLE 8.2 Growth in Higher Education by Type of Institution, 2010–2011 to 2018–2019

Type of institution	*Number of institutions (Count)*			*Total enrolment (100,000)*			*Share of enrolment*	
	2010–11	2018–19	*% Change*	2010–11	2018–19	*% Change*	2010–11	2018–19
Universities	621	993	*59.9*	51.9	74.9	*44.2*	28.3	20.7
Colleges	16499	39931	*142.0*	115.5	264.7	*129.1*	62.9	73.3
Stand-alone Institutions	11139	10725	*-3.7*	16.3	21.5	*31.4*	8.9	5.9
Total	28259	51649	*82.8*	183.8	361.0	*96.4*	100.0	100.0

Source: AISHE 2010–2011 and 2018–2019. Surveys are listed by reference year rather than year of publication.

increased its share of total enrolment at the cost of both universities and stand-alone institutions. Both the number of colleges and their enrolment have more than doubled over the decade.

Twenty-first-century changes: privatisation

A second major feature of recent changes has been the privatisation of HE. The decisive moment came in the early years of this century: the 11th Five-Year Plan document reported that, in 2006, for the first time in the history of independent India, the majority of enrolment in higher education was in private institutions.[6] This was a major shift given that higher education (as different from school and vocational education) had always been exclusively associated with the state. Since then, the trend has intensified greatly, as shown in Table 8.3.[7]

The privatisation of enrolment has followed the privatisation of institutions, particularly colleges. Nearly four-fifths of higher education enrolment is accounted for by colleges, and this proportion has increased slightly from 77% in 2012–2013 to 78% in 2018–2019.[8] The majority of colleges were already privately owned in the early 2000s, and that proportion went up to about 75% in 2012–2013 and further to about 78% in 2018–2019.[9]

Column 5 of Table 8.3 shows that, in the span of six years covered here, total college enrolment increased by more than 69 lakhs (or 6.9 million), and that more than 75% of this increase was due to private colleges. In the same period, university enrolment went up by more than 16 lakhs (or 1.6 million), and a little more than half of this increment (53%) was in the private sector. If this trend continues, we can expect an acceleration in the private share of enrolment in both colleges and universities.

In terms of a static comparison between the two time points shown in Table 3, we can see (in columns 3 and 4) that the share of the private sector in university enrolment has increased from about 17% to almost 25%, while the private share in college enrolment has gone up from 63% to 66%. Considering colleges and

TABLE 8.3 Enrolment in Government and Private Institutions, Universities, and Colleges, 2012–2013 to 2018–2019

	Type of institution	*2012–2013 (000s)*	*2018–2019 (000s)*	*Increase (000s)*	*Percent increase*
Col.1	Col.2	Col.3	Col.4	Col.5	*Col.6*
Universities	Government	4864	5633	769	*15.8*
	Private	979	1854	875	*89.3*
	All	5844	7487	1643	*28.1*
	% Private	***16.8***	***24.8***	***53.2***	
Colleges	Government	7188	8889	1701	*23.7*
	Private	12361	17577	5215	*42.2*
	All	19549	26465	6917	*35.4*
	% Private	***63.2***	***66.4***	***75.4***	
Total	Government	12052	14522	2470	*20.5*
	Private	13341	19431	6090	*45.6*
	All	25393	33952	8560	*33.7*
	% Private	***52.5***	***57.2***	***71.1***	

Source: For Universities, Table 50 of AISHE 2018–2019; for Colleges, Table 5(a) in AISHE 2018–2019 and 2012–2013.

universities together, the private share has increased from almost 53% to about 57%, but the private share of the increase over this period is as much as 71% (column 5).[10]

It must be emphasised that these figures underestimate the private sector's share since the bulk of non-reporting institutions for the AISHE surveys are private ones. Moreover, stand-alone institutions, which account for roughly 10% of total enrolment in higher education are not considered here, and they are overwhelmingly private. However, these figures do provide a broad overview of the gradual advance of private over public higher education during the past two decades.

3 Has massive expansion made Indian higher education more inclusive?

We now consider the consequences for inclusion of this unprecedented growth of the higher education sector. Considered first are the specific groups on which state policy has focused—women, and the disadvantaged castes and tribes. Second, the cost of higher education is taken up. The early drive to make higher education affordable has lost considerable momentum in recent decades, with the elite sections of the state sector raising fees quite substantially, especially in the lucrative fields of management and technical education. Economic reasons continue to be the most important trigger for dropping out of higher education. Finally, the gender question is examined in a disaggregated context, which shows that despite the encouraging performance overall, significant gaps remain in gender equity.

Changes in the social composition of higher education

In overall terms, the recent growth has worked to significantly alter the social composition of Indian HE, with the increasing inclusion of groups that were until recently almost completely excluded or greatly under-represented. The entry of new groups was facilitated by the 93rd Amendment to the Constitution, which extended OBC reservations to elite 'institutions of national importance' and central universities. Although it took some years to take effect, by the second decade of the 2000s, its impact was being felt. Table 8.4 shows the change in the GERs for broad groups over the past two decades. While men (considered as an undifferentiated group) have always been ahead, the table shows that both the Scheduled Tribes and especially the Scheduled Castes have not only raised their GERs significantly in absolute terms, they have also reduced the gap relative to the national average. Women have been (overall) the big success story of the past two decades, with enrolment now higher than the national average, and slightly higher than the male GER, though sharp differences remain across disciplines.

However, Table 8.4 has certain limitations. First, the data is not disaggregated enough—groups like OBCs and Muslims are not shown separately because GERs are not reported routinely for them. Second, the GER itself is age-dependent (since the denominator of this ratio is the 18–23 age group) and this may understate the enrolment of disadvantaged groups who tend to take longer to complete courses or enrol when they are older. Table 8.5 tries to address these limitations.

Table 8.5 shows the share of different social groups in total HE enrolment—it considers all enrolled students regardless of their age. In addition to the groups represented in Table 8.4, data are shown for OBCs, Muslims, Other Minorities (mainly Christians, Sikhs, Buddhists, and Jains), and Persons with Disability.[11] However, unlike all the other groups, the group called 'Upper Caste Hindus' is neither officially recognised nor explicitly counted. I have computed data for this group as a residual, by subtracting the total of all the other groups from the grand total. This is now a common practice in both academic and other contexts, and it provides a robust estimate for a socially critical group that is otherwise always anonymous.

TABLE 8.4 Gross Enrolment Ratio for Various Social Groups, 2010–2011 to 2018–2019

Social groups	*Gross Enrolment Ratio (GER)*		*Group GER as % of national average GER*	
	2010–2011	*2018–2019*	*2010–2011*	*2018–2019*
Women	17.9	26.4	92.3	100.4
Men	20.8	26.3	107.2	100.0
Scheduled Tribes	11.2	17.2	57.7	65.4
Scheduled Castes	13.5	23.0	69.6	87.5
National average	*19.4*	*26.3*	*100.0*	*100.0*

Source: AISHE for respective years. GER = Percentage of the population aged 18–23 that is enrolled in higher educational institutions.

Table 8.5 shows that, relative to share of the general population, the Upper Caste Hindus is the only group that is over-represented, all others are more or less under-represented. Some groups, like Persons with Disability and Muslims, continue to be severely under-represented. However, comparing the two years, it is clear that the share of all groups other than Upper Caste Hindus has risen, while that of the latter is falling. Women are the only group that cuts across all categories (i.e., all other groups include women within them). Considered as a separate group, women are also closest to achieving proportional representation in HE overall, though this overall average conceals sharp differences across disciplines and faculties. Women are already the majority in some disciplines and fields like general education (especially the humanities and social sciences) and in education, but they continue to be greatly under-represented in most professional and technical disciplines.

The disaggregation of social groups that Table 8.5 offers still does not address the question of differential access to different types of HE institutions. This is an important issue since the 'massification' literature (mentioned in the beginning) indicates that existing inequalities can be reproduced in the form of elite capture of high-quality or elite institutions, leaving the substandard ones for disadvantaged groups. Table 8.6 tries to overcome this problem.

Table 8.6 begins to tackle this issue, though it cannot address it directly or comprehensively. It shows the social composition of the student body in different types of universities and colleges. In other words, it provides the same data as Table 8.5 but disaggregated across types of institutions.[12] Five types of universities are distinguished: Central Universities and Institutions of National Importance (INI, which include the IITs, IIMs, and so on) are funded by the central

TABLE 8.5 Percentage Share in Total University and College Enrolment of Various Social Groups, 2010–2011 to 2018–2019

Social groups	*Percentage share in total university enrolment*		*Percentage share in total population*
	2010–2011	*2018–2019*	
Women	44.0	48.6	48.5
Scheduled Tribes	4.4	5.5	8.6
Scheduled Castes	11.1	14.4	16.6
Other Backward Classes	27.6	36.3	42.0
Muslims	3.8	5.3	14.2
Other Minorities	1.8	2.1	4.5
Persons with Disability	0.2	0.2	2.2
*Upper Caste Hindus**	*51.1*	*36.5*	*~20.0*

Note: *Upper Caste Hindus estimated as residual.

Source: For enrolment shares, AISHE; for population shares, NSSO for OBC; and Census 2011 for rest (except UC-H).

TABLE 8.6 Representation of Women and Social Categories in Student Enrolment by Type of University or College, 2011–2012 and 2018–2019

Type of university or college	*Women*		*Scheduled Castes*		*Scheduled Tribes*		*Other Backward Classes*		*Persons with Disability*		*Muslims*		*Other Minorities*		*'Upper Caste' Hindus*		
	11–12	*18–19*	*11–12*	*18–19*	*11–12*	*18–19*	*11–12*	*18–19*	*11–12*	*18–19*	*11–12*	*18–19*	*11–12*	*18–19*	*11–12*	*18–19*	*Change*
Universities																	
Central Univs	44.3	47.4	9.3	13.8	3.6	4.1	11.8	16.6	0.3	0.6	1.2	7.4	0.7	1.6	73.5	56.6	***-16.9***
Inst. of Nat. Imp.	17.7	23.9	12.6	13.3	5.7	6.3	20.8	26.8	0.7	1.2	0.3	2.2	0.4	0.8	60.2	50.6	***-9.6***
State Univs	41.1	47.6	11.6	11.1	2.9	3.3	27.9	32.7	0.1	0.3	2.8	5.1	0.7	1.3	54.0	43.3	***-10.7***
Cen+State OpenU	40.8	41.2	12.8	12.8	7.2	7.7	31.3	27.8	0.0	0.1	0.3	0.2	0.1	0.1	48.3	51.3	***+3.0***
Private Univs	33.9	41.8	3.1	10.8	1.5	4.8	16.5	26.8	0.1	0.2	1.7	3.5	3.0	0.8	74.3	61.7	***-12.6***
All India Univs	*39.8*	*42.9*	*10.4*	*10.7*	*4.0*	*4.6*	*25.3*	*25.5*	*0.1*	*0.2*	*1.8*	*2.7*	*0.9*	*0.8*	*57.6*	*51.7*	***-5.9***
Colleges																	
Central U Coll	54.3	53.6	10.5	10.5	19.5	24.5	20.2	23.9	0.2	0.4	3.0	4.7	3.4	8.5	43.4	27.9	***-15.5***
State Pub U Coll	46.5	51.0	12.5	15.4	4.1	5.2	31.3	39.1	0.2	0.2	4.6	5.8	2.0	2.3	45.5	32.3	***-13.2***
All India Colleges	*46.8*	*51.1*	*12.4*	*15.2*	*4.7*	*5.7*	*30.9*	*38.7*	*0.2*	*0.2*	*4.5*	*5.8*	*2.0*	*2.5*	*45.5*	*32.2*	***-13.3***

Note: 1. 'Upper Caste' Hindus obtained as residual. 2. 'Stand Alone' institutes giving diplomas and certificates not included. 3. Some university types combined: 'State Univs' = State Public Univs + Institutions Established Under State Acts + Deemed Univs-Govt + Deemed Univs Govt Aided; 'Private Univs' = State Pvt Univs + State Pvt Open Univs + Deemed Univs-Private + Others.

Source: Based on AISHE 2011–2012 and 2018–2019, Tables 27 and 28.

(national) government, and roughly correspond to the elite sector of Indian HE. State Universities are funded by state governments, and Open Universities (distance education) are funded by both states and centre. Private Universities in India are of very uneven quality, with a few maintaining very high standards, but the majority are mediocre if not substandard. Though they may offer some undergraduate degrees, universities are mostly devoted to postgraduate (master's level and higher) education. Colleges are exclusively undergraduate institutions (though a few master's degrees may be offered) and account for almost 80% of total enrolment in HE. By contrast, the Central Universities' share is 2%, while that of INI is less than 1%, so that the elite sector of Indian HE accommodates only 3% of all students. It should be kept in mind therefore that quantitatively colleges are far more important, but qualitatively—that is, in terms of the degree of social mobility they offer—universities are dominant.[13] 'Stand Alone' institutions that offer diplomas and certificates lower than the bachelor's degree are not considered here as the data on them is incomplete and unreliable.

As can be seen in Table 8.6, all groups other than Upper Caste Hindus (UCH) have registered an increase in their share. The stranglehold of the UCH in Central Universities, Private Universities, and State Universities is being eroded, with the fall in UCH share being the highest for Central Universities at almost 17%. The decline in the UCH share is also significant in both Central and State university colleges at around 13%, and this sector accounts for almost four-fifths of total enrolment. There is a decline in the UCH share in the Institutions of National Importance as well, though there seems to be an increase of about 3% in Open Universities which will need further examination.

The most important feature of Table 8.6 is that the UCH share in the State Colleges, which account for about 75% of total enrolment, has now fallen to less than one-third. Though the UCH share here is still comfortably more than their estimated share of the total population, this implies, in all probability, that a significant number of students from social groups eligible for reservation have been able to enter the 'unreserved' category.[14] This is an encouraging sign as it is the long-term goal of reservation policy to secure the diversification of the unreserved category so that it reflects the social composition of the larger society.

Positive trends of this kind should not blind us to the continuing under -representation of all groups other than the UCH. Persons with Disability are still largely excluded from HE given that their current presence in both universities and colleges amounts to roughly one-tenth of their share in the Indian population. Muslims are almost as badly off—their current share in university enrolment is less than 3%, while it is about 6% in colleges, compared to their 14% share in the national population.

Since discrimination and exclusion are relevant for faculty as well, Table 8.7 provides data on gender and caste community of the faculty. Broadly speaking, from the point of view of inclusion, the social composition of faculty is lagging behind that of students, though it is headed in the same direction. The last (rightmost) column of Table 8.7 shows that the share of UCH is declining in all types

TABLE 8.7 Representation of Women and Social Categories in the Faculty, by Type of University or College, 2011–2012 and 2018–2019

Type of university or college	*Women*		*Scheduled Castes*		*Scheduled Tribes*		*Other Backward Classes*		*Persons with Disability*		*Muslims*		*Other Minorities*		*'Upper Caste' Hindus*		
	11–12	*18–19*	*11–12*	*18–19*	*11–12*	*18–19*	*11–12*	*18–19*	*11–12*	*18–19*	*11–12*	*18–19*	*11–12*	*18–19*	*11–12*	*18–19*	*Change*
Universities																	
Central Univs	26.3	27.5	6.9	10.0	5.0	6.8	6.5	13.8	0.7	1.0	13.8	18.4	1.6	8.4	66.3	41.6	-24.7
Inst. of Nat. Imp.	15.9	15.3	3.4	6.5	0.8	1.5	4.5	12.8	0.2	0.4	1.7	2.9	0.6	4.6	89.0	71.4	-17.6
State Univs	27.7	31.3	8.2	11.0	1.6	2.9	14.3	23.9	0.4	0.4	2.4	6.1	2.3	8.4	71.2	47.2	-24.0
Cen+State OpenU	33.2	37.7	13.4	12.5	4.4	2.9	15.1	21.3	0.2	0.4	2.8	3.3	0.7	3.5	63.6	56.1	-7.5
Private Univs	39.6	37.9	2.9	3.6	0.9	1.0	15.1	22.5	0.2	0.1	1.5	3.7	3.6	9.4	76.0	59.7	-16.3
All India Univs	*32.3*	*32.9*	*5.5*	*6.6*	*1.5*	*2.1*	*13.4*	*21.7*	*0.3*	*0.3*	*2.9*	*5.3*	*0.3*	*8.6*	*76.4*	*55.3*	*-21.1*
Colleges																	
Central U Coll	48.1	49.0	6.6	8.2	15.5	20.4	13.1	19.3	0.9	0.6	2.5	3.9	5.0	23.0	57.3	24.6	-32.7
State Pub U Coll	39.5	39.8	6.8	8.9	1.6	1.8	22.8	33.7	0.5	0.3	3.2	5.5	3.1	8.6	62.4	41.2	-21.2
All India Colleges	*39.8*	*40.1*	*6.8*	*8.9*	*2.1*	*2.4*	*22.5*	*33.2*	*0.5*	*0.3*	*3.2*	*5.5*	*0.0*	*9.0*	*65.4*	*40.7*	*-24.7*

Note: 1. 'Upper Caste' Hindus obtained as residual. 2. 'Stand Alone' institutes giving diplomas and certificates not included. 3. Some university types combined: 'State Univs' = State Public Univs + Institutions Established Under State Acts + Deemed Univs-Govt + Deemed Univs Govt Aided; 'Private Univs' = State Pvt Univs + State Pvt Open Univs + Deemed Univs-Private + Others.

Source: Based on AISHE 2011–2012 and 2018–2019, Table 30.

of institutions during the decade covered, though the starting points are different across types of institutions. Not surprisingly, Institutions of National Importance have had the highest concentration of UCH faculty – as much as 89% in 2011–2012, and this has come down to about 71% in 2018–2019, indicating that there is still a long way to go here.

Scheduled Castes, Scheduled Tribes, Other Backward Classes, Muslims, and Other Minorities have all increased their shares across all university and college types. However, in general, Private Universities are seen to be the least inclusive for these groups, while Central Universities are the most inclusive. Women are only nearing one-third share overall in universities and have a 40% share in college faculty, showing that they lag behind the advances made in terms of representation of women among the student body. Despite the undoubted gains in diversification, it is clear that a fully inclusive faculty body is still some distance in the future, especially in the universities where the overall share of the UCH is still a comfortable 55%, well over double their estimated share in the total population.

The cost of higher education and class exclusion

Of all the various forms of exclusion, the economic is the easiest to grasp intuitively—indeed, it is often taken for granted. Despite this, however, compiling authoritative statistical evidence for economic exclusion is not as easy as one might expect, especially for higher education. From a statistical point of view, educational fees and expenses are inherently more difficult to track than enrolment. There is no centralised database for data on what educational institutions charge their students, and AISHE does not collect this type of information. Until recently, scholars have relied mostly on macro data from the national accounts to estimate expenditure on higher education by households and by the government. Though the NSSO's household sample survey data has been available since the mid-1980s, it is only in the last decade that it has been detailed enough to allow for the disaggregated analysis needed to address questions of inequality and exclusion. Access to unit-level data has been especially important in enabling such analyses.

Privatisation is the single most important factor affecting the cost of education in India. In the first two decades after Independence, that is, roughly until the end of the 1960s, education at all levels was state-supported. The shift towards the privatisation of schooling began in earnest in the 1960s and was established by the 1970s. The same shift began a decade later in higher education, but the state sector remained dominant until the 1990s. As discussed earlier, the twenty-first century has seen the rapid privatisation of higher education, along with the narrowing of differentials between state-supported and private institutions, particularly in relation to costs.

In Table 8.3, we had seen the public–private shares of enrolment from the point of view of educational institutions, as represented by the AISHE. In Table 8.8, we see the public–private shares of enrolment from the perspective of households as represented by the NSSO sample surveys. Government Institutions (GIs) include those administered by local bodies (such as municipal corporations or panchayats). Private Aided Institutions (Ais) are those that receive some financial (and other) assistance from the government, but this has been declining over time. Private Unaided Institutions (UIs) are wholly private, even though the state often helps such institutions as well through various direct and indirect subsidies and unlevied taxes. The 75th Round of 2017–2018 and the 71st Round of 2014 are the two most recent NSSO surveys specifically on education. Though the enrolment figures shown here are not strictly comparable (because of definitional changes between the two surveys explained in the Appendix), they do provide an overall sense of how the share of the government institutions is declining.[15]

Both years show that government institutions have the minority share of enrolment in both the rural and urban sectors, with the share in the latter being significantly less than in the rural sector. However, on subjects like enrolment, the institution-based AISHE data are more reliable, and so Table 8.3 is a better guide to the pace and extent of privatisation than Table 8.8, the latter only broadly confirming the trends in the former.

Since private investment in higher education is a for-profit venture, it has naturally been largely restricted to the lucrative markets for technical and professional degrees. But in terms of sheer numbers, 'general' education remains by far the larger category, accounting for 75–80% of total enrolment. This is corroborated by NSSO data during 2017–2018, which suggests that 76% of total enrolment at the graduate or higher levels is in general subjects; but if diplomas and certificates below graduate level are also counted as part of higher education, then the share

TABLE 8.8 Higher Education Enrolment by Type of Institution (Graduate Level and Above), 2014 and 2017–2018

Type of institution	*Estimated enrolment (000s)*			
	Rural		*Urban*	
	2014	*2017–2018*	*2014*	*2017–2018*
Government	6,985	8,071	4,461	5,349
% share	*48.1*	*49.9*	*38.2*	*41.1*
Private Aided	3,280	3,903	3,286	3,278
% share	*22.6*	*24.1*	*28.1*	*25.2*
Private Unaided	4,250	4,209	3,934	4,389
% share	*29.3*	*26.0*	*33.7*	*33.7*
Total enrolment	14,514	16,183	11,681	13,015
% share	*100.0*	*100.0*	*100.0*	*100.0*

Note: The figures are not strictly comparable: 2017–2018 includes diplomas while 2014 excludes them; 2017–2018 age group is up to 35 years, whereas 2014 is up to 29 years.

Source: Computed from data in NSSO Reports 585 (2017–2018) and 575 (2014).

of general education becomes as high as 96%![16] But high enrolment numbers for general education do not necessarily indicate a preference for it—they suggest that it is more of a refuge for those who cannot afford the expensive technical or professional courses that are increasingly offered in private institutions.

Privatisation has led to a significant increase in the cost of education overall, and particularly in the technical-professional courses. However, it is also true that state institutions too have been relentlessly privatising parts of their own institutional space with innovations like 'self-financing' courses and 'affiliation fees' for subordinate institutions. This process has gone so far that scholars admit that the distinction between public and private institutions may be blurred today. Tables 8.9 and 8.10 try to illustrate these tendencies using NSSO data from the three most recent surveys on education.

Table 8.9 provides an initial view of the difference between state-funded education and private education. It shows average expenditure per student on general education in three different types of institutions at different levels. Although this chapter is about higher education, a comparison with costs at different levels—the Primary and the Higher Secondary—is helpful for getting a sense of what it means in financial terms for a student to enter higher education. Higher education is restricted here to general (as different from technical/professional) education and is split between the graduate and postgraduate levels, because this subdivision has been provided in the two most recent surveys. These figures are in Rupees at current prices, so they have not been adjusted for inflation.

Interpreting these tables requires us to focus on three points. First, primary education in GIs is a useful reference point since it is the level at which the state provides maximum assistance—it is what educational costs would look like if they were borne socially rather than privately. However, the level of state support starts to decline as we move up the educational levels, so even within GIs, we see average private expenditure per student rising quite significantly from primary to higher secondary and then to the graduate and postgraduate levels. Second, average expenditure increases at each level of education, as we move from GIs to AIs to UIs, being uniformly the highest for the last at all levels and in both the rural and urban sectors. But because of the first point, the gap between GIs and private institutions (of both kinds) is widest at the primary level and (generally) begins to narrow as we move up levels, being the narrowest at the postgraduate level. In other words, higher education involves significant financial burden on households regardless of the type of institution, but obviously this burden is higher in AIs and especially in UIs. The third point is that these are sample survey data, and given the realities of the Indian situation, sample sizes are relatively small at the postgraduate level, and may therefore be unreliable when disaggregated further (as they are here by type of institution).[17]

Table 8.10 tries to clarify and highlight the main conclusions to be drawn from Table 8.9 by converting the figures for average expenditure into index numbers. Index numbers help to show the proportionate change relative to the reference group or category—here, the average expenditure in GIs in each year at each

TABLE 8.9 Average Annual Expenditure Per Student on General Education, by Sector, Level of Education, and Type of Institution, 2007–2008, 2014, and 2017–2018

Sector	*Sector and level of education*	*Government institutions*			*Private Aided institutions*			*Private Unaided institutions*		
		2007–2008	*2014*	*2017–2018*	*2007–2008*	*2014*	*2017–2018*	*2007–2008*	*2014*	*2017–2018*
(1)	*(2)*	*(3)*	*(4)*	*(5)*	*(6)*	*(7)*	*(8)*	*(9)*	*(10)*	*(11)*
RURAL	Primary	410	965	1,092	1,928	6,452	9,603	2,889	7,907	10,623
	Higher Secondary	3,333	6,056	6,144	4,148	10,803	10,371	7,359	13,988	17,537
	Graduate	4,810	8,753	9,516	5,726	11,730	12,820	8,050	17,093	16,485
	Postgrad & above	8,988	11,403	13,117	11,250	14,224	17,483	17,665	25,372	20,928
URBAN	Primary	1,012	2,149	2,413	4,249	11,881	15,800	5,787	14,242	19,315
	Higher Secondary	4,933	9,668	10,074	8,869	20,066	26,905	15,520	30,810	34,383
	Graduate	6,336	11,560	12,448	6,783	16,993	22,949	13,637	26,380	25,204
	Postgrad & above	9,471	13,580	15,974	8,424	20,978	22,594	16,091	29,661	32,249

Source: Based on NSSO survey data: computations using unit-level data for 2007–2008 (64th Round), and published results for 2014 and 2017–2018 (71st and 75th Rounds, respectively).[18]

TABLE 8.10 Index Numbers of Average Annual Expenditure Per Student on General Education

Sector	*Sector and level of education*	*Government institutions*			*Private Aided institutions*			*Private Unaided institutions*		
		2007–2008	*2014*	*2017–2018*	*2007–2008*	*2014*	*2017–2018*	*2007–2008*	*2014*	*2017–2018*
(1)	*(2)*	*(3)*	*(4)*	*(5)*	*(6)*	*(7)*	*(8)*	*(9)*	*(10)*	*(11)*
RURAL	Primary	100	100	100	470	669	879	705	819	973
	Higher Secondary	100	100	100	124	178	169	221	231	285
	Graduate	100	100	100	119	134	135	167	195	173
	Postgrad & above	100	100	100	125	125	133	197	223	160
URBAN	Primary	100	100	100	420	553	655	572	663	800
	Higher Secondary	100	100	100	180	208	267	315	319	341
	Graduate	100	100	100	107	147	184	215	228	202
	Postgrad & above	100	100	100	89	154	141	170	218	202

Note: Columns 3, 4, and 5 could have been omitted, but are included for ease of interpretation.
Source: Computed from data in Table 9. See Appendix for details.

level of education—which is equated to the base value of 100. Reading from left to right along each educational level, we can compare the average expenditure in AIs and UIs to the average expenditure in GIs at the same level. For example, taking the first row for the Primary level in the Rural sector, we can see that in 2007–2008, the average expenditure for primary education in AIs was 4.7 times higher (index number=470, divided by base=100) than that in GIs; in 2014, it was almost 6.7 (6.69) times higher; and in 2017–2018, it was almost 8.8 (8.79) times higher. We can read the numbers for UIs for the three years in the same way, and know what multiple they represent relative to average expenditure in GIs.

The most obvious conclusion to be drawn from Table 8.10 (also visible in Table 8.9, but presented more sharply in Table 8.10) is that GIs are much less expensive than either of the two kinds of private institutions. (There is only one cell in the table that is less than 100, the reasons for which are discussed here in connection with sample size issues.) But a second striking fact about Table 8.10 is that the rows for Primary level in the Rural and Urban sectors are exceptional—the index numbers in these two rows are much higher than those in the rows below them in each sector. This is because of the high level of state support for Primary level education, which allows private expenditure by households to be very low (at this level) in GIs, which in turn causes the index numbers for AIs and UIs at this level to be relatively high. The level of state support declines as we move to the higher levels, particularly the last two that are part of higher education, and that is why the index numbers for the other levels are much smaller, being (generally) smallest for the graduate and postgraduate levels. In short, from the point of view of students, higher education in GIs is much more expensive than school education in GIs, so that the gap between GIs and private institutions narrows at this level.

Finally, some caveats need to be mentioned about the sample survey data on which both Tables 8.9 and 8.10 are based. Sample sizes for the postgraduate and above level tend to be relatively small, so that further corroboration is needed before too much weight is placed on this data, particularly when they seem anomalous or odd. For example, Table 8.10 shows that in 2007–2008, average expenditure at the postgraduate level in AIs was actually *lower* than that in GIs by about 11% (index number is 89). For the postgraduate level in 2007–2008, the sample size for GIs, AIs, and UIs, respectively, were 118, 26, and 13 in the Rural sector, and 217, 60, and 23 in the Urban sector. The sample size for AIs and UIs is particularly low, and the data here requires more detailed investigation that is beyond the scope of this chapter.

Thus, what we have learnt so far from Tables 8.9 and 8.10 is that higher education is much more expensive than school education in all types of institutions, and that it tends to be even more expensive in private institutions, particularly UIs. Given the trend towards privatisation discussed earlier, this suggests that poorer students will find it more and more difficult to afford higher education. However, we need further evidence to make a more precise and substantiated argument about economic exclusion.

Table 8.11 provides a rough sense of the class composition of those currently attending courses in higher education. It does this by distributing the cohort of those engaged in higher education across the quintiles of monthly per capita consumption expenditure (MPCE) of the households they belong to. MPCE data has long been used as a proxy for income (and more broadly for class), given the

TABLE 8.11 Class Composition of Students in Higher Education

Quintiles of MPCE	*Rural*			*Urban*		
	2007–2008	*2014*	*2017–2018*	*2007–2008*	*2014*	*2017–2018*
Poorest 20%	5.9	6.9	10.7	4.7	7.1	11.7
20–40%	8.2	10.3	15.6	10.2	11.3	15.2
40–60%	12.6	17.3	17.2	17.9	18.0	17.6
60–80%	20.0	23.5	22.8	26.7	26.0	21.9
Richest 20%	52.9	41.9	33.7	40.5	37.8	33.4
All	*100.0*	*100.0*	*100.0*	*100.0*	*100.0*	*100.0*

Note: Higher Education is defined as degrees at graduate level and above, not including diplomas. Columns may not add up to 100 due to rounding errors.
Source: Computed from data in NSSO Reports 532, 575, and 585. See Appendix for details.

difficulties with collecting income data directly in a country like India. Because consumption expenditure ignores income and wealth, it tends to understate inequality given that the rich spend proportionately less of their income than the poor who may often be spending beyond their income. Simply put, the poor may be accumulating debt, and the rich may be accumulating wealth, but both remain invisible when we look at consumption expenditure. Despite this drawback, consumption expenditure is for practical reasons much more reliably collected through surveys than income, and that is why it is used very frequently in the analyses of inequality.

One way to interpret Table 8.11 is to see it as a sign of hope. The bottom two quintiles (the poorest 40% of the sample) have steadily increased their presence in higher education across the three survey years, and in both the rural and urban sectors. The reverse is true of the top two quintiles (or the richest 40%) with just one exception (2007–2008 to 2014 in the rural sector). The gap between the top and bottom quintiles is also narrowing steadily in both sectors. In 2007–2008 in rural India, the ratio between the first and fifth quintiles was roughly 1:9, and this came down to about 1:6 in 2014 and roughly 1:3 in 2017–2018. For the urban sector, this ratio declined from 1:8 to a little over 1:5 in 2014, and a little less than 1:3 in 2017–2018. On the other hand, the same data could be used to underline how sharp inequalities are even as late as 2017–2018, when there are roughly three times more students from the richest quintile in Indian higher education than students from the poorest quintile.

Apart from the disadvantages already mentioned, NSSO survey data has another drawback when used to study subjects like higher education. The surveys were designed, and they remain, highly sophisticated instruments for a detailed study of poverty, including extreme poverty. Since higher education is not a site where the poorest sections of the population predominate, it is not a site where NSSO data is at its most illuminating. However, given that the unit-level (or household and individual level) data from some of these surveys is now available to researchers, some effort can be made to reshape the survey data. Table 8.12 tries to stretch out the higher end of the class structure by separating out the top two deciles, and it telescopes the lower end by making the first two size classes include three deciles each. Compared to Table 8.11, Table 8.12 provides more detailed information on the richest deciles; however, since unit-level data is not yet available for 2017–2018, it is limited to only two years.

Table 8.12 provides a somewhat different perspective on the class composition of Indian higher education. In the rural sector, it broadly agrees with the hopeful picture presented in Table 8.11, showing a decline in inequality through the rise in the enrolment share of the three groups up to the 80th percentile, and a decline in the share of the top two deciles. However, Table 8.12 offers much less optimism in the urban sector, where there is hardly any change. The shares of the top two deciles remain almost identical between 2007–2008 and 2014, and the shares of the lower groups are also more or less constant. Since the urban sector is obviously the major player in higher education, this is a sobering view. Table 8.12 also

TABLE 8.12 Class Composition of Higher Education, 2007–2008 and 2014

Divisions of MPCE	*Rural*		*Urban*	
	2007–2008	*2014*	*2007–2008*	*2014*
Poorest 30%	9.5	11.6	10.7	11.9
30–60%	17.4	23.0	22.3	23.4
60–80%	21.3	24.7	27.5	25.2
80–90%	19.9	14.5	17.2	17.5
Richest 10%	32.0	26.2	22.4	22.0
All	*100.0*	*100.0*	*100.0*	*100.0*

Note: Higher Education is defined as degrees at graduate level and above, not including diplomas.
Source: Computed from unit-level data, NSSO Rounds 64 and 71. See Appendix for details.

highlights the concentration of privilege (if entry into higher education is counted as such) at the very top of the economic spectrum. The top one-tenth (richest 10%) have a disproportionate share of the enrolment, which has fallen from roughly one-third to a one-fourth in the rural sector, and is maintained at more than one-fifth in the urban sector.

The intersections of class, caste, community, and gender

The previous sections have discussed the implications of the rapid expansion of Indian higher education for the inclusion of hitherto excluded groups, and the economic aspects of access. In this section, the intersections of social and economic dimensions of exclusion (or inclusion) are taken up, beginning with a brief overview of the most salient groupings that will help analyse the inequality in the Indian context. The official statistics tend to report on the legally recognised categories, which are usually unidimensional. For example, the NSSO reports on religion and official caste categories separately, and until unit-level data become available, it was not possible to cross-tabulate the two. Obviously, there are many ways in which groups can be demarcated, and the method chosen here involves six groups, four of which are the result of cross-tabulation.

The Scheduled Tribes (STs) and Scheduled Castes (SCs) are well-known official categories created and formalised before Independence by the colonial state, albeit in partial response to indigenous demands.[19] Although every significant social grouping in contemporary India is certain to be deeply differentiated along class, regional, community, and other lines, these two groups retain enough social coherence that it is not necessary to subdivide them for the sort of analysis undertaken here. In recent decades, Muslims in India have emerged as an officially denied but empirically robust marginalised group according to all the usual yardsticks. For this reason, Muslims are treated as a single community here with the sole exception of those who fall within the ST category.[20] Treating Muslims as a single category requires them to be taken out of the Other

Backward Class (OBC) category, where they account for about 10% and 12% of the rural and urban OBCs. However, in recent times, Muslim-ness as an identity marker has become almost overwhelming, drowning other markers. Hence, the OBC category minus Muslims is today a more coherent category, despite the huge internal differences that remain. The OBCs are perhaps the least coherent of the official categories now operative in India. The remaining two categories are the Upper Castes (UC), the most elusive social grouping in statistical terms. They are not officially recognised and must be arrived at as a residual. Here the UCs are divided into two parts, the Other Minorities (mainly Christians, Sikhs, Jains, and others who are neither Hindu nor Muslim), and the Hindus. The former group is economically well off but very small in size, while the latter is the most dominant group in Indian society.

Table 8.13 provides an initial sense of the intersection of social and economic inequality in higher education through a comparison of the average (mean) expenditure per student on higher education of different social groups expressed as a percentage of the UC-Hindu figure. We can see that caste inequalities are quite strong, particularly in the urban sector where the mean expenditure of the STs and SCs is only a little more than half that of the UC-Hindus. In fact, in the urban sector, the two UC groups are clearly above all others, with a minimum difference of about 20%. In the rural sector, groups other than ST and SC are fairly close to the UC-Hindu average, while UC-Other Minorities are obviously far ahead. Mean expenditure on higher education is perhaps the simplest measure of inequality, and its importance increases with the increasing privatisation and the fading of the state as a source of inexpensive higher education.

However, averages can be misleading, and it is necessary to get a more detailed sense of the distribution of expenditure on higher education across social groups. This is provided in Figures 8.1 and 8.2, which graph the deciles of expenditure on higher education by different social groups in the rural and urban sectors, respectively.[21]

Table 8.13 had suggested (through a comparison of mean expenditure) that the Muslims and OBCs are both very close to the UC-Hindu group. Figure 8.1

TABLE 8.13 Index of Mean Expenditure on Higher Education by Social Groups, 2014

Social groups	*Rural*	*Urban*	*All India*
All-Scheduled Tribes	65.6	56.2	50.8
All-Scheduled Castes	64.5	53.3	50.5
Non-ST-Muslims	94.3	65.9	73.7
OBC-Non-Muslims	96.3	80.7	80.0
UC-Other Minorities	269.1	122.2	164.4
UC-Hindu	*100.0*	*100.0*	*100.0*
All Groups	92.9	84.1	82.2

Source: Computed from unit-level data for the NSSO 71st Round survey. See Appendix for details.

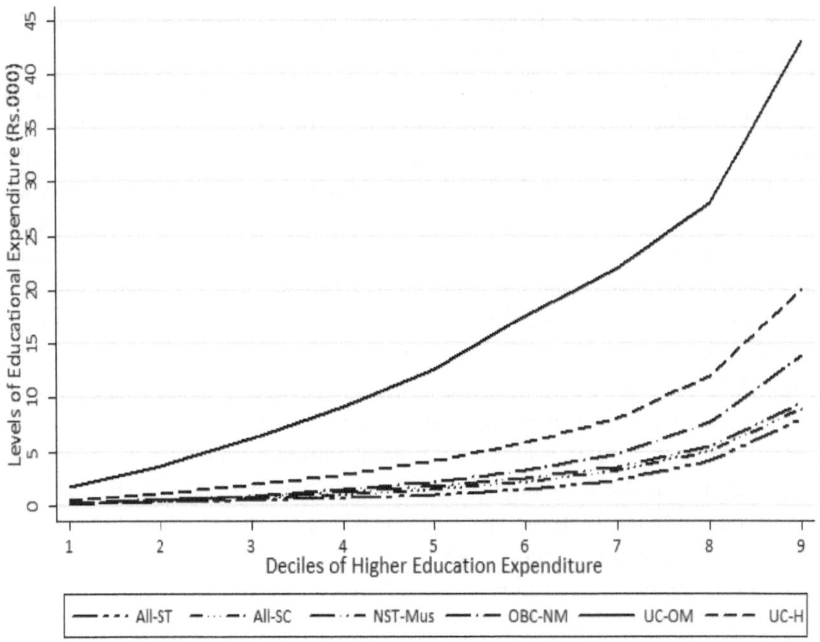

FIGURE 8.1 Deciles of Higher Education Expenditure by Social Groups, 2014, Rural

Source: Computed with unit-level data from the 71st Round Survey of the NSSO.

corrects this impression by showing us that the OBCs are clearly spending more on higher education after about the 7th decile, whereas Muslims remain indistinguishable from the STs and SCs. The massive difference between the UC-Other Minorities group and the rest is explained by the fact that rural upper caste Christians and Sikhs (who would form the bulk of this group) are known to be very prosperous. However, this should be balanced against their small number relative to other groups. There is clearly a relatively well-off segment among the rural OBCs at the upper end of the distribution.

Figure 8.2 shows that caste inequalities are much sharper in the urban sector. Not only is there less of a difference between the two UC groups but the difference between them and the other groups is also quite significant. Moreover, the difference between the two UC groups and the others is visible throughout the distribution, showing that the upper castes outspend other communities at every level. Muslims and SCs are clearly the least privileged (measured by levels of spending on higher education) groups in urban India.

Table 8.14 provides yet another snapshot of economic inequalities across social groups, this time in terms of shares in aggregate expenditure on higher education and in total enrolment. The social gradations in Indian society are broadly

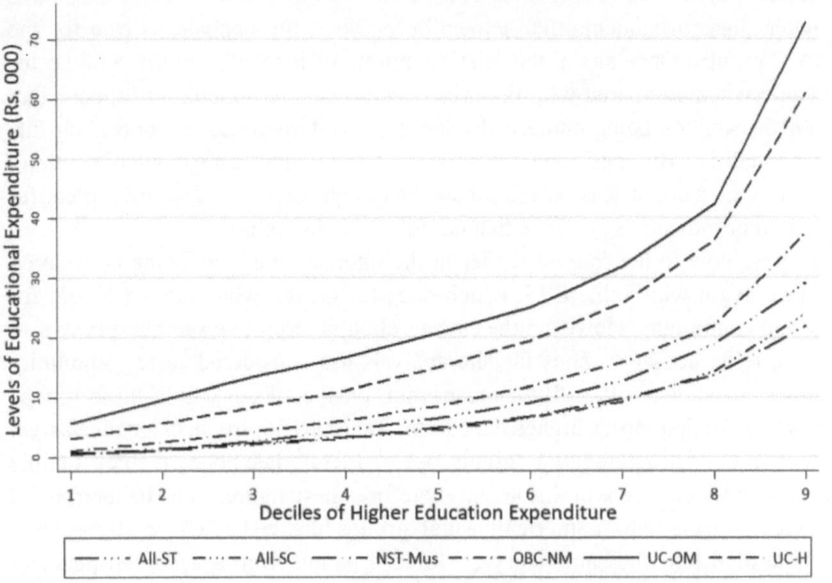

FIGURE 8.2 Deciles of Higher Education Expenditure by Social Groups, 2014, Urban

Source: See Figure 8.1.

TABLE 8.14 Community Shares in Total Expenditure and Total Students, 2014

Caste and community groups	*Rural*		*Urban*		*All India*	
	% Total Edu. Exp.	*% Total students*	*% Total Edu. Exp.*	*% Total students*	*% Total Edu. Exp.*	*% Total students*
All-Scheduled Tribes	8.9	12.6	5.1	7.6	6.1	9.8
All-Scheduled Castes	10.3	14.8	6.4	10.2	7.5	12.2
Non-ST-Muslims	8.3	8.2	8.8	11.2	8.8	9.9
OBC-Non-Muslims	37.5	36.2	29.2	30.5	32.2	33.0
UC-Other Minorities	7.5	2.6	4.9	3.3	6.0	3.0
UC-Hindu	27.5	25.6	44.2	37.2	38.9	32.0
All Groups	*100.0*	*100.0*	*100.0*	*100.0*	*100.0*	*100.0*

Source: Computed from unit-level data for the NSSO 71st Round survey.

reflected in the all-India columns, where all the groups from STs to OBCs have a higher share of students than expenditure, while the opposite is true for the two UC groups. Once again, the relative muting of inequality in the rural sector is visible when compared with the urban sector. It is reasonable to suppose that the OBC category, being numerically large and differentiated, is concealing further inequalities. But until robust methods of disaggregation are available nothing more may be said, at least at the macro level considered here, despite plentiful anecdotal or indicative evidence that confirms this hypothesis.

Turning now to the role of gender in the interaction effects being considered here, we begin with Table 8.15, which does for gender what Table 8.13 did for caste and community. However, the caveats about interpreting sample survey data must be reiterated here. Thus far, the analysis has considered caste-community groups as a whole, with a further restriction on the subset within these groups currently participating in higher education. Table 8.15 introduces gender as yet another level of disaggregation, giving rise to a legitimate concern about sample counts in individual cells at this level. Therefore, these figures must be interpreted with care, especially for numerically small groups like the UC-Other Minorities.[22]

Table 8.16 tells the same story as Table 8.14 but from a gendered perspective. In Table 8.14, we had looked at community shares in aggregate expenditure on higher education and in shares of aggregate enrolment, but without regard to gender; in Table 8.16, we are again looking at community shares, but this time, we are looking not at entire communities but at the share of women (in aggregate higher education expenditure and in community enrolment) within each community. Once again, we see that the female share of students is higher than the share of total expenditure for all groups in both sectors with the single exception of rural UC-Other Minorities. Table 8.16 reassures us that the picture presented in Table 8.15 is not an artefact.

But both tables are subject to the larger considerations involved in interpreting women's participation in higher education. Together with the enrolment data presented earlier in this chapter, the statistical evidence seems to suggest that women are a group who demonstrate the success of policy initiatives and point to a higher level of overall development. However, this suggestion cannot be taken

TABLE 8.15 Female Mean Expenditure on Higher Education as Percentage of Male, 2014

Social groups	*Rural*	*Urban*
All-Scheduled Tribes	87.1	75.6
All-Scheduled Castes	85.5	79.5
Non-ST-Muslims	64.8	65.1
OBC-Non-Muslims	94.4	78.5
UC-Other-Minorities	146.0	68.9
UC-Hindu	74.9	78.5
All Groups	*89.8*	*77.3*

Source: Unit-level data, NSSO 71st Round.

TABLE 8.16 Female Share of Total Expenditure and Total Students in Higher Education, by Social Groups, 2014

Social groups	*Rural*		*Urban*	
	% of total expenditure	*% of total students*	*% of total expenditure*	*% of total students*
All-Scheduled Tribes	36.8	40.1	43.8	51.2
All-Scheduled Castes	36.1	39.8	39.0	43.9
Non-ST-Muslims	26.5	35.3	32.0	41.9
OBC-Non-Muslims	36.7	38.0	39.0	44.7
UC-Other-Minorities	59.7	51.5	43.9	52.8
UC-Hindu	31.5	37.5	38.1	43.5
All Groups	*36.1*	*38.5*	*38.7*	*44.6*

Source: Computed from unit-level data, NSSO 71st Round.

at face value in the Indian context, where higher education for non-poor and/or upper-caste women performs peculiar functions that are easily misinterpreted. The 'narrowing of the gender gap' in Indian higher education does not represent 'empowerment' in any simple sense. Even where the numbers are strongly in favour of women—such as the UC-Other Minorities data in Tables 8.15 and 8.16—further contextualisation is needed to uncover their social meaning. This is especially true given two all-important facts that impact women's lives in India, namely, compulsory marriage and very low levels of paid employment.[23] To put it sharply, gender parity in higher education means little if advanced degrees are seen as an investment in the marriage market rather than in 'empowerment.'

4 Conclusion: what statistics can and cannot reveal

Against the historical backdrop of higher education as an engine of inequality-reducing mobility, and the more recent evidence of its 'massification' in India, the limited objective of this chapter is to examine the impact of statistical expansion on social inclusion as revealed by the available macro-data. The two main data sources used here are the All India Survey on Higher Education (AISHE) and the National Statistical Office (NSO, formerly the National Sample Survey Organisation, or NSSO) survey data. The period covered is mostly the past two decades, the specific years being determined by the survey years, particularly the NSSO surveys.

The statistics reveal that the most successful aspect of the massive expansion of Indian higher education is what may be termed as 'enrolment inclusion.' This is revealed by both the AISHE and NSSO data, and points—by and large—to the steady improvement in the overall Gross Enrolment Ratios, as well as the increased shares in enrolment of groups that were under-represented earlier. 'Enrolment inclusion' has been most prominent for women (when treated as a single homogenous category), and is true—more or less—for all other groups as well. However, Persons with Disability and Muslims remain severely under-represented in most sites of higher education even today, and the inclusion of women is uneven across caste, community, and class.

Statistics on the cost of higher education are harder to interpret because of their inherent complexity, but suggest overall that there has been a significant increase over the past 15 years. Though this has been difficult to establish clearly, the data suggest that the state's role in subsidising higher education has been eroded, so that the gap between costs at private and government institutions has been narrowing. However, privatisation has been a major engine driving costs, and as the private sector accounts for a larger and larger proportion of total enrolment, the cost of higher education is set to rise even more steeply in the near future. The changing dynamic of the field suggests that the distinction between public and private higher education needs to be reconsidered. Disaggregation by caste and community groups reveals continuing economic inequalities inflected by social identities. Though the rural sector has seen an overall narrowing of gaps between the poorer and the richer groups, in the urban sector, the caste gap remains sharp and seems to be resisting change.

A careful reading of the narrative presented by the macro data underlines the need for contextual understanding. The true meaning of statistics, that is, their real impact on social groups and on the life chances of individuals can only be understood through rigorous contextualisation. This obviously requires qualitative studies and ethnographic approaches, including accumulating insights on the role of higher education drawn from research that did not intend to study it. These 'accidental,' or more accurately transversal, insights could be quite useful in providing depth to the inevitable flatness of quantitative data.

Consider the questions raised earlier in connection with the gender data, for example. Unless we interpret them against a broader backdrop that includes the fall—alarming because of already low absolute levels—in the proportion of women who are able to obtain paid employment, the marked enrolment-inclusion of women would be grossly misinterpreted. This is not to say that these numbers become meaningless when juxtaposed with the employment data, but to insist that their meaning is not self-contained but depends crucially on the surrounding environment.

To take an equally important example, consider the data on the cost of education at different levels given in Tables 8.9 and 8.10. Taken at face value, these tables seem to show quite clearly that government institutions are less expensive than private ones, especially at the school level. However, the full meaning of these differences and their social impact requires information that is external to that data set. We need to know that government schooling has long been abandoned by all but the poorest groups, but government higher education remains in high demand, especially in elite institutions. We need to imagine a dynamic process that leads households to invest huge amounts in school education, particularly at the higher secondary level in order to access the relatively inexpensive higher education in government institutions. To put it differently, there may be very little continuity in terms of students between the higher secondary and the graduate and postgraduate levels of government institutions. At most well-regarded public universities and colleges, the severe competition for entry ensures that most of the student body will consist of those educated in expensive private schools. An ironic switching of places happens when those who went to government schools because they could not afford private schooling are forced into expensive private higher education of indifferent quality because they cannot score the impossibly high grades needed to enter public universities.

In sum, statistical data on social issues has the inevitable effect of 'dis-embedding' the data from its social context, without which its full meaning or implications can never be understood. This is the strength of social statistics—bracketing the social context to isolate specific quantitative information is a virtue, not a weakness or fault. We cannot expect statistics to do what they were not intended to do—it is the job of the researcher to counter the dis-embedding effect by re-inserting the data in its proper social context so that its meaning can reveal itself. This may require additional studies that use methods other than quantitative measurement and aggregation. The entire effort is by its nature collective rather than individual, requiring many scholars across many disciplines with many different methodological orientations.

It is this kind of collective multidisciplinary effort that is required in order to understand the global phenomenon of the 'massification' of higher education in its varied local contexts. This chapter seeks to be part of this larger effort at a time when a global pandemic has suddenly transformed—perhaps permanently—the very definition of 'higher education.'

Notes

1 In its broad contours, this is an old and well-known argument in India. See Jayaram (1979), who cites a version of this from the 1971 resolution on national policy on education, which in turn cites the Report of the Education Commission of 1964–1966. For a recent version of this argument, see Deshpande and Apoorvanand (2018).

2 There is a large literature; for an influential subset on one explanation—the theory of 'effectively maintained inequality' or EMI—see Lucas (2001, 2017); McKeever (2017).

3 See, for example, Mok and Jiang (2016) for China and Varghese (2015) for India.

4 The exemplary work of Tilak and Choudhary (2019) attempts to address similar questions based on an analysis of unit-level data from the 64th and 71st Rounds of the NSSO surveys. However, in this chapter, I take a slightly different approach and have more limited objectives.

5 For a more detailed version of the following argument, see Deshpande (2013).

6 The Planning Commission of India no longer exists, nor do five-year plans. According to the Ministry of Human Resource Development (MHRD), in 2006, 63.2% of higher education institutions were privately owned and they accounted for 51.5% of total enrolment in higher education (Planning Commission, 2008: 23).

7 For some of this data is only available from AISHE 2012–2013 onwards, hence the starting point of the comparison is slightly different in this table from that in earlier ones. Also, Stand-Alone institutions are excluded here for lack of robust data; some of the proportions may therefore not match those in other tables.
8 As per AISHE data, excluding Stand-Alone institutions.
9 Not shown in Table 3; these figures are based on AISHE 2012–2013 and 2018–2019, respectively.
10 These figures are broadly supported by NSO data which suggest that the split between private and public enrolment is roughly 54% and 46%, respectively. The NSO estimate includes both aided and unaided private institutions, at the graduate and above level (including diplomas), for ages up to 35 years. The difficulties of comparison between the NSO samples and the AISHE census-type data base are too complex to discuss here. See Statement 11 (RU) in NSO (2019: 26).
11 One caveat should be noted about categories like Muslims and Other Minorities, which in the AISHE surveys (as well as the NSSO surveys) only includes those Muslims (and Christians and Sikhs) who do not come under the official caste/tribe categories of SC, ST, or OBC. In other words, religion-based categories here are essentially the 'upper-caste' section of the community. However, in some of the NSSO surveys, unit-level data is made available, so researchers can do their own cross-tabulations, which is what I have done later in this chapter. But the AISHE data do not have this facility, so the published cross-tabulations must be used.
12 However, since the institutionally disaggregated data only became available in AISHE from 2011–2012, the initial time point of comparison is slightly different from Table 8.5, where it is 2010–2011.
13 Data on 'Stand Alone' institutions that offer diplomas and certificates lower than the bachelor's degree are not considered here as the data on them is incomplete and unreliable.
14 The total share of reservation seats cannot exceed 50% according to a 1993 Supreme Court judgement. Though some state governments have managed to circumvent this limitation, the odds are that if two-thirds of students are not from the UCH, then at least some are making it without benefit of reservation.
15 The three main NSO surveys used here are Education in India: 2007–2008, based on the 64th Round, results published in NSSO Report No. 532; Education in India 2014, based on the 71st Round, results published in NSSO Report No. 575; and Household Social Consumption on Education in India: 20017–2018, based on the 75th Round, results published in NSSO Report No. 585.
16 Computations (not shown here) based on Table 30 in Report No. 585 of 2020. See NSSO, 2020.
17 Sample counts for the postgraduate and above level: a) 64R, 2007–2008: 687, or 0.7% of those currently attending all levels of education; reference age group: 5–29 years; source: Table 11, Appendix A, p.A-113 in NSSO Report 532. b) 75R, 2017–2018: 3,937, or 1.3% of those currently attending at all levels of education; reference age group: 3–35 years; source: from Table 30, Appendix A, p. A-309 in NSSO Report 585. Note that reference age group is significantly higher (+6 years) for 2017–2018, which is particularly relevant for the postgraduate level, and hence partially explains the much higher sample size compared to 2007–2008.
18 Columns 4,7,10: Taken from 71R, Report 575, Education in India (published 2016), Appendix A, Table 36, 'Average expenditure (₹) per student during current academic session pursuing general course by level of education for each type of institution,' p.A-294; Columns 5,8,11: Taken from Statement 22, 'Average expenditure (₹) per student pursuing general education by levels of current attendance and type of institution,' in NSSO Report Key Indicators of Social Consumption in India: Education, based on NSSO 75th Round, July 2017 to June 2018 (published 2019), p. 27 [Note that reference age group is up to 35 years for 75th Round].

19 STs may include persons of any religion; SCs are restricted to Hindus, Sikhs, and Neo-Buddhists.

20 The intersection is relatively small. In the NSSO 2014 (71st Round) survey, less than 4% of rural Muslims are STs, and this figure drops to under 1% in the urban sector. Among STs, Muslims carry slightly more weight, being a little more than 4% in rural and about 2.5% in urban India in the 2014 survey sample.

21 The graphs in Figures 8.1 and 8.2 are based on unit-level data from the NSSO 71st Round survey of 2014. Prescribed sample weights are applied to obtain the deciles of educational expenditure, which are in current Rupees.

22 The cell counts for males and females in higher education for UC-OM are 97 and 103 in the rural and 151 and 169 in the urban sectors. These are the lowest cell counts among all groups, but UC-OM is the only group where the cell count for females is greater than that for males in both sectors. Thus, these results are usable, but must be treated with care.

23 See John (2012) and Kannan and Raveendran (2019) for elaboration of these points.

References

AISHE (various years). *All India Survey on India Higher Education*, Ministry of Human Resource Development, Government of India, New Delhi. Surveys are referred to by their reference years. The surveys for following years have been cited: 2010–11, 2011–12, 2012–13, 2018–19.

Altbach, P. G. (1968). "Student Politics and Higher Education in India," *Daedalus*, vol. 97(1), 254–273.

Deshpande, S. (2013). "Caste Quotas and Institutionalised Inclusion in Indian Higher Education," in Deshpande, S. and U. Zachariah eds., *Beyond Inclusion: The Practice of Equal Access in Indian Higher Education*, New Delhi: Routledge: 13–48.

Deshpande, S. and Apoorvanand (2018). "Exclusion in Indian Higher Education Today," in *India Exclusion Report 2017–18*, New Delhi: Centre for Equity Studies and Yoda Press: 191–218.

Dreze, J. and S. Amartya (2013). *An Uncertain Glory: India and its Contradictions*, Princeton: Princeton University Press.

Jayaram, N. (1979). "Higher Education, Inequality and Social Change in India," *Sociological Bulletin*, vol. 28(1–2), 46–58.

John, M. E. (2012). "Gender and Higher Education in the Time of Reforms," *Contemporary Education Dialogue*, vol. 9(2), 197–221.

Kannan, K. P. and G. Raveendran (2019). "From Jobless Growth to Job-Loss Growth: Gainers and Losers During 2012–18," *Economic and Political Weekly*, vol. LIV(44), 38–43.

Lucas, S. R. (2001). "Effectively Maintained Inequality: Educational Transitions, Track Mobility and Social Background Effects," *American Journal of Sociology*, vol. 106(6), 1642–1690.

Lucas, S. R. (2017). "An Archaeology of Effectively Maintained Inequality Theory," *American Behavioral Scientist*, vol. 61(1), 8–29.

McKeever, M. (2017). "Educational Inequality and Apartheid in South Africa," *American Behavioral Scientist*, vol. 61(1), 114–131.

Mok, K. H. and J. Jiang (2016). *Massification of Higher Education: Challenges for Admissions and Graduate Employment in China*, Working Paper No. 5, Centre for Global Higher Education, Economic and Social Research Council (ESRC), England.

NSO (2019). *Key Indicators of Household Social Consumption on Education in India*, New Delhi: National Statistical Office, Government of India.

NSSO (2010). *Education in India 2007–08: Participation and Expenditure*, National Sample Survey Organisation, Report No. 532, New Delhi: Ministry of Statistics and Programme Implementation, Government of India, May.

NSSO (2015). *Status of Education and Vocational Training in India, 2011–12*, National Sample Survey Organisation, Report No. 566, New Delhi: Ministry of Statistics and Programme Implementation, Government of India, September.

NSSO (2016). *Education in India 2014*, NSSO Report No. 575, New Delhi: Ministry of Statistics and Programme Implementation, Government of India, March.

NSSO (2020). *Household Social Consumption on Education in India*, NSSO Report No. 585, New Delhi: Ministry of Statistics and Programme Implementation, Government of India, July.

Planning Commission (2008). *Eleventh Five Year Plan 2007–2012*, "Social Sector", New Delhi: Government of India, vol. II.

Tilak, J. B. G. and P. K. Choudhary (2019). *Inequality in Access to Higher Education in India between the Poor and the Rich: An Analysis of 64th and 71st Rounds of NSSO Data (2007–08 and 2013–14*, Working Paper CSD 1/2019, New Delhi: Centre for Social Development.

Varghese, N. V. (2015). *Challenges of Massification of Higher Education in India*, CPRHE Research Papers No. 1, New Delhi: Centre for Policy Research in Higher Education, National University of Educational Planning and Administration.

9

EDUCATION TO INCLUDE THE FIRST EDUCATED GENERATION IN AN UNEQUAL SOCIETY IN BANGLADESH

Kazuyo Minamide

1 Introduction

> *Shamsu,*[1] *a friend of mine from a village in Jamalpur, a northern district of Bangladesh, decided to stop his education and migrate to work in the city when he passed the Higher Secondary Certificate (HSC). He had lost his drive to continue studying because he could not imagine what he would do even after higher education. His friends who had already started to earn money, predominantly working in the garment industry, also pressured his thoughts on the matter. Just before he left for Dhaka, he told me, 'After I got the HSC with my hard work, I feel sad to work at a garment factory and get the same salary as other workers who only graduated from primary school.'* [From my field notes in 2012]

In modern societies, 'Education for All' is unquestionably among the strongest slogans. Bangladesh is no exception. Rather, since independence in 1971, education has been targeted as a key factor for development. In particular, since the 1990s, governments and the private sector, including NGOs and local communities, have aimed for education expansion across the country (Jalaluddin et al., 1997; Unterhalter et al., 2003). As a result of multiple stakeholders' efforts, mass primary education has been achieved, making children the first in their family to attend a formal school, the so-called 'first educated generation.' Furthermore, since the beginning of this century, Bangladesh has experienced significant economic growth, which is largely attributable to the export-oriented garment industry and remittances from overseas Bangladeshi migrant workers. Because most wage labourers in garment factories are in their 20s, one might infer that the first educated generation, who started to attend school in their childhood in the 1990s, has contributed directly to economic growth. Consequently, according to the numbers, formal education appears to be successful in advancing economic growth at the national level.

DOI: 10.4324/9781003304760-12

However, when considering class-wise economic growth, the socio-economic gap has visibly expanded: the first educated generation, which has newly migrated from rural areas to urban cities, that is, the new class in the capitalist economy, is far from constituting 'the urban middle class,'[2] which has emerged in cities with a new lifestyle. Labourers, who strongly support economic growth with their large population, are motivated to attend schools in villages. They then migrate to work in the city; however, their educational experience is ineffective in regard to creating a better life.

If this is the case, then for whom and for what is this education intended? I conducted anthropological fieldwork in a rural village to examine individual experiences of the first educated generation from their childhood in the 2000s to the present day, when they are in their 20s. Similar to Shamsu, none highly regard work at the bottom of the global economy, predominantly in the ready-made garment industry. However, none deny the importance of education, although they are unable to enjoy the practical effectiveness of their own. How do they consume, understand, and accept their educational experiences in terms of their respective life strategies? As described herein, I would like to discuss the paths of their lives from their educational experience to their economic opportunity, particularly the paths chosen by young men.

Many academic and semi-academic studies have been conducted in Bangladesh to examine female garment workers (Kabeer and Mahmud, 2004; Siddiqi, 2000, 2009; Ashraf, 2017; Prentice and Neve, 2017) because most workers in the industry are women. Their problematic working conditions and social inequalities are discussed globally. In these contexts, male stakeholders usually appear to be counter-agencies forcing women to work in these difficult situations. However, a number of male workers also work in the industry, not only at the management level but also as these women's colleagues. Alternatively, they begin working as labourers initially and gradually improve their position. This chapter presents a specific examination of young men who, with their educational experience, migrate from rural villages to cities to seek job opportunities. In Bangladesh, a patriarchal society, men are presumed to be the main income earners at home. Economic independence is expected to be a priority in their lives. How their educational experience can improve their economic opportunities is expected to be crucially important for men to be independent. In this study, the different paths followed by men and women are also clarified.

First, the social background and uniqueness of the generation in question, those born in the 1990s in Bangladesh, must be explained. I discuss how education expansion has created an unequal structure and how the global economy has placed this generation, the so-called first educated generation, in a struggle between education and opportunity. Next, based on my fieldwork experience, I examine how subjectivity accepts the ideology of education and makes use of it for their respective life strategies. Education includes the first educated generation in the capitalist economy but not in a way in which they can enjoy their educational career. Nonetheless, they have ideologically accepted values of education and have alternatively had prospects for better lives in their villages, although the benefits are not yet specific.

2 The 1990s generation and their social background

The generation born in the 1990s in rural areas in Bangladesh was specifically examined in this study. As described earlier, this generation has mostly grown up during the rapid expansion of mass primary education. Following their education, many have migrated to work in urban areas to support national economic growth, which indicates that they are the key generation to examine the connectivity between education and economic growth in Bangladesh. I briefly characterise the social background of this generation from birth to the present.

The 1990s, 20 years after Bangladesh's independence in 1971, were the turning period of the country politically, economically, and socially. In 1990, after 15 years of autocracy, the combination of the longstanding 'people power' opposition movement and pressure from international donors secured the end of Ershad's rule (Lewis, 2011: 19). The first national election after liberation was then held. The generation born immediately after that is commonly designated as the 'post-autocracy' or 'post-Ershad regime' generation (Prashanta, 2013). Following the revival of democracy, the country has vacillated between socialism and capitalism, between secularism and Islamisation, and between nationalism and globalism (Van Schendel, 2009; Riaz, 2017).

Because Bangladesh received enormous amounts of international aid beginning immediately after independence, foreign support and donors retain a strong presence in people's daily lives. Under the neoliberal trend of development, donors who prefer 'civil society under a small state' partnered with NGOs without going through the government (Lewis, 2011: 110). The establishment of NGOs by local elites also became noticeable shortly after independence, and these NGOs have continued to grow. Both national and international NGOs have delivered global concerns directly to local people. In the 1990s, these NGOs focused mainly on rural development through various approaches. They emphasised the improvement of individual human capital to reduce poverty, and their development approaches have directly influenced people's lives and mindsets. With reference to Sobhan (2007), Lewis (2011: 161) noted that 'from a political economy perspective, an additional problem is that recent poverty-reduction efforts have preferred to focus on individualised approaches that seek to strengthen what Sobhan calls "the agency role of poor".' Poverty reduction efforts have emphasised decreasing infant mortality, increasing primary school enrolment, and improving socio-economic status of women through microcredit activity. These can be regarded as clearly responding to international organisations' 'Millennium Development Goals.' Bangladesh appears to be 'a success story' from the perspective of the global development industry. These individualised approaches are anticipated as important factors that can be used to assess how individuals of the first educated generation have personalised their educational experience and established their lives.

3 Education expansion with inequality

Among all development approaches, large-scale expansion of education across the country had the greatest impact on the generation of the 1990s. When Bangladesh emerged as a nation state in 1971, in its constitution, the state asserted a commitment to make educational equity for all its citizens as basic human rights. Also, education has been one of the most prior areas of intervention from the aid and development agencies. With the Convention on the Rights of the Child issued by the UN in 1989, the 'Education for All' conference held in Thailand in 1990 marked a turning point in the movement to promote basic education throughout the world. Furthermore, in human capital-based approaches, education enrolment itself has become the primary aim (Andaleeb et al., 2011).

Since Bangladesh's independence, primary education and improvement of the literacy rate have been pursued as top issues. Multiple providers have engaged in expanding formal education in various ways (Jalaluddin et al., 1997). As a result, schools of several different types—not only government schools and private schools but also non-formal primary education (NFPE) schools run by NGOs and madrasas, which are Islamic educational institutions—have emerged simultaneously since the beginning of the push to universalise education. Furthermore, students and their parents had to choose which school to attend (Minamide, 2005).

The overall school enrolment rate has increased due to the efforts of multiple stakeholders. The primary school enrolment rate in the 2000s (when the generation of the 1990s went to school) was approximately 95%. Moreover, with the support and pressure of international aid, the primary school enrolment rate for girls has increased dramatically, finally exceeding that of boys.

However, this diversity of schools in Bangladesh's education system has been criticised in terms of the quality of education that may be provided. The fact that each provider has motivated people to come to schools in different ways, responding to different people's interests, has also left gaps in educational quality. Substantial disparities have been discussed primarily among the three streams of education: the majority of schools that teach in Bengali, the English medium schools only for privileged children, and the madrasas.

As the enrolment rate rose, the quality gap became increasingly apparent. To standardise educational quality, in 2007, the government began administering a national examination, the Primary School Certificate (PSC), for students to take at the end of their five years of primary education. In 2010, it also began administering the Junior School Certificate (JSC) examination, which was taken in eighth grade. Both of these examinations are taken in addition to the completion exam for the Secondary School Certificate (SSC) after ten years of education. The exam system also shifted from memorising to selecting answers. However, the examination policy, which aimed to establish quality assurance, was confusing for schools, particularly in rural areas, and widened the existing disparities between urban and rural areas.

Contrary to the stated goal of providing primary education, seats in secondary schools are limited. Many students who graduate from primary schools have no access to higher levels of education. One reason may be the limited number of stakeholders involved in secondary education, as development approaches primarily emphasise basic education and NGOs have no authority to run secondary schools. Symbolically, the government administration is also divided between the Ministry of Primary and Mass Education and the Ministry of Education which administers secondary education and beyond.

Despite the limitations in the improvement of secondary education, higher education reform has been implemented since the 1990s. Public universities have increased in number from 9 in 1991 to 50 in 2022 and are primarily located in urban settings. In addition, once the private university act was enacted in 1992, private universities began to open in cities. Today, 108 institutions operate in Bangladesh.

On the other hand, in rural areas, affiliated colleges under the National University have been increasing rapidly since the 2000s. Unlike other public universities, these colleges have no authority to organise their curriculum or conduct exams. They are dependent on their affiliating board at the National University for all curricula and exams. There are two types of affiliated colleges: honours colleges and degree colleges. Honours colleges offer four-year courses for undergraduate education and one-year master's degree programme, whereas degree colleges are an extension of secondary education in the arts, sciences, and commerce, with three-year courses for undergraduate education and two-year master's degree programmes. In rural areas, degree colleges are more popular among those who aim to obtain a certificate by taking exams without regularly attending classes. Many male students work in cities and return just before annual exams, whereas female students who have already married study at home and take exams.

Considerable differences exist between public and private universities and affiliated colleges as well as between honours and degree colleges in terms of the content of the education and the lifestyle of the students. Although students at many universities today, both public and private, are from different districts across the country, after migrating from their original communities to urban cities, they live in dormitories with their friends and enjoy a so-called 'campus life.' They gain knowledge, networks of new friends and contacts, and perhaps a new sense of values that clearly differ from those prevalent in rural communities. After acquiring this new intellectual and social capital, they attempt to climb the social class ladder. Although they are not guaranteed gainful employment, at a minimum, they can imagine working in a 'white-collar job' and target that as a goal. However, the number of such students is extremely limited (Oshikawa and Minamide, 2016).

Figure 9.1 depicts the shortcomings of universal education, most prominently that most individuals from the 1990s generation quickly disappear from the education stage after completing primary school. More than half leave education by the end of tenth grade, and only 4% remain enrolled at the stage of higher education.

It can be said that universal education has actively instilled the educational ideology in the 1990s generation; however, they appear to retain it only in regard to

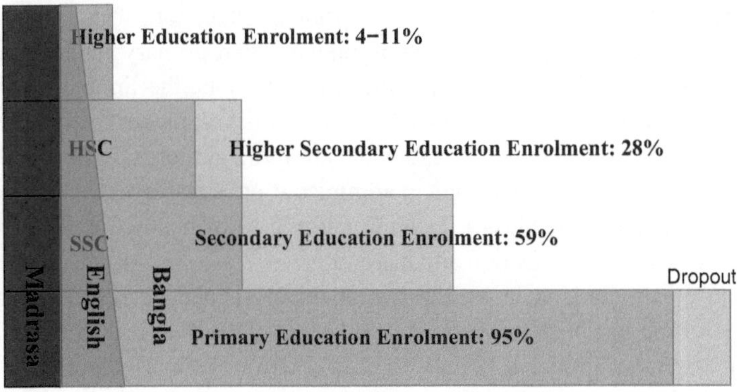

FIGURE 9.1 Education System and Enrolment in Bangladesh

Source: BANBEIS (2011, 2018).

the primary education level. The lack of qualitative standardisation among types of schools and the quantitative gap separating primary and secondary education, as described earlier, constrain their opportunities.

The job market in contemporary Bangladesh is biased: it is centred on a particular industry and lacks a step-by-step social structure to reward educational experience. I further elucidate this difficulty in the next section.

4 Unwilling opportunity in a global economy

Bangladesh's economy has grown at an annual rate of over 6% consistently since 2004. The country is considered one of the 'next 11' countries that are expected to promote economic growth in the twenty-first century, along with BRICS (Brazil, Russia, India, China, and South Africa). However, this economic growth has been attributable almost entirely to two sources: remittances from overseas migrant workers and the ready-made garment industry.

According to data from 2017, more than one million workers from Bangladesh are engaged in overseas employment in several countries, predominantly Middle Eastern countries, primarily as semi-skilled or unskilled labourers (BBS, 2018: 96). Within the country, more than four million workers are employed at over 5000 garment factories (BBS, 2018: 98). Although agriculture is Bangladesh's major industry, employing 40.6% of the population, manufacturing is growing rapidly, currently accounting for 14.4% of the labour force. The ready-made garment industry, including apparel and knitwear, constitutes 45.5% of the manufacturing industry (BBS, 2018: 187) and accounts for 82% of national exports (BBS, 2018: 98). Currently, the country is the second-largest ready-made garment exporter in the world.

However, severe and problematic working conditions in factories that have not been adequately improved are discussed not only outside Bangladesh but also within its society. Industrial tragedies such as building collapses and factory fires have laid bare such factories' working conditions and have invited pressure to develop both domestic and international initiatives focused on improving them (Barua and Ansary, 2017; Siddiqi, 2016). However, 'although initiatives . . . improve building safety and create new mechanisms for expressing worker grievances, they leave untouched the fundamental conditions of the industry: long hours and punishing conditions, with very little leverage for workers to change their circumstances' (Ashraf and Prentice, 2019: 105). That is the case because 'Bangladesh's comparative advantage in the global economy is its low labor costs,' and 'this labor has been actively cheapened by processes of labor precarization: suppressing mobilization and keeping wages and labour standards low' (Ashraf and Prentice, 2019: 101).

Despite the severe reality and even negative image of such factories, hundreds of thousands of young people from villages, who often have no better option, continue to migrate to work in them. According to Ashraf,

> the rapid expansion of the sector depended on a mass influx of workers from rural areas into Dhaka's factories and employs more than four million workers, of whom nearly 80% are women, and who are rated among the world's cheapest labour force.
>
> *(Ashraf, 2017: 82)*

Therefore, these individuals have been ideologically motivated to attend schools in a system that includes considerable disparities beginning at the primary level. A quantitative limitation of secondary education and beyond exists. Moreover, the emerging job markets for the new class are also biased, emphasising the garment industry, which is strongly influenced by the global economy and which forces workers to subsist as low-wage labourers. Less than 4% of the generation can realise professions based on their educational experience and 96% cannot enjoy the effectiveness of their educational experience in their professional lives.

In a sense, the development approaches coloured by the global trend of human capital improvement have, ironically, created 'the world's cheapest labour forces' in the global economy. Have they been included in education solely for the sake of the global economy? This was not the intention. How, then, do they understand and utilise their educational experiences over the course of their lives? In the next section, based on my field research results, I introduce their perspectives and prospects for a better life.

5 Rural youth, their limited education and their temporary jobs

From 2000 to the present, I have conducted anthropological research in rural Bangladesh, including year-long fieldwork. Specifically examining children's socialisation and the effects of their educational experience on the course of their lives, I followed particular groups of children from childhood to adolescence and early adulthood. During long-term observation in 2000 and 2003–2004, I experienced everyday life in a rural village. I attended a primary school founded in 1991 by a Bangladeshi NGO called Basic Development Partners (BDP). I studied in a fourth-grade classroom with my 'classmates,' who were my interlocutors (Minamide, 2014). Since then, I followed the life courses of 38 children (19 boys and 19 girls): 22 students who were in the fourth grade in 2000 and 16 students who were in the fourth grade in 2003 (Oshikawa and Minamide, 2016). Their family backgrounds were similar: their parents were engaged primarily in agriculture, either farming their own land or as employees of landowners. Most of the children I followed were of the first educated generation in their respective families, creating a massive gap in educational experience between them and their parents (Minamide, 2015: 36–37). After graduating from primary school, most went directly to high school; however, a large number left before completing secondary education.

Figure 9.2 depicts the educational level attained by all 38 children according to enrolment level. Although many of the children (30 of 38) who graduated from primary school proceeded to high school (secondary education), nine left before completion. In all, 21 students completed secondary education up to the tenth grade (17 without repeating a year and 4 repeating in the middle). About 60% (13) of students who completed education up to the tenth grade passed the SSC exam.

For most rural youth, SSC appears to be the last point at which they retain their school lives. Many girls got married after SSC, irrespective of whether they passed; moreover, many young men started to work regardless of whether they were enrolled in a college. Only three students passed the HSC without a gap. Only one male student went on to an honours college. None of my 38 friends[3] went on to study at a university.

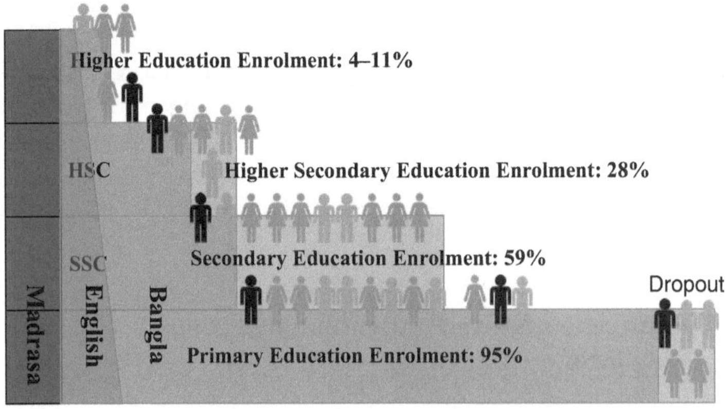

FIGURE 9.2 Mapping the Educational Experience of 38 Children

Sources: BANBEIS (2011, 2018) and author's survey from 2000 to 2016.

Although their turning points for deciding to leave education are diverse, overall, many of the young men migrated to cities to work in garment factories, whereas many young women got married. Although 70–80% of the workers in Bangladesh's garment factories are women, most urban migrants from my research area were young men. Only 2 of the 19 girls worked in the city. The geographical features of their home villages in eastern Jamalpur might explain this unusual situation. The land elevation in the area is higher than that in other districts in Bangladesh. Rice cultivation is active throughout the year. Seasonal labour migration to urban areas used to be common practice in Bangladesh during the rainy season when it was difficult to cultivate the land, but the lower risk of flooding in this area means that the people there have not needed to migrate seasonally (Minamide, 2015: 36). Today, however, because the demand for cash income has increased and because job opportunities other than agriculture are few in the village, men (the family breadwinners) tend to migrate to the cities, where they can get jobs. Apart from cases of extreme poverty, women do not migrate to work; rather, they maintain their family life in the village.

Boys left the village at various points, sometimes returning once and leaving again (Minamide, 2015: 41). Among the 19 young men in all, 10 are working in and around Dhaka and 6 live in the village. Although they moved to Dhaka at different times, most are working in the garment industry under similar conditions. They were frustrated initially to work under the same conditions, irrespective of their varying educational levels (Minamide, 2015: 42).

As described earlier, jobs in the ready-made garment industry, where many young men work, are not viewed in a positive light because of the severe working conditions, including low wages. In addition, as described by Shamsu at the beginning of this chapter, because their educational background is irrelevant, it is not a job they want to have after completing some level of education. Rather, many young people take such work as a 'temporary job' because they have no better alternative (Minamide, 2018). Moreover, since the 1980s, the average age of workers in the garment industry has remained in the mid-20s, demonstrating that working in garment factories is a way for young people to spend their transient youth period. Many friends from the village are now working in garment factories, but none plan to continue doing so as their life work.

6 Temporary strategies and plans for a 'better life'

How have these individuals accepted their present situation working in the garment industry? What prospects do they have for their future?

Despite the lack of a direct correlation between their educational attainment and their ability to work in specific jobs, none of my friends from the village denied the importance of their educational experience, believing that it will contribute to improving their future. Some regret having stopped their education midcourse and a few continue to seek opportunities to return to school for higher education. A young man who passed the SSC examination and started working in a garment factory told me, 'I studied at school to be a good man, not to destroy my life. Based on my educational experience, I can try my best to obtain a better life.' Although they cannot imagine the specific benefits that their education will have for their life courses, they generate some meaning for education on their own and adopt it as necessary in their lives. Next, I introduce several cases illustrating how they compromise in regard to their present situation and how they consider their future plans.

The case of Zakir

Zakir, a friend in the village, migrated to the city to work at a garment factory after passing the SSC. He worked for one and a half years but subsequently gave up and returned home once. He migrated again after several months and then married a woman in his original village several years later. He now lives and works in the city by himself; his wife lives in the village with her family-in-law. Zakir regularly sends remittances to his family. His father was able to buy agricultural land and rebuild their house with these remittances.

Similar to others, Zakir wants to return to his village and start a business after working in the city for a couple of years and saving money. Recently, he told me, 'I will return to the village after earning money in Dhaka for a few more years, but I will not be able to do agriculture like my father. It's too tough! I will start some agriculture-based business. I am thinking of cultivating fish in our ponds.' He then asked me if I had any information regarding how and where he might be able to train for such a business.

The case of Faruk

Another young man, Faruk, appears to be more settled with his job in the city than Zakir. His father, a rickshaw driver in the village, suddenly passed away when Faruk was studying in seventh grade. Due to the loss of his father's support, he abandoned his education and migrated to the city of Dhaka, where he began working in a garment factory, to support his family as the only son. Soon thereafter, he moved to a T-shirt printing factory, where he received a slightly better salary than at the garment factory, although he had to work for 12 hours a day, including a 1-hour break, in day/night shifting. First, he was a helper supporting a machine operator. He then gradually acquired skills sufficient to become an operator. During the 12 years since he started to work in the industry, he has continued to job-hop among seven factories after receiving information regarding factories with better hiring conditions, particularly a better salary. In the intervals, while he was transferring jobs, he spent some time in the village to rest. Now, because a labour force for the garment industry is in high demand in Bangladesh, he has been able to find work easily with his experience and proper skills. Nevertheless, he was never satisfied with his working conditions. He told me that he could have received a better salary if he had an SSC certificate when he moved from his fifth workplace to his sixth. His explanation indicates that such individuals' educational career can result in a better salary but only when they already have professional skills.

Although Faruk seems to be building his career step by step in the city, his prospects have remained in the village. Recently, he married a village woman whom his family chose as his partner. Before his marriage, he planned to rebuild his house, where his mother lived alone. His new family would also live there in the future. To my knowledge, over the last five years, he has been saving money for his house. Although he has not yet decided whether he will return to the village or continue living in the city, his sense of belonging clearly lies in the village.

The case of Shimul

Even with no idea regarding specific possible jobs, some young men attempt to earn a degree at a degree college and seek opportunities for better jobs while working in garment factories. Another young man, Shimul, spent several years in the village seeking white-collar job opportunities after completing his HSC. He searched job advertisements in newspapers and applied to jobs he found and asked his relatives and peers, including me, to introduce any opportunity but experienced no success. He ultimately began working in a garment factory but continued his studies at a degree college to obtain a degree. As described earlier, degree colleges do not have regular classes; the students attend college only before and during the annual exams. He obtains permission from his employer to be absent from work for a month (without salary) and returns to the college to take the exams. He believes that getting a degree can help him to get jobs that are better than his garment job. When I asked him what type of job would be a possibility, he mentioned being an NGO worker.

The case of Apu

Apu has already returned to the village. He stopped his education immediately after completing primary education and was then trained as a woodworking carpenter in the village. After a few years of carpentry training, he migrated to Dhaka, where he subsequently worked in the garment industry for four years. He then returned to the village and began working at a carpentry workshop. Recently, he has been working independently as a carpenter to receive orders in the village directly. When I inquired as to prospects for his future, he immediately responded to me, 'I am happy if I can continue to live in this way.'

The case of Salam

Salam is a tinsmith. He dropped out of school in the fourth grade and began working at his elder brother's bakery in the town near the village. He shifted jobs one after another before being trained as a tinsmith. During the five years preceding the interview, he had apparently settled as a tinsmith in the village, where he runs his workshop with a small number of staff members. However, he is waiting for a chance to migrate overseas as his next step. He told me,

> It would be difficult to run a household without earning abroad. I want to migrate overseas for several years and save money; then, I will start any business in the village. That is the quickest way to be successful in my life.

If I were to rank them by educational career, then Shimul (and Shamsu, who was introduced in the introduction), with his HSCs, would be considered more educated than others, followed by Zakir with an SSC, Faruk, who studied up to seventh grade, Apu, who only completed primary education, and Salam, who dropped out of fourth grade. Except for Salam, they have all experienced work in urban settings, primarily in the garment industry. Although their starting salaries differed depending on the timing with which they began working (the base salary has been revised relative to inflation year by year), their educational careers did not alter their initial working conditions. None were willing to work in the industry. For most of them, except for Apu, who had already returned to his home village and started his own business, it seems that 'temporariness' is the common mindset that they employ to accept their present situation. They seek better opportunities for their future. Although they have experienced work in urban settings, they have no model for their future in the city. Their prospects, such as engaging in agriculture-based business or working as NGO workers, have been imagined in rural contexts. Even overseas migration is regarded as a process of doing business in the village. The geographical features of their respective villages, with the potential for active agriculture, might also enable them to retain their identity as well as their future prospects in the village.

However, it might be said that even their involuntary temporary strategy serves as one stage in their respective life paths, which is markedly different from the situation for female workers. As Ashraf (2017) has argued, women who have experienced working in the garment industry, called 'garment girls,' are regarded negatively in society as 'extremely poor' people who have no means to subsist other than working in the industry. Some conservatives even present negative images of them: they do not follow the gender-related social norms in terms of their working conditions. The case at my research site has also indicated that it would be more acceptable for women to get married earlier even without income than to work and earn money in the garment industry. In contrast, whether extremely poor or not, all men are expected to gain economic independence before marriage. They cannot marry without earning income through some type of job. Although the image of young men working in the garment industry is also unfavourable, temporary engagement in the industry is still recognised as a process by which they seek independence.

7 Conclusion

The contemporary young generation born in the 1990s in Bangladesh has been the target of continuous development initiatives and has been involved in education. However, the improvement of individual human capital, but without preparing opportunities to use that capital, has brought about frustration among the first educated generation. Although the universalisation of education has motivated them to aim for 'better lives,' certain structures are preventing the value of that education from being universally enjoyed. The lack of standardisation among types of schools and the lack of a step-by-step social structure that would allow individuals to achieve according to their educational attainment limit their opportunities. In particular, although many young people work in the garment industry, global economic forces always place them at the bottom in terms of providing cheap labour without appreciating their educational background. In addition, because the economy of contemporary Bangladesh has been overly dependent on this single industry, such individuals have lacked variation in their job opportunities that would allow them to enjoy step-by-step achievement.

It can be said that the first educated generation has been included in a meritocratic society that places value on individual academic careers. Nevertheless, from the very beginning, the opportunities that they have newly received at school are far from equal in both quantitative and qualitative terms. Whereas the education systems and situations shape their opportunities, the development approach to individual human capital under the neoliberal trends imbues them with the discourse of 'self-responsibility.' As a result, they are forced to struggle with their situation, such as by working in the garment industry, on their own. Their approach to managing this unsatisfactory situation is to assume it as temporary. Although they cannot yet imagine the goal of that temporary situation, the ideology of education keeps them focused on their prospects for a better future.

Acknowledgement

This study was funded by the Japan Society for the Promotion of Science, project fund 16KK0045.

Notes

1 All names in this chapter are pseudonyms to preserve privacy.

2 The emergence and impact of the 'urban middle class' in relation to Bangladesh's economy have been discussed by numerous scholars. However, the focal class to discuss in this chapter is quite different from that phenomenon.

3 As I explained in regard to the methodology by which I conducted my fieldwork, I have built a relationship/rapport with my interlocutors since their childhood, and I believe that they have accepted me as their friend. In this sense, I use the term 'friend' to refer to my interlocutors.

References

Andaleeb, S. S., H. R. Khan, and M. Ahmed eds. (2011). *Education and National Development: Selected Papers from the 2008 and 2009 Conferences on Bangladesh at Harvard University*, Dhaka: The University Press Limited.

Ashraf, H. (2017). The Threads of Time in Bangladesh's Garment Industry: Coercion, Exploitation and Resistance in a Global Workplace, *Ethno Scripts*, vol. 19(2), 81–106.

Ashraf, H. and R. Prentice (2019). "Beyond Factory Safety: Labor Unions, Militant Protest, and the Accelerated Ambitions of Bangladesh's Export Garment Industry," *Dialectical Anthropology*, vol. 43(1), 93–107. https://doi.org/10.1007/s10624-018-9539-0

BANBEIS (Bangladesh Bureau of Educational Information and Statistics). (2011). *Bangladesh Education Statistics 2010*, Dhaka: Ministry of Education.

BANBEIS (Bangladesh Bureau of Educational Information and Statistics) (2018). *Bangladesh Education Statistics 2017*, Dhaka: Ministry of Education.

Barua, U. and M. A. Ansary (2017). "Workplace Safety in Bangladesh Ready-Made Garment Sector: Three Years after the Rana Plaza Collapse," *International Journal of Occupational Safety and Ergonomics*, vol. 23(4), 578–583.

BBS (Bangladesh Bureau of Statistics) (2018). *Statistical Yearbook Bangladesh 2017*, Dhaka: Ministry of Planning.

Jalaluddin, A. K., A. Mushtaque, and R. Chowdhury eds. (1997). *Getting Started: Universalizing Quality Primary Education in Bangladesh*, Dhaka: The University Press Limited.

Kabeer, N. and S. Mahmud (2004). "Globalization, Gender and Poverty: Bangladesh Women Workers in Export and Local Markets," *Journal of International Development*, vol. 16, 93–109.

Lewis, D. (2011). *Bangladesh: Politics, Economy and Civil Society*, New York: Cambridge University Press.

Minamide, K. (2005). "Children Going to Schools: School-Choice in a Bangladeshi Village," *Journal of the Japanese Association for South Asian Studies*, vol. 17, 174–200.

Minamide, K. (2014). *'Kodomo iki' no jinruigaku: banguradeshu nouson syakai no kodomotati (Anthropology of 'Child-sphere': Children in a Bangladesh's Rural Society)*, Kyoto: Showa-do. (in Japanese)

Minamide, K. (2015). "The First Educated Generation as 'Social Transformers' in Rural Bangladesh: An Overview from Their Childhood to Adolescence in a Village of Jamalpur," *Nrivijnana Patrika (Journal of Anthropology)*, vol. 20, 33–51.

Minamide, K. (2018). "Seeking *New Life* in Bangladesh: Do Rural Migrating Youth 'Urbanize' after Moving to the City?" *Nrivijnana Patrika (Journal of Anthropology)*, vol. 23, 11–26.

Oshikawa, F. and K. Minamide eds. (2016). *'Gakkouka' ni mukau minami ajia: kyouiku to syakai henyo ('Schoolized Society' in South Asia: Education and Social Change)*, Kyoto: Showa-do. (in Japanese)

Prashanta, T. (2013). "Defining a Generation: Making Sense of Our Lives and Times, Before and Beyond Shahbagh," https://opinion.bdnews24.com/2013/03/03/defining-a-generation-making-sense-of-our-lives-and-times-before-and-beyond-shahbagh/

Prentice, R. and G. D. Neve eds. (2017). *Unmaking the Global sweatshop: Health and Safety of the World's Garment Workers*, Philadelphia, PA: University of Pennsylvania Press.

Riaz, A. (2017). *Lived Islam & Islamism in Bangladesh*, Dhaka: Prothoma Prokashan.

Siddiqi, D. (2000). "Miracle Worker or Woman Machine? Tracking (Trans) National Realities in Bangladeshi Factories," *Economic and Political Weekly*, vol. 35(21–22), L11–L17.

Siddiqi, D. (2009). "Do Bangladeshi Factory Workers Need Saving? Sisterhood in the Post-Sweatshop Era," *Feminist Review*, vol. 91(1), 54–174.

Siddiqi, D. (2016). "Before Rana Plaza: Toward a History of Labor Organizing in Bangladesh's Garment Industry," in Crinis, V. and A. Vickers eds. *Labour in the Clothing Industry in the Asia Pacific*, London: Routledge: 60–79.

Sobhan, R. (2007/2010). *Challenging the Injustice of Poverty: The Need for Structural Change in South Asia*, New Delhi: SAGE Publications India.

Unterhalter, E. et al. (2003). "A Fragile Dialogue? Research and Primary Education Policy Formation in Bangladesh 1971–2001," *Compare*, vol. 33(1), 85–99.

Van Schendel, W. (2009). *A History of Bangladesh*, Cambridge: Cambridge University Press.

10

BECOMING DALIT

Ambedkarite Movements and Inter-caste Marriages in and Around Nagpur

Tatsushi Nemoto

At 11:30 am on 8 March 2019, I interviewed a Dalit woman, U.M., who had married a Muslim man, C.K., in 2012.[1] We met in the living room of a common friend's house. The friend had left for work, leaving his wife, son, daughter, and us. The woman, a former Buddhist, talked about her marriage: 'Both families opposed our dating and crises arose repeatedly. My family was often informed by others that we were seen together. And every time my paternal uncle heard this, he would beat me without asking me anything. One day, my paternal uncle suddenly started repeatedly thrashing my right leg with a teacup.' U.M. peered into my eyes and caressed her right leg as she spoke: 'My paternal uncle never listened to me and beat me almost every day. All my family members were opposed to our dating. Even now, when I think about it, I feel very scared.' U.M. clutched her head in her hands as she wept.

1 'Dalit' as an open category

This chapter explores the word 'Dalit,' which has undergone numerous redefinitions in India, to present a viewpoint called 'Becoming Dalit' by combining discussions of Dalit Studies—especially Dalit feminism—with scholarship on inter-caste marriages. As a first step, we examine the category of 'Dalit.' According to Guru, 'categories have a trajectory of their own' and 'travel along a path full of challenges, counter-challenges, contradictions, and transformations' (Guru, 2001: 97). Hence, these categories 'change their meaning, connotation, and significance from time to time and place to place, depending upon the specific socio-economic and ideological context, and the politics of the users who formulate them' (Guru, 2001: 97). Therefore, when discussing a category, rather than applying a monolithic, fixed meaning to it, one must consider: the local historical, social, and political contexts; the relation between categories; the positions that

DOI: 10.4324/9781003304760-13

users occupy and discuss the category's transformation process. These discussions may enable us to predict how these categories will be redefined in the future.

The word Dalit, which literally means 'broken,' is primarily used to refer to those castes in India that have historically been subjected to the practice of 'untouchability.' That is, the category of 'Dalit' is rooted in the historical, social, and political experiences of the 'untouchables.' However, the term does not include only those castes; 'its great capacity to reach out to larger sections of people' must be recognised (Guru, 2001: 99). Similarly, Dhanda emphasises that the word Dalit is not a synonym for ex-untouchables or Scheduled Castes (SCs) but 'a political term of self-reference' that can involve all 'oppressed' peoples (Dhanda, 2012: 101). Thus, while the word Dalit is derived primarily from the experiences of ex-untouchables, there are certain blank spaces at the edge of its definition that leaves the category open to reinterpretation. Moreover, as Rao states, the Dalit category makes evident '*the historical structures and practices of dispossession that experientially mark someone as Dalit*,' and simultaneously, it designates '*someone seeking to escape those same structures*' (emphasis in original) (Rao, 2009: 16). Put simply, Dalits are not only those who are exposed to discrimination but also those who protest these discriminations.

Dalit feminism is the 'most powerful challenge' to the seemingly undifferentiated category of 'woman' in India since the mid-1990s (Velaskar, 2016: 392). It has contributed towards redefining the category of Dalit. Dalit feminism emphasises that 'Dalit women' do not occupy the same place as dominant-caste Hindu women in society. When Dalit women raise demands for 'women's unity' alongside dominant-caste Hindu women, it obscures the oppression that Dalit women are subjected to, in the patriarchal caste hierarchy as ex-untouchables. Simultaneously, Dalit women cooperating with Dalit men for Dalit unity obscures 'the more intimate forms of control by dalit men over the sexual and economic labour of "their" women' (Rao, 2003: 1). Therefore, Dalit women must 'talk in a different way' (Guru, 1995: 2548). Subordinated by caste hierarchy, gender inequality, and the economic class pyramid, Dalit women are triply burdened; furthermore, they are bound by multiple societal norms. Rege designates this situation as 'multiple patriarchies' (Rege, 2003: 95). Despite being called Dalit, the experiences of Dalit women are not commensurate with those of Dalit men. Dalit feminism has enabled the reinvention of the male-created definition of Dalit by examining the perspective of Dalit women.

2 Caste hierarchy and inter-caste marriage

In 'a long history that ranges from the debates on *sati* and the age of consent in the nineteenth and early twentieth centuries, to child marriage and rape in contemporary times, the question of women's capacity to consent and the meanings of "consent" outside of marriage' have been matters of public debate (Krishnan, 2015: 68). Inter-caste marriage has been a major part of this debate. According to Uma Chakravarti, caste hierarchy and gender inequality are 'the organising principles of the Brahmanical social order,' and the purity of women guarantees the purity of a caste and its position in the caste hierarchy (Chakravarti, 1993: 579, 585). Similarly, Chowdhry observes that the control of female sexuality is at the centre of caste and kinship codes, and 'bestowal of this sexuality in marriage is critical to patriarchal forces and their concern with caste purity, caste status, power, and hierarchy' (Chowdhry, 1997: 1019). Male relatives, such as fathers, uncles, and brothers, maintain the purity of the caste and the hierarchical order by controlling women's sexuality and by finding marriage partners for women from within a socially acceptable community. Therefore, 'caste ideology (endogamy) is the very basis of the regulation and organisation of women's sexuality' (Rege, 2003: 94–95).

In societies where such norms circulate, an arranged marriage, where parents select their child's marriage partner, is considered more ideal than a love-based marriage. Whereas an arranged marriage is considered 'a religious ritual' that is approved by family, relatives, and the community, and is 'blessed by God with the gift of love,' a love marriage is widely considered 'a most unholy union' (Mody, 2008: 8). The cases that raise more violent condemnation among love marriages are inter-caste marriages, especially those in which there are elopements (Chowdhry, 1997: 1022). Inter-caste marriage of a female family member signifies to the male relatives of the woman that they have no control over her sexuality. Indeed, the 'ideology of female guardianship is essentially an ideology of control' (Chowdhry, 1997: 1025); however, the opposition to love marriage is often masked as 'concern' of the family about 'cultural differences' with people from other castes, thus effectively concealing patriarchal norms while preserving caste boundaries. What is viewed as most dishonourable is the case of 'a high-caste woman involved with a lower-caste man' (Chakravarti, 1993: 584). Elopements of caste Hindu women with Dalit men often engender violent reactions.

As indicated by several studies, the primary issues related to inter-caste marriages are 'honour' and 'masculinity' (Chowdhry, 1997, 2004, 2007; Rao, 2003). The masculinity of the caste is outlined 'both by the degree of control men exercise over women and the degree of passivity of the women of the caste' (Kannabiran and Kannabiran, 1991: 2131). A woman who transgresses the norms of caste endogamy by eloping with a lower-caste man 'not only breaches and damages this "male honour" but also underlines the value she herself places on such a concept' (Chowdhry, 2004: 84). Thus, love marriage couples are engaged in a 'silent revolution' (Dhanda, 2012) that attempts to push the limits of 'Indian' morality and 'Indian' marriage (Mody, 2002: 255). However, women who violate the norms of arranged marriage are abused in their immediate surroundings as 'sexually promiscuous' and attract little sympathy from family members or local communities, even when the couple faces marital problems (Grover, 2009: 29). As bringing back a runaway girl, who undermines local norms, into the traditional network of a wider community is often difficult (Chowdhry, 2004: 78), 'physical elimination of the girl can be the only "honourable" option' for her family and relatives (Chowdhry, 2004: 78). Thus, a woman attempts to rewrite the multiple patriarchies and demonstrate her agency by choosing an inter-caste marriage. However, this results in her losing her social connections with her family and confronting the risk of a violent situation.

3 Becoming Dalit

This chapter attempts to synthesise aspects of Dalit feminism with those of studies on inter-caste marriage, to discuss the phenomenon of becoming Dalit. Drawing from the discussion on 'becoming minoritarian' (Deleuze and Guattari, 2013: 339) presented in *A Thousand Plateaus*, the chapter views becoming Dalit as a means of filling the blank spaces in the definition of the category of Dalit and thereby, redefining it. According to Guru, various categories that have the same objective and share 'the same positive utopia of creating a society free from coercion, exploitation, and dehumanization' represent multiple Dalit identities (Guru, 2001: 107). This outlook necessitates redefining the category of Dalit for a common purpose through tension-filled negotiations among these various categories. For example, according to Rege, the category known as 'Dalit women' should not be considered 'an automatically unitary group' that confronts the 'same problems,' but as an emerging group 'in a context of struggles and a viable oppositional alliance' (Rege, 2006: 77). This perspective leads to reconsiderations regarding the definitions of the categories 'Dalit' and 'Dalit women.' The negotiations among these categories have led to a revision of the meaning of Dalit, allowing it to potentially reach 'the level of social ontology' (Guru, 2001: 105).

Deleuze and Guattari's discussion about 'becoming' elucidates the meaning of this alliance. According to them, the alliance is not a correspondence between relations, a resemblance, an imitation, or an identification (Deleuze and Guattari, 2013: 277). Instead, it implies 'two simultaneous movements,' or 'an asymmetrical and indissociable block of becoming' (Deleuze and Guattari, 2013: 340). Dipesh Chakrabarty's argument on 'fragments' further elucidates their discussion. According to Chakrabarty, we visit the subaltern not to understand 'fragmentary' in 'the sense of fragments that refer to an implicit whole,' but rather to study 'fragments that challenge not only the idea of wholeness but the very idea of the "fragment" itself (for if there were not to be any wholes, what would the "fragments" be "fragments" of?)' (Chakrabarty, 1995: 757). Consequently, the alliance is understood as a collaboration between these fragments that challenge the idea of wholeness; a collaboration that produces for us something we 'have never thought before' (Dave, 2014: 446).

Additionally, it is crucial to understand that becoming minoritarian occurs through this alliance. According to Haraway, 'becoming is always becoming *with*' in 'the collaborative, complex, processual, and performative relationships' (emphasis in original) (Haraway, 2008: 137, 244). Dave emphasises that 'becoming' is 'an act of bordering in which both (original) categories are revealed to be infinitely other than what they are' (Dave, 2014: 448). This becoming is not something that is fixed in hierarchy; rather, it keeps moving to transform itself and occupies a place on both sides of the alliance. According to Deleuze and Guattari, the conjunction 'and . . . and . . . and . . .' brings sufficient force to shake the verb 'to be' (Deleuze and Guattari, 2013: 26).

The observations on Dalit feminism by Rege, who does not come from the Dalit community, become important in this context. Rege says, 'we do not argue that non-Dalit feminists can "speak as" or "for" the Dalit women but they can "reinvent" themselves as Dalit feminists' (Rege, 2003: 99). Similarly, according to Dhanda, a woman becomes 'a Dalit' not simply because of her location within the gendered and coloured hierarchies but through her praxis (Dhanda, 2012: 101). Rege and Dhanda's reinvention of themselves through their own praxis can be understood as 'becoming minoritarian.' If these understandings are correct, are caste Hindu women who chose inter-caste marriages with Dalit men, then becoming Dalit through the alliance with their marriage partners?

This chapter discusses Dalit inclusion in Nagpur and a neighbouring village named U in contemporary India, from the perspective of both Dalits and caste Hindus. It defines Dalit inclusion as an attempt by Buddhists or ex-untouchables to incorporate caste Hindus into their anti-discrimination movements. Specifically, this chapter examines a water purification project conducted by Buddhists, which can be reframed as the sharing of food or water among different castes; it also investigates inter-caste marriages between caste Hindu women and Dalit men, which can be seen as an alliance that shakes the logic of descent in local society.

Although many caste Hindus became regular customers of the water purification project, inter-caste marriages, which deviate sharply from social norms, disrupted the society and subjected the Buddhists to criticism from caste Hindus. This necessitates an examination of whether the sharing of food or water, and inter-caste marriages can support collaboration and mutual self-transformation among caste Hindus and Dalits. The concluding part of this chapter presents a discussion of the accounts given by a caste Hindu woman who married a Dalit activist, and a former Buddhist woman who married a Muslim man.[2] The discussion examines the becoming of these two women, who, through their inter-caste marriages, drew 'the diagonal' that traverses the vertical and horizontal coordinates (Deleuze and Guattari, 2013: 346) of caste, gender, and economic class hierarchy.

4 Ambedkar, untouchable liberation movements and inter-caste marriage

B.R. Ambedkar (1891–1956), also called 'Babasaheb' or 'Father of the Untouchables' in India, was born a member of the Mahar caste which was subjected to 'untouchability.' After returning home from studying in the United Kingdom and the United States, Ambedkar started the Mahad Chavdar Tank Satyagraha in 1927. At a meeting there, he said to the participants, 'Hindu society should be reorganised on two main principles: equality and absence of casteism.' In response to his speeches, the 'untouchables' who participated in the meeting burned the *Manusmriti* or *The Laws of Manu* to denounce casteism (Keer, 1971: 99–100).

The classical legal text *Manusmriti*, which was written in Sanskrit, states the following about inter-caste marriages in Chapter III-13: 'A Śūdra may take only a Śūdra woman as wife; Vaiśya, the latter and a woman of his own class; a Kṣatriya, the latter two and a woman of his own class; and a Brahmin, the latter three and a woman of his own class' (Olivelle, 2005: 108). Chapter III-14 adds, 'Not a single story mentions a Brahmin or a Kṣatriya taking a Śūdra wife even when they were going through a time of adversity' (Olivelle, 2005: 109).

Opposing the norms depicted in *Manusmriti*, Ambedkar explores how caste could be abolished in his 1936 book *Annihilation of Caste*.[3] He suggests that it is not the sharing of food or water between different castes, but inter-caste marriage is the 'real remedy' (Ambedkar, 2010: 67). Inter-caste marriages, which deviated from local norms, had the power to overturn the patriarchal social order called the caste hierarchy. Among inter-caste marriages, those between Brahmin women and 'untouchable' men were, indeed still are considered, the most problematic. Under such social conditions, Ambedkar insisted that the 'fusion of blood' through inter-caste marriage 'can alone create the feeling of being kith and kin' between different castes (Ambedkar, 2010: 67). In 1948, Ambedkar remarried Savita (1909–2003), a 39-year-old Brahmin physician. It was a marriage between a man at the bottom of the caste hierarchy and a woman of the highest caste. Examining Ambedkar's words and actions from the ideological perspective of the Dalit movement, we can re-evaluate his remarriage with Savita as signifying a realisation of his ideas about the annihilation of caste. However, as discussed in greater detail later, Ambedkar's remarriage and Savita's name are rarely discussed in contemporary Nagpur. On rare occasions, it is mentioned that most Buddhists, except those who married a person from another caste, evaluate the remarriage negatively.

Ambedkar served as the first law minister of India after its independence and was the chairman of the Constitution Drafting Committee. The Constitution of India, which came into effect in 1950, includes the prohibition of discrimination on grounds of religion, race, caste, sex, or place of birth (Article 15); the abolition of untouchability (Article 17); and affirmative action for SCs and Scheduled Tribes (STs), such as the reservation of seats in the House of the People and in the Legislative Assemblies of the States (Articles 330 and 332).[4] Furthermore, in 1950, the Indian parliament discussed the Hindu Code Bill. Ambedkar, as the law minister, oversaw the presentation of the facets of the Bill and particularly defended 'the very idea of equality for women in marriage, divorce, adoption, and property rights' (Zelliot, 2003: 212). Although Ambedkar resigned from the cabinet in 1951, the Hindu Code Bill was passed as acts in 1955 and 1956. It included clauses on the 'abolition of caste in the matter of marriage and adoption' (Zelliot, 2003: 213).

5 Male-dominated Dalit movements

The Dalit movements that succeeded Ambedkar's movement following his death in 1956 have employed '*the model of permanent struggle through the exacerbation, rather than the resolution, of difference*' (emphasis in original) (Rao,

2009: 158). Consequently, in the post-Ambedkar era, Dalit personality has been characterised prominently by 'the emotions of violence, bewilderment, and rage' (Nagaraj, 2011: 212). Simultaneously, these Dalit leaders have continuously subordinated and suppressed the 'independent political expression of dalit women' (Guru, 1995: 2549), whereby Dalit politics is 'imagined as male' and as 'a masculinist anticaste politics' (Rao, 2009: 54). During my fieldwork, which was conducted in Nagpur for two years, I observed that whereas the speeches at large Buddhist assemblies or festivals were mostly made by male activists, most participants who chanted at the Buddhist temples everyday were women. Consequently, there exists a disjuncture between the thoughts of Ambedkar who fought for women's rights, and the practices of the male Buddhist activists or 'Ambedkarites.' The Buddhist movement is, therefore, a patriarchal movement where women often have a subordinate role.

A comparison of the evaluations of Ambedkar's two marriages by Buddhists in contemporary Nagpur shows that the current Dalit movements are also based on stereotyped perceptions of gender roles. Savita was Ambedkar's wife during his tenure as the chairman of the Constitution Drafting Committee in the 1940s and helped him organise a mass conversion ceremony in 1956. However, in contemporary Nagpur and village U, it is the portrait of Ramabai (1898–1935) that is always placed next to that of Ambedkar. Ramabai belonged to the Mahar caste and married Ambedkar at the age of 9 in 1906. Ramabai not only managed housework for their children and relatives but also collected cow dung for fuel to provide for her family when Ambedkar went to London for his studies. Whereas Savita's name is uttered only rarely, Ramabai's struggles are praised by Buddhists. Similarly, while Buddhists celebrate Ambedkar's and Ramabai's birthdays each year in Nagpur and village U, Savita's is not. Furthermore, rumours that Savita murdered Ambedkar still abound among Buddhists, despite the conveyors of these rumours themselves explaining that it is baseless. Whereas Ramabai is known among Buddhists as a model 'wife who supported the activities of Ambedkar by taking care of their family,' they rarely discuss what Savita thought, talked about, or practised.

6 Nagpur city and village U

Confrontations among castes seem to have increased since the 1990s in India. Simultaneously, the rise of Hindu nationalism has become more apparent. The market liberalisation policies adopted since 1991 have accelerated high fluidity under globalisation. This 'neoliberal capitalism has been felt quite unevenly across time, regions, sectors, castes and classes' and has 'altered existing social relations in India' (Münster and Strümpell, 2014: 4). Under such circumstances, the self-consciousness of Dalits has been raised using affirmative action, such as the reservation system. Some lower-caste people have attained high-ranking jobs with authority and economic power, such as positions in the Indian Administrative Service (IAS) or the Indian Police Service (IPS), or as doctors, politicians, or university professors. Additionally, the Bahujan Samaj Party (BSP), which has lower castes or Dalits as its power base, expanded its power considerably in Uttar Pradesh and the party's national president, Mayawati (born in 1956), became the first Dalit woman chief minister of India in 1995.

In contemporary India, Nagpur is a centre of both the contemporary Dalit and Hindu Nationalist movements. Hundreds of thousands of Dalits, led by Ambedkar in 1956, converted from Hinduism to Buddhism in Nagpur, in a place currently located on the south side of the city, where a huge pagoda has been built. The place of the mass conversion is called 'Deekshabhoomi,' which means 'land of conversion.' Furthermore, hundreds of Buddhist temples exist in the area with statues of Ambedkar. At the same time, the headquarters of the Hindu nationalist organisation, Rashtriya Swayamsevak Sangh (RSS), is located on the east side of the city.

The effects of the mass conversion are revealed by India's 1961 Census, which showed that the number of Buddhists in India increased from 182,823 in 1951 to 3,250,227 in 1961. During this period, the percentage of Hindus decreased from 85% to 83.5%. In the same period in Maharashtra, the number of Buddhists increased from 2,487 to 2,789,501, and the percentage of Hindus decreased from 89.5% to 82.2% (Mitra, 1965: 482–485). According to India's 2011 Census, of Nagpur's population of 2,405,665, Hindus numbered 1,699,322 (70.6%), Buddhists 374,537 (15.6%), Muslims 287,436 (11.9%), Christians 27,569 (1.1%), Jains 21,689 (0.9%), and Sikhs 16,369 (0.7%). Nagpur has an extremely high percentage of Buddhists compared to India as a whole, for which the figure is only 0.7%. Village U in the Nagpur district is situated several kilometres away from the city of Nagpur. According to the 2011 Census, out of the 3,217 people (574 households) in the village, the numbers of SCs and STs were 535 (16.6%) and 547 (17%), respectively.[5]

As of 2013, there were five Brahmin households and no Kshatriya or Vaishya household in village U. Other Backward Classes (OBCs) accounted for more than half of the total village population, and over half of the OBC households belong to the Kunbi caste; the rest include Malis and Telis, among others. All SC households, excluding one Mang caste family, belong to the Mahar caste. After the members of the Mang family converted to Buddhism in 2014, all SCs in village U became Buddhists. The Hanuman Temple is the largest temple in the village, and Hindu festivals are celebrated at the square in front of it. Whereas there are two Buddhist temples, one of them is old, rarely used, and is outside the village. The village also hosts a boarding school for ST students, managed by the RSS. A Christian and a Muslim household are also present, both of which arrived from outside the village.

7 Dalit inclusion 1: drinking water purification project

In 2001, a Buddhist or Dalit organisation called Multipurpose Society for Justice (MSJ) was founded in village U. In 2013, the organisation had 15 Buddhist members, all of whom were male. Over the years, the contamination of drinking water by industrial wastewater from a nearby steel plant and a power station led to severe water scarcity in the village. Following protests by the MSJ in 2013, a new reservoir was built away from the contaminated one. The organisation then started a water purification project in 2014, for which the Buddhists received financial and technical aid from overseas. As part of the project, MSJ added powder flocculants, which reduced harmful materials in the water, and distributed the purified water to the villagers at a low price (20 litres daily at 100 rupees per month). As of December 2014, the project had 121 households as its customers; one in every five households participated in the project. Among those households, 31 were OBCs, 39 were SCs, 48 were Tribal (STs, Nomadic Tribes, and Denotified Tribes), and 3 were Brahmin households. In April 2015, the number of customers increased to 150 households, and the entire operation costs 30,000 rupees per month. Consequently, a monthly deficit of approximately 15,000 rupees arose. Subsequently, MSJ decided to end the project in January 2017. The activists' explanation regarding the project is presented below. The first narrative is from an oil company worker (forties, male); the second is that of the MSJ president (thirties, male).

OIL COMPANY WORKER: Although caste Hindus do not give us water, we nevertheless distribute water to them. Lord Buddha taught us not to hate anyone. If you read the Constitution of India, then you can understand that Babasaheb [Ambedkar] framed the Indian Constitution not only for untouchables but also for Shudras. If we hate Brahmins and do not give them water, it will make us bad people. Even though other people hate us, if we do well for everyone in the village, they will respect us. This is the only way to bring a change in other people. If we do a good job, then they can change, and other villagers will respect us.

MSJ PRESIDENT: The Constitution of India, as drafted by Babasaheb [Ambedkar], granted every person the right to receive education, and envisioned equality and liberty for everyone. Although Brahmins have oppressed us, the Constitution prohibits discrimination. Now that Buddhists outnumber Brahmins, we could behave like kings. However, the Constitution makes everyone equal. Without the Constitution, we could retaliate, but we follow the Constitution. . . . If we perform good actions, then those who oppressed us will realise that discriminating against us is wrong. . . . There is still discrimination against us, such as not having a meal at our wedding ceremonies. However, our relationship with OBCs has gradually improved through our project. If we do a good job, then others will also respect us.

In light of these narratives, one can reframe this water project as the sharing of food or water among different castes. In 1927, Ambedkar launched Chavdar Lake Satyagraha and struggled against caste Hindus in Mahad to gain access to a public reservoir for the 'untouchables.' Contemporary Dalit activists share these historical memories of discrimination against 'untouchables' by caste Hindus, who did not allow them to use public tanks. However, MSJ distributed purified drinking water to residents of village U, irrespective of their religion or caste, in accordance with 'justice, liberty, equality, and fraternity,' as framed by Ambedkar in the preamble of the Indian Constitution. In other words, through this water project, Ambedkarites aimed to earn respect as 'egalitarian Buddhists' by having caste Hindus receive water from the hands of Dalits. According to these activists, people from other castes will respect them if they do the right thing, despite the hatred they harbour against Buddhists. In other words, for these activists, caste Hindus become indispensable because they make Dalit activists feel dignified by receiving their water.[6]

8 Equality before God

Caste Hindus such as Brahmins or OBCs in the same village who received the water from MSJ activists did not do so on the grounds of equality under the law. Rather, they accepted the water because of the logic of equality before God. Caste Hindus who purchased drinking water from the Buddhists provided the following narratives. The first is by L., a Brahmin woman (thirties) who works in her family-owned general store. The second is that of V., a Kunbi caste (OBC) woman (forties) who works in her family-owned general store.

L.: I do not believe that I should not receive water from Buddhists or SCs. I also do not believe that I should not let them in my house. I learned about moral behaviour from my parents. My husband thinks the same way. Older generations believe that they should not touch SCs, receive water from them, or let them in their houses. However, these are old traditions. . . . [To get on a minibus going to the farms] Buddhists gather every day in front of my shop. If they ask for water, I give them water. My daughter also goes to a school managed by Buddhists. Hindus, Muslims, Buddhists, Sikhs, and Jains are friends. I have no problem with the SCs because God is one for everyone. The older generation does not accept them, but the educated, studied with followers of other religions and castes in schools and universities, and developed friendships.

V.: I do not believe that I should not receive water from SCs. I think there are no differences between various castes and religions, and all are one. I learned about it from my parents. . . . I came from Nagpur and had lived there with Buddhists and other people. I learned of the festival celebrated on April 14 [for Ambedkar's birthday] from the Buddhists. At the time of [the Hindu festival] Diwali, they donated some things to us, and during the Dussehra festival, my family distributed clothes to the Buddhists [for celebrating the mass conversion in 1956]. Sometimes, we ask Buddhists to join our family events. I do not know about the older generation, but my parents did not teach me to discriminate against them, or that any difference exists between us and them.

A Teli caste (OBC) man (sixties), who is a retired government officer, said, 'I have read the books on Christianity, Buddhism, and Babasaheb [Ambedkar] and learned the importance of equality. Those who don't give water to SCs have an antiquated mentality.' In fact, on the altar in his general store that he opened after his retirement, a portrait of Buddha and Ambedkar's book *The Buddha and his Dhamma* were placed next to a statue of Hindu goddess Lakshmi and portraits of the local saints, such as Sai Baba of Shirdi.

While the Buddhist activists and caste Hindus have fostered mutual relations, there exists a disjuncture in their interpretations of equality. Unlike Buddhist activists who shared the water based on notions of equality and justice, caste Hindus received the water and accepted the existence of Buddhists based on cultural memory that affirms 'equality before God.' This disjuncture demonstrates that despite the efforts of the Buddhists to redefine equality by sharing food or water with caste Hindus, equality did not necessarily become redefined in the way that Buddhists intended.

9 Dalit inclusion 2: inter-caste marriage

Inter-caste marriages, especially those between a Brahmin woman and a Dalit man, can be an effective means of overturning the caste hierarchy and gender inequality, and rewriting these patriarchal social orders. Its effectiveness is demonstrated by the emasculation and loss of honour felt by higher-caste men due to these marriages. They attempt to avoid this by inflicting harsh punishments on Dalit men, their relatives, and higher-caste women. However, these inter-caste marriages have become more common because of 'the new social pressures generated in the wake of the democratising process'—reservations and greater educational and economic opportunities becoming accessible to lower-caste groups (Chowdhry, 1997: 1023). Consequently, a conflict has arisen in contemporary India between traditional expectations for status derived from caste and individual aspirations, which derive power from new norms such as 'egalitarianism, citizenship, and entitlement' (Chowdhry, 2007: 296).

This study specifically investigates the inter-caste marriages of Dalit male activists and considers their experiences in the context of the Ambedkarite movements. The first case is explained by a Dalit activist (forties) who married a Brahmin woman (forties) in 1995. The second case is narrated by a Dalit activist (thirties) who married a Kunbi caste (OBC) woman (thirties) in 2014.

Dalit activist H. is a government servant living in a Buddhist residential area in Nagpur. H. joined a Dalit activist group in 1988 and currently manages a vocational training school for economically disadvantaged people. He started working for a bank in 1993, where he met his colleague, A., a Brahmin, who would later become his wife. Her family strongly objected to their marriage. Her grandfather P., who was a famous RSS leader, was the one most strongly opposed to their union. H.'s family also initially objected to their marriage; however, they gave their approval a few months later. In 1995, H.'s family conducted the entirety of their wedding ceremony, in which none of A's relatives participated. The relations between both families improved after 14 years, when A.'s grandfather P. died of an illness. Today, A. and H. have a son and a daughter; both children visit A.'s parents freely. H. said the following about inter-caste marriages:

> I would like to advise other Buddhists to choose their marriage partners from other castes. If other castes choose Buddhist marriage partners, Buddhists need to accept them as well. Thereby, Buddhism will spread and we will no longer be called 'Mahar Buddhists'. Inter-caste marriages are absolutely necessary. If Buddhism spreads through inter-caste marriages, then caste discrimination will cease to exist.

Activist D. is a manager in a car manufacturing company and lives in a Buddhist residential area in Nagpur. D. has been involved in social movements since 1998 and has held classes to educate SCs, STs, and OBCs since 2009. His wife, U., who belongs to the Kunbi caste, came from the adjacent Wardha district. U. had moved to Nagpur for higher education. They met when they both joined the master's degree programme in Social Work, in 2007. Despite their parents' opposition to the marriage, they gathered numerous social workers and politicians and had a court marriage in Nagpur, in 2014. D. and U. were 28 and 25 years old, respectively, when they married. They now have a 5-year-old son. D.'s parents have already accepted their marriage, but U.'s family has not. Even six years after their marriage, U.'s parents refuse to meet her. Activist D.'s insights on inter-caste marriage are presented as follows:

> OBCs deny Buddhism. . . . They agree to let their members marry SCs, such as Chamar, Bhangi, and Mang, but they do not accept their marriage with Ambedkarite Buddhists because Buddhism challenges Hinduism. . . . To abolish casteism, sharing of food and inter-caste marriage are insufficient. The only solution is to spread Buddhism among them. . . . I have never persuaded my wife's family to accept our marriage because the OBC families believe in superstition; if we talked with them, we know exactly what would happen in the future.

Ambedkarites such as H. and D. tried to explain their marriages in the context of anti-discrimination movements to abolish caste. According to Rao, 'the politicization of everyday life beyond the realm of formal politics' was central to Dalit's postcolonial identity, and inter-caste marriages remain 'a biopolitical frontier for caste emancipation' (Rao, 2009: 215, 360). However, if inter-caste marriages between caste Hindu women and Dalit men are viewed solely from the perspective of the emancipation of Dalits, caste Hindu women can be trivialised as 'tools' to spread the ideology of Dalit movements. That is, contemporary male-dominated Dalit movements continue to ignore these women's 'autonomy' over their bodies (Chowdhry, 2004: 70). For that reason, we will later examine these inter-caste marriages from the women's perspective.

10 Struggles among men over honour and masculinity

Inter-caste marriages between caste Hindu women and Dalit male activists lead to conflicts over honour and masculinity between caste Hindu male relatives and Dalit activists. The former struggle to control a woman's sexuality by limiting their choice of marriage partners, whereas the latter are engaged in male-dominated Ambedkarite movements that have explicitly posited inter-caste marriage as the remedy for caste discrimination. Details of the elopement and inter-caste marriage between T., an OBC woman of the Mali caste, and R., a Dalit activist of the Mahar caste in village U are presented in the next paragraph. Both individuals' parents are farmers. T., who completed a Bachelor of Science degree, has an elder brother and an elder sister. R. has three elder brothers and an elder sister. Their marriage is the second inter-caste marriage among the village's Buddhist men in the past two decades.

T. met R. for the first time in 2009, when they were aged about 15 and 25, respectively. Because T. attended the school and used the library that the Buddhist organisation MSJ managed, they gradually became close. In 2014, rumours of their intimate relationship had spread in the village; T. was around 20 at the time, and by then, R. had become a prominent leader in the village and was the vice-chairman of the Panchayat of village U. T.'s parents arranged a marriage for her with another man within six months of her elder sister's marriage. Consequently, T. and R. eloped from the village in February 2017. Following this, OBCs held Caste Panchayats several times in the village; for about a year, the Buddhists, who were usually invited to the events of the OBCs such as wedding ceremonies, were 'socially boycotted' by the OBCs who were the majority community in the village. During that time, T. and R. had to stay in another city near the village, where they often starved. They returned to the village when T. became pregnant a year after their elopement.

Both T. and R. took a long time to narrate their experiences regarding the elopement and inter-caste marriage. We examine R.'s narrative here and discuss T.'s experiences in the next section. R. narrated the following:

> Our marriage was really difficult. We left the village for a year. . . . After we returned to our village, my sister did not allow us to live on our family land, which is why our house is at the edge of our village. My family did not allow me to attend my sister's engagement ceremony or enter my parents' house. . . . Our life was very hard. We were extremely poor during the year we were not in the village. We had no idea what to do during the first month. We slept in a different place every night. After a while, we rented a room in a nearby city, O., but we did not have enough food to eat and went

> to sleep hungry for several nights. . . . After we left the village, the OBCs discussed how to respond to our elopement. They could have killed us. Had we returned after a month, both of us would have been killed. . . . After N. was born, our relationship with my family improved. They started to visit our house.

It can be discerned from the narrative above that the family members of R. and T. disowned them following their elopement. It took a long time for R. and T. to find a room to rent in an unfamiliar city. At times, they were unable to find food enough to feed themselves. They returned to the village after T. became pregnant. After their son was born, R.'s mother visited their house and looked after him. R.'s sister allowed him to join her wedding ceremony and enter his parents' house. It can be said that their son's birth solved their difficulties; however, R.'s father has not yet permitted R. to use their family's agricultural land. Moreover, their house is located neither in the residential area of the Hindus nor in that of the Buddhists. It stands apart from all other houses at the very edge of the village. The only Muslim house in village U is the one closest to theirs.

T. has been in a weaker position than her husband in this inter-caste marriage. As of September 2019, two-and-a-half years after their elopement, she cannot meet her family inside the village. She talks with her mother on the phone, but if she wants to meet her mother face to face, they must meet in Nagpur, which is several kilometres from the village. R.'s family, by contrast, has gradually accepted their marriage since his son's birth. However, for T., the relationship with her family has not changed by any marked degree since their return. 'Social taunts' directed at inter-caste marriages are 'a lifelong affair' (Chowdhry, 2004: 80), especially for women's family and relatives.

11 Dalit inclusion seen from a woman's perspective

When one has a lower status in the social hierarchy, 'their disadvantaged position grants them a certain epistemic privilege over others' (Guru, 1995: 2549). For example, Dalit women who are oppressed by multiple patriarchies, such as casteism and gender inequality, might be recognised 'as having the greatest interest' in challenging these patriarchies (Rege, 2006: 73). According to Rege, narratives by Dalits on their life histories are '*testimonios*,' which establish 'a right to speak both for and beyond the individual, and contest explicitly or implicitly the "official forgetting" of histories of caste oppression, struggles, and resistance' (Rege, 2006: 13). If this is true, then what is the status of a caste Hindu woman who moved 'downwards' by marrying a Dalit man and thereby dishonoured her family? What struggles are included in her experiences?

A higher-caste woman who elopes with a Dalit man often loses her relationship with her family. She finds herself in a situation in which her male relatives feel they have lost their sense of honour. An OBC woman, T., who married a Dalit activist, R., now volunteers her time, teaching economically disadvantaged children in their village. She made the following remarks in an interview:

> R. was a person of good character; and he was smart, so I came to like him. However, my parents and brother opposed our marriage. They did not speak to me after we returned to the village. One day, I decided not to speak to them. I thought they would speak to me if I had a happy life. Now, my family has started speaking to me. Babasaheb [Ambedkar] and Lord Buddha said: 'We should not discriminate against anybody'. Everyone should follow their teachings. . . . We have a goal, to be recognised by others as the best couple in the village. If we realise our goal, then our future will be good. . . . I learned many things from Babasaheb's books. I read *Annihilation of Caste*, *Riddles in Hinduism*, and *The Buddha and His Dhamma*. . . . I think if other people want to talk with us after seeing our life, they can visit us. We do not have to be the first to approach other people. When we lived in city O., we had very difficult days. Every day was a fight for survival. When we did not have enough money to buy soap for washing, R. cried. . . . I had to face hunger even though N. was in my belly. I was very anxious about it. My body trembles with fear when I recall those days. So, I try not to remember anymore.

Although Ambedkar emphasised the importance of inter-caste marriages for the abolition of caste, not all aspects of marriage between Dalit activists and caste Hindu women can be said to have resulted from the ideology of Ambedkarite anti-caste movements. T.'s statements that 'R. was a person of good character; and he was smart, so I came to like him' reveal that there are other ethics and logic involved, that explain their marriage, other than the ideology of Ambedkarite movements. However, such movements have connected their ideology with these marriages and politicised them as marriages between 'different castes.' In this situation, despite having knowledge of several discourses, such as the ideology of the Ambedkarite anti-caste movements, the Brahmanical patriarchy, and the preamble of the Indian Constitution, T. expressed a sentiment that is not necessarily consistent with these discourses.

The narrative revealed her 'unemphatic, ad hoc, subaltern rewriting' (Spivak, 1988: 308) of the multiple forms of patriarchy. Male relatives who wanted to maintain the purity of their caste by controlling women's sexuality broke off their relationship with T. when she married a Dalit man. However, in her narrative, T. said, 'One day I decided not to speak to them.' That is, T. decided not to have any relationship with her family members. Her testimonial described how her choice of having an inter-caste marriage made her male relatives lose their sense of honour and masculinity. So long as she survives and does not abandon her choice of partnering or collaborating with a Dalit man, her existence can breach and damage caste hierarchy and gender inequality. Thus, the woman continues to be excluded. T.'s testimonial also indicated that her husband R. felt emasculated because of his inability to provide for his wife, even though he enhanced his sense of masculinity by damaging her male relatives' sense of honour. In fact, T. saw her husband R. crying many times because of their difficult life after the elopement.

T.'s position is difficult to understand from a perspective of hierarchies of caste and gender because she tries to move diagonally, traversing the vertical and horizontal coordinates of caste and gender hierarchy. In the Indian context, if the word Dalit indicates those who have experienced coercion, exploitation, and dehumanisation, and denotes those who have the same drive of creating a utopian society free of those aspects, then it can be argued that T., who has experienced exclusion from her family and caste community and who has criticised multiple forms of patriarchy and caste discrimination, is in the process of becoming Dalit. Consequently, an OBC woman, T., who moves diagonally by marrying a Dalit activist, R., would be attempting to fill some of the blank spaces in the definition of the Dalit category, thereby redefining it by becoming Dalit herself.

12 Returning to multiple possibilities

According to Dave, at the time of emergence, 'anything is possible, but by virtue of that introduction of potential, something must be chosen' (Dave, 2011: 658). Moreover, the struggle for radical activism 'lies between the multiple potentials in a moment of social emergence and the simultaneous introduction of closure and commensuration' (Dave, 2011: 659). Therefore, the direction of individual efforts and social movements to change the present situation is defined by difficult struggles in the transition from multiple potentialities to the actualisation of one of these potentialities. Following this argument, the concluding part of this chapter presents a discussion of the narrative taken up at the beginning of this chapter, of a formerly Buddhist woman U.M., who married a Muslim man. We examine her struggle to turn one potentiality into an actuality, and vice versa.

The formerly Buddhist woman U.M. married a Muslim man, C.K., in 2012. U.M. works at a pharmaceutical company in Nagpur. Originally, C.K. was a friend of U.M.'s cousin. They started dating around 2001, when U.M. finished her 12th standard. Both families strongly opposed their dating (her father, who is conventionally responsible for her marriage, had already passed away in 1998). Every time her paternal uncle became aware that U.M. had been with C.K., he would beat her without allowing her to speak. In 2009, U.M. pursued MBA after completing her undergraduate course in pharmacy. She and C.K. had a court marriage in Nagpur in 2012 without notifying anyone in the family. Over the next two years, they saved money, bought gold, and prepared household items. In 2014, when U.M. turned 29, they married according to Islamic law. After the marriage, U.M. converted to Islam, changed her name from U.M. to N.K., and stopped celebrating festivals such as Holi and Diwali.[7] None of her relatives joined her wedding ceremony. Only maternal uncles and a maternal cousin came for the reception after the ceremony. Their son was born in 2016, but except for her maternal aunt, members from neither family came to see their son. U.M. has been able to increase her income from 3,500 rupees per month in 2010 to 49,000 rupees per month presently, despite receiving no support from either family. Even now, eight years after their marriage, the two families never meet. About her marriage, U.M. said,

> I converted to Islam after marriage and changed my name to N.K. Following Islamic tradition, we had to do that. I liked C.K.; I did that because C.K. asked. However, now I think it was not necessary to change my name. . . . I forgot my identity. When I was asked what my name was, I had no idea if I should say U.M. or N.K. I think it is strange that only I have to throw away various things and change many things. If you get married to a person from a different caste, then both must change. I like clothes such as those worn by Westerners, but I have worn Islamic clothes ever since I got married. I did not know how to behave and got confused. Even though my husband did not have to throw away anything, I had to abandon many things. . . . When someone gets married with a person from a different caste, the husband [husband's life] remains the same; only the wife [wife's life] changes. When we choose inter-caste marriage, the community does not let us go anywhere. . . . People cannot change themselves without being strong. C.K. must become stronger and change himself. He has to do what his wife's caste does. Then he will understand what I have had to abandon.

My interview with U.M., which started at around 11:30 am, lasted until around 2 pm. She talked almost without rest. Finally, U.M. said, 'Being a woman, being a girl, is very complicated. I am very happy to be able to talk with you because I have a dream of turning my story into a book.' As a Dalit woman, U.M. is ranked low in gender, caste, and economic class. Since 1991, when the Indian government changed direction to promote economic liberalisation, U.M. managed to enhance her education level considerably and has attempted to overcome her economically inferior status. She was, therefore, able to start earning 49,000 rupees a month. Despite being exposed to violence from her paternal uncle, she was able to realise the marriage she desired, even as the confrontation between caste groups and that of religious communities intensified in the 1990s. After her marriage, U.M. converted from Buddhism to Islam and changed her name from U.M. to N.K., in accordance with the desires of her spouse.

However, gradually, she came to be unaware of who she was and faced an identity crisis. She moved away from actuality and retuned to multiple possibilities. As part of her struggle, following the advice of a Yadav caste (OBC) woman who got married with a Buddhist man, U.M. chose to change her name from N.K. to U.M. again. The ethics of U.M., who claimed that 'C.K. must strengthen and change himself. He must do what his wife's caste does. Then he will understand what I have abandoned by now' overlaps with the idea of 'alliance' or 'a block of becoming' discussed by Deleuze and Guattari (2013). Similar to the OBC woman T. in village U, U.M. used limited discourses, such as 'clothes like those of Westerners' and 'Holi' to express herself in a way that existing norms could not completely explain, and thereby tried to remake patriarchal hierarchies.

Thus, the question arises whether only the woman remakes herself through inter-caste marriage. This chapter discussed the relation between Dalit movements and inter-caste marriages using U.M.'s narrative. A woman choosing to maintain her inter-caste marriage can act as an objection to multiple patriarchies. In T.'s case, both her male relatives and her marriage partner R. lost their masculinity because of their inability to be her 'guardian.' Therefore, men must face pressure to become other than what they are, as a result of inter-caste marriage. If not only women but also male activists who choose inter-caste marriages remake themselves and draw the diagonal that traverses the hierarchy, then the male-dominated and patriarchal Dalit movements can be transformed from their present state.

Acknowledgement

This work was supported by JSPS KAKENHI; Grant Numbers: JP26870075, JP16H03533.

Notes

1 Some proper nouns have been abbreviated and some details such as dates have been changed for anonymity in this chapter.
2 'Caste' in this chapter is a translation of a word the local residents use: 'jati.' 'Jati' refers to 'a community' or 'a group of people.' Local residents of Nagpur refer to a marriage between Muslims and Buddhists, which is discussed in this chapter, as a type of inter-caste marriage because inter-religious marriage involves men and women from different groups.
3 *Annihilation of Caste* was originally Ambedkar's manuscript prepared for his speech at the 1936 annual conference of the Jat-Pat-Todak Mandal of Lahore. However, Ambedkar was unable to deliver the speech because the reception committee of the conference considered his criticism of caste and his idea of conversion from Hinduism described in the manuscript unacceptable and chose to cancel the conference (Ambedkar, 2010: 36). In that same year, the English manuscript was published and translated into major Indian languages.
4 India.gov.in, National Portal of India. *The Constitution of India*. www.india.gov.in/sites/upload_files/npi/files/coi_part_full.pdf (accessed 24 October 2018).
5 Office of the Registrar General and Census Commissioner, India. *Census of India 2011*, www.censusindia.gov.in/2011census/population_enumeration.html (accessed 16 September 2015).
6 In the words of Nagaraj, for Buddhist activists, MSJ's drinking water project incorporated 'the Ambedkarite model' of 'self-respect' by which Dalits restore their dignity by themselves without the help of caste Hindus, and 'the Gandhian model of self-purification' by which interactions between Dalits and caste Hindus erase the notion of 'untouchability' from the caste Hindu's heart (Nagaraj, 2011: 78–80, 140).
7 The Dalit movements that follow the teachings of Ambedkar in contemporary Nagpur define Holi and Diwali as 'Hindu festivals' and convince Buddhists to stop celebrating these 'Hindu festivals' because they converted to Buddhism. Nevertheless, some Buddhists still partake in these 'Hindu festivals' even though they are aware of the ideology of Ambedkarite activists. Nemoto (2014) discusses the relations between 'Hindu festivals' and Buddhist culture in detail after the Dalit mass conversion in 1956 by

investigating the invention of Buddhist culture and the two forms of conversion among contemporary Buddhists in Nagpur.

References

Ambedkar, B. R. (2010). "Annihilation of Caste with a Reply to Mahatma Gandhi," in *Dr. Babasaheb Ambedkar Writings and Speeches Vol. 1*, Mumbai: Dr. Babasaheb Ambedkar Source Material Publication Committee: 23–96.

Chakrabarty, D. (1995). "Radical Histories and Question of Enlightenment Rationalism: Some Recent Critiques of 'Subaltern Studies'," *Economic and Political Weekly*, vol. 30(14), 751–759.

Chakravarti, U. (1993). "Conceptualising Brahmanical Patriarchy in Early India: Gender, Caste, Class and State," *Economic and Political Weekly*, vol. 28(14), 579–585.

Chowdhry, P. (1997). "Enforcing Cultural Codes: Gender and Violence in Northern India," *Economic and Political Weekly*, vol. 32(19), 1019–1028.

Chowdhry, P. (2004). "Private Lives, State Intervention: Cases of Runaway Marriage in Rural North India," *Modern Asian Studies*, vol. 38(1), 55–84.

Chowdhry, P. (2007). *Contentious Marriages, Eloping Couples: Gender, Caste, and Patriarchy in Northern India*, New Delhi: Oxford University Press.

Dave, N. N. (2011). "Indian and Lesbian and What Came Next: Affect, Commensuration, and Queer Emergences," *American Ethnologist*, vol. 38(4), 650–665.

Dave, N. N. (2014). "Witness: Humans, Animals, and the Politics of Becoming," *Cultural Anthropology*, vol. 29(3), 433–456.

Deleuze, G. and F. Guattari (2013). *A Thousand Plateaus: Capitalism and Schizophrenia*. B. Massumi (trans.), London and New York: Bloomsbury.

Dhanda, M. (2012). "Runaway Marriages: A Silent Revolution?" *Economic and Political Weekly*, vol. 47(43), 100–108.

Grover, S. (2009). "Lived Experiences: Marriage, Notions of Love, and Kinship Support amongst Poor Women in Delhi," *Contributions to Indian Sociology*, vol. 43(1), 1–33.

Guru, G. (1995). "Dalit Women Talk Differently," *Economic and Political Weekly*, vol. 30(41/42), 2548–2550.

Guru, G. (2001). "The Language of Dalit-Bahujan Political Discourse," in Shah, G. ed., *Dalit Identity and Politics*, New Delhi: Sage Publications: 97–107.

Haraway, D. J. (2008). *When Species Meet*, Minnesota: University of Minnesota Press.

Kannabiran, V. and K. Kannabirann (1991). "Caste and Gender: Understanding Dynamics of Power and Violence," *Economic and Political Weekly*, vol. 26(37), 2130–2133.

Keer, D. (1971). *Dr. Ambedkar: Life and Mission*, Mumbai: Popular Prakashan.

Krishnan, S. (2015). "Agency, Intimacy, and Rape Jokes: An Ethnographic Study of Young Women and Sexual Risk in Chennai," *Journal of the Royal Anthropological Institute*, vol. 22(1), 67–83.

Mitra, A. (1965). *Census of India 1961, Volume I India, Part II-C (i) Social and Cultural Tables*, New Delhi: Manager of Publications.

Mody, P. (2002). "Love and the Law: Love-Marriage in Delhi," *Modern Asian Studies*, vol. 36(1), 223–256.

Mody, P. (2008). *The Intimate State: Love-Marriage and the Law in Delhi*, London and New York: Routledge.

Münster, D. and C. Strümpell (2014). "The Anthropology of Neoliberal India: An Introduction," *Contributions to Indian Sociology*, vol. 48(1), 1–16.

Nagaraj, D. R. (2011). *The Flaming Feet and Other Essays: The Dalit Movement in India*, London, New York and Calcutta: Seagull Books.
Nemoto, T. (2014). "Creating a New Meaning for Buddhist Rituals: Two Forms of Religion and Conversion among Contemporary Indian Buddhists in Nagpur City," in Wong, H. W. and K. Maegawa eds., *Revisiting Colonial and Post-Colonial: Anthropological Studies of the Cultural Interface*, Los Angeles: Bridge21 Publications: 131–158.
Olivelle, P. (2005). *Manu's Code of Law: A Critical Edition and Translation of the Mānava-Dharmáśāstra*, Oxford: Oxford University Press.
Rao, A. (2003). "Introduction: Caste, Gender and Indian Feminism," in Rao, A. ed., *Gender and Caste*, New Delhi: Kali for Women: 1–47.
Rao, A. (2009). *The Caste Question: Dalits and the Politics of Modern India*, Berkley and Los Angeles: University of California Press.
Rege, S. (2003). "A Dalit Feminist Standpoint," in Rao, A. ed., *Gender and Caste*, New Delhi: Kali for Women: 90–101.
Rege, S. (2006). *Writing Caste/Writing Gender: Reading Dalit Women's Testimonios*, New Delhi: Zubaan.
Spivak, G. C. (1988). "Can the Subaltern Speak?" in Nelson, C. and L. Grossberg eds., *Marxism and the Interpretation of Culture*, Urbana: University of Illinoi Press: 271–313.
Velaskar, P. (2016). "Theorising the Interaction of Caste, Class and Gender: A Feminist Sociological Approach," *Contributions to Indian Sociology*, vol. 50(3), 389–414.
Zelliot, E. (2003). "Dr Ambedkar and Empowerment of Women," in Rao, A. ed., *Gender and Caste*, New Delhi: Kali for Women: 204–217.

11

DO 'ISLAMIC NORMS' IMPEDE INCLUSIVE DEVELOPMENT OF WOMEN?

A Case Study of Islamic Education for Women in Rural Bangladesh

Ai Sugie

1 Introduction

To address this chapter's question, 'Do Islamic norms impede inclusive development of women?' one must consider the diverse meanings of 'Islamic norms' and 'inclusive development of women' (White, 2010). 'Gender and development' are important elements of inclusive development. Development studies have emphasised slogans such as 'gender equality' and the 'empowerment of women' (Rauniyar and Kanbur, 2009). Nevertheless, although Western and secularist views and Islamic views are not necessarily opposed or mutually contradictory (Gardner, 1998; White, 2010; Bano, 2017), 'gender equality' based on the modern Western view might be counter to Muslimahs' 'welfare' or 'well-being.' Moreover, the application of modern Western views might be a factor that lowers the percentage of school attendance and employment for women. For example, school attendance and employment among women in Iran increased after the Iranian Revolution. Iranian parents felt comfortable sending their daughters to work and school because of Iran's segregation of men and women (Sakurai, 2001). What, then, is an 'inclusive development' of Muslimahs?

Generally, in Western or secularist perspectives, gender is based on socially or culturally constructed differences or inequality between men and women. According to this view, gender equality can be achieved through social or cultural reform. Muslims generally believe that Allah creates men and women and ordains their differences and relations. Consequently, the controversial issue in Islamic gender perspectives is how Allah creates the differences and relations between men and women. It is important for exemplary Muslims to understand the basis for the legitimacy of their norms, as described in the following subsection. Therefore, an examination of Islamic norms is required.

DOI: 10.4324/9781003304760-14

Ambiguity of Islamic norms

Many researchers regard Islam as a discourse (Asad, 1986; Ahmed, 1992; Mahmood, 2005; Minesaki, 2009) or practice (Sadiki, 2004). The discourse and practice approaches to Islam both transcend the dichotomies reflected in terms such as 'elite/popular,' 'text/practice,' and 'Islam/islams' and emphasise their continuum, as well as the ambiguity of Islamic ideals (cf. Mahmood, 2005). However, this view might engender the misunderstanding that conduct or customs that clearly conflict with the Quran, such as terrorism and honour killing, are also attributable to Islam; Tsujigami (2011) demonstrates that any discourse can be justified in the name of Islam by quoting various and contradictory male and female Muslims' discourses on gender. Therefore, this chapter divides Islamic discourse into 'Islamic norms based on sources of the Shariah' and 'norms established by Muslims' (cf. Mir-Hosseini, 1999).

'Sources of the Shariah' refers primarily to the Quran and secondarily to the Hadith.[1] The latter comprises records of the prophet Muhammad's words and deeds. These texts are ambiguous, even when the polysemic nature of Arabic is taken as a given. Therefore, these texts and practices have been interpreted in diverse ways. Muslims decide their code of conduct based on interpretations of sources of the Shariah. Consequently, legitimate Islamic norms might differ across legal schools, periods, and regions because interpretations are influenced by each region's historical background and culture (Eidhamar, 2018).

'Norms established by Muslims' are generally believed to be based on Islam, but they are not based on any sources of the Shariah. Norms established by Muslims include local customs. For example, rural Bangladesh has many norms concerning women that have no basis in sources of the Shariah, such as the common saying 'women's heaven is at their husbands' feet.' In fact, the original words in the Hadith differ, as described in the section 5. Some Islamic norms are mutually contradictory. It is not uncommon for Muslims to contest the legitimacy of Islamic discourse (Mahmood, 2005). Therefore, the important issue is who insists on what kind of Islamic discourse, and whose interpretation serves as its basis.

Differences and power relations between men and women in Islam

In the Quran, men differ from women because Allah created the two distinctively (cf. Wadud, 2006):

> O mankind, indeed We have created you from male and female and made you peoples and tribes that you may know one another. Indeed, the most noble of you in the sight of Allāh is the most righteous of you. Indeed, Allāh is Knowing and Aware.
>
> *(Quran Al-Hujurāt 49:13)*[2]

However, power relations are controversial in various interpretations of the Quran. For example, two different interpretations are presented in the following verse:

> Divorced women remain in waiting [i.e. do not remarry] for three periods, and it is not lawful for them to conceal what Allāh has created in their wombs if they believe in Allāh and the Last Day. And their husbands have more right to take them back in this [period] if they want reconciliation. And due to them [i.e. the wives] is similar to what is expected of them, according to what is reasonable. But the men [i.e. husbands] have a degree over them [in responsibility and authority]. And Allāh is Exalted in Might and Wise.
>
> *(Quran Al-Baqarah 2:228)*

What this study calls the 'male-centred interpretation' posits that men *always* have authority over women. It often enforces gender roles based on the separation of internal (home) and external environments. Men do outside work, such as subsistence or economic activities; women do inside work, such as housework and child-rearing. However, the 'alternative interpretation,' as it is called in this study, posits that men and women have equal rights based on their differences (Al-Buti, 2006). In this view, the differences between men and women do not justify the superiority or inferiority of one gender or the other but show instead that they were created to complement each other. Supporters of the alternative interpretation allow women to work outside with *purdah* (veiling).

The male-centred and alternative positions are two interpretative poles. Historically, men have interpreted sources of the Shariah and have constructed a male-centred interpretation (Mernissi, 1991; Ahmed, 1992). However, this male-centred Islamic discourse space has been shaken because female Islamic education and religious activities have become popular in various countries, as explained in the next subsection.

Muslimah participation in the Islamic discourse space

Although several Hadith clearly approve the pursuit of education and knowledge for both male and female Muslims,[3] female education has been restricted. Nevertheless, female education has been promoted and has spread along with Islamic revivalism since the late 1970s. Demand for both formal and informal studies of Islamic texts has emerged and has steadily expanded in both Muslim majority countries and Muslim diaspora communities in the West (Bano and Kalmbach, 2012; Bano, 2017) and Muslim minority countries such as China (Jaschok, 2012). For example, Al-Azhar University, a world-leading authority in Islamic education, has been admitting female students since 1961 (Mahmood, 2005). Islamic schools for women have been established in Iran since the 1980s (Sakurai, 2001). Such Muslimah involvement in Islamic education and religious activities has been linked to political changes, including state formation and Muslimahs' access to higher education and increasing social mobility (Kandiyoti, 1991; Begum,

2015; Bano, 2017). The spread of mass education and print capitalism (Anderson, 2006), as well as the rise of the urban middle class, have vitalised social and religious reformation movements (Eickleman, 1992).

Muslimahs who have received higher modern education in Western universities have deconstructed traditional male-centred Islamic discourse and have sought to reinterpret sources of the Shariah from the female perspective since the 1980s (Mernissi, 1991; Ahmed, 1992; Mir-Hosseini, 1999; Wadud, 2006). Their work has been designated as 'Islamic feminism.' It rejects both the images of women offered by Western feminists and Muslims who blindly support the male-centred interpretation, and it seeks to expand Muslimahs' rights (Rhouni, 2010; cf. Abu-Lughod, 2013).[4]

In addition to offering theoretical examinations of Islamic discourse and historical accounts of its male-centred characteristics, previous studies have also examined how the recently flourishing female Islamic education has affected women's status, gender relations, and Islamic discourse space by exploring Muslimahs' lived experiences. Researchers have discussed how this movement can be understood and evaluated. The feminist research can be broadly divided into two types: (a) critical analyses of views or images of women constructed in dominant discourses or nation-building processes, as well as the development projects of religious authorities or governments (Kandiyoti, 1991; Moghadam, 1994; Jeffery and Basu, 1998; cf. Abu-Lughod, 1998) and (b) evaluations of women-centred religious reforms or social movements that resist or reconstruct conventionally male-dominated Islamic discourse and religious activities (Mahmood, 2005; Minesaki, 2009; Sakurai, 2011). In particular, many researchers have been engaged in studies on female Islamic education since Mahmood's (2005) pioneering study in Cairo and have described Muslimahs' participation in Islamic study circles as an agentive act (Kalmbach, 2008; Ahmad, 2009; Bano and Kalmbach, 2012; Bano, 2017). Some of these studies point out the structural limitation whereby Muslimahs tend to follow a male-centred interpretation rather than reinterpret or challenge it. However, Muslimahs' agency, which is engaged with Islamic education platforms described by earlier studies in various countries, implies the possibility of seeking alternative modernities within the Islamic frame of reference. Moreover, the Islamic knowledge they acquire in Islamic study circles, including even male-dominated Islamic discourse, are not obstacles but rather resources, or bases upon which to raise women's status and dignity (Huq and Rashid, 2008). For example, the discourse that 'Men are in charge of women' based on the Quran (An-Nisā' 4:34) seems to allow male domination of women. However, women can assert their right to be fulfilled materially, physically, and emotionally by their husbands. Although Islamic feminists tend to dismiss the male-centred interpretation and to insist on the significance of reinterpretation by Muslimahs themselves, such opposition to male-centred interpretation and reinterpretations is not necessary or feasible for Muslimahs, as suggested by the empirical studies that demonstrate how Muslimahs follow the male-centred interpretation. For example, some Muslimahs prefer to stay at home rather than work outside their home in order to fulfil their duties as homemakers and to satisfy their husbands; these Muslimahs consciously choose the male-centred interpretation and do not wish to reform Islamic norms in radical ways. Moreover, the interpretations of ordinary women, those who have not received higher Islamic education, might be dismissed by men or religious authorities. It might be better to appropriate the dominant or authorised interpretations.

Inclusive development of Muslimahs

The first step towards an inclusive development of Muslimahs is women's participation in the Islamic discourse space—that is, the process of interpreting sources of the Shariah and the construction and examination of diverse Islamic discourse. The inclusive development of Muslimahs means that women can participate in religious activities and can refer to Islamic discourse in whatever form they desire. Individual Muslimahs should be free to select their own interpretations and Islamic discourse. One woman might work outside her home whereas another might concentrate on family caregiving, while in turn demanding economic support from her husband. Although these two examples represent extremes, Muslimahs should become accustomed to the diversity of interpretations and Islamic discourse in order to contest their legitimacy. Bano (2017) calls this search the 're-democratisation of Islamic knowledge' and highlights the roles played by influential and elite Muslimahs in mixing Islamic traditional ideals with their moral superiority and optimality in their modern lives (cf. Wadud, 2009). Muslimahs need to receive Islamic education on an equal basis with men, learn the various interpretations and Islamic discourse, and obtain the intellectual resources and authority required to discuss and negotiate the legitimacy of Islamic discourse. This negotiation is what Mahmood (2005) calls the 'politics of piety.'

Has Bangladesh also experienced a flourishing of female Islamic education and religious activities? If it has, does this help enhance the inclusive development of Muslimahs?

2 Islam and women in Bangladesh

Rokeya Begum (1880–1932) is often described as the first feminist activist in East Bengal (now Bangladesh). She accused men of using religion to dominate women and established the first Muslimahs' school in Kolkata. However, such movements were limited to charismatic individuals such as Begum. It took nearly a century after her era for female education and religious activities to begin to expand.

Bangladesh won its war of liberation with help from India and became independent from Pakistan in 1971. The policy of the new country was secularism because it followed Indian policy and had experienced anti-liberation violence during the war, including a massacre that was said to have been caused by an Islamist political party. However, Islam has been gradually instrumentalised in national politics since the end of the Mujibur administration (1971–1975), under pressure from oil-producing countries in the Middle East, which are important donor countries for Bangladesh. The use of Islam in national politics is based on the need for national integration (Huque and Akhter, 1987). The Ziaur administration (1977–1981) removed the ban on the establishment of Islamist parties. The Ershad administration (1983–1990) pursued an explicit Islamisation of the public sphere. Islamic education was introduced to public education, and Islam became the state religion in 1988. Since that time, Islam has been a prominent feature in politics and in all administrations and parties (Takada, 2006; Togawa, 2014). During this shift in politics, the government's policy towards women was 'contradictory' (Kabeer, 1991) and 'opportunistic' (Sobhan, 1994). It reconciled the programmes of 'Women in Development' of Western countries with the demand for restrictions on female activities by Muslims who supported the male-centred interpretation. However, such a policy and the expansion of Islamic education did not benefit women, who were generally excluded from educational opportunities (Kabeer, 1991: 136). Although two female heads of two major political parties have held the reins of government since the 1990s, their policies towards women did not differ from the earlier 'opportunist' one.

However, women's social and spatial mobility have increased since the 1990s, driven by both direct encouragement from development agencies as well as macro-level socio-economic changes such as the spread of education and the growth of the labour market in agriculture and the garment sector (Kabeer, 2002). Grameen Bank and non-governmental organisations (NGOs) have organised women for social and political empowerment and have lent small loans/microcredit since the late 1970s. Many studies have examined the effects of such activities. They have concluded that microcredit and the organising of women have empowered them through income generation and asset building, although these efforts have not changed the patriarchal structure (Todd, 1996; Dowla, 2006; cf. Sugie, 2019b).

Islamist parties have become key players in national politics. Riaz (2004) demonstrates how Islamists increased their power in both the political sphere and in broader society in the 1990s. Violence against and the suppression of women were symbolic of the Islamist movement. Acts of violence against women and NGOs by *fatwabazi* occurred frequently throughout Bangladesh, including one incident in the 1990s in the village where Rokeya Begum was born. *Fatwa* originally meant a *mufti's* advice or recommendation based on Shariah, which has no binding power; however, it was strongly enforceable though not necessarily based on Shariah in rural Bangladesh. Moreover, an independence ceremony held by a secular NGO was attacked by *madrassah* students in the Brahmanbaria district in 1998. This conflict exposed the struggle between secularist NGOs and Islamist groups. Researchers have explained the background of these incidences by pointing out the rapid growth, commercialisation, and interference in politics of microcredit-centred NGOs in the 1990s (Togawa, 2014) as well as the reactions of influential figures and religious authorities to the increased mobility of women and the poor (Takada, 2006).

Consequently, while the mobility of women increased, Islamist oppression of women also increased. However, this era also saw increased female participation in Islamist political groups, religious practices such as *purdah*, and religious activities such as *tablighi jama'at* and *talim* (*ta'leem*). *Tablighi jama'at* is a religious reformation movement in which a group goes to mosques in various places and preaches about Islamic creeds and norms.[5] *Talim* is a weekly Islamic lecture for local neighbourhood women given in a house by a female preacher, enabling women to join the male-dominated religious sphere (Huq and Rashid, 2008; Begum, 2015, 2016).[6] Female religious activities have become more popular in Bangladesh, two decades later than in other countries, partly because the country has been experiencing macro-level economic growth and the spread of mass education since the 1990s (Sen, 2003). While Islamic revivalism emerged and became influential in other countries during the 1970s, Bangladesh has remained extremely disordered and impoverished because of the disasters and political struggles of that period (Gardner, 1998).

Some researchers have argued that Islamist activities, including female ones, have undermined the tradition of Sufism, which is often believed to be female-friendly (cf. Sobhan, 1994), as well as the achievements of NGOs on behalf of women's empowerment, and that the rights of all women, including non-Muslims and those unable to follow *purdah* due to poverty, have been violated (Rozario, 2006; Miaji, 2010). Indeed, this argument might be valid if we consider that some influential Islamists insist that women must not receive education or work outside the home. However, other researchers have offered positive evaluations of recent women-centred religious activities such as *tablighi jama'at* and *talim*. In the case presented by Begum (2015, 2016), Muslimahs themselves interpret the Quran and insist on their right to conduct religious activities outside the home. Siddiqi (2017) asserts that women's participation in religious activities such as *talim* can lead to a sense of agency, although he concludes that women's agency in the *tablighi jama'at* remains strictly limited by the male-centred interpretation. Consequently, there is no consensus understanding of how female religious activities should be viewed based on subjective and objective evaluations of women's positions.

I conducted fieldwork in several Bangladeshi villages where Muslimahs held *talim* frequently. This chapter presents an exploration of the *talim* situation and examines how this movement can be evaluated. We discuss about not only those who attended *talim* but also those who did not, and examine the position and potential of Islamic education with respect to the diverse women in the area. Specifically, we examine whether *talim* contributed to the inclusive development of Muslimahs or impedes their participation and initiative by enforcing a male-centred Islamic discourse.

3 Study area and research methods

The study area includes seven villages; the main ones are villages B, M, and K in the Tangail district, located about 80 km northwest of Dhaka (Map 11.1).[7] It has been a Hindu-dominated area, although Muslims have also lived there since at least the end of the nineteenth century. Their numbers have increased since the 1960s because of immigration.[8] Muslims who have been regarded as 'different *jati*,' and considered unmarriageable by other local Muslims have resided in villages surrounding the area (Sugie, 2016). They were called '*Sanaidar*' locally. They traditionally serve as musicians on ceremonial occasions. Almost all such Muslims have suffered from poverty, illiteracy, and discrimination.

I conducted fieldwork intermittently in the area between 2011 and 2018. A Muslim household survey was conducted in village B, along with interviews and participant observation of *talim*. I have participated in *talim* with my little daughter and sometimes with a female research assistant since 2017. I am a Japanese woman who converted to Islam when I married a Bangladeshi Muslim whose house was located near the study area. Therefore, preachers and participants of *talim* treated me as a student of Islam rather than as a researcher. Religious books used in *talim* (Begum, 2018; Hemayet Uddin, 2017) were also analysed.

4 Channels of Islamic discourse

There were 16 mosques and five *madrassahs* in six villages (except village K) during the survey period, although only 4 mosques were built by 1918 (Map 11.1). Opportunities to learn Islamic knowledge have increased along with

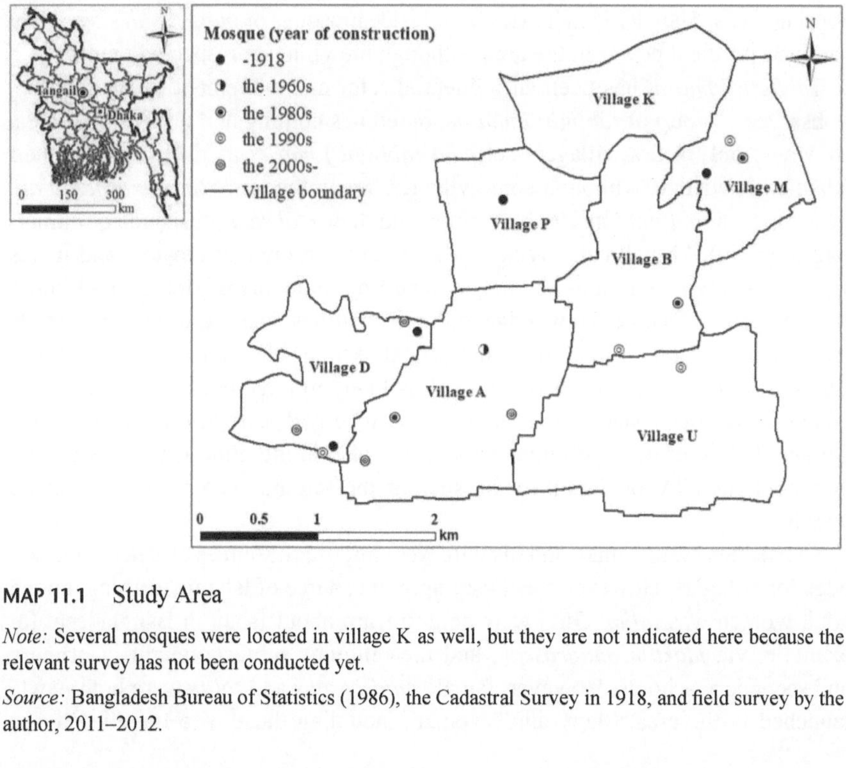

MAP 11.1 Study Area

Note: Several mosques were located in village K as well, but they are not indicated here because the relevant survey has not been conducted yet.

Source: Bangladesh Bureau of Statistics (1986), the Cadastral Survey in 1918, and field survey by the author, 2011–2012.

macro-level economic growth and the flourishing of cooperative religious activities in this area (Sugie, 2019a). I asked about the source of Islamic knowledge in 48 Muslim households in village B.[9] Most households answered the 'mosque or imam and his wife.' Although there is generally no space for women in mosques in Bangladesh, women also asked the imam's wife about Islamic norms. Imams were also teachers of *maktab*, in which children learned basic Arabic and how to read the Quran.

The '*madrassah*' was also an important centre of Islamic education for villagers. Villages M and P had *a madrassah.* Both villages had a *Hafiz madrassah,* the graduation requirement of which was a full recitation of the Quran. Moreover, there were two *Deobandi qwami madrassahs* in village M and one *furqania madrassah* in village P.[10] All five *madrassahs* were built in 2007. One *Deobandi qwami madrassah,* built in 2012, was for girls, whereas the *furqania madrassah,* built in 2007, was for both boys and girls. The educational qualifications of almost all the imams and *madrassah* teachers were the upper *dakhil* (equivalent to SSC[11]) or *Hafiz* (reciter of all verses of the Quran). Although none had ever studied abroad, the founder of the male *Deobandi qwami madrassah,* locally called 'Nurul *mufti,*' had graduated from the *Hatjahari madrassah,* a well-known and influential Islamist *madrassah* in the Chittagong district. The two *Deobandi quami madrassah* were built and managed privately by this man and his wife, whereas all *Hafiz* and *furqania madrassah* were maintained by each *samaj.*[12] Therefore, the *Hafiz* and *furqania madrassah* teachers and imams were employed by *samaj* from neighbouring areas. They lived in houses built inside mosques or *madrassah* sites. They had little political power in the area, although the villagers respected them.

Tablighi jama'at has been an influential reformist movement in Bangladesh. I observed a group of *tablighi jama'at* sometimes coming and going in the area. However, only a few villagers selected *tablighi jama'at* as the source of their Islamic knowledge. Although some villagers knew the term '*masturat jama'at,*' which means *tablighi jama'at* by women and their *mahram* (husbands or unmarriageable kin),[13] Muslimahs living in the area had rarely participated, and it was reported that female groups had never come from other areas. However, all those who preached Islamic knowledge or their families had experienced *tablighi jama'at* and/or *hajj*, as mentioned in the next section. Therefore, the recent flourishing of *tablighi jama'at* in Bangladesh is likely to have indirect effects on the Islamic discourse space in this area. Those who had learned directly from the Quran, Hadith, or other religious books were also in the minority. Moreover, no one mentioned TV or digital media such as the Internet as a source of Islamic learning.

Consequently, the imam and his wife were important sources of Islamic knowledge for villagers. However, the most important source of Islamic learning among adult women was *talim.* Girls were able to learn about Islam in Bangladesh, for example, via *maktab*, *madrassah*, and the religious subjects taught in primary and secondary schools. However, female *madrassahs* and *talim* were both newly launched in the area. Many adult women, including those who travelled to the region from other areas to marry, could not learn even basic Islamic knowledge or Arabic. Many villagers reported, 'I never heard about *talim* once. It has been increasing for a decade.' *Talim* diffused randomly in this area: Some villages had several *talim*, whereas others had none. The introduction of *talim* to this area is described in the next section.

5 *Talim* as the source of Islamic discourse

Preachers of talim

Socio-economic background

There were two types of *talim* in the area: One was held weekly by a female preacher in her house from 10 a.m. to the prayer after noon; the other was held irregularly by a family who brought a female preacher and who treated the audience to snacks at their house. This study focused on the former. I attended the *talim* held in villages M and K. This subsection presents the socio-economic backgrounds of the two preachers and their Islamic discourse.

The *talim* preacher in village M was addressed as '*caci*' (aunt) but was referred to as 'Shaif *maulana*'s wife' by participants; this chapter uses the latter term. She was a 50-year-old housewife who had passed Class Eight. She lived in village M and had never performed *hajj* or *masturat jama'at*. Her husband was 60 years old, had passed *maulana* (equivalent to a university degree), and had performed *hajj* in 2018. He had been employed as an imam in a mosque in the neighbouring sub-district, living away from his family. Her unmarried son was a *Hafiz* and *madrassah* student completing *dawra-e-Hadith* (equivalent to a master's degree). Her elder daughter was married and had given birth to a baby when I conducted the fieldwork. The elder daughter's husband had also passed the *maulana* and often participated in *tablighi jama'at*. Her younger daughter was a student in Class Five. Shaif *maulana*'s wife was busy taking care of her daughters and a grandchild because all male family members were living in other areas for work or school. Therefore, she sometimes had to cancel the *talim*. At such times, other women preached in her place. Her household owned at least two acres of farmland and a house in the town where her husband was living. She began the *talim* in 2003 for the 'people's virtue.' She also said, 'Now, women are learning well [about Islam]. There are many women who do not know about things like *haram* and the way of ablution [*wudu*].'

The *talim* preacher in village K was addressed as '*kaki*' (aunt) and referred to as 'Khuda *maulana*'s wife.' She was a 53-year-old homemaker who had passed *hafiza* (female reciter of all verses of the Quran) and *dakhil* (equivalent to SSC). She was living in a rented house in the capital city of Tangail and travelled weekly to village K with her husband for the *talim*. She had performed *hajj* in 2017 and *masturat jama'at* with her husband. Her husband was 60 years old and had passed *dawra-e-Hadith*. He had been an imam and *madrassah* teacher in various areas; then, he taught local people about Islam at informal study meetings. He had worked in Saudi Arabia for five years and had performed *hajj* with local people many times through his connection with a *hajj* travel agency. The two daughters of Khuda *maulana*'s wife were married, but her three sons were all unmarried. The eldest son joined a company after passing the Bachelor of Science (BSc). The youngest son was studying to complete the Bachelor of Arts (BA). Only the middle son had passed the *maulana*; he worked as a *madrassah* teacher, like his father. The household had about two acres of farmland. They owned a house under construction in the capital city of Tangail.

The concept of *talim* was introduced in village K from another area. Habib imam's wife began the *talim* in village K. It was the first *talim* in the area. Her younger sister married an imam in the neighbouring sub-district and saw *talim* held in that area. She advised Habib imam's wife to hold one. She then started the *talim* in village K with her husband's help. However, she asked Khuda *maulana*'s wife to preach instead of her because she became sick. Consequently, Khuda *maulana*'s wife began the *talim* in 1992 'for Allah and to spread Islamic knowledge.' She also said, 'All Muslims must learn about Quran and laws legalised by Allah and invite everyone.'

Islamic discourse by female preachers

Almost all the Islamic discourses of the two preachers were mutually contradictory (Table 11.1), as in the case of White (2010). However, what Khuda *maulana*'s wife said regarding the differences and relations between men and women was often heard from other women, including the imam's wife and female *madrassah* teacher. Neither of them was able to find their Islamic discourse in sources of the Shariah and the religious books used in the *talim* such as Begum (2018) and Hemayet Uddin (2017). For example, Shaif *maulana*'s wife said, 'I do not know in which parts of the Quran and Hadith these are written. I can't find them in religious books. It will take time to search which parts. My husband can say because he is *maulana*,' and 'If I do not know something, I ask Nurul *mufti* [the abovementioned *madrassah* male teacher].' The female preachers' Islamic discourse was different from what was written in the religious books. For example, those books say that women can take an outside job or business with *purdah* and that, when a wife demands a divorce from her husband because of his failure to provide sexual or economic satisfaction, the divorce is obligatory (*wajib*). Consequently, the preachers seem to follow the Islamic discourse of their husbands, Nurul *mufti*, or other people, rather than sources of the Shariah and religious books. However, it is noteworthy that they did not force women to be blindly subordinate to their husbands and spoke about how to correct a husband's faults or escape their violence, as presented in Table 11.1.

Teaching contents

In the *talim* in village M, the preacher and participants recited the words of prayer (*dua*) or verses of the Quran together. Some Hadith and religious stories were

TABLE 11.1 Islamic Discourse on Women and Gender Relations of Female Preachers

	Shaif maulana's wife (village M)	*Khuda maulana's wife (village K)*
1. Differences and relations between men and women	Men and women are equal before Allah. Knowledge and intelligence are also endowed equally.	Men are higher than women. Wives must follow what their husbands say. Men are superior in every respect, such as in physical power and courage.
2. Difference in amounts of Islamic knowledge between men and women	Women do not know as much as men. Men can learn well if they go to *madrassah* and obtain degrees. If women could also go to *madrassah*, they could learn well too. However, we did not go. Women have no opportunity. Intelligence is the same (as men), but women have no opportunity.	Ten women's intelligence is equal to one man's intelligence. It is said in Hadith.
3. Women outside the home	Women must stay at home.	Women must not go far from their house without being accompanied by men.
4. Gender roles and women working outside the home	Now everyone works outside with *purdah*. However, I do not know how it is judged in Islam. (Working outside is) not allowed, at least without the husband's permission. First, (women) must complete their housework.	Men work outside. Women can also work both inside and outside. (Women) can go to the bazaar and anywhere else.
5. Solution for husbands' faults and violence	A wife's master is her husband. She can go to heaven if (she) follows what her husband says. It rarely happens that what she learned from *talim* and what her husband says are mutually contradictory. In the case in which (her husband is) wrong, they must ask a great Islamic scholar what is right.	A wife must be patient and pray to Allah that her husband will become good. Even so, if (he) does not become good, she can divorce him. Although a husband can divorce according to Hadith, a wife can also divorce. It's based on a law of the government. [I said, 'Many women do not know that.'] So, I hold the *talim*. It is obligatory for women to receive education as well.

Note: These are the female preachers' answers to questions the author asked before the *talim* in villages M and K.
Source: Field survey by the author, 2018.

taught using religious books. Then, the preacher led the congregation in prayer after noon. The content of the *talim* in village K was almost identical, with the addition of prayer in Bengali (*munazat*) and calling the roll. Khuda *maulana* sometimes gave a short lesson to participants from the other side of a cloth. The relationship between the preachers and participants was not hierarchical. Participants were able to ask questions in the middle of the lesson. Although the preachers encouraged practising what they preached in the *talim*, they did not force anyone to do it and left things entirely up to the participants.

Women's status and rights were discussed while emphasising the virtue of obedience to and caring for the husband. For example, the Hadith of 'Heaven lies under mothers' feet for children' (Sunan An-Nasa'i) was featured one day. The preacher said, '[This Hadith is for] sons and daughters equally. Without a mother living happily, one cannot go to heaven. [Mother's] happiness becomes the effort to enter heaven [*ebadot*]. However, many good deeds one does, a person cannot enter heaven if the person's mother is unhappy. Mother is the most valuable. The second is the husband and then the mother-in-law.' In addition, the preacher heard that one participant became pregnant with a girl before the beginning of the *talim*. She was pleased and said to the participant, 'Girls are good. Girls will be mothers and play the respectable role of teaching about Islam to children.' These words, which are rarely heard from other women in the area, are important in changing the persistent social preference for male babies.

Although the gender role assignment by which men work outside the home to earn money and women work at housekeeping and child-rearing was unquestioned in the *talim*, the preachers explained the importance of attending *talim* and other religious practices for women. Khuda *maulana*'s wife emphasised that Allah told Muslims to spare at least two hours for religious activities during the day and that they had to spend time thinking not only about wealth and family in the present world but also about the future world.

By contrast, I have also listened to preaching in Islamic conferences and *talim* by male imams and *madrassah* teachers, and found that they emphasised only women's obligations such as *purdah* and obedience to the husband or father and seldom described women's rights or honourable status. They also suggested that women did not need to go outside the home for religious activities because their housework and prayers to Allah for their family had the same value. Consequently, Islamic discourse of the male and female preachers partly corresponded, but their teaching contents were starkly different.

Participants and changes in their lives

A total of around 50 to 60 participants came from houses near to the preachers' and neighbouring villages. The attendance roll for the *talim* in village K included more than 100 names. Participants were not limited to the rich but included poor people, such as widows who made their living working as servants (Table 11.2). A few participants had educational qualifications above SSC or had experience working outside the home, such as in garment factories and NGOs. Although most participants usually assigned priority to housework, many women still attended the *talim*, even with their children or infants. Widows, who generally needed less time for housekeeping and taking care of the family, participated actively. They went from house to house to invite their neighbours and regularly attended *talim* in other villages as well. The participants were always almost identical: They were likely to be women whose families were pious and allowed them to attend *talim* or widows who were isolated from other family members.

The main purpose of participating in *talim* was to learn about religious norms and practices (Table 11.2). Most participants told me that their religious minds and practices became more devotional and correct by attending *talim*. Aside from its effect on individual piety and knowledge, *talim* also served unintentional social functions. Participants often updated and exchanged information and consulted preachers about their daily problems.[14] Here, I discuss two incidents observed in the *talim* to demonstrate its effects on women's lives. When Khuda *maulana*'s wife was calling the roll, she found that a woman named Amena had not attended for a while and asked the other participants about her. One participant said, 'Amena said [to me], "I am so worried about the payment of weekly installments [for microcredit], so I can't sit down at the *talim* with an easy mind". So, I advised Amena to withdraw her membership [from the microfinance institute]. Then, Amena [quit and] told me that it was good for her to quit and that she wanted to come to the *talim* again.' Then, the preacher explained that happiness-seeking in the present world made her suffer more and preached about the prohibition against paying or receiving interest in Islam. Although the participant's advice might have been only one of the reasons why Amena withdrew her membership, this incident suggests that the *talim* and its participants had some influence over life choices.

However, another incident demonstrates that preachers and participants of the *talim* seldom interfered directly with other participants' family matters. A widow commonly called 'Liton's mother' (Liton is her eldest son) had attended the *talim* in village K since it began. She had become sick and had difficulty walking but attended the *talim* as long as possible and was respected by other participants. However, none of her sons supported her economically. She died of disease in August 2018. The *talim* held immediately after Liton's mother's death was dedicated to praying for her. A participant who had attended Liton's mother's last moments cried and spoke in detail about the event, and blamed her sons for not taking care of her. Khuda *maulana*'s wife listened to her story and then warned all the participants, including her, not to say anything bad about anyone, even clearly guilty persons, because it was a severe sin in Islam.

As described earlier, the *talim* provided a place where women deepened their solidarity by discussing daily problems. It was particularly meaningful for isolated widows to engage in social interactions and to feel a sense of belonging. However, neither the preachers nor participants ever protested the violation of a woman's rights by her family or took action to resolve problems as previously reported (Begum, 2015, 2016; White, 2010). Moreover, although the *talim* contributed to

TABLE 11.2 Examples of the *Talim* Participants

	Jusna (village M)	*Mina (village M)*	*Bulbuli (village K)*	*Nurjahan (village K)*
1. Age	50	50	45	50
2. Education	Class 4	No	No	No
3. Occupation	Homemaker	Domestic helper	Homemaker	Homemaker
4. Family structure	Three persons: husband 50 years old, passed Class 4, farmer; daughter married and living separately; both elder and younger sons unmarried, passed HSC and migrant workers in Kuwait; child of daughter, Class 8 student	One person: husband deceased; son and daughter married and living separately	Two persons: husband 55 years old, passed Class 5, farmer; all three daughters married and living separately; youngest daughter, *qawmi madrassah* student in Tangail city; son, *Hafiz madrassah* student	Two persons: husband deceased; elder son and daughter married and living separately; younger son, migrant worker in Dubai; younger son's wife
5. Income source	Farming	Domestic help	Farming	Remittance from younger son
6. Attendance rate	Sometimes (she was busy helping with her grandchild's studies).	Every week for five years	Every week for nine or ten years	Every week since the beginning of *talim* in this area
7. Purpose	To be able to pray and read the Quran properly	Everyone goes, to be able to pray properly.	To learn about Islam correctly such as prayer, fasting, obligation (*wajib*), the mode of ablution (*wudu*), four (kinds of) *purdah*	To learn (about Islam) correctly
8. Permission from family	My husband lets me go. (He) assigns priority to housework but allows me to go to *talim*.	I have come (to *talim*) when my husband was alive. Then he let me go.	(Family members) are not against (my attending *talim*). Father-in-law and mother-in-law are deceased. I go to *talim* after finishing cooking and taking care of the cows.	My husband told me to go to *talim*.

	Jusna (village M)	Mina (village M)	Bulbuli (village K)	Nurjahan (village K)
9. Changes in life through *talim*	(My life) has changed drastically in all aspects, such as in prayer and fasting. I follow what my husband says. This morning, I could not read the Quran because I took care of my husband's meals, but I will read after cooking *Insha Allah*.	Allah developed (my life).	(My life) has changed by going to *talim*. I consider Islam. I pray.	(My life) has changed drastically. I learned that (Muslims) must not tell a lie, must not eat through theft, and must eat by separating *halal* and *haram*.
10. Changes in relationship with family	I have a very good relationship with my husband. We do not quarrel. My husband could not understand anything if I were not (with him). My husband is very good.	My daughter used to go to *talim*, too. My son's wife also comes to *talim*.	My relationship with my son and daughter became good . . . (they) follow what I say. Although I cannot recall everything I learn in *talim*, I tell them what I can remember and to follow it. I tell them to pray.	The relationship became good. My (younger) son's wife will come (to *talim*). I invited (her). I always come to *talim* and invite various women.

Note: I selected these four participants as typical cases considering their age, village of residence, family composition, etc. The underscored persons in the family structure were living with the participants. 'Four (kinds of) *purdah*' means that Muslimah should be veiled in different ways in four types of situations. For example, when there are only Muslimah(s), she need not hide her hair, but specific parts of their body must be hidden.

Source: Field survey by the author, 2018.

individual learning about Islam, the increase in participants' religious knowledge was not observed to improve or redefine their status or relationship with their family, unlike what is observed in Huq and Rashid (2008).

The Muslimahs who regularly attended *talim* intended to obtain religious knowledge and learn correct practice, a motivation driven by the desire to satisfy Allah and ensure happiness after death. In short, the ultimate meaning of 'inclusiveness' for them is to enter heaven. The sisterhood and solidarity of Muslimahs come from their devotion to Allah, not from resistance to masculinity or gender inequality. The Muslimahs do not pursue social achievements in this world, such as enhancing or protecting their rights; any such social achievements are merely the unintentional side effects of *talim*.

Background and reasons for not attending talim

Many women did not attend *talim*, even in neighbouring houses. Non-participants told me that they could not attend because of housework, child-rearing, or a lack of anyone who could mind the house because the male members worked or were students; they only rarely described reasons related to piety. As the preachers and some participants said (Tables 11.1 and 11.2), women had less time to spend on religious activities because of persistent gender roles and spatial division, according to the male-centred interpretation of sources of the Shariah (Begum, 2015, 2016). Furthermore, women who belonged to the *Sanaidar jati* (the discriminated Muslim group) did not participate in *talim*. One *Sanaidar* woman said to me, 'This area provides little opportunity to learn [about Islam]. It's a matter of education. How can we let children study even though we can't feed them properly? Everyone is poor. I can [pray] because I went to *maktab* and learned how to pray *namaz* when I was living in my parents' house. I also taught my daughters. However, most women do not even know how to pray *namaz*. An imam came from village P to teach Arabic to adults, but no one attended.' Although I have mentioned that poor women also participated in *talim*, the main reason *Sanaidar* women could not spare time for religious activities was their struggle with poverty. They could not afford to participate in Islamic learning, even though there was an opportunity in their villages. This group has not benefited from the macro-level social and economic improvements (Sugie, 2016). Many of those women had to walk around the neighbouring villages to beg or engage in physical labour, in addition to housework and child-rearing. They were unable to give their children sufficient education, including Islamic learning, and their lack of Islamic knowledge and practice reinforced or reproduced the discrimination against them (Sugie, 2016). Considering the case of *Sanaidar*, Rozario (2006) presents a valid argument that those who are unable to follow Islamic norms because of poverty might be more socially disadvantaged due to the flourishing of Islamic education. A certain standard of religious practices, such as performing daily prayers or following *purdah*, guarantees or improves social involvement and status; Sugie (2019a) describes such a local social system as an 'Islamic locale.' Those who cannot afford these practices might face discrimination or social exclusion.

6 Conclusion

This chapter explored the Islamic discourse space and women's participation in rural Bangladesh by treating the case of *talim* in several villages in the Tangail district. To conclude, I will examine the background of the flourishing of *talim* and discuss how this activity can be understood with respect to the inclusive development of Muslimah. Although I could not explore the process in detail because of space constraints, religious activities have increased and become more cooperative since the late 1980s in this area (Sugie, 2019a). *Talim* is regarded as a movement that demonstrates how Islamic practices and activities have become more open and accessible. Such changes, including the increase in *talim*, have not been led by the government, Islamist parties, or other wealthy Muslim majority countries, but by bottom-up movements among rural Bangladeshis. The fact that the discriminated women could not afford to participate in *talim* or other Islamic learning and that the female preachers of the *talim* were more or less wealthy shows that the macro-level social and economic developments since the 1990s have been important preconditions for the growth and spread of this movement.

The *Talim* was an important place to learn about Islam for adult women, given the limited opportunities for their Islamic education. The necessity and significance of female Islamic education were asserted in the *talim*. Female preachers' husbands also helped. However, higher Islamic educational qualifications were obtained only by men. The female preachers were wives of imams who had received higher Islamic education, but they themselves lacked it. Therefore, neither the participants nor the female preachers were on the equal footing required for them to discuss the legitimacy of Islamic discourse with such men. They merely followed them. Consequently, the women neither challenged the male-centred interpretation nor reinterpreted sources of the Shariah. This result is different from that seen in other cases in Bangladesh (Huq and Rashid, 2008; Begum, 2015, 2016). However, the Islamic discourse in the *talim* was ambiguous and could not be reduced to a male-centred one, as in the narrative offered by some Islamists who oppose female education and outside employment. The Islamic discourse in the *talim* included women's rights and did not enforce blind obedience to the husband.

Although the *talim* provided a venue where women could discuss their daily problems and deepen their solidarity, the preachers and participants did not directly interfere with family problems. Therefore, the *talim* has improved individual Islamic knowledge and practice, but it has not had significant effects on women's status and relationships with their families. Consequently, the *talim* has contributed to the spread of Islamic discourse from the perspective of women. However, it remained inadequate for achieving the inclusive development of Muslimahs given the gender gaps in Islamic educational attainment and in social statuses and lives. Moreover, the *talim* participants tended to be limited to those who were more or less free from the scourge of poverty and were able to afford time for religious activities, and whose family members approved of female Islamic education. It could not include all women as participants.

Nevertheless, I would like to evaluate the *talim*'s social meanings positively and anticipate its potential for advancing the inclusive development of Muslimahs, even though they themselves did not see *talim* as a way to enhance their rights or destabilise men's authority, as is seen in previous studies. The existence of female preachers is not a sufficient condition for constructing and spreading Islamic discourse on women's honourable status and rights, but it is a necessary condition considering that the Islamic discourse of male preachers tended to focus only on women's duties, such as *purdah* and housework, and obedience to male family members. Islamic learning circles such as the *talim* were the only places where Muslimahs can regularly gather for a purpose and construct good relationships with other women beyond their neighbourhood and relatives (Metcalf, 1998; White, 2010).[15] As described in Section 4, mosques in Bangladesh generally have no spaces for women. Female religious practices are personalised in private spaces. The existence of places such as the *talim*, where Muslimahs can learn about Islam directly from and create relationships with other women, is important for learning a diverse Islamic discourse and developing 'chosen' relationships (Kabeer and Huq, 2010). Moreover, given the backlash against the increased mobility of women in the 1990s mentioned earlier, *talim* supported by local religious authorities is a realistic way to help female religious activities to expand women's rights and spheres of activity in the conventional male-dominated framework and to push back against male privilege and authority of constructing Islamic discourse gradually (Sakurai, 2011)—that is, to promote inclusive development of Muslimahs.

As described in Section 2, there is a two-decade gap in the flourishing of female Islamic education between Bangladesh and other countries. *Talim* has been held in the area for nearly 20 years, but no generational change among preachers and participants has occurred. A few Muslimahs in their teenage years and twenties were studying for higher degrees in Islamic education during the study. They may eventually be able to compete with imams or male *madrassah* teachers. *Talim* will facilitate the inclusive development of Muslimahs more efficiently when female preachers appear who have higher Islamic educational qualifications and who can understand and navigate the diversity and ambiguity of Islamic discourse.

Turning back to the question posed in the title of this chapter, we answer that Islamic norms are diverse and ambiguous. Some Islamic discourse, particularly male-centred discourse, might impede the inclusive development of Muslimah. However, female Islamic education represents an opportunity to change or appropriate male-centred Islamic discourse and its space, although the case of *talim* in the study area remains at the germination stage. When Muslimah can negotiate the legitimacy of Islamic discourse, Islamic norms themselves will offer an occasion and resource for the inclusive development of Muslimah.

Acknowledgements

My sincere appreciation is extended to the teachers who gave me valuable comments and advice at the 2018 INDAS–South Asia International Conference and its preliminary seminar. I would like to express my gratitude to those residing in the Bangladeshi villages I visited during my fieldwork for their warm cooperation. This study was supported by a Grant-in-Aid for JSPS Fellows (Number 16J05363).

Notes

1 The explanation of other sources of the Shariah is omitted here.
2 This chapter cites the translation of the Quran available at https://quranenc.com/ja/browse/english_saheeh (accessed 11 January 2022).
3 One example is the following: Anas Bin Malik claimed that the messenger said, 'Seeking knowledge is a duty upon every Muslim' (Sunan Ibn Mājah).
4 Some scholars who underwent traditional Islamic education have also contributed to our understanding of women's status in Islam by rejecting the assumption that Islam inherently includes discrimination against and disadvantages for women (e.g., Al-Buti, 2006), although their works are rarely cited in the Western and Japanese academic communities.
5 See Metcalf (1998) and Begum (2015, 2016) for details.
6 *Talim* is also held irregularly as one activity of *tablighi jama'at*.
7 Some Muslims belong to Hanafi schools and others to ahl-e Hadith in this area. However, this area is more or less neutral in terms of Islamic beliefs and practices relative to other areas such as Chittagong, where '*Wahabis*' (a reformist sect) have had a strong influence (Hara, 1991), and Sylhet, wherein Islamic purism has become prominent due to the large number of migrants to London and Middle Eastern countries (Gardner, 1998).
8 The Muslim population in each village in 2011 was the following: 1,405 in village K, 1,142 in village M, 645 in village B, 1,298 in village P, 461 in village U, 1,093 in village A, and 958 in village D (Bangladesh Bureau of Statistics, 2015).
9 When the interviewee was a man, I asked about the source of Islamic knowledge for women as well, and vice versa. Sugie (2019a: 9) presents relevant details.
10 Deobandi, a reformist group of the Sunni sect, seeks to revise Muslim beliefs and practices by emphasising strict adherence to the *Hanafi* legal cord. Several types of *madrassah* exist in Bangladesh; among them, *qawmi madrassah* has a unique curriculum composed mainly of Arabic lessons, whereas *furkania madrassah* provides fundamental Islamic knowledge and Arabic. Neither is included in the formal education system.
11 SSC stands for 'Secondary School Certificate.'
12 Although *samaj* generally means 'society' or 'association' in South Asia, the term is used to refer to the informal social unit that conducts cooperative dispute settlement and religious activities in Bangladesh.
13 Begum (2015, 2016) describes *masturat jama'at*, which is conducted only by women.
14 Participants also consulted Khuda *maulana* from the other side of the wall when he was waiting in another room during the *talim*. He taught the Arabic words to prayers (*dua*) and gave *tabiz* (charms with a verse of the Quran written on a piece of paper) to women to solve their problems.
15 NGOs organised women and implemented social mobilisation and political empowerment programmes until the 1980s. However, NGOs have leaned on microcredit and have abolished those programmes to ensure their organisations' financial sustainability since the 1990s (Sugie, 2019b).

References

Abu-Lughod, L. ed. (1998). *Remaking Women: Feminism and Modernity in the Middle East*, Princeton, NJ: Princeton University Press.

Abu-Lughod, L. (2013). *Do Muslim Women Need Saving?* Cambridge: Harvard University Press.

Ahmad, S. (2009). *Transforming Faith: The Story of Al-Huda and Islamic Revivalism among Urban Pakistani Women*, Syracuse, NY: Syracuse University Press.

Ahmed, L. (1992). *Women and Gender in Islam: Historical Roots of a Modern Debate.* New Haven, CT and London: Yale University Press.

Al-Buti, M. S. R. (2006). *Women between the Tyranny of Western System and the Mercy of the Islamic Law*, Beirut: Dar al-Fikr al-Mouaser.

Anderson, B. (2006). *Imagined Communities: Reflections on the Origin and Spread of Nationalism*, London: Verso books.

Asad, T. (1986). "The Idea of an Anthropology of Islam," *Qui Parle*, vol. 17(2), 1–30.

Bangladesh Bureau of Statistics (1986). *Small Area Atlas of Bangladesh: Mauzas and Mahallahs of Tangail District*, Dhaka: Bangladesh Bureau of Statistics.

Bangladesh Bureau of Statistics (2015). *Bangladesh Population and Housing Census 2011 Community Report Zila: Tangail*, Dhaka: Bangladesh Bureau of Statistics.

Bano, M. (2017). *Female Islamic Education Movements: The Re-democratisation of Islamic Knowledge*, New York: Cambridge University Press.

Bano, M. and H. Kalmbach eds. (2012). *Women, Leadership, and Mosques: Changes in Contemporary Islamic Authority*, Leiden and Boston: Brill.

Begum, M. A. (2015). "Negotiation for Extended Gender Roles in Islam: Women in Tablighi Jamaat in Bangladesh," PhD thesis. Hiroshima University.

Begum, M. A. (2016). "Reconfiguring Boundaries and Gender Relations in the Religious Sphere: The Women in an Alternative Group of Tablighi Jamaat in Bangladesh," *International Journal of South Asian Studies*, vol. 8, 49–72.

Begum, M. A. (2018). *Wajay Niswan ba Mohilader Waj (Women's Sermon)*, Dhaka: Al-Eshaque Prokashani. (in Bengali)

Dowla, A. (2006). 'In Credit We Trust: Building Social Capital by Grameen Bank in Bangladesh," *Journal of Socio-Economics*, vol. 35, 102–122.

Eickleman, D. F. (1992). "Mass Higher Education and the Religious Imagination in Contemporary Arab Societies," *American Ethnologist*, vol. 19(4), 643–655.

Eidhamar, L. G. (2018). " 'My Husband is My Key to Paradise.' Attitudes of Muslims in Indonesia and Norway to Spousal Roles and Wife-Beating," *Islam and Christian–Muslim Relations*, vol. 29(2), 241–264.

Gardner, K. (1998). "Women and Islamic Revivalism in a Bangladeshi Community," in Jeffery, P. and A. Basu eds., *Appropriating Gender: Women's Activism and Politicized Religion in South Asia*, New York and London: Routledge: 203–220.

Hara, T. (1991). *'Paribar' and Kinship in a Moslem Village in East Pakistan*, Tokyo: Institute for the Study of Languages and Cultures of Asia and Africa.

Hemayet Uddin, M. (2017). *Ahkamun Nisa (The Things to Do for Woman)*, Dhaka: Maktabatul-Ashraf. (in Bengali)

Huq, S. and S. F. Rashid (2008). "Refashioning Islam: Elite Women and Piety in Bangladesh," *Contemporary Islam*, vol. 2(1), 7–22.

Huque, A. S. and M. Y. Akhter (1987). "The Ubiquity of Islam: Religion and Society in Bangladesh," *Pacific Affairs*, vol. 60(2), 200–225.

Jaschok, M. (2012). "Sources of Authority: Female Ahong and Qingzhen Nusi (Women's Mosques) in China," in Bano, M. and L. Kalmbach eds., *Women, Leadership, and Mosques: Changes in Contemporary Islamic Authority*, Leiden and Boston: Brill: 37–58.

Jeffery, P. and A. Basu eds. (1998). *Appropriating Gender: Women's Activism and Politicized Religion in South Asia*, New York and London: Routledge.

Kabeer, N. (1991). "The Quest for National Identity: Women, Islam and the State in Bangladesh," in Kandiyoti, D. ed., *Women, Islam and State*, Philadelphia: Temple University Press: 22–47.

Kabeer, N. (2002). *The Power to Choose: Bangladeshi Women and Labor Market Decisions in London and Dhaka*, London and New York: Verso.

Kabeer, N. and L. Huq (2010). "The Power of Relationships: Love and Solidarity in a Landless Women's Organisation in Rural Bangladesh," *IDS Bulletin*, vol. 41(2), 79–87.

Kalmbach, H. (2008). "Social and Religious Change in Damascus: One Case of Female Islamic Religious Authority," *British Journal of Middle Eastern Studies*, vol. 35(1), 35–57.

Kandiyoti, D. ed. (1991). *Women, Islam and State*, Philadelphia: Temple University Press.

Mahmood, S. (2005). *Politics of Piety: The Islamic Revival and the Feminist Subject*, Princeton, NJ: Princeton University Press.

Mernissi, F. (1991). *The Veil and the Male Elite: A Feminist Interpretation of Women's Right in Islam*, Cambridge: Perseus Books.

Metcalf, B. (1998). "Women and Men in a Contemporary Pietist Movement: The Case of the Tablighi Jama 'at'," in Jeffery, P. and A. Basu eds., *Appropriating Gender: Women's Activism and Politicized Religion in South Asia*, New York and London: Routledge: 107–122.

Miaji, A. B. (2010). "Rural Women in Bangladesh: The Legal Status of Women and the Relationship between NGOs and Religious Groups," PhD thesis, Lund University.

Minesaki, H. (2009). "Gender Strategy and Authority in Islamic Discourses: The Female Preacher Case Studies in Contemporary Egypt," *Journal of Gender Studies*, vol. 12, 77–91. (in Japanese)

Mir-Hosseini, Z. (1999). *Islam and Gender: The Religious Debate in Contemporary Iran*, Princeton, NJ: Princeton University Press.

Moghadam, V. M. ed. (1994). *Gender and National Identity: Women and Politics in Muslim Societies*, London and New Jersey: Zed Books Ltd., Karachi: Oxford University Press.

Rauniyar, G. and R. Kanbur (2009). "Inclusive Growth and Inclusive Development: A Review and Synthesis of Asian Development Bank Literature," *ADB Occasional Paper*, vol. 8.

Rhouni, R. (2010). *Secular and Islamic Feminist Critiques in the Work of Fatima Mernissi*, Leiden and Boston: Brill.

Riaz, A. (2004). *God Willing: The Politics of Islamism in Bangladesh*, Lanham, Boulder, New York, Toronto and Oxford: Rowman & Littlefield Publishers.

Rozario, S. (2006). "The New Burqa in Bangladesh: Empowerment or Violation of Women's Rights?" *Women's Studies International Forum*, vol. 29(4), 368–380.

Sadiki, L. (2004). *The Search for Arab Democracy: Discourses and Counter-discourses*, London: Hurst & Company.

Sakurai, K. (2001). *Gendai Iran: Kami no Kuni no Henbo (Contemporary Iran: Chang in the land of God)*, Tokyo: Iwanami-shoten. (in Japanese)

Sakurai, K. (2011). "Women's Empowerment and Iranian-style Seminaries in Iran and Pakistan," in Sakurai, K. and A. Fariba eds., *The Moral Economy of the Madrassah: Islam and Education Today*. London and New York: Routledge: 32–58.

Sen, B. (2003). "Drivers of Escape and Descent: Changing Household Fortunes in Rural Bangladesh," *World Development*, vol. 31(3), 513–534.

Siddiqi, B. (2017). *Becoming 'Good Muslim': The Tablighi Jamaat in the UK and Bangladesh*, Singapore: Springer Nature.

Sobhan, S. (1994). "National Identity, Fundamentalism and the Women's Movement in Bangladesh, in Moghadam, V. M. ed., *Gender and National Identity: Women and Politics in Muslim Societies*, London and New Jersey: Zed Books LTD, Karachi: Oxford University Press: 63–80.

Sugie, A. (2016). "Persistence and Change in Occupational Groups among Muslims in Rural Bangladesh: A Case Study of Sanaidar Jati in Tangail District," *International Journal of South Asian Studies*, vol. 8, 73–102.

Sugie, A. (2019a). "Disembedding Islamic Locale: The Spread and Deepening of Islamic Knowledge in Rural Bangladesh," *Journal of Urban and Regional Studies on Contemporary India*, vol. 5(2), 1–21.

Sugie, A. (2019b). "Solidarity Economy Versus Neoliberalism? Microcredit in Rural Bangladesh," *Journal of Business and Economics*, vol. 10(9), 811–824.

Takada, M. (2006). *Bangladesh Minshuu Shakai no Muslim Ishiki no Hendo: Desh to Islam (Fluctuation of Muslim Identity Consciousness in the Popular Society of Bangladesh: Desh and Islam)*, Tokyo: Akashi Shoten. (in Japanese)

Todd, H. (1996). *Women at the Center: Grameen Bank Borrowers after One Decade*, Dhaka: University Press.

Togawa, M. (2014). "Islam and NGOs in Bangladesh: A Case Study of the Attack on the Independence Ceremony at Brahmanbaria in 1998," in Togawa, M. and S. Nejima eds., *Islam to NGO: Minami Asia kara no Hikaku Kenkyu (Comparative Studies from South Asia), NIHU Research Series of South Asia and Islam*, vol. 6: 19–70. (in Japanese)

Tsujigami, N. (2011). *Gendai Saudi Arabia no Gender to Kenryoku: Foucault no Kenryokuron ni Motoduku Gensetsu Bunseki (Gender and Power in Contemporary Saudi Arabia: A Discourse Analysis from the Perspective of Foucauldian Theory of Power)*, Tokyo: Fukumura Shuppan. (in Japanese)

Wadud, A. (2006). *Inside the Gender Jihad: Women's Reform in Islam*, Oxford: Oneworld Publications.

Wadud, A. (2009). "Islam Beyond Patriarchy Through Gender Inclusive Qur'anic Analysis," in Anwar, Z. ed., *Wanted: Equality and Justice in the Muslim Family*, Musawah: An Initiative of Sisters in Islam: 95–112.

White, S. C. (2010). "Domains of Contestation: Women's Empowerment and Islam in Bangladesh," *Women's Studies International Forum*, vol. 33(4), 334–344.

12

FROM 'FAILED DEVELOPMENT' TO 'INCLUSIVE DEVELOPMENT'?

Views of Ethnic/Caste Minority Women

Seika Sato

1 Introduction

'Developing the country (*desh vikas*)' has been a national credo of Nepal since its opening up to the international order in the early 1950s. Initially set by the government administering the country at that time, the credo has been carried on as a national project through regime changes, from the *Panchayat* regime through 'democratic' ones that rose to dominance in 1990, to the present day. Over the years, it has come to be embraced as doing what is necessary to achieve the betterment of people's lives, with concomitant 'economic growth' and 'modernisation,' by practically every citizen across cultural and social diversity, different economic standings, and political convictions.

The prevalent faith in 'development' does not mean that the project has not been criticised. In fact, another consensus on 'development' that emerged through decades of exercises in Nepal is that the project largely 'failed,' at least up to the present day. Well over a half century of developmental interventions in Nepal have fallen far short of delivering its people raised living standards meeting their expectations. A few academic arguments that criticise 'development' per se as structural violence aside (Shrestha, 1997; Tamang, 2004),[1] the Nepali people, from elites down to the grassroots level, have been criticising 'development' not because they see it as an unwelcome intervention that might be inherently devastating for people's livelihood but because they see it failing to deliver people its promised benefits (Leve, 2007: 158–159), although views vary as to why efforts have failed (Bista, 1990; Panday, 2009 [1999]).

What was deemed a prominent 'failure' of development in Nepal was, apart from (or on top of) the overall insufficient level of gross economic growth, the uneven distribution of fruits of 'development,' that, far from levelling the pre-existent degree of economic disparity, instead boosted the sense of deprivation

DOI: 10.4324/9781003304760-15

in more sections of the country. While demands for rectification of inequality had not been altogether absent under the *Panchayat* era, they gained far more strength and visibility after its end with the democratisation movement in 1990, which paved the way not only for the liberal political environment but also for extensive foreign developmental interventions that often accompanied ideas such as equality, justice, and human rights. People came to be more aware of disparity or discrimination and to expect more of equality to prosper, irrespective of their former standing in society. That growing expectation found its forcible expression through a decade-long Maoist uprising in 1996–2006 and then got carried on to mainstream politics with Maoists' joining it. Around the turn of the century, the demand took up the new slogan 'inclusion,' which established itself as a shared platform for 'New Nepal' to be built through progressive social and political reforms, if not by 'revolution' anymore. 'Failed development' was therefore reformulated as 'exclusionary' practices that must be made 'inclusive' to succeed, in economic and other terms.

Who were deemed 'excluded' in developmental exercises in Nepal? Whereas newly developed class stratification in the capitalist economy seems to be gaining prominence in recent decades (Liechty, 2002, 2012), other disparities and discriminations based on ascribed identities (caste, ethnicity, region, gender, etc.) have persisted, while constantly undergoing reconfigurations in relation to class. Consequently, broadly speaking, two competing views exist on *who* are excluded (and thus who should be addressed for 'inclusion'): one view regards the gaps between ascribed categories as significant (DFID and the World Bank, 2006; Onta, 2005) while the other specifically examines the gap separating the haves and the have-nots (Aasland and Haug, 2011; Madjdian, 2018; Biswakarma and Mangrati, 2017). Admittedly, class and ascribed identities cut across each other, and their relative significance is *not* to be categorically predetermined. In the contemporary public discourse in Nepal, however, the overwhelming emphasis is put on the former, giving leverage to the calls for 'inclusion' of those identity-based groups.

It is particularly interesting that what has been called for (and put into practice to some extent, as described below) so far under the banner of inclusion is almost solely the 'representation' of hitherto 'excluded' groups based on such identities as caste, ethnicity, region, or gender in various public arenas, especially in (but not limited to) electoral politics. Institutionalisation of proportional representation of various identity groups, that is, instalment of reservation system in accordance with each group's population ratio, has been vigorously sought after, at the cost of demands for other possible measures to achieve inclusion, not to mention demands based on class (Drucza, 2014; Sato, 2015a). The current politics of inclusion in Nepal practically turns out to be tantamount to identity politics.

Given the circumstances outlined earlier, several questions present themselves: 'Exclusion' of what kind has actually been perpetrated on which sections of population in the course of 'development' in Nepal? After the call for 'inclusion' gained its impetus, was any progress made towards 'inclusion'? If it was, then how was it achieved? What are the remaining issues to be solved?

The forms of inclusion and exclusion or (dis)engagement with developmental practice are diverse among diverse populations in Nepal. Conflicting trends can coexist even in a single community. The fact forces us to boil the question down to examine the more specific section(s) of Nepali society at the moment. Here we limit our scope to two groups: Janajati[2] women and Dalit women. They are the groups situated at the intersection of multiple exclusions, those in terms of gender and caste or ethnicity, and are definitely deemed as belonging to the more 'excluded' part of Nepali society. Let us restate the questions as follows: How have women of caste or ethnic minorities (Janajati and Dalit women) been 'excluded' (sidelined, disadvantaged, and marginalised) in the course of 'developing the country' in Nepal? How have they been (dis)engaged with developmental practice? Is their 'inclusion' actually in progress, amidst the introduction of an 'inclusion' agenda? We explore these questions by delineating their patterns of engagement with 'development' (Section 3) and then identifying the emerging momentum to 'inclusion' (Section 4). However, first, we start by sketching their current state of inclusion and exclusion in Nepali society by reviewing their statistical and discursive profiles (Section 2).

2 The state of Janajati and Dalit women's 'inclusion and exclusion': indices and discourse

Statistical profiles

We refer here to the *National Social Inclusion Survey 2012*, a large-scale sample survey designed to measure and compare wide-ranging aspects of life, from 'human development' through political participation to family and community relations, found among diverse Nepali populations, conducted by a team of Nepali scholars based in the Department of Sociology and Anthropology at Tribhuvan University, the country's oldest establishment in the field (Gurung et al., 2014). The survey itself was apparently inspired by the 'inclusion' agenda now being enacted, and employing the terms of disaggregation in line with it, such as caste, ethnicity, region as well as gender, when relevant. Consequently, the survey presents important advantages for reference if one tries to understand the state of a given group on the current 'inclusion' agenda in Nepal.

On average, Janajati (women)'s living standards, as elucidated through such indices as access to healthcare, educational status, house or land ownership, and household expenditure, seem to be approximately equal to the national mean (see Figure 12.1 for household expenditure). Actually, the group as a whole is not especially worse off in Nepali standards, although deviation across different (or even within) Janajati groups is huge. Although some Janajati, such as Thakali, Byasi, Sherpa, and Newar (the last one is shown separately in the figures) score at the Nepali top level, others, such as Raute, Chepang, and Munda, hover around the national bottom. It is noteworthy that they, along with Madhesi, appear to be subject to linguistic (or cultural, in extension) exclusion in Nepal, which is dominated by Nepali-speaking people from hills (Figure 12.2).

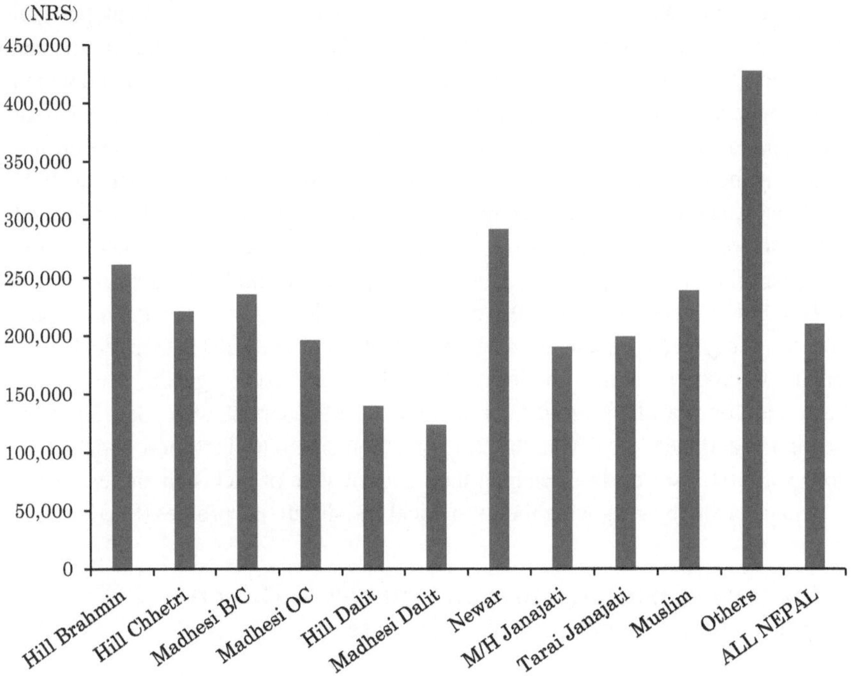

FIGURE 12.1 Average Annual Household Consumption Expenditure (NRS)

Source: Gurung et al., 2014: 68, FIG. 4.23.

Speaking of gender relations within each group, the presence of gender disparity and gender-based violence among Janajati is demonstrated clearly by the data. Contrary to the widely shared image of 'gender equality' in Janajati societies in Nepal (see the next section), Janajati women's status within their own community is apparently not on par with that of their male counterparts, either in public or domestic settings. For example, their educational achievement is lower than that of men (Figure 12.3). Moreover, the incidents of domestic violence are not especially few against Janajati women (Figure 12.4), although the latter figure is invariably based on subjective reports, which does not necessarily reflect objective incidence of violence.

The living standards of Dalits are definitely stagnating at the national bottom (Figure 12.1). Statistics also reveal that Dalit women are the more disadvantaged in their own communities. Their educational achievement is lower than men in their group; they are demonstrably subjected to domestic abuse (Figures 12.3 and 12.4). Furthermore, Dalits continue to be adversely affected by caste discrimination; they are prone to be abused by 'higher' caste people (Figure 12.5). While such incidents can happen to both genders, it is noteworthy that women are more likely to be adversely affected by such incidents because they often happen in such mundane public encounters during activities mostly conducted by women, such as collecting water, going to temple, or shopping (Kharel, 2010: 73). While

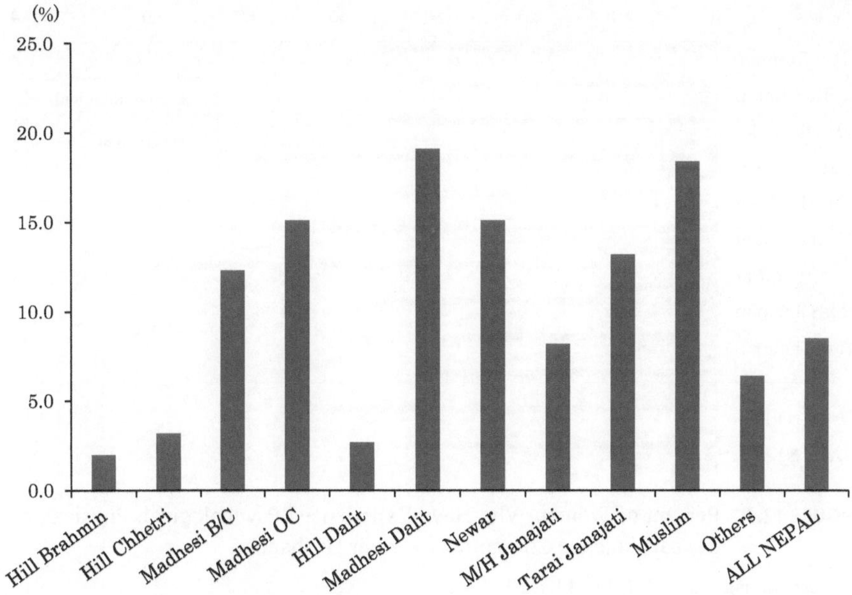

FIGURE 12.2 Percent of Respondents Who Lost Opportunities Due to Language by Social Groups

Source: Gurung et al., 2014: 103, FIG. 6.4.

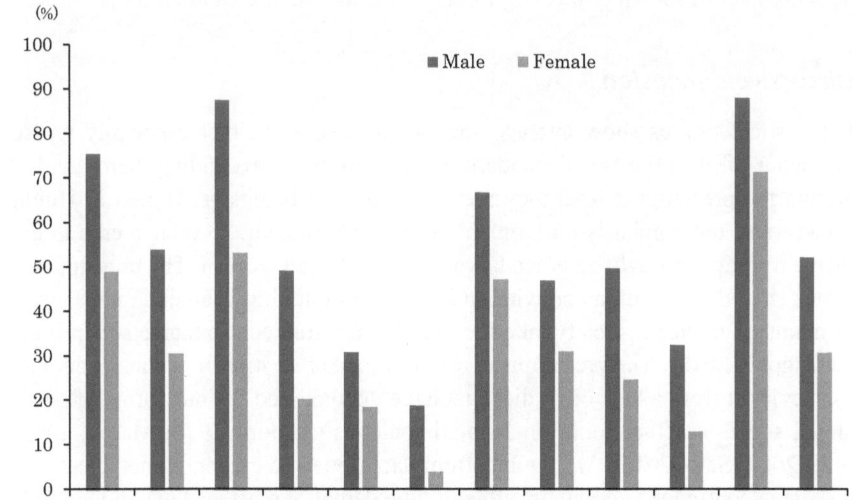

FIGURE 12.3 Percent of Population Aged 18 &+ Years Who Have Completed at Least 8th Grade of Education by Sex

Source: Gurung et al., 2014: 50, FIG. 4.6.

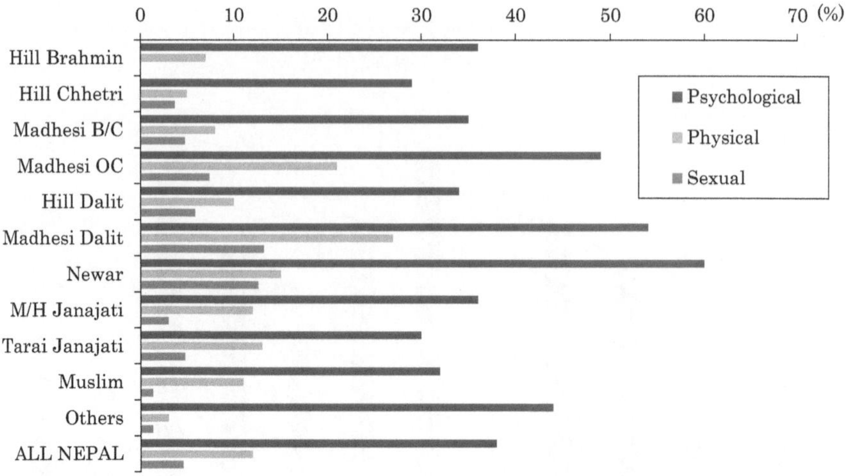

FIGURE 12.4 Percent of Women Who Have Experienced Psychological, Physical, or Sexual Violence Committed by Their Husbands

Source: Gurung et al., 2014: 143, FIG. 7.17.

the stagnating position of Dalits (women) as a whole is not disputable, regional and other disparities among Dalits are also noteworthy. Dalits (women) of Madhesh are overall shown to be even worse off, as all the figures illustrate.

Discursive dimension

If statistical figures show average Janajati women as neither especially worse nor better off than the Nepal standard, then discourses surrounding them revolve around the presumption that they are *not* oppressed beings as women in Hindu society are; the emphasis on women's nearly equal status to their men's is the theme routinely brought up when talking about Janajati women. The presumption seems shared both within and without Janajati communities: Janajati men as well as mainstream Nepal society take the premise for granted (Tamang, 2008; Tumbahangphe, 2010). The presumption cannot be taken at its face value, of course, as is evident from a host of studies that have documented various forms of patriarchal social structure found in Janajati societies (Andors, 1976; March, 2002; Stirr, 2009; Sato, 2015b)[3] as well as from data reviewed earlier. Nonetheless, the discourse continues to circulate, effecting the denial of existent Janajati women's need to raise *their own voice* in the face of their actual marginalisation within their own communities.[4]

At the same time, Janajati women are generally regarded as 'backward and uneducated' in the present 'developmental' order of Nepali society, which justifies their overall subordinate position in the order. As ignorant and innocent beings,

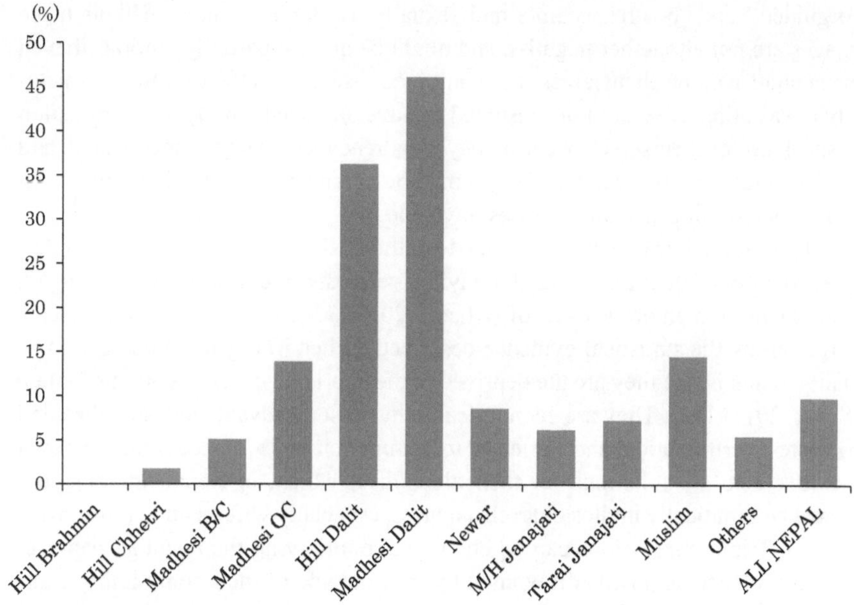

FIGURE 12.5 Percent of Respondents With Experience of Verbal Abuse in the Community by Other Social Groups

Source: Gurung et al., 2014: 118, FIG. 6.17.

they are seen as 'fit' to be guided and protected by the more knowing, powerful people: their 'high-caste' sisters, for example. A case in point is found in the discourse on 'girl trafficking' to India flourished in the 1990s. The victims were believed to be disproportionally from Janajati communities and were often represented as such. 'Rescue' of young women who were presumed to be 'victimised' because of their poverty and undereducation (or lack of 'development') would more often engender their disempowerment rather than the opposite.

A very intriguing fact is that they are seen to be prone to sexual victimisation not only because of their ignorance or innocence but also because of the way they essentially are. It seems only natural for dominant Hindus to think that women are sexually exploited *because they deserve it.* Combined with exoticism as well as casteism, Janajati women's presumed equality with men or freedom from their controls translates readily into their imagined sexual openness or being 'promiscuous and not respectable' (Caviglia, 2018: 82–83). That imagined character could actually funnel as well as justify their sexual exploitation by men from dominant groups.[5]

Here, we find seemingly inconsistent, but nonetheless interconnected discursive representations of Janajati women: 'independent women enjoying equal status to their male counterparts,' 'backward and uneducated women who must be guided,' and 'not respectable and sexually available women.' Although the images are not altogether negative and might be at least partially embraced even by Janajati women themselves, the combined discursive effect on them is actually devastating: they are not presumed to have any need, ability, or justification to speak up for themselves because they are already free, largely uneducated, and fundamentally not respectable. They would be deprived of having their own voice and rendered, for practical purposes, invisible.

'Dalit women are "thrice" excluded on the basis of class, caste and gender' (Bishwakarma, 2004: 2). In fact, that saying is almost a cliché heard time and again when Dalit women are spoken of (Kharel, 2010: 32–33, 223). It actually seems borne out by the statistical evidence described earlier. The general perception of Dalit women is that they are the deprived of the deprived, or 'Dalits among Dalits' (Sunar, 2011: 108). They are economically the most disadvantaged, still shackled by caste discrimination, and subjected to domination and violence from their own menfolk who are infamous for their alcoholism which, in Nepali imagination, almost automatically invites quarrelsomeness, especially wife-beating (BK, 2013: 27, 40). Triple oppressions can be combined, multiplying the resultant damage. Sexual violence against Dalit women by men outside of their community, arguably not a rare occurrence, is a case in point, where a woman's triply oppressed status in terms of class, caste, and gender constitutes the backdrop against which the crime and misconduct get perpetrated easily. In fact, a Dalit woman might well be prone to be victimised because she is a woman, because she had no choice but to go outside to earn (Sato, 2017b), and because she could be silenced easily based on her low caste and class status.[6]

While Dalit women are regarded as being at the bottom of the social ladder and as victimised by the *de facto* culturally sanctioned violence, another thread of prevalent discourse surrounding them would turn the perceived vector of violence upside-down. They are popularly imagined as being 'not respectable,' 'overly sexual,' and 'promiscuous' (Cameron, 1998) and are therefore deemed to embody the 'sinful' and 'dangerous' nature among others presumably shared by women as a whole in Hindu culture (Bennett, 1983). According to this conception, it is they who would perpetrate destructive effects on others rather than the other way around, by seducing men in particular and by poisoning people in general, the latter leading to the reportedly disproportionate accusation of witchcraft against Dalit women.

Whereas the representation of 'perpetrator' appears not to be readily reconcilable with that of 'victim,' both images easily conjoin to exacerbate Dalit women's plight. In the narrative of this image complex, if they become abused, sexually or otherwise, it is they who invited the action by themselves; they become victimised *because they are bad.* By imposing certain inherent 'nature' onto Dalit women, their actual plight is effectively transformed into something they deserve.

Consequently, Dalit women are regarded as extremely pitiful but nonetheless dangerous; they are the victims but are potential perpetrators. Ambivalence prevails, and after all, doubles the suffering of Dalit women. From their own perspective, prevailing is not ambivalence but straightforward discursive and often real exclusion that enforces and justifies their marginalisation in society.

To sum up, Janajati and Dalit women have been represented, although differing in terms of details, as the ambivalent 'Others' in popular Nepali discourse; they may not always be treated negatively, nonetheless they mostly remain deprived of their own voice, that is, *representation* by themselves. With this state of Janajati and Dalit women in mind, one can turn to the contours of their engagements with 'development' that have unfolded in Nepal to date.

3 Janajati and Dalit women's engagements with 'development'

Extremely varied though they may be, Janajati and Dalit women's engagements with 'development' can be broadly categorised into one of the following forms: not being developed, being developed, or being adversely affected by development. In this section, the expected commonalities in their experiences are delineated against the backdrop of their state of being outlined earlier.

Not getting developed

Given that 'development' has been a national project for well over a half century, it is almost inconceivable that there remains any place in Nepal where no 'development' has ever occurred in one form or another. A common narrative heard in the more remote parts of Nepal, however, is that which deplores lack thereof: people talk of 'no school,' 'no hospital,' 'no road,' 'no electricity,' 'no development programme,' etc. When people perceive gross deficiency of development and talk openly about that, developmental practice is actually there, if only in the form of people's unfulfilled expectations for it. People are already subsumed under the developmental regime only to sense its absence around them.

Many men and women from Janajati communities are prone to be relegated to this near disengagement with development because of their 'distance' from Nepali mainstream society in geographical, cultural, and linguistic terms. Their traditional environs are invariably located in the remote rural areas (the major exception being Newar) and they are, by definition, distinct from the mainstream in their traditional culture and language, which constitute barriers against outside intervention, developmental or otherwise.[7]

If Janajati communities get excluded from 'development' because of their geographical and cultural distance, Dalit women and men get excluded because of their caste status as 'untouchables,' even when they do constitute the part and parcel of dominant Nepali-speaking Hindu society. They have been excluded from a multitude of sociality, from such a simple practice of commensality or socialisation at home or other places through worship in a temple, not to mention conjugality. Developmental practice made still another moment to effect their social exclusion. Various social restrictions on Dalits and their generally disadvantaged position in society are expected to affect their engagements with development adversely. One can readily imagine that developmental programmes would skip their community routinely, as if theirs were located in as remote places as Janajati's.

'Not being developed' might take still another form. Even if Janajati and Dalit (women) are formally included in the developmental target, they could be *effectively* excluded from accessing its benefits. This might happen in two ways. First, people who are more favourably positioned in the targeted locale with more adequate cultural, social, or economic capital, which in turn is based on their caste, ethnic, class, or gender status, can usurp and channel the benefits of development; those who are already advantageously positioned would get more benefits at the cost of those positioned disadvantageously. Consequently, disparity between haves and have-nots would be amplified. Those who really need the intervention may well just be left behind.[8] Dalits almost invariably, and Janajati often, are the more disadvantageously positioned in mixed caste and ethnic settings. If Dalits or Janajati are generally positioned unfavourably, it is true to a greater degree for their womenfolk.

Secondly, Janajati and Dalit (women) can become effectively excluded from 'development' because the interventions are not designed to suit their actual needs and capacities. As a rule, developmental interventions come from 'outside' and are subsequently mediated by Nepali-speaking high-caste elites in Kathmandu, who are expected to be neither well informed nor motivated to become well informed to address the reality on the ground. Programmes are often fatally detached from the grassroots reality and become hopelessly irrelevant to the local context, grossly neglecting the cultural difference (especially in the case of Janajati) or class standing (especially in the case of Dalits) of expected participants. A case in point, for example, is a programme for education of female children. Engaging in the programme incurs, for example, 'a triple expense' for poor Dalit households if not for others: the cost of the education, the missed earning opportunity, and the increased price of dowry (Patel, n.d.: 27), which are difficult to be properly compensated with subsidies provided by the programme alone. The same programme cannot be equally effective across different caste, ethnic, and class standings.

Getting developed

If 'not getting developed' would definitely make communities marginalised in the national developmental order, then becoming an integral part of the order would not necessarily mean that they are now freed from marginalisation. For many Janajati or Dalits, actually, it simply means that they would be included in the order *at its bottom*.

As pointed out time and again on a global scale (Escobar, 1995) as well as in the context of Nepal (Pigg, 1996), becoming incorporated into developmental regime is tantamount to getting positioned as the object of the intervention, as those who are 'lagging behind,' 'uneducated,' 'not understanding,' and who therefore must 'get developed.' Development is such a project that would constantly require and create the rank of people who are labelled as 'not' or 'less' developed to go on. When they 'get developed' at all, Janajati and Dalits find themselves in subordinate positions vis-à-vis those who drive the operation, almost invariably high-caste Hindus. The power balance between those who 'develop' and those who 'get developed' could be so skewed that it is as if the benefits of development are provided as a 'mercy' of superiors to their inferiors, as a Dalit critic once pointed out (Aahuti, 2014: 176).

Neoliberal developmental regime is well known to have made 'women' the major target for intervention. That does not mean that women were made to spearhead the project. Rather, women now have been directly subsumed under the regime to be objectified and used as a means to further economic growth (Tamang, 2004). Many rural-based, ethnic, and caste minority women have been incorporated into the regime only to be given the least powerful position within it, whereas some elite women, mostly of urban middle-class high-caste background, did 'get developed' sufficiently and made their way to influential positions over time.

Disparity emerges not simply between those who lead the operation and those who get developed in it. People implicated into the developmental order would now get differentiated and stratified in more minute terms in accordance with the *degree* of getting developed, which would be measured mainly by the way they consume in a capitalist economy. With the massive inflow of foreign aid after 1990 that grossly expanded developmental base, some women from Janajati and Dalit communities also made their way into more powerful positions in developmental industries. Whereas a few educated Janajati women assumed leadership roles in NGOs, a host of NGOs focused solely on Dalit (women's) issues were established around that time (Cameron, 2007), in which some educated Dalit women did secure a place.[9] Now Janajati and Dalit women's involvement with development is far from uniform, although their tendency to concentrate at the bottom of the order remains unchanged. A cynic described the situation as one in which some favourably positioned women are 'marketing the misery' of their fellow, less favourably positioned, sisters (Sunar, 2011: 107, 115).

Suffering from development

Consequently, the experience of engagement with development might be more or less disheartening for Janajati and Dalit women at large. The most substantially and intensely disastrous form of engagement with development, however, would be the case in which their traditional livelihood actually gets irreversibly damaged as a direct or indirect result of developmental operations, whether entirely or partially, in abrupt or gradual form. The adverse effects might well diverge between Janajati and Dalits (women).

Many Janajati ancestral homelands are located in parts of the country that were not easily accessible by outsiders. As developmental processes progressed, cases emerged in which Janajati communities were forced to discontinue their traditional ways of livelihood or were even displaced from their habitat. The first and by far the major incident in this line was the case of displacement of the Tharu people, a Janajati community of Terai region, who lost most of their land and became marginalised in their own place by the inflow of immigrants from the hills following the eradication of malaria from the region in the 1960s. Although taking place on a more minor scale, incidents of developmental encroachment on the rights of Janajati individuals or communities continue to this day, resulting from either a hydropower plant or power line installation, road construction, mining, or establishment of national parks, etc. (LAHURNIP, 2017a, 2017b). While non-Janajati people might also be adversely affected by those encroachments, given many Janajati homelands' geographical location and their marginalised position within the country, it does make sense that they are prone to be targeted for 'sacrifice' by the more powerful people in the name of the greater cause of 'developing the country.' We also note here that it may well be Janajati women more than men who are adversely affected when their traditional livelihood becomes disrupted. That is true because, especially in recent years when we see men from rural areas increasingly emigrate (often to foreign countries) to earn, it is women who are more likely to get left behind to carry on their traditional livelihood at home (LAHURNIP, 2017a: 99).[10]

Dalits' suffering can be expected to take a different form from that of Janajati. Whereas Janajati are likely to be adversely affected by concrete developmental interventions, Dalits are likely to be besieged by the result of a much larger trend whose parts those interventions would constitute: marketisation. Dalit communities are well known to have once subsisted on their caste-determined occupations, providing goods or services to their specific patrons. People increasingly cease to rely on this mode of provision and turn instead to the market to fill their needs, making it impossible for Dalits to continue their traditional livelihood. While there are cases in which Dalits were able to adapt to, or even make good use of, the newly created monetised economy while capitalising on the skills fostered through their traditional occupations,[11] many merely lost their age-old ways of life with no viable alternative means of subsistence (Kharel, 2010: 139).

Consequently, many Dalits have been displaced from their traditional livelihood for the slim chance of making a better living in the freedom of marketplace, although poorly equipped with the capital they were able to build on, either in the form of skills, education, money, or social networks. Nonetheless, they might still be grossly disadvantaged in the capitalist economy because of their status in the old caste economy. They could even be 'punished' or ostracised for practising new occupations outside of their tradition.[12] Being neither allowed to stay in their former place nor able to venture forth to experience new opportunities presumably opened up with the onset of 'development,' many Dalits appear now to have been caught up in a double bind.

4 Momentum for 'inclusion'

In 1936, the country's arguably most adored author to date, Laxmi Prasad Devkota, wrote, 'A human being becomes noble by heart, not by caste/ethnicity (*jat* in Nepali)' (in his 1936 masterpiece, *Muna Madan*). Since the country's integration into the modern international order in the 1950s, it basically proceeded to institutionalisation of equality and democracy, although the road was full of setbacks. The 1961 constitution abolished discrimination based on caste; the 1991 constitution reinstated democracy, declared gender equality, and recognised Nepal's ethnic and linguistic pluralism. Since that time, multitudes of laws had been implemented to materialise those mandates. The current 2015 constitution further widened the vision with the 'inclusion' concept.

Momentum for 'inclusion' is not limited to the words of law, of course. Through decades of its practice, 'development' has brought some positive change in people's livelihood and has laid the groundwork for further change, if not at the level of people's expectations and certainly with the gross disparity across populations. Today, more parts of the country than ever before have access to such fundamentally important infrastructure and services as transportation, basic healthcare, and primary education. Some of the population have achieved higher education and have achieved middle-class status in the increasingly economically developed Nepal society. If not getting opportunities at home, people now turn to the outside world and sustain their hopes for prosperity and class mobility. Apparently, decades of developmental practice have achieved some betterment of Nepali livelihood *in absolute terms*, which is the sort of betterment that the Human Development Index, for example, can assess.

The point is, however, that improvement in absolute indices does not necessarily match people's perception of the progress achieved in 'inclusion.' As described at the outset, development in Nepal is invariably regarded as having 'failed' to date, not because it failed to make any effect on people but because it actually did, either by exacerbating people's feelings of deprivation (by 'not getting developed') or by (de)grading them to such disempowering positions of being 'backward' villagers (by 'getting developed'), if not by disrupting people's age-long livelihood and making them 'adversely affected by development.'

Consequently, calls for inclusion have mounted. To date, they almost exclusively revolve around gaps across different identities (caste, ethnic, regional, and gender) and their proportional representation (mainly) in electoral politics. Of course, minority groups are also demanding other remedies such as implementation of development programmes specifically targeted at such groups. Nevertheless, priority at the moment is apparently being assigned to the issue of representation; most people seemingly expect, perhaps naively, that inclusion in other fields of lives would follow suit once inclusion in politics is realised. We now review in turn what has happened with respect to political representation of Janajati and Dalit women.

Janajati women

For Janajati movement as a whole or at least for some major Janajati groups, one focus during the process of constitution writing was the federal restructuring with installation of 'ethnically identified' states. After the agenda went off, the issue of institutionalisation of Janajati's 'proportional representation' in governmental bodies came to be the main issue for the movement. The women's movement had been demanding their proportional share (Acharya, 2010), too, which now acquired the mandate in a clause of the new constitution that confirms women's right to participate in 'all state structures and bodies on the basis of the principle of proportional inclusion' (38(4)). The Janajati women's movement, for its part, is also demanding first and foremost their share of representation proportional to their presence, trying to establish their separate identity and avoid dissolution into that of either 'Janajati' or 'women' (Rai, 2017). The question is how far their demands have translated into reality.

In the present electoral system, the proportional representation (PR) seats of House of Representative (HoR) and State Assemblies (SAs), which constitute (roughly) 40% of all seats, with the rest being elected by First-Past-The-Post (FPTP) system, are divided among six 'inclusion groups[13]'in accordance with their population ratio (national Janajati ratio is 28.7%). The Election Act mandates that half of PR candidates for each 'inclusion group' be women, which means that the mandatory reservation for 'Janajati women' is institutionalised for the first time in Nepali history. In the 2017 HoR and SA elections under this system for the first time, however, they ended up still vastly under-represented because of their gross failure to win outside of their mandatory PR seats. Janajati women were able to hardly compete for a party candidacy, much less win a seat, in the FPTP constituency. Actually, the same applies to larger 'Janajati' or 'women' as well. Both groups, along with other minority groups allocated with reserved seats, ended up under-represented at the cost of men from 'Khas Arya,' the so-called 'high'-caste Hindus from hills, who maintained their age-old dominance in spite of the unprecedented institutionalisation of 'inclusion.'[14]

For the local election held in the same year, the outlook for Janajati women was even grimmer. The newly introduced reservation policy for local bodies stipulates that two out of five ward members, including one ward chair, must be women, of which one is from Dalit community, and that parties must have at least one woman candidate for either mayor or deputy mayor (chair or deputy chair) for (rural) municipalities. Although an unprecedented 14,339 women in all became part of local government, nearly all were elected to seats reserved for women. Among them, 19.9% were from Janajati (Paswan, 2017), who turned out to be under-represented again, even among women. The reservation of one of two female ward member seats for Dalits cut deeply into the share not only of Janajati women but also of all non-Dalit women.[15]

From a long-term perspective, Janajati women are making progress, although limited, to fairer representation, along with other or 'larger' minority groups such as 'Janajati' or 'women.' Nevertheless, the progress is still a far cry from the achievement of proportional representation in electoral politics, still less in other public arenas. One might wonder whether the limit of success can be attributed to the current narrow focus on achieving representation by mandatory reservation. The point is examined further as one turns to address the case of Dalit women.

Dalit women

The Dalit movement in Nepal, which more often than not took its inspiration from its counterpart in India, has raised the demand for reservation early on (Aahuti, 2014: 161). They demanded not only 'fair' (i.e., 'proportional') representation but also 'special rights' or 'additional rights with compensation' (Basnet and Darnal, 2007; Aahuti, 2014: 184, 187, 245). Whereas the contents of 'special' or 'additional' rights to be granted on top of fair representation seem varied or not yet well developed among different authors, the logic for demanding the 'special' provision is sufficiently plain. They are intended to address the reality of economic, social, and cultural oppressions perpetrated on Dalits for 'thousands of years,' which is deemed as incomparable in its magnitude with those experienced by other disadvantaged communities such as Janajati.

In the 2017 election for HoR and SAs, Dalits (women) also ended up far short of gaining proportional representation, similarly to Janajati and other inclusion groups. The overwhelming dominance of Khas Arya men in FPTP, where no seats are reserved for any group, made any prospect for other minority groups to obtain balanced representation remote.

In the election for local governmental bodies held the same year, however, the picture was different. As described earlier, the new rule of game set in the Election Act stipulates that two out of five ward members (including the ward chair) must be women, of which one must be Dalit. For Dalit women, whose official population ratio is just around 7% of the total Nepali population, 20% of ward member seats are reserved.[16] The provision led to the unprecedented presence of Dalit women in elected positions: Dalit women occupied 47.4% of the total 14,339 seats won by women as a whole (Paswan, 2017).[17] Dalit women, for the first time in Nepali history, became the minority group that realised *over*-representation by far exceeding (almost *three times* larger than) their population ratio vis-à-vis the whole nation. When Dalit women have been described repeatedly as being subjected to *triple* oppressions, it is as if they now had broken out of them and had obtained a disproportionally large presence, if only in this particular context of local electoral politics.

In this case also, however, they remain remarkably *under*-represented in that they failed to register in any position (ward chair, mayor or chair of (rural) municipality or its deputy) outside of their reservation. The picture appeared grimmer for Dalit women than for non-Dalit women on this front. Whereas the number of Dalit women elected outside of their reservation remained nil, some non-Dalit women candidates did get elected, although they were few.[18]

In this circumstance, it is more than obvious for everyone that this scale of Dalit women's representation was realised only by introducing mandatory seat reservation for them.[19] It would have been entirely impossible without that concession. In this context, what appears remarkable about this representation is that it can be taken as an exceptionally clear showcase for what reservation can or cannot achieve, that is, the possibility of reservation politics (or limit thereof).

The Dalit women's movement welcomed the provision and embraced it as an important opportunity to further their presence in politics and to push their agendas forward, including the mainstreaming of Dalit women in developmental practice. Celebrating the great victories Dalit women were bound to win, Dalit women organisations were quick to start efforts to turn their presence into substantive power for change. One emphasis of their endeavours is the capacity building of those elected representatives (*Samavesi Drishti*, 2018a; *Margadarshan*, 2017/2018). Courses on basic knowledge and skills necessary to function in the position were organised at multiple sites across the country for Dalit women ward members, not a few of whom testify that they had never spoken their mind in public or that they were not even aware of the necessity to understand what was on a paper before signing it, on top of being unable to read it in the first place (*Samavesi Drishti*, 2018c, 2018d). Another point of emphasis is on the building of an environment in which Dalit women, with due capacity and motivation, can actually do their work. The range of issues in this regard is so broad that it would practically require an overhaul of the whole society. Nonetheless, transformative efforts were launched already, among others with the most familiar sociality at hand (that is, women's relationship with 'household head') (*Samavesi Drishti*, 2018b). Dalit women's movement is striving, to the extent that their capacity and resources will allow them, to make the best use of their abruptly enlarged presence, which has been realised by virtue of the reservation policy. They are certainly determined not to let conservatives boast by saying, 'We did give them the chance, but they could not (use it)' (Sunar, 2018: 10).

Their task ahead must be emphasised as a formidable one. Conservatives who are for maintaining the status quo would have agreed to the deal in the first place because they calculated that the possibility was extremely low that Dalit women's presence, substantial as it was, would translate into their actual power. As these people may have fully understood, formal representation alone is generally insufficient to empower a marginalised group. While Dalit women's organisations are spearheading the development of enabling capacity as well as environments for Dalit women representatives, the conservatives might have been trying to contain the power of representation, either by recruiting Dalit women representatives who are neither able nor willing to work for Dalit women in the first place, by hampering their capacity-building and environment-building efforts, or by squarely obstructing those representatives' endeavours by 'binding their hands and feet' (Tamang, 2018).

If Dalit women representatives cannot make a difference with their magnitude of presence, then the conservatives will make a strong case that presence, after all, means nothing and that therefore the provision for reservation can afford to be scrapped. The claim against the provision can be made forcibly building on this particular case of Dalit women, given that their scale of representation cannot be too small to have effects; in consequence, the reservation policy might be repealed one day.

It must be emphasised, however, that we are witnessing a case showing with exceptional clarity that the achievement of 'inclusion' is *not solely* dependent on representation (the case is neither the first nor sole example in this regard, of course). Although balanced representation might be the only reasonable outcome if society is truly 'inclusive' at all, it is not the goal in itself but only one means, albeit an important and perhaps essential means, to achieve such society. Inclusion of Janajati and Dalit women (or of any group) would proceed only if politics of reservation expands and combines with substantive efforts on other fronts, such as their own capacity building, building up of enabling environment, fairer distribution of resources, and transformation of social discourse that (mis)represents them in mainstream society. Such combined efforts will truly enhance their 'representation.' While such efforts, parts of which were reviewed briefly herein, have been underway, the efforts might be neither sufficiently strong nor sufficiently comprehensive even to uphold the present momentum for inclusion, that is, the provision of reservation for political representation.[20]

5 Concluding remarks

One must return to the question presented at the outset: Are Janajati and Dalit women becoming more 'included' in the Nepali social order, which has professedly proceeded on a 'development' track for well over a half century?

We have observed on the whole in this study that they had been 'excluded' or marginalised in their engagements with 'development' in particular, and in the Nepali social order heading for 'development' in general. As the calls for inclusion mounted around the turn of the century, momentum for change gained strength, notably around the issue of political representation. The resultant introduction of some mandatory reservations in electoral positions for minority groups including Janajati and Dalit (women) did translate into more balanced representation. Nevertheless, to date, no minority group has achieved a level of representation proportional to their population, except for the case of Dalit women for local bodies for which mandatory seats were set far above their population rate. The fear seems real, meanwhile, that even that achieved representation might not duly translate into their actual inclusion, or worse, might get lost amidst a swelling conservative backlash if efforts for inclusion in political representation are not combined successfully with those on other fronts as well.

Janajati and Dalit women are standing at the crossroad of exclusion and inclusion, and will continue to do so, for the foreseeable future.

Notes

1 Their arguments were inspired, in turn, by the critical discourse in developmental studies circulating globally, such as that presented by Ferguson (1990) or Escobar (1995).
2 Janajati (or Adivasi Janajati, Indigenous Nationalities in English) are ethnic communities that claim they are the original dwellers on the soil of Nepal preceding the arrival of now dominant caste Hindus from India and have lived outside of Hindu caste order, fundamentally retaining their own culture and language. After the 'unification' of Nepal (and especially after the promulgation of the Country Code in 1856), they were put under the caste order in the middle range between 'high-caste' and 'untouchable' groups by the state (Höfer, 1979).
3 It is also true, however, that some academic discourse did endorse and perpetuate the popular image of egalitarian gender order among Janajati (e.g., Watkins, 1996; Kattel, 2016), the credibility of which is largely eroded by the concrete facts presented in the very studies themselves.
4 Sato (2017a: 281–286) provides a discussion related to this point.
5 The case in point is the Janajati women from Helambu (Hyolmo), who are 'famous' for their 'stunning' beauty (Caviglia, 2018, for their ethnography, see Sato, 2015b). The area is known to have provided women to serve in the palaces of aristocratic Rana families in Kathmandu historically, which, later in the age of 'development,' became infamous for allegedly high incidence of 'girl trafficking.'
6 Even in rare cases in which sexual encounter between Dalit woman and man of 'higher' birth is not simply the former's sexual exploitation by the latter but which involves some mutuality and leads to inter-caste conjugal relationship, noteworthy is that Dalit women would still be likely to face the kind of exclusion that would not be experienced by either Dalit men or Janajati women, not to mention their male partners; they might well not be accepted as a member of her partner's family because of their 'untouchable' status. The curious combination of perfect acceptance of Dalit women in trade of sex with strong social repudiation of them appears to hold widely in Nepal. One might be reminded of Badi, a Dalit caste, the women of which have traditional occupations that are nothing other than trade in sex.
7 Some Janajati from high Himalayas, notably Sherpa, however, have actually made favoured targets for foreign aid/development, precisely because of their remoteness and the 'exotic' attraction associated with it.
8 An impressive episode can be presented here. In a conversation at his home in the outskirts of Kathmandu valley, a Dalit man showed a bucket with a sign of a well-known INGO on it to the author, saying, '(After the 2015 earthquake made his house of mud and stone unlivable) Aid did come here. Those who have (in his neighbourhood) got the house – we got this.' (in August 2018).
9 With expansions in Dalit (women) organisations, positions are also being filled by those from outside of Dalit (women) communities, given that a good command of English is the prerequisite to fill these positions in the larger, well-funded (I)NGOs (Kharel, 2010: 184).
10 Women constituted only 5.26% of total labour emigration from Nepal in the official account for the year 2016/2017 (Ministry of Labour and Employment, Government of Nepal, 2018). Given this overall prominence of male over female emigrants, the situation is presumably not so different in Janajati communities, although the gender ratios of emigrants might be quite varied across communities.
11 Kharel (2010) reports on cases of successful musicians in modern music industry from the Damai caste, whose traditional occupation was performance of ritual music and tailoring.
12 Folmar (2007) reports such cases. In one of them, a Dalit man's new business (running a tourist hotel) was vandalised by enraged locals; in another, a Dalit commercial singer simply had to hide her caste identity for fear of ruining her career.
13 They are Khas Arya, Dalit, Madhesi, Tharu, and Muslim, apart from Adivasi Janajati.

14 Women occupied slightly fewer than 30% of all entire seats in HoR, which represented a dramatic rise from 5.9% before Maoists joined mainstream politics in 2006, but a rollback, if small, from the attainment in the last national election (for Constituent Assembly, held in 2008).
15 It cut deeply into Dalit men's representation, too.
16 The population size of Dalits has been the issue of contention for many years. Some estimates hold that the Dalit population is much larger than the official tally (Cameron, 2007: 25).
17 Women were greatly outnumbered by men in elected local government positions, 35,041 in total, with all the mandatory representation for women in ward member seats (40%) as well as in mayor, chair, and deputy positions (50%).
18 Only 7 out of 263 mayor seats were held by women (6 are Khas Arya; 1 is Madhesi), for example (Paswan, 2017).
19 In actuality, the provision's constitutional grounds are unclear (Vollan, 2018: 109). It was presumably a deal, reached among different parties amidst their conflicting interests and intentions, who try to promote *or* disprove the politics of reservation.
20 Apparently the rise of 'backlash' against 'inclusion' appears to be widely felt (Limbu, 2018), starting already in the drafting process for the current constitution.

References

Aahuti (2014). *Varna System and Class Struggle in Nepal*, Kathmandu: SAMATA Foundation.

Aasland, A. and M. Haug (2011). "Perceptions of Social Change in Nepal: Are Caste, Ethnicity, and Region of Relevance?" *Journal of Asian and African Studies*, vol. 46(2), 184–201.

Acharya, M. (2010). "Changing Discourse on Women's Movement: A Critical Lookback," in Dahal, D. R. and C. D. Bhatta eds., *Multiverse of Nepal's Democracy: Contents and Discontents*, Kathmandu: Friedrich-Ebert-Stiftung: 85–126.

Andors, E. (1976). "The Rodi: Female Associations Among the Gurungs of Nepal," PhD Dissertation, Columbia University.

Basnet, P. and S. Darnal eds. (2007). *Bisheshashikar ra Arakshanko Rajniti (Politics of Special Rights and Reservations)*, Kathmandu: Jagaran Media Center.

Bennett, L. (1983). *Dangerous Wives and Sacred Sisters: Social and Symbolic Roles of High-Caste Women in Nepal*, New York: Columbia University Press.

Bishwakarma, P. (2004). "The Situation Analysis for Dalit Women of Nepal," National Seminar on 'Raising Dalit Participation in Governance' organized by Centre for Economic and Technical Studies in cooperation with Friedrich-Ebert-Stiftung, May 3 and 4, 2004 Lalitpur. http://dalits.nl/pdf/TheSituationAnalysisForDalitWomenOfNepal.pdf (accessed July 11, 2019)

Bista, D. B. (1990). *Fatalism and Development: Nepal's Struggle for Modernization*, Hyderabad: Orient Longman.

Biswakarma, G. and R. Mangrati (2017). "Dalit Youths' Perception Towards Their Current Employment in Nepal," *Contemporary Voice of Dalit*, vol. 10(1), 84–97.

BK, A. B. (2013). *The Stigma of the Name: Making and Remaking of Dalit Identity in Nepal*, Kathmandu: Himal Books for Social Science Baha.

Cameron, M. (1998). *On the Edge of the Auspicious: Gender and Caste in Nepal*, Urbana & Chicago: University of Illinois Press.

Cameron, M. (2007). "Considering Dalits and Political Identity in Imagining a New Nepal," *Himalaya, the Journal of the Association for Nepal and Himalayan Studies*, vol. 27(1), 13–26.

Caviglia, L. (2018). *Sex Work in Nepal: The Making and Unmaking of a Category*, London and New York: Routledge.

DFID and the World Bank (2006). *Unequal Citizens: Gender, Caste and Ethnic Exclusion in Nepal*, Kathmandu: DFID/World Bank.

Drucza, K. (2014). "A Garden of Different Flowers: Recognition and Representation in Nepal's Social Inclusion Agenda," in Zeynep, G. E. ed., *New Opportunities and Impasses: Theorizing and Experiencing Politics* (Politsci'13 Conference, Conference Proceedings, October 31–November 2, 2013, Istanbul University). Istanbul: DAKAM Publishing: 48–67.

Escobar, A. (1995). *Encountering Development: Making and Unmaking of the Third World*, Princeton: Princeton University Press.

Ferguson, J. (1990). *The Anti-Politics Machine: 'Development,' Depoliticization, and Bureaucratic Power in Lesotho*, Cambridge: Cambridge University Press.

Folmar, S. (2007). "Identity Politics Among Dalits in Nepal," *Himalaya, the Journal of the Association for Nepal and Himalayan Studies*, vol. 27(1), 41–53.

Gurung, Y. B., B. R. Suwal, M. S. Pradhan, and M. S. Tamang (2014). *Nepal Social Inclusion Survey 2012: Caste, Ethnic and Gender Dimensions of Socio-Economic Development, Governance, and Social Solidarity*, Kathmandu: Central Department of Sociology/Anthropology, Tribhuvan University.

Höfer, A. (1979). *The Caste Hierarchy and the State in Nepal: A Study of the Muluki Ain of 1854*, Innsbruck: Universitat Verlag Wagner.

Kattel, S. P. (2016). "Practice of Democracy and Justice in Simple Society: Can We Learn Lesson from the Kisan Community of East Nepal?" in Pokharel, B., J. Rai, and M. S. L. Tamang eds., *Nepali Anthropology: New Direction and Contributions (Seminar Proceedings)*, Kathmandu: Central Department of Anthropology, Tribhuvan University: 397–428.

Kharel, S. (2010). "The Dialectics of Identity and Resistance among Dalits of Nepal," Ph.D. Thesis, University of Pittsburgh.

LAHURNIP (Lawyers Association for Human Rights of Nepalese Indigenous Peoples) (2017a). *Nepalma Adivasi Adhikar Hananka Ghatna*, Kathmandu: LAHURNIP.

LAHURNIP (Lawyers Association for Human Rights of Nepalese Indigenous Peoples) (2017b). *Study on the Impact of the Upper Trishuli-1, 216 MW Hydropower Project on the Indigenous Communities of Rasuwa*, Kathmandu: LAHURNIP.

Leve, L. (2007). "Failed Development' and Rural Revolution in Nepal: Rethinking Subaltern Consciousness and Women's Empowerment," *Anthropological Quarterly*, vol. 80(1), 127–172. www.jstor.org/stable/4150946 (accessed July 11, 2019)

Liechty, M. (2002). *Suitably Modern: Making Middle Class Culture in Kathmandu*, Princeton: Princeton University Press.

Liechty, M. (2012). "Middle-Class Déjà vu: Conditions of Possibility, from Victorian England to Contemporary Kathmandu," in Heinman, R., C. Freeman, and M. Liechty eds., *The Global Middle Classes: Theorizing through Ethnography*, Santa Fe: School for Advanced Research Press: 271–300.

Limbu, S. T. (2018). "Reimagining Inclusion," *The Kathmandu Post*, June 1, 2018. https://kathmandupost.ekantipur.com/news/2018-06-01/reimagining-inclusion.html (accessed July 11, 2019)

Madjdian, D. S. (2018). "Gender, Intra-Household Food Allocation and Social Change in Two Himalayan Communities in Nepal," in Niehof, A. et al. eds., *Diversity and Change in Food Wellbeing: Cases from Southeast Asia and Nepal*, Wageningen: Wageningen Academic Publishers: 153–175.

March, K. (2002). *If Each Comes Halfway: Meeting Tamang Women from Highland Nepal*, Ithaca and London: Cornell University Press.

Ministry of Labour and Employment, Government of Nepal (2018). "Labour Migration for Employment: A Status Report for Nepal: 2015/2016–2016/2017," https://asiafoundation.org/wp-content/uploads/2018/05/Nepal-Labor-Migration-status-report-2015–16-to-2016–17.pdf (accessed July 11, 2019)

Onta, P. (2005). "Assessment of Policy and Institutional Framework for Addressing Discrimination Against Adivasi Janjatis (Indigenous Nationalities) in Nepal and a Review of Public Discourse and Action of the Adivasi Janjati Social Movement," Unpublished draft of Chapter 9 of the Gender and Exclusion Assessment (GSEA) Report, Kathmandu, February.

Panday, D. R. (2009) [1999]. *Nepal's Failed Development: Reflections on the Mission and the Maladies*, Kathmandu: Nepal South Asia Centre.

Paswan, B. (2017). "Data Reveals Local Elections a Disaster for Gender Equality," *The Record*, October 27, 2017. www.recordnepal.com/wire/features/data-reveals-local-elections-a-disaster-for-gender-equality/ (accessed July 11, 2019)

Patel, L. ed. (n.d.). *Dalit Women in South Asia: Access to Economic Rights*, Kathmandu: ADRF (Asia Dalit Rights Forum)/FEDO (Feminist Dalit Organization)/UN Women.

Pigg, S. L. (1996). "The Credible and the Credulous: The Question of 'Villagers' Beliefs' in Nepal," *Cultural Anthropology*, vol. 11(2), 160–201.

Rai, K. ed. (2017). *Pahichanko Khoji: Adivasi Janajati Mahilaka Samajik, Sanskritik ra Rajnitik Sandarbha (2018–2073)*, Kathmandu: Indigenous Media Foundation.

Sato, S. (2015a). "Hosetsu no Haijo Suru Mono: Kaikyuron teki Nepal no Kanosei (What is Excluded from 'Inclusion': Envisioning Nepalese Society from the Perspective of Class)," *Teikyo Journal of Sociology*, vol. 28, 1–31.

Sato, S. (2015b). *Kanojotachi tono Kaiwa: Neparu, Yorumo Shakai ni okeru Raifu/Sutori no Jinruigaku (Conversing with the Yolmo Women: An Anthropology of Life/Story in Nepal)*, Tokyo: Sangensha. (in Japanese)

Sato, S. (2017a). "Soko ni 'Onna' wa Itaka? Neparu Minshuka no Dotei no Ichidanmen (Has 'Woman' Been There? A Profile of Democratization in Nepal)," in Nawa, K. ed., *Tenkanki Neparu ni okeru 'Hosetsu' no Shoso (Aspects of 'Inclusion' in Nepal amid Political Transitions)*, Tokyo: Sangensha: 257–295. (in Japanese)

Sato, S. (2017b). "Still Out of Place? Women in Public Spaces in Contemporary Nepal," in Shinoda, T., T. Inoue, and T. Suda eds., *Social Transformation and Cultural Change in South Asia: From the Perspectives of the Socio-Economic Periphery*, Tokyo: The Institute for Oriental Studies, Daito Bunka University: 221–244. (in Japanese)

Shrestha, N. R. (1997). *In the Name of Development: A Reflection on Nepal*, Lanham: University Press of America.

Stirr, A. (2009). "Exchanging Songs: Migration, Gender and Nation in Nepali Dohori Performance," PhD Dissertation, Columbia University.

Sunar, D. (2018). "Nirvachan Parinam: Dalitka Lagi Asalagdo," *Samavesi Drishti*, vol. 1(1), 10–11.

Sunar, P. (2011). "Dalit Women and Social Exclusion in Nepal: A Concern for Social Justice," *Nepali Journal of Contemporary Studies*, vol. 11(2), 103–119.

Tamang, P. (2008). *Hamro Nepal: Sanghiya Loktantrik Ganatantra*, Kathmandu: Mulyangkan Prakashan Griha.

Tamang, S. (2004). "Nepalma Vikase Narivad," in Deschene, M. and P. Onta eds., *Nepalko Sandarbhama Samajsastriya Chintan*, Kathmandu: Himal books for Social Science Baha.

Tamang, S. (2018). "'They've Given Us the Chair but Bound Our Hands and Feet': Embedding Elected Female Representatives in Institutions in Nepal," *Studies in Nepali History and Society*, vol. 23(2), 309–352.

Tumbahangphe, S. (2010). *Nepalma Mahila Andolan*, Biratnagar: Vani Prakashan.
Vollan, K. (2018). "The 2017 Local Elections in Nepal: An Unusual Framework with Expected Consequences," *Studies in Nepali History and Society*, vol. 23(1), 103–127.
Watkins, J. C. (1996). *Spirited Women: Gender, Religion and Cultural Ideology in Nepal Himalaya*, New York: Columbia University Press.
Samavesi Drishti (by Center for Dalit Women/Dalit Mahila Kendra Nepal) (2018a). "Dalit Mahila Pratinidhiko Kshamata Abhivriddhi Pariyojna Suru," vol. 1(1), 3.
Samavesi Drishti (by Center for Dalit Women/Dalit Mahila Kendra Nepal) (2018b). "Dalit Mahila Janapratinidhika Gharmulisanga Abhimukhikaran," vol. 1(3), 12.
Samavesi Drishti (by Center for Dalit Women/Dalit Mahila Kendra Nepal) (2018c). "Talima Sahabhagi Janapratinidhiharuko Anubhav," vol. 1(3), 15.
Samavesi Drishti (by Center for Dalit Women/Dalit Mahila Kendra Nepal) (2018d). "Hamita Bolna Janne Bhayau," vol. 1(4), 1.
Margadarshan (by FEDO (Feminist Dalit Organization)/Dalit Mahila Sangh) (2017/18).
Margadarshan (vikram sambat 2074 Poush). "Mahila Sadasyalai Samman tatha Abhimukhikaran," vol. 12(17), 21.

13

DESTITUTION IN OLD AGE

Living Through Asymmetrical Relations

Sae Nakamura

1 Introduction

Population ageing coupled with ever more fluid and changing family relations is a social dynamic confronted in many parts of South Asia today. It is not rare that one comes across local newspaper articles alerting readers to the 'future scenario' of aged society, stuffed with numerical expressions and statistical charts. For example, in Sri Lanka as of 2012, the percentage of the population aged 60 and older is around 12.4%; it is estimated that one in four people will be over sixty by 2041. Presumably, Sri Lanka would face a graver dilemma of old age than other neighbouring countries because of its highest longevity (life expectancy at birth 75.0–72.0 for male and 78.6 for female) and lowest fertility rate (crude birth rate 15.6/1000) in South Asia.

Concern about the old age burden is expressed plainly in what is called 'old-age dependency ratio.' It indicates a proportion of older persons in relation to that of working age; the higher the ratio, the greater the potential burden on the state and society. There is a sharp increase in the old-age dependency ratio in Sri Lanka. It is expected to be as high as 45.5% two decades from now. It is regarded as posing a severe threat and challenge to the national economy (e.g., *Sunday Times*, 21 September 2008).

Whereas such indicators might enable us to aggregate social trends and envision a 'probable' future, it does so at the cost of objectifying old age in solely economic terms. Old age is regarded as a difficulty simply because it is a potential burden or 'cost' imposed on the economy. It does not necessarily tell us how one can better face it if that was a difficulty at all. In other words, a vision of a 'probable' future, however precisely sketched, would still leave us with some exceedingly complex questions. How can old age be conceptualised in a time characterised by increasing longevity and booming health industries? How should

DOI: 10.4324/9781003304760-16

intergenerational relations be designed when the fluidity of family relations is the norm? Does a way of conceptualising old age exist, not as an isolated entity but as a 'being-in-time,' which would nurture our imagination about a 'possible' form of future[1]?

It must be clarified at the outset that this chapter, with the consideration described earlier in mind, alludes to a rather different kind of 'inclusivity' compared to that presented in other chapters of the volume. Put simply, the key concern of this paper is about the nature of an *inclusive society that adopts existential vulnerability and human transience as one of its fundamental values*. The author will specifically describe a residential institution for elderly people in Sri Lanka, designated as *vädihiti nivāsa* in Sinhala, as a case to explore this idea. Before illustrating ethnographic vignettes with relevant details, the next few sections briefly reflect broader debates about inclusion and exclusion in old age. They suggest what new questions might be raised by examination of institutional lives in Sri Lanka.

2 Debating inclusion and exclusion in old age

The exclusion of older persons is generally conceptualised as a problem of 'ageism.' Ageism is defined as stereotyping, prejudice, and discrimination against people based on their age (WHO, n.d.). Where ageism is normalised, one who fails to avoid oldness is bound to experience disapproval and exclusion from the public sphere. As a counterargument to ageism, the 'successful ageing' movement appeared as early as the 1990s. It emphasised the high cognitive and physical function capacity of older persons and insisted that they be more engaged in social interaction, which is enabled by, but simultaneously would have a positive effect on, their physical and cognitive health conditions (Rowe and Kahn, 1997). Closely tied to this concept was the idea of 'productivity' of older persons. Akin to the logic of 'inclusive neoliberalism' which aims to tackle poverty by 'making markets work for the poor' through legal and regulatory arrangements (Craig and Porter, 2003), successful ageing movements pushed institutional reforms that opened up labour markets for the 'young-old.' 'Working longer, living better' is a slogan now widespread not only in North American and European countries, but also in Japan, and possibly in other Asian countries, that have experienced industrialisation and population ageing.

As the concept became popular, however, successful ageing discourses, initially aimed at overcoming the exclusion of older persons, have presented a rationale for 'selective exclusion' of certain groups of people. Those who were excluded were destitute, frail, or perhaps senile older persons who were fully dependent on others. In *Successful Aging as Contemporary Obsession* (2017), Lamb et al. elucidate that 'successful ageing' discourses flourished in a specific cultural–historical condition, characterised by an unprecedented demographic shift of population ageing, breaking down of welfare states, and rise of the neoliberal state and citizens. Staying independent, healthy, and productive became highly valued not only for the well-being of the individual but also because it would support economic viability and minimise the burden on part of society (Lamb et al., 2017). Consequently, gerontology has not dealt adequately with the question of 'real' old age (Gilleard and Higgs, 2010; Lamb et al., 2017). When productive activity and well-being in old age is the dominant ideology in academic gerontological circles (Katz, 2000: 135), 'real' old people might easily be underrepresented, except in medical discourses or accusative claims against the dehumanising effects of health industry including nursing homes.

One might explain such a tendency to under-represent the aged bodies as underpinned by North American culture, which, according to Kleinman and Benson (2006), emphasises individual agency and autonomy while denying human limits, which include frailty, senility, and death itself. Such attitudes related to old age and frailty might also be contextualised in broader philosophical concerns. In the Western philosophical traditions, egalitarian relations between rational subjects are often regarded as the basis of ethical intersubjective relations. Justice here is regarded as a 'contract' or 'exchange' between relative equals, both of whom are similarly independent and autonomous. Consequently, legal and institutional arrangements were created through conflict to ensure equal rights and participation for socially disadvantaged people.

However, such logic might not be applicable to 'real' old people. In fact, the aged senile body-self could be a deviation and a potential threat to the ideal figure of individuals as social participants and consumers. A philosophy of 'inclusivity' from the vantage point of 'ageing' then, should be capable of addressing real, distinct, and sometimes unavoidable differences and asymmetries that are prevalent in actual human conditions. This leads us to the question of ethics in asymmetrical relations, as explained later.

3 *Vädihiti Nivāsa:* residential institution as a problem or potential?

To sketch out a form of social inclusion that embraces transience and vulnerability as its fundamental value, however speculatively, the author turns to ethnographic accounts gathered during a 24-month period of fieldwork (2007–2010) conducted at several *vädihiti nivāsa* around the suburbs of Colombo.

Vädihiti nivāsa, or 'old age homes' in Sinhala, are facilities where individuals separated from their families and loved ones for various reasons are provided with shelter, sometimes until they pass away.[2] The author notes that family networks centred on parent–child relationships still fulfil a strong supportive function in many parts of the island (Silva, 2004). In fact, only a fraction of the older people of Sri Lanka live in these facilities. For example, as of 2009, only about 15,000 out of a population of two million residents aged 60 and older lived in the 185 registered nursing facilities nationwide (Higuchi, 2012). However, they are seen to be increasing, causing a certain sense of anxiety and concern among people in the country.

It might sound inappropriate to choose residential institutions as sites to discuss 'inclusion' of older persons. This impropriety is especially apparent when reflecting upon the fact that old-age residential institutions have long been the subject of study precisely because they figure as a site of '*exclusion*' both in popular imaginary and academic discourses. For example, nursing home ethnographies, which mainly flourished in the United States, attempted to address problems of dehumanisation in institutional settings. They disclosed the brutalising effect of institutionalisation (Goffman, 1961) and assessed it mainly in terms of bureaucratisation of care, objectification of aged bodies, and the 'social death' experienced by nursing home residents because of these processes (Gustafson, 1972).

In scholarly works examining South Asia such as India and Sri Lanka too, institutionalisation is generally dealt with along with a sense of discomfort. However, how they differ in conceptualisation represents an important difficulty. In South Asia, institutionalisation figures as a difficulty not quite because of its bureaucratisation or objectification of residents' bodies, but more because the residents are separated from a person's kin and relatives (Nalini, 1997; Eriyagama, 2000; Kalavar and Jamuna, 2008). The scenario in which the problem of ageing is posed as that of the modern family (Cohen, 1999) emerges repeatedly in both popular and academic discourses because it symbolises the disintegration of traditional family relations. Popular discourses on 'traditional' family care based on the logic of long-term reciprocity are iterated in Protection of the Rights of Elders Act, which is the backbone of the formal Old Age Policy in Sri Lanka. Adopted in 2000, the Act stipulated the obligation of the child towards the child's parents. The establishment of a 'maintenance board,' which was introduced as an arrangement for elderly parents to petition for the support from their children, was symbolic of this.

As such, those who are separated from family, such as residents at institutions, are 'excluded' from such accounts of ideal old age. During fieldwork, the author came across Buddhist monks who often used the figure of *vädihiti nivāsa* residents to illustrate the worth of parents and importance of old age support by the children. In other instances, social visits by school students were meant to teach them the plight of these 'abandoned' parents and to make them think of a solution to the social predicament, which would begin by 'raising awareness' of young people about the value of elderly people and parents.

In contrast to these negative representations, what caught the author's eyes first was a miscellaneous group of people, who at first glance the author could not understand who they were or what they were doing, coming and going in and out of the premises. Soon later, especially after the author was given a room to stay and volunteer in the premises as staff, it became clear that the *nivāsa* was a site of *samāja sēvā* (or social service) where various actors and things gathered and intersected to support the lives of the residents. Groups of school students, college student volunteers, and sometimes employees of private firms visited frequently as a part of their CSR activities. Relatives, friends, and former co-workers, if they are up to the task, were always welcome to visit and to respond to the mental and material needs of residents. The most prevalent form of support was a direct gift of food and necessary utensils designated as '*dāna*,'[3] given by the public living circumjacent to the institution, or who had travelled a long distance to visit acquaintances, be it staff or residents.

Residential institutions are often represented as a place of separation and loneliness. In many respects, such an account seems to hold true. However, if seen from a different angle, *vädihiti nivāsa* appears as a potential site which embodies a kind of 'encounter' of different body-selves. As will be examined, such encounter gives fresh meaning or value to life (or death) in residential institution. Moreover, as such encounter is beyond the reach of biopolitical control, it opens a space for subject transformation—transformation of the subject's relationship with oneself, others, and the world. What will be delineated in the rest of this article is the nature of this 'encounter,' taking place in seemingly highly asymmetrical relationships. In particular, the author will first examine interaction among residents and the *dāna* donors (Section 4), and subsequently into the end-of-life care where the staff figures at the centre (Section 5). By turning to these ethnographic details, the author hopes to reflect on ethical questions related to asymmetricity and inclusivity (Section 6).

4 Living through asymmetrical relations: *Dāna* practices and aesthetics

Whereas fee-based facilities for the affluent are flourishing in the suburbs of Colombo, most *vädihiti nivāsa* found island-wide are free and reduced-cost facilities. These facilities are inhabited by individuals either with no income/savings, or those who receive retirement or survivors' benefits but who are unable to afford the whole living expenses.[4] In most of the cases, the main income of these free and reduced-cost facilities is donation. Table 13.1 shows a breakdown of the yearly income of a residential institution in a highly populated town located about 20 kilometres south of Colombo,[5] in which the author was privileged to conduct long-term fieldwork as a volunteer worker. According to its annual report, in 2008–2009, more than 60% of its income was generated from donations, most of which are offered through *dāna* or the daily provision of free meals, medicines, and clothes.[6]

Presumably, the dominant recipient of *dāna* in Sri Lanka is the Buddhist monks. The monks are conceptualised as *punnyakettam* ('field of merit' in Pali) in the popular understanding of Buddhism. Therefore, the act of *dāna* to them is assumed to be an exceedingly meritorious act for a lay Sinhala Buddhist. Merit accrued from the gift of veneration is presumed to benefit one either in this life or in the afterlife (Heim, 2004). However, the main reason for giving *dāna* to *vädihiti nivāsa* is somewhat different. A certain understanding exists that residents are '*asaranai*.'[7] Put simply, it is a gift of food and goods based on 'pity' that supports the lives of the residents at *vädihiti nivāsa*,[8] not veneration.

TABLE 13.1 Yearly Income of a *Vädihiti Nivāsa* (2008–2009)

	%
Dāna	54
Residential fee	13
Rent income of real estate	13
Subsidy from Ministry of Social Welfare	7
Other donations	6
Fundraising	4
Deposit interests	2
Others	1

Note: 'Rent income of real estate' derives from buildings attached to the institution, where small shops are operated.

At one time, the author felt uncomfortable with a gift based on the feeling of pity for others. In the context of gift theory in anthropology, this can be thought of as a difficulty of non-reciprocity. Actually, in the foreword to M. Mauss's *The Gift* (1990), Mary Douglas explains why charity or the so-called 'pure gift' ends up harming its recipients (Mauss, 1990: vii). When the donor expects to receive nothing in return, the donor subconsciously blocks the response from the recipient, forcing dependence on the recipient. Charity then becomes a 'gift of control,' as a means by which to achieve the donor's self-actualisation. Denying reciprocity entails the danger of creating a relation of superiority and subordination.

How were the residents living through such an asymmetrical relationship? Regarded from the eyes of the residents, *dāna* is a mundane but important occasion. For one thing, for many residents, 'food and T.V. programmes' are everyday pleasures. Not a few reported that they had given up meat or dessert items such as ice cream or yoghurt. However, when they were served, many enjoyed eating them occasionally. When sweets such as candy were added to the food items, residents were keen to preserve them inside their jars, neatly kept inside their cupboards. On days when *dāna* is not available, residents are served modest food. When such days are repeated, some residents would outwardly complain about the food, others would quietly take some toffee from the secret jar.

Apart from attention to the food itself, *dāna* was also important because residents' daily chores were coordinated according to the traffic of people who would come and go for *dāna*. Donors visiting *vädihiti nivāsa* were a common scene; the visit usually happens once or twice, or in some cases, five times a day: breakfast, tea, lunch, afternoon tea, and finally dinner. Residents had to prepare for the ritual on each occasion. For example, one female resident would wake up immediately before six in the morning. After she has a brief wash, she adjusts her clothes, neatly combs her hair, and knots a bun. She goes out to the backyard to pick two bowls of jasmine flowers, one of which she uses for her *mal pūjāwa* (flower offering) to a small Buddha statue on top of her low cupboard, and another to be decorated carefully and kept on the altar in the cafeteria for the *dāna* ritual. Other residents would prepare food vessels, candles, incense sticks, and wait sitting in the corridor. As soon as the donors come through the gate and greet the Matron at the office, an announcement is made for all to come into the dining hall for *pūjāwa*. A resident who was a retired teacher, wearing black-rimmed glasses, would come in and sit at the front, and asks the donors to light the incense and put the vessels on the altar before she starts chanting.

The *dāna* ritual at *vädihiti nivāsa* is a kind of memorial service (or merit transference service) for deceased people. When the donors make a reservation for *dāna*, they are asked for whom this is meant, and matter-of-factly respond by giving the name of their late family member. Many choose to give *dāna* on the death anniversary or the birthday of the departed, and repeaters visit the same institution annually on the same date. In the ritual, the merit accrued from their act of *dāna* would be transferred to the deceased, as well as to the donors, so that they are blessed with good health, prosperity, and longevity in this and the next life, and ultimately reach *nibbāna* devoid of decay and death. *Dāna* ceremony is called by the residents '*pin dīma*' in Sinhala, which literally means 'merit giving.' In Pali, it is termed *pin anumōdanā*. When the recipients consist of many Buddhists, it was always the case in which a particular sutra for *pin anumōdanā* is chanted in unison by the residents.

What is interesting about such ritualised space of *dāna* is that the residents behave as if they are religiously superior beings, like *upāsaka/upāsika*, or pious lay Buddhists who follow eight or ten precepts. For example, residents wear white clothes, which are symbolic of *upāsaka/upāsika*, only at mealtimes. The ceremony is prepared and led by one or two persons who can chant the wordings of merit transference fluently. In return, the donors display respect and esteem through bodily and verbal expressions, sometimes kneeling down and touching the feet of the residents. Here, the relation between 'benevolent donor' and 'destitute older people' seems to transform through the *dāna* practice, albeit temporarily and conditionally.

The actual behaviour and course of interaction between donors and residents differ depending on various factors such as architectural elements, institution size, and form of *dāna*.[9] Whereas subtle differences exist in the way they mutually interact, overall, *dāna* seems to urge both the donor and recipient to behave in a specific way, with certain attitudes, so that the act of *dāna* would be accomplished righteously. There is attention to the aesthetics of *dāna*, or generally accepted dispositions and appropriate modes of giving, which people strive to follow (Heim, 2004). Not only do the donors strive to make good gifts. The residents are also expected to behave as good recipients: they retain the attitude that they will receive whatever they get, in a manner that would not spoil the donor's feelings, at least in front of the donors. In an extreme case, the residents would not criticise the donors even if the *dāna* was rotten and spoiled, as in the following case.

Case 1: Rotten dāna

> One day there were many more leftovers than usual; I was wondering why. One resident came up to me; and as she poured her leftovers into the pan she said, 'Salad and curry; both are spoiled. Inedible!' Then another came and said, 'Wow I wish I could eat more! It's so tasty!' Because I had a surprised look on my face, she whispered, 'It's a joke, Sae. Oh no, how can anyone eat these!' Right behind her were the donors, going around the room and greeting the residents. The female resident who had 'joked' to me turned around and greeted them with a smile, glorifying their merit. The donors put their hands together in front of each of the residents. Then they left the home jovially. It seemed that the donors were quite poor from their mode of dress. The staff described that 'these days it's too hot, so we cannot avoid this. Perhaps they cooked a little bit too early'. When serving for ourselves (as I was dining with floor staff), I was merely asked whether I would have bean curry and the salad. No one explicitly criticised the donor who brought the day's *dāna*.

In fact, such *dāna* is not necessarily desirable. Seen objectively, people might say that it's not meritorious at all. However, the ceremony proceeds, and the residents transfer the merits to the departed as requested. The case implies that the residents and staff alike perceive their role as a respectful recipient, in Pali '*punnyakettam*,' irrespective of what they receive, thereby making the dāna practice something more than the mere act of alms-giving to beggars.

Even if a transformation of the relation between 'benevolent donor' and 'destitute older people' were not apparent, the *dāna* ritual can unveil the fact that the donors are also 'in need' of care and concern. The ritual functioned as a mechanism to prompt donors to share personal loss or longing for their passed ones, which is acknowledged and shared by the residents. Such an act of acknowledgement can sometimes be disquieting for the residents, as in the following case.

Case 2: Dāna for late son

> An old couple had given *dāna* every year for two decades for their late son who died at the age of twenty-one. The son is said to have joined the army and lost his life in the civil war fought between LTTE (Liberation Tigers of Tamil Eelam) and the Sri Lankan army. The old couple brought the portrait of their deceased son to the ceremonies. While participating in the rituals, they held the portrait in their hands. A female resident, the retired teacher, who had been leading the ritual showed apparent unrest by making several mistakes in the words. Some criticised that she was getting senile. However, at the end of the ceremony, she said, '*Pav*, *anē*. What should I do . . . ?' Then she stroked the shoulders of the old couple, standing there for a while.

Here, the word '*pav*' means sin, the antonym of '*pin*' or merit. However, in addition to this usage, '*pav*' is a mundane expression uttered when one is witness to others in a helpless, defenceless, or precarious condition.[10] Generally, it is the donors who feel '*pav*' for the residents who are '*asaranai*,' who need someone else to support their lives. However, here, it is the resident who feels and utters '*pav*' for the donors. The vignette reveals that *dāna* ritual at times instigates a space where everyone is acknowledged as potentially *pav* ('needy') in an insecure journey of life called *samsāra*.

The most frequent use of the word '*pav*' was visible through interaction with animals. Feeding cats, dogs, birds, or crows that come and go, or which are either temporarily or permanently living at the premises, was a part of their daily chores. Residents would share their meals saying, 'if we do not give them enough food, there is nothing to eat. *Pav*.' They left a portion of their meal, and when the food was over, mixed them well using fingertips. When fish and meat were scarce, some would mix their own powdered milk to make it tastier. At some institutions, because of this feeding habit, there were so many cats that the committee members tried to ban the practice. However, the residents continued the practice in secrecy. The cats continued to live with them as family. At other institutions which had fewer residents, everyone gave away a portion of their meal, just as monks do, which was fed to various animals living nearby. Such practices were enabled by the physical environment of the *nivāsa*, which was surrounded by small lanes and marshlands, distant from the main street. They walked around to feed the cat's family in the back of the building, dogs in the next house, and those staying around a nearby temple.

The author has described asymmetrical relations at the core of *dāna* practices. However, simultaneously, there is apparently a distinct kind of 'equality' or reciprocity emerging in certain contexts. Potentially all parties, whether donor, resident, or animal, are *pav*. They all must share food and *pin*[11] for their insecure journey of life. Although it was not apparent all the time, residents were potentially both takers and givers in a chain of gift-giving and caring. The way the residents interacted with the donors varied; their acts of caring would take various forms aside from the mundane act of performing the rituals or sharing food.[12]

5 Senility, dying, and care

In *vädihiti nivāsa*, apart from charitable gift relations, asymmetry of another kind is apparent in the treatment of frail residents by the staff. As illustrated later, in the institution where the author stayed as a volunteer, most of the residents passed away at *vädihiti nivāsa* itself. Those who once washed their body and clothes, cleaned their room and public space, in the course of time, were to receive physical assistance from roommates and staff, and gradually lose their appetite, and quietly take their last breath. Such clinical reality of end-of-life care can engender ethical issues precisely because of the asymmetrical power relations it holds. Gradual loss of cognitive and physical and mental abilities might render a person incomprehensive to others, whereas one would be compelled to hand over control over the body, to allow others to intrude over the boundary of the body. Danger always looms that the act of care can be a gift of control, ignoring the distinct voice of the dying. In the worst case, the dying might be labelled as not fully human.[13] At least initially, the staff seemed to the author to care very little about the 'needs' or the voice of these residents. Sometimes, right in front of these frail residents, they said that 'it's not worthwhile living like this.' Such a statement reminded me of the scenario of 'social death' at nursing homes in the United States, where older people were denied their human dignity, and became treated as objects or lifeless 'things' long before their physical death.

After visiting the *vädihiti nivāsa* for months conducting interviews with the residents, the author was accepted as volunteer staff and was given accommodation on the premises. In the course of this study, the author had learnt to handle the work of assisting with meals, excretion, and bathing, with help from other floor staff. In the last few months, the author was told to look after a 'sick room,' in which frail old residents were staying. End-of-life care was done through oral feeding alone. Typically, several weeks after changing to liquid meals, death was inevitable. Because of the constant lack of time and labour, it was rare that we were present at the time of death. The clinical situation there continued to be disturbing. The author was not accustomed to the natural processes of decay and dying, which was surely one reason for this bafflement. However, what was most perplexing was the floor staff's response to the suffering of dying residents, as the author described earlier. During the fieldwork, particularly after witnessing the strong emotional response of one floor staff member to the suffering of a dying resident, the author gradually acknowledged a personal response to suffering that was narrow and limited in scope.

Case 3: desperation with life

> It was March: a very hot and humid season. Perhaps because of the weather, many residents were approaching death. Three male residents and two female residents were being fed a liquid diet, being unable to swallow well. One such resident was a male resident called Gamage *sīya* (grandfather). Underneath his bed was a spittoon to cough out his phlegm, which was relentlessly disturbing him.
>
> One evening, as I entered the kitchen, I saw Nilanthi (a member of the floor staff who had been working at the home for eight years and was just about to get married and leave) sitting and talking with an elder member of the floor staff in the pantry. As soon as Nilanthi took notice of me, she related what she had witnessed. When Nilanthi went to feed him, Gamage sīya had been lying on the floor. It seemed that he had tripped over his spittoon; he was smeared with his phlegm; the whole room was filled with a filthy odour.
>
> As she talked, her eyes were filled with tears. Then she said to me, 'right before my marriage, I felt despair with life. I am fed up with life (*kalakillak athi vela, jīvithe epā vuna*),' and then she fell silent for a while. Another staff member told me to go back to my room.

This was the first time the author witnessed one of the floor staff exhibits a strong emotional response to the suffering of dying residents. After this event, the author began listening to Nilanthi and her colleagues to understand what her words meant. As the author gathered narratives of the staff, the author was exposed to a new understanding of the relation between the floor staff and the home residents.

Nilanthi told me that she was 'fed up with life,' that she felt despair with life. Her emotion was expressed in the word '*Kalakirīma*.' Etymologically, *kalakirima* is derived from the words *kāla* and *kriyā*, literally meaning 'the termination of time,' that is, death. However, in its popular form, it refers to a sense of hopelessness or despair with life (Obeyesekere, 1985: 144). However, why did she feel *kalakirīma*?

S: The other day when Gamage *sīya* fell, you told me that you felt *kalakirīma*. Could you tell me why you felt like that?

N: I feel *Kalakirima* here because of the suffering (*dukh*), which *āchila* (grandmothers) and *sīyala* (grandfathers) go through. <u>To me, it is very difficult to bear their suffering</u>. Just a glance at them makes me feel so sad (*dukha hithenawā*).

Here, let us consider what she means by saying 'To me, it is very difficult to bear their suffering.' Why did she have to bear the suffering of residents at all?

S: Why do you feel *kalakirima* when you see them suffer?

N: When you get old, Sae, you say that people turn out to be like little kids (*podi lamayi wagē*). In our Home (*nivāsa*) too, it happens. When *āchi* and *sīya* behave like children, we get upset at once and scold them. At such time what I feel is that I am also ageing. As I get older, and if I turn out to be in such a state (*mē thaṭṭuwata vätunoth*), I wonder if I could ever bear that situation. Probably, I cannot. When I feel that I cannot face such a situation, I feel despair with life.

Her statement clarifies that it is *not* that she was feeling helpless because she was incapable of relieving their suffering, as the author was. To put it simply, what had led her to be 'fed up with life' was the projection of the residents' suffering during ageing and decay onto herself. However, it is noteworthy that Nilanthi was referring not only to the universal suffering of age and decay. She further said,

> We will certainly be as old as our *grandmothers* and *grandfathers* someday. Won't we, Sae? And I think . . . <u>what if I happened to live my last days here, at *this* Home? What if I had to come to *this place*?</u> When I think like this, I feel very sad.

Here, Nilanthi is not only talking about the universal truth of ageing but is also referring to her possible fate, that she might be spending her old age and death in an institutional setting, 'at *this* Home,' where she now lives and works. There are at least two reasons she feels 'very sad' when she thinks she might come to 'this Home.' One is that life in this Home is not easy. Nilanthi related to me the following:

> Most of the time, everyone seeks to stay cheerful, but Sae, it's not easy to bear this humdrum life in such places as this. Eat and sleep, eat and sleep.

> This routine makes them fed up. You can't freely go out on your own; we only take them to temples, churches, or hospitals. Even if you try to talk with other people, only a trivial misuse of a word can lead to a quarrel. You wait and wait for your family to visit you but no one is really coming and you feel so lonely. Little by little your mental state gets worse.
>
> *(mānasika vätenawā)*

Another reason is that, if one is to enter *vädihiti nivāsa*, meaning that one has to live with a past that hurts a lot.

> These elders are recondite/impenetrable (*guptai*). They have many things undisclosed. Take Podi Nona āchi for example. It's been a long time since she came here. However, now she is incapable of communicating with others. None of us know about her property, brothers and sisters, etc. Now, there's a reason for her silence. She refuses to talk about them. If you start talking about family backgrounds, then *āchila* (grandmothers) will get upset. However, living with these secret pasts can engender such symptoms as high pressure or lack of appetite.

This statement clarifies that the aetiology of the weakness or illness was in some way or other associated with the residents' past ailments, often arising from family disputes. For example, whereas forgetfulness was explained as a natural result of neurons dying out, psychological breakdowns were explained using both the Ayurvedic concept of the body and the aetiology particular to institutionalised elders that suggests that their mental status (*mānasika tattva*) decreases because of their experience of being abandoned by their family, or because of ruminating too much on such depressing memories. However, this was not a mere objective evaluation of the condition of a resident; it was also something that connected the floor staff's subjectivity with that of the residents.

That all floor staff, including Nilanthi, had some form of family difficulty (mostly economic), might have added to the likelihood that they might follow a similar fate to that of the residents at the home. All nine staff members' father or mother either died in the war, were ill in bed, or were unable to work. Most had come from economically disadvantaged family backgrounds; about half of them were from orphanages. Nilanthi told me that she had given up on her dream of becoming a doctor because of her father's illness. When she was a teenager, the Red Cross had come to her school to do a demonstration of the medical profession. At this time, Nilanthi first had contact with medical kits and professionals. She felt very excited and since then had been determined that she would become a doctor one day. However, as she was preparing for her A level exam, her father became severely ill. The entire household faced enormous difficulty. It was then that she thought of working to support her mother, who was also getting weaker, instead of studying to further her dream of becoming a doctor. The floor staff knew very well about each other's backgrounds and difficulties, so did the matron, and even some of the residents. In addition, some older staff were present, including the matron and office workers, who were unmarried and were determined to live alone. Although Nilanthi was readying to be married soon, she said she *might* still happen to live alone, enter an institution, live with an unspeakable past, and finally die apart from her family.

When the staff perceives the suffering of the residents to overlap with their future selves, their care practice was envisaged as the care they themselves would receive in their possible future. For Sinhala Buddhists, logic to support care for one's aged parents is derived from the concept of *karma* and retribution. The logic goes that if one looks after parents well, such a good deed will be rewarded in kind when one gets older, and that our own children will look after us well. Floor staff narratives revealed a somewhat different but similar logic:

> When I grow old and . . . let's say if I did not marry my fiancée, or was widowed and had no one to look after me, and if I came to this Home, then the people here would treat me in the same way as I treat people here now. This really happens.
>
> *(Nilanthi)*

> If I did not get married, and lived my life alone, and if I came to live here, because of the good that I do to the parents (residents) here, those who will be here will serve me well. I think like this.
>
> *(Chandima, 28 years old)*

Here, the continuity or commonality of 'me (floor staff)' and 'you (dying resident),' provides a basis for meaningful care practice. In a situation that posed a challenge to their conventional cultural framework under which parents should be cared for by their children, they had creatively adopted the logic of *karma* and parental care in the context of care for the destitute elders and thus rendered the practice meaningful.

What is interesting in this ethnographic account is that Nilanthi's bodily self was afflicted as *if* she comprehended Gamage sīya's suffering, when, in actuality, his suffering was solely unimaginable: when she uttered the word *kalakirima* and was filled with desperation, her body was afflicted by the suffering of another embodied being, Gamage sīya. However, she also stated that his suffering stayed undisclosed and recondite (*guptai*), and therefore was something she could never grasp. How is it possible that the other's unimaginable suffering might unsettle her to such an extent that she felt 'desperate with life'? The key to understanding this point is the concept of contingency. In her reflexive account narrated after the event, Nilanthi expressed a feeling of presumed interchangeability. In other words, she felt that 'the future in which I shall be placed in *his* situation is quite imaginable.' From her accounts, one assumes that in rendering such 'subjunctive reality' (Bruner, 1986) credible, the concept of *karma* and retribution played a crucially important role. However, if the author were to describe what had happened at that very moment when she saw Gamage sīya lying on the floor smeared with phlegm, the author doubts it is the case in which Nilanthi was merely 'imagining' her possible future. Probably, Nilanthi, although unintentionally, *was* Gamage sīya ('I *am* you'). Therefore, she was experiencing an intercorporeality in which she was in a 'reversible' (Nishimura, 2001) relationship with, or was inseparable with the body-mind of Gamage sīya. Through such an affective, intercorporeal encounter with Gamage sīya, coupled with the logic of *karma* and contingency, the dying resident's pain and suffering invoked the 'Other (or otherness) within oneself,' leaving the floor staff feeling unease and despair, but also experiencing continuity with the residents. In feeling the sense of *kalakirima*, the floor staff do not lose sight of the afflicted person in front of them; rather, they are stilled by the sense of the depth and proximity of one's vulnerability and made to face the sheer reality of life. It was such dissolution of the self, and a kind of hesitant but unyielding hope found therein, that seemed to pose an alternative to our understanding of 'ethical' in encountering the dying other.

6 Envisioning social inclusivity based on our existential vulnerability

Lives and deaths at *vädihiti nivāsa* reveal the sheer vulnerability and unavoidable asymmetries prevalent in the actual human condition. However, each resident, irrespective of their past, was provided with a space to live his/her life. They passed away, acknowledged for their unique character and their suffering. It was not a space of social death. Rather, it was a place for encounters. What is achieved or at least encouraged to be achieved in these encounters through the concrete act of gift-giving or end-of-life care was the acknowledgement of the contingency of life, and the collective effort to make positive changes in one another's future lives. The author has tried to describe that this space of encounter was endorsed by the performativity of the cultural tools coupled with the ability of the body-self to sense and acknowledge another's suffering. This created an 'inclusive' social space for those who happened to be 'excluded' from mainstream social values in their later and *last* stages of life.

The kind of 'inclusivity' emerging from this chapter is rather vague and lacks sufficient elaboration. However, the author would like to end by mentioning how it might enrich our project of understanding and envisioning the state of inclusion in South Asia or elsewhere. As it was manifested in a successful ageing movement, a standardised mode of understanding 'inclusivity' exists in terms of incorporation of disadvantaged groups into economic and political activities. Some have criticised that inclusion of this kind is underpinned by the neoliberal economic policies, and thus would end in widening inequalities. One established solution is to intervene, at the state level, to adjust inequality by ensuring the excluded group the equal rights and participation in the public sphere. This is a necessary intervention. However, simultaneously, it runs the risk of unconsciously privileging the dominant representation of 'what it means to be fully human,' just like young (or young-old) Americans who abhorred a state of dependence and discounted the 'real' old age. What is left out of these considerations is the rich social domain in which interactions among various actors open up creative ways of dealing with complex social and ethical dilemmas. The novelty of the vision on 'inclusivity' emerging from the case study of *vädihiti nivāsas* probably lies in demonstrating to us how mutuality was retained even in asymmetrical power relations. The mutuality here was not present all the time; it was not prescribed. It was rather actualised as one nurtures and deepens sensibility to 'the otherness within,' of becoming something else while keeping track of oneself.

Notes

1 The use of the adjectives 'probable' and 'possible' is derived from Arjun Appadurai's work, which examines the tension between the 'ethics of possibility' (hope, aspiration, and desire) and the 'ethics of probability' (systematised rationalities, risk management, and cost/benefit) (Appadurai, 2013; Fischer, 2013).

2 The word *vädihiti* consists of *vädi* (more) + *hiti* (to have existed), and can be translated as 'elder,' whereas *nivāsa* means 'home' or 'residence.' Translated into English, one obtains an expression such as 'house of the elderly' or 'residence of the elders.'

3 *Dāna* or *dān* is a familiar concept and practice in many parts of South Asia. It connotes the virtue of generosity and giving of alms in Hindu, Jain, and Buddhist traditions. For Sinhala Buddhists, the most familiar form of *dāna* is alms given to Buddhist monks; local Sinhala Buddhist people are obliged to support nearby temple(s) by giving meals (*dāna*) regularly.

4 Looking only at those facilities registered with the government as of 2006, 146 out of 171 facilities (85%) were of free and reduced type, with 5,536 out of 6,014 residents (92%) living at these facilities (National Secretariat for Elders, 2006).

5 Residents of the home were from various socio-economic backgrounds, which can be grouped roughly into three: those from 1) lower class, without any income/savings nor anyone to look after them; 2) lower-middle class, who might have one's own/spouse's pension, but who cannot manage to live with them; and 3) upper/upper-middle class, many of whose children work abroad, and who can afford to stay in private rooms. A majority (67.3%) were those who never made payments. Several others (14.4%) were making monthly payments, but two-thirds of them (9.8%) were recipients of government income security schemes for poor people and widows. The rest had paid only the initial admission fee. With regard to their marital status, 40% had never married, 7% were legally divorced, 60% had no child, and 26% had only one or two children, whereas the average number of children of their generation was 5.5. Two-thirds were female residents, many of whom were widows (Nakamura, 2017).

6 How well an institution succeeds in collecting *dāna* determines the capacity (how many can be given shelter) and indeed the very survival of the institution is dependent on how well an institution succeeds in collecting *dāna*. This particular institution, occupied by more than 150 residents at the time of the survey, was among the most 'successful' cases.

7 '*Asaranai*' is a term in which '*a*,' denoting the negative, is added to the Sanskrit '*śaraṇa*' or the Pali '*saraṇa*,' which means roughly 'restoration, house, refuge, or shelter.'

8 Rather than economic conditions, people seem to show strong empathy towards one's fate of not being able to spend old age with one's own family.

9 The different forms of *dāna* can be largely categorised into three. They are 1)'brought-in *dāna*,' in which the donor is asked to prepare meals beforehand, 2)'in-kind *dāna*,' in which the donor brings dry rations and/or goods in kind, and 3) 'in-cash *dāna*,' the form of *dāna* that only requires paying for a meal. Among various types of *dāna*, 1)

brought-in *dāna* involves many of the instances of aesthetic attentiveness, clichés, and gestures that are manifest in *dāna* practice to the respected, that is, monks. The brought-in *dāna* was mainly performed at small-scale institutions with less than 30 people. If the *dāna sālāwa* (or dining room) is spacious enough, then donors would lay a rug and sit on the floor, while a resident would sit on a chair in the front and perform *pūjawa*. Such a ritual set-up resembles the *dāna* practice performed for Buddhist monks. The difference in height and posture can transform the relationship between two parties. However, in more populous institutions, in-cash *dāna* was practiced more often. If there is not enough space, then the donors would keep standing while the residents perform the ritual on the chair. As such, the transformative quality of the *dāna* encounter might depend on the design of the building, whether it resembles that of religious institutions such as meditation centres, or that of hospitals or workhouses, a legacy from the colonial era (Nakamura, 2011).

10 This usage is understandable if we turn to the fundamental meaning of *pav* or '*pāpa*' in Pali, which denotes all beings as incomplete and impermanent (Boyd, 1975).

11 This does not simply mean 'sending' the merit to the deceased. A recipient of *dāna*, as well as those who helped *dāna* to be accomplished, including those who simply rejoiced at looking at the deed *(anumōdanti)*, are potential receivers or sharers of the merit accruing from the act.

12 Ānanda sīya (grandfather), an ex-teacher and principal of government schools, often shared his wit and knowledge when conversing with donors or staff. The author still remembers the sarcastic look on Ānanda sīya's face when he described that one female resident, who performed the ritual for him, failed to choose the 'right' word for the pin transference. '*Shaktimak* is physical power! How can you succeed in academic achievements with *shaktimak* alone? You need *buddhimak*. *Buddhimak* was the right word.' Later he gave me a book of *nikāya* (Pali Canon on Buddhist teachings) for study by the author, struggling with the thesis.

13 In terms of power relations in clinical contexts in the West, debate on social death led to gradual penetration of a 'person-centred approach' in medical practices surrounding disease, ageing, and death. As Sharon Kaufman argues, since the 1950s, 'the idea that the patient is an *experiencing person*—someone with a deep, psychic interior who lives in and is shaped by a social world and *who must articulate needs, desires, and an identity*—had developed for several decades in American psychiatry and psychology as the influence of Freud's work was taken up in clinical practice. . . . [The] patients now had a voice within a medical discourse; the patient was now the *patient-as-person'* (Kaufman, 2006: 66–67, emphasis added). The idea of the 'patient-as-person' was not only for those who were able to speak up for themselves; it also incorporated the frail and ageing bodies because old age came to be viewed as the effect of disease on the body (Kaufman, 2006: 78). Therefore, according to Kaufman, older people were no longer allowed to be a '*dying person*,' but were now seen from the perspective of the 'patient-as-person,' awaiting their 'needs' or 'feelings' to be comprehended and responded. Such trends in healthcare practice and discourse acted as if to counterbalance the negligent, problematic attitudes of the past: the sort described in a series of nursing home monographs.

References

Appadurai, A. (2013). *The Future as Cultural Fact: Essays on the Global Condition*, London: Verso.

Boyd, W. J. (1975). *Satan and Mara: Christian and Buddhist Symbols of Evil*, Leiden: E.J. Brill.

Bruner, J. S. (1986). *Actual Minds, Possible Worlds*, Cambridge, MA: Harvard University Press.

Cohen, L. (1999). *No Aging in India: Alzheimer's, the Bad Family, and Other Modern Things*, Berkeley: University of California Press.

Craig, D. and D. Porter (2003). "Poverty Reduction Strategy Papers: A New Convergence," *World Development*, vol. 31, 53–69.

Eriyagama, V. (2000). "A Sociological Analysis of the Problem of Old Age in Sri Lanka," Diss. University of Peradeniya. (in Sinhala).

Fischer, T. (2013). "An Ethics of Possibility and a Positive Anthropology," *Anthropological Observations . . . On Economics, Politics and Daily Life*. (personal blog). http://anthropologicalobservations.blogspot.com/2013/11/an-ethics-of-possibility-and-positive.html (accessed May 10, 2019)

Gilleard, C. and P. Higgs (2010). "Aging without Agency: Theorizing the Fourth Age," *Aging and Mental Health*, vol. 14(2), 121–128.

Goffman, E. (1961). *Asylums: Essays on the Social Situation of Mental Patients and Other Inmates*, New York: Anchor.

Gustafson, E. (1972). "Dying: The Career of the Nursing Home Patient," *Journal of Health and Social Behavior*, vol. 13, 226–235.

Heim, M. (2004). *Theories of the Gift in South Asia: Hindu, Buddhist and Jain Reflections on Dāna*, New York and London: Routledge.

Higuchi, M. (2012). "Koreisya to fukushi: yutakana chiiki syakai to kyusokuna koureika (Elderly and Welfare: Rich Local Community and Rapid Population Ageing)," in Sugimoto Y., F. Takakuwa, and S. Suzuki, eds., *Suriranka wo shiru tameno 58 shou (Fifty-Eight Chapters to understand Sri Lanka)*, Tokyo: Akashi Publisher: 153–157. (in Japanese)

Kalavar, J. M. K. and D. Jamuna (2008). "Interpersonal Relationships of Elderly in Selected Old Age Homes in Urban India," *Interpersona*, vol. 2(2), 193–215.

Katz, S. (2000). "Busy Bodies: Activity, Aging, and the Management of Everyday Life," *Journal of Aging Studies*, vol. 14(2), 135–152.

Kaufman, S. R. (2006). *And a Time to Die: How American Hospitals Shape the End of Life*, Chicago: University of Chicago Press.

Kleinman, A. and P. Benson (2006). "Culture, Moral Experience and Medicine," *The Mount Sinai Journal of Medicine*, vol. 73, 834–839.

Lamb, S. ed. (2017). *Successful Aging as a Contemporary Obsession: Global Perspectives*, New Brunswick, NJ: Rutgers University Press.

Lamb, S., J. Robbins-Ruszkowski, and A. Corwin (2017). "Introduction: Successful Aging as a Twenty-first-Century Obsession," in Lamb, S. ed., *Successful Aging as a Contemporary Obsession: Global Perspectives*, New Brunswick, NJ: Rutgers University Press: 1–24.

Mauss, M. (1990) [1925]. *The Gift: The Form and Reason for Exchange in Archaic Societies*, London: Routledge.

Nakamura, S. (2011). "Suriranka no jizengata rojin home to dana (Dāna and the Philanthropic Elderly Home in Sri Lanka)," *South Asian Studies*, vol. 23, 100–120. (in Japanese)

Nakamura, S. (2017). *Kyoou suru sintai: suriranka no roujin sisetu vadihiti nivasa no minzokushi (Communicative Body: An Ethnography of Elderly People's Homes, Vädihiti Nivāsa in Sri Lanka)*, Kyoto: Nakanishiya Publishers. (in Japanese)

Nalini, B. (1997). "Institutional Care for the Aged: The Issues and Implications," in Chakravarty, I. ed., *Life in Twilight Years*, Calcutta: Kwality Book Company: 63–77.

National Secretariat for Elders (2006). *List of Elder's Homes 2006*. Colombo: Ministry of Social Services and Social Welfare.

Nishimura, Y. (2001). *Katarikakeru shintai: kaigo kea no genshogaku (Communicating Body: Phenomenology of Nursing Care)*, Tokyo: Yumiru Publisher. (in Japanese)
Obeyesekere, G. (1985). "Depression, Buddhism, and the Work of Culture in Sri Lanka," in Kleinman, A. and B. Good eds., *Culture and Depression: Studies in the Anthropology and Cross-Cultural Psychiatry of Affect and Disorder*, Berkeley and Los Angeles: University of California Press: 134–152.
Rowe, J. W. and R. Kahn (1997). "Successful Aging," *The Gerontologist*, vol. 37(4), 433–440.
Silva, T. (2004). "Elderly Populations, Family Support and Intergenerational Arrangements," in UNFPA and Population Association of Sri Lanka eds., *Ageing Population in Sri Lanka: Issues and Future Prospects*, Colombo: United Nations Population Fund in association with the Population Association of Sri Lanka: 45–75.
The Sunday Times (2008). "Impending Problems of an Ageing Population," September 21, 2008. www.sundaytimes.lk/080921/Columns/eco.html (accessed 30 July 2019)
World Health Organization (n.d.). "Homepage on Ageing and Life-Course," www.who.int/ageing/ageism/en/ (accessed 31 July 2019)

14

UNIVERSAL BASIC INCOME AND LAND RIGHTS FOR WOMEN

An Anti-capitalist Critique

Nivedita Menon

This chapter will examine the growing approval for cash income grants in India and how these proposals tie in with another important policy development—individual land rights for women. In brief, the argument is that the thrust of both policies is essential to transform all forms of collective wealth into individual property, to render all forms of wealth alienable, to convert wealth into monetary form, and ensure that all this alienated, monetised wealth is fully visible to, and available to the state for taxation and to be mobilised for capitalist investment. The drive towards 'inclusion' into the capitalist framework, in other words, is precisely the problem.

1 Universal basic income and basic income grants

For some time now, the argument for cash income grants has been made in India by broadly left-wing as well as neoliberal economists. A relevant distinction to note before proceeding is the one between Universal Basic Income (UBI) and Basic Income Grants (BIG). UBI refers to proposals for minimum cash incomes provided to *every* citizen or resident of a country, BIG refers to targeted income grants to the most vulnerable sections of the population. Such proposals come from economists of both Left and Right, and take somewhat different forms accordingly.

The next two subsections examine neoliberal and left-wing arguments for UBI/BIG.

Neoliberal arguments for UBI/BIG

Neoliberal economist Surjit S Bhalla wrote supporting the idea of a state-provided basic income targeting the bottom 50% of the population (2017). The proposal positively counter-posed direct transfer of a minimum cash income to individual

DOI: 10.4324/9781003304760-17

bank accounts, against poverty alleviation policies such as the Public Distribution Scheme (PDS) and the Mahatma Gandhi National Rural Employment Guarantee Act Scheme (MGNREGAS).[1] The argument is that such schemes are riddled with corruption, and only a small fraction of food or wages intended for the poor actually reach them. On the other hand, 'a guaranteed minimum income to all (population, adult, worker or variant thereof)' would be 'an efficient redistribution of income' (Bhalla, 2017).

Bhalla suggested sources for the government to draw the resources for this policy—partly by scrapping PDS and MGNREGA, and partly from the increased personal income tax collection he expected annually to result from the demonetisation policy.[2] This last claim was made without any supporting analysis or evidence, when in fact within a month, 80% of the banned currency had entered the banking system, thus giving the lie to the government's claim that most of the banned currency was 'black money' (Agencies, 2016).

From this position, the argument precisely is *not* for Universal Basic Income (UBI), but for targeted Basic Income Grants (BIG), or limited cash transfers to those identified as the poorest. Similarly, an earlier editorial in *the Financial Times,* for instance, while stating the UBI is a 'bad idea,' agreed that cash transfers, 'which is what UBI boils down to . . . can fix many of India's distorted policies,' that is, government subsidies. But cash transfers should not be universal, they should be 'directed at only the poor or for facilities that primarily benefit them' (*Financial Times* Editorial, 2016). Bhalla and *Financial Times*, thus, are both arguing for targeted cash transfers through BIG rather than for UBI.

The Economic Survey 2017, on the other hand, made a strong case for UBI as a radical measure to alleviate poverty, although not for immediate implementation, as a chief economic adviser in the Finance Ministry, Arvind Subramanian said. He too stated that the cost of it would have to be met by dismantling existing welfare schemes. A prerequisite to implementing UBI, said the *Economic Survey*, is 'JAM'—Jan-Dhan accounts, Aadhaar, and Mobile.[3]

The Jan-Dhan Yojana set up in 2014 is a 'financial inclusion' scheme under which 15 million bank accounts were opened with no minimum balance, in order to provide 'universal and clear access to banking facilities.' The Aadhar Card or UID is a Unique Identification biometric system which has *de facto* become necessary to access government benefits. Mobile phone coverage is essential for mobile banking, as otherwise innumerable physical branches of banks would have to be opened. All these three imply greater state surveillance, monetising of all incomes and linking of incomes to the banking system. As we have seen especially from 2008, the banking sector is most susceptible to the shocks administered by global capitalism (Bello, 2018). It has also been argued that formalising the economy, making it entirely legible to the state, links it closely to the world capitalist system, and renders it riskier for the ordinary person. The still ongoing global economic crisis has least affected the informal sectors in poorer countries, including India, as even the World Bank has acknowledged (Nigam, 2013: 528–529).

There is a long history of conservative and libertarian arguments for guaranteed or universal basic income, arising from an idea that it reduces government intervention in social welfare schemes. Milton Friedman in *Capitalism and Freedom* (1962) proposed a guaranteed income, which he termed a 'negative income tax,' arguing for the following benefits: reduction of government bureaucracy; efficiency of free markets in which people vote with cash, as it were; and enabling people to do work that cannot bring in a living wage in a market economy, such as charity and volunteer work. Friedrich Hayek (1981), a libertarian philosopher, supported the idea that the state should ensure a minimum income for everyone, in a society in which state interference would be minimal, and the twin pillars of free market and private property were protected.

In India, one kind of critique of targeted basic income grants is made on the grounds of its *implementability*. It is argued that the technology required is not adequately tested and has 'caused large-scale disruptions and exclusions among the poor and the under-privileged' (Banerjee, 2017). There is also the well-documented problem of fraud in Aadhar cards (DNA Correspondent, 2016).

One commentator argues that 'the very fact that UBI has been pitched as a "post-industrial state" scheme is precisely because it hinges on comprehensive banking and technological connectivity, as well as digital infrastructure,' when all these factors are missing in India. Even banking systems have very shallow coverage, and despite policy pushes such as the Jan-Dhan Yojana, 45% of Indians still don't have a bank account and distrust the banking system (Chakraborty, 2017).

There is, however, another more substantive critique of neoliberal arguments for basic income grants, which emerges from a broadly left-wing *support* for UBI in principle.

Left-wing arguments for UBI/BIG

Guy Standing, labour economist, author of *The Precariat: The New Dangerous Class* (2011), is one of the key proponents of Universal Basic Income from the Left. Standing also supports BIG, under specific conditions explained below. Standing's conception of the 'precariat' includes the large sections of the global population, the millions of people who have simply fallen out of the net of global corporate capital, which has rendered them superfluous to its needs. Standing had in 2011, worked with Renana Jhabvala of SEWA (Self Employed Women's Association) in India, to launch two pilots to test the impact of basic income grants, funded by UNICEF, with SEWA as coordinator. Standing believes that basic income grants 'will work optimally with good public services and social investment, and that they would operate better if implemented through a Voice organization, i.e., a body giving members the capacity to act in unison' (Standing, 2013). In this case, the 'Voice organisation' was SEWA.

Jhabvala (2016) cites studies by SEWA Bharat in Madhya Pradesh and Bihar, which showed that due to 'leakages,' many central schemes reached less than 25% of the people. Jhabvala thus appears to be more open, unlike Standing, to the idea of direct income grants *replacing* subsidies and government schemes. Interestingly,

Arvind Panagariya of National Institution for Transforming India (NITI Ayog), which replaced the Planning Commission and is meant to provide a road map for neoliberal restructuring of the economy, cited Jhabvala to reject *The Economic Survey* proposal for UBI as unfeasible, and to suggest targeted BIG (Panagariya, 2017).

It is thus not clear that Jhabvala and Standing share the same understanding of what BIG is meant to achieve, because from the point of view of a Standing-inspired BIG, proposals to *replace* government schemes and policies with cash transfers are not acceptable. The reasons to reject this are evident in this article by Angshukanta Chakraborty, for example,

> Unconditional and direct cash transfers do not discriminate between varying situations which might make cash benefits less helpful and benefits in kind, such as food, maternity benefits, schooling, healthcare, guaranteed employments, etc. more desirable. Another major issue with UBI replacing existing PDS is that in case of situations like drought, famine, crop loss, extreme inflation, natural disasters, wars and other casualties, in-kind benefits are far more effective than meagre cash transfers. Guaranteed jobs and nutrition, as well as schooling, are better indicators of a family beating the poverty trap with government help, rather than being handed over a little bit of money in lieu of the former.
>
> *(2017)*

Economist Reetika Khera, who has been active along with Jean Dreze in the Right to Food Campaign, agrees with Guy Standing that universal basic income grants are desirable, but not at the cost of existing social benefits. Khera argues for a phased implementation of UBI, 'a sensible way of making UBI affordable. Two existing schemes and entitlements – pensions for the elderly, widows and disabled persons and universal maternity entitlements – can be thought of as a universal basic income for these demographic groups' (Khera, 2016).

Jean Dreze sees the apparent consensus on UBI on the right and left as masking deep differences. For the Left, according to him, UBI is part of a comprehensive social security system that would also include universal healthcare, free education, good public services, some transfers in kind (e.g., school meals), and other forms of social support. For the right, on the other hand, UBI is to accompany deep cuts in other social programmes such as the PDS and the National Rural Employment Guarantee Act (NREGA). He points out that some neoliberal UBI advocates have already made an explicit case for dismantling both (Dreze, 2017).

UBI within a capitalist horizon

Dreze, Khera, and some other Left proponents of income grants seem to see these at best as limited measures within the limitations of the current political economy. But there are stronger Left arguments for UBI, which like neoliberal arguments, assume both the omnipresence and inescapability of capitalism.

Guy Standing's argument for UBI is the best illustration of this. Based on the understanding that a large proportion of the world's population has become dispensable for capital, 'more decent jobs' is simply not the answer. The precariat is a class-in-the-making, but unless it becomes a class-for-itself with effective agency, the anger and anxiety that lie at its heart could lead to 'a politics of inferno' (Standing, 2011: vii). Standing traces the first stirrings of the global precariat to May Day 2001 in Europe, where hundreds of thousands of mostly young people marched to demand free migration and a universal basic income, demands that had little to do with traditional unionism.

Standing's argument (Standing, 2015) is that globalisation, technological change, and government policies have created a world in which 'the income distribution system of the twentieth century has broken down and it will not come back,' and 'real wages will continue to stagnate and fall.' Technology has not destroyed work *per se*, it is just that the precariat does 'more and more work, much of which is unrecorded, unrecognised and unremunerated.'[4] The precariat is both victim and hero, for its politics is a politics of defiance. But

> They are becoming a new dangerous class. They are prone to listen to ugly voices, and to use their votes and money to give those voices a political platform of increasing influence.
>
> *(Standing, 2011: 1)*

The UBI is meant to give people the basic security which would take them away from this dangerous direction and make them 'work harder and more productively, not less.'[5]

Standing's rationale for the UBI, thus, is predicated on changed requirements of capital that render redundant large sections of populations globally. But it is also justified on the grounds that without such security, the precariat is dangerous, prone to be drawn to 'irrational' right-wing mobilisation. In other words, neoliberalism needs to redistribute some of its super-profits if this precariat is to work 'more productively,' and not push society towards 'a politics of inferno.' Capitalism is thus assumed to be inescapable and omnipresent. No other solution seems possible to him than capitalism re-enveloping the precariat it has abandoned. And the precariat he sees as having no option but to sell its labour power to capital.

The other well-known left-wing proponent of UBI is Kathi Weeks who in *The Problem with Work* (2011) ties in the idea of UBI with a critique of work itself, which she argues has been culturally overvalued. In a later interview, she explains that this ethic of work has undergirded an economic system of wealth for a few who work very little, and 'poorly paid and all-consuming waged work for the rest.' According to Weeks, 'Where a strong work ethic is a key element of productivity, our willingness to call these values and modes of being into question is a potentially effective mode of rebellion' (Weeks, 2016).

Drawing on Marxist feminist literature on social reproduction, Weeks develops the idea of social reproduction as referring to 'all the social, cultural and subjective infrastructures on which the more narrowly conceived structure of production (that is, work covered by the wage) depends, just as a smaller parasite lives by drawing sustenance from the body of a stronger host.' Thus, maintaining the two separate spheres of waged work and social reproduction becomes conceptually impossible. Both 'work' and 'family' have failed as inclusive and sustainable social forms. As Weeks conceives of it, 'the political movement for a basic income can be advanced as a way to open conversations about what counts as work, about the value of different kinds of work, and also about what else besides work we might want to do with our time, what other models of care, creativity and cooperation we might want to build' (Weeks, 2016). While existing welfare measures envisage the reintegration of beneficiaries into the labour market, BIG assumes a basic income to take into account the fact that most people will not ever get work, or the opportunity to labour, and that this could be a positive thing.

While Standing and Weeks believe that new forms of solidarities and political utopias would emerge from the guarantee of a basic income, they do not address the fact that the very provision of this income would require capitalism to carry on its (ecologically devastating) business as usual, and all wage receivers would have to be fully legible to the state. Indeed, it has been explicitly argued by some on the Left that BIG would help to solve the crisis of falling demand in the capitalist economy, a crisis that can no longer be dealt with by the three methods of stimulating demand hitherto used—war, rise in wages, or higher levels of private debt. And as technological progress enables growing production alongside vanishing jobs, only BIG can ensure that the global economy keeps ticking—'By giving every citizen a monthly cheque, a Basic Income Guarantee will be as fiscally stimulative as World War II without requiring the murder of millions' (Streithorst, 2015).

With this last critique, we move towards an entirely different set of problems with UBI, which can be articulated from a point of view that does not assume capitalism to be inevitable, as both proponents and opponents of capitalism have tended to believe. Rather, it is worth recognising that capitalism has to be built painfully with heavy state intervention, a fact recognised by one of the most articulate and powerful proponents of capitalism of the late twentieth to twenty-first century, Hernando de Soto, who made it his life mission to understand 'why capitalism triumphs in the West and fails everywhere else,' and to redress the situation by getting states 'everywhere else' to adopt policies that would enable capitalism to triumph (de Soto, 2000).

Let us move now to understanding state-led support in India for individual land rights for women, in the context outlined earlier. Here too, we see a state-led and global capital guided project to establish individual rights to land, make land alienable and to render it accessible to domestic and global capital for corporate projects.

2 Land rights for women as a capitalist agenda

Bringing women into the ambit of individual property rights has long been one of the key issues in feminist practice and scholarship. What happens to the feminist understanding of land rights for women in the face of large-scale land acquisitions for corporate globalisation? The only real challenge to capitalist ambitions is posed by collective ownership of land and strong assertions of the commons. What does this recognition mean for feminist campaigns for individual land rights for women?[6] At this moment in time, several kinds of political movements and several strands of scholarship from the end of the twentieth century onwards, for about three decades or so, are coming together to alert us to a need for a shift in feminist perspective on land rights for women.

Land struggles in India

Let's begin with what we learn from struggles against the accelerated and large-scale land acquisitions by the state for use by private corporations. Activists in these movements and scholars engaged in understanding land relations are increasingly coming to the recognition that the Indian state is now very amenable to joint *patta*s (title deeds), which has been the main demand of women's movements for decades—that is, joint title deeds for husband and wife to family land. However, as Smita Gupta argues, while joint *pattas* are important, sole preoccupation with them is a problem, thrust upon us by international agencies with a neoliberal agenda. The women's movement must, says Gupta, focus far more on dispossession, land-use change, lack of access to commons, and depletion/degradation of the commons. Small individual plots in a context of rising and widespread agrarian distress will in fact, increase women's drudgery. Gupta believes that collective farming with state support is the way forward (Gupta, 2018). Individual land rights, whether to men only or also to women, restrict farmers to family plots by giving them formal title deeds, even joint *patta*s; while the state takes control of common and public lands. Enclosures, evictions, and land-use policies are all state strategies for taking over common and public lands, and of course, title deeds are no magic potion against land acquisition. Rather, individual title deeds facilitate land acquisitions by the state. Furthermore, it has long been understood in the context of land reforms that 'joint *patta*' in effect sidelines the question of land redistribution and in that sense, is not a radical agenda. As Mercia Andrews, land rights activist from South Africa, puts it, no effective land struggle is possible without breaking up the nuclear family.[7]

Roma, an activist with All India Union of Forest Working People, is opposed to the *patta* as such, which she sees as looking at land use and ownership exclusively through the prism of the family. In her experience, she says, only collective ownership can fracture patriarchy, and her organisation works with movements that collectively cultivate land. Such a movement would be a movement of the landless, not of middle and upper peasantry. There is thus, in this understanding, a contradiction between the interests of upper caste peasants who own land and the interests of the landless, largely Dalits, who use common lands. In her understanding then, an alliance of marginal farmers and landless needs to be built, and this would have to address the caste divide as well.[8]

Common lands that embody historical layers of customary use rights are the biggest challenge to market relations, and prime among such lands are forests. It is in this context that land occupation movements by castes and tribes traditionally excluded from agriculture must be viewed and understood—for example, the occupation of Muthanga forest lands in Kerala by adivasis, violently evacuated by police in 2003. CK Janu, Chairperson of the Adivasi Gothra Maha Sabha that spearheaded this struggle, said in an interview, 'Adivasis are the real owners of land . . . . [Our main slogan is] the right to live in the land where we are born till death' (Gatade, 2005).

This 'occupation' of lands by the poor is in fact a *reoccupation* of common lands which were turned into state-owned land overnight through colonial legislations such as the Indian Forest Acts of 1878 and 1927, equally fiercely enforced by the post-independence Indian state as well. Globally, the trend is towards the legitimisation by states and World Bank institutions, of property titles for the poor and for women, even as these states engage in large-scale land acquisition in the interest of extractive capital. We will see that this is not a contradiction, and how the first works in the interests of the second. Is there then, a disjuncture between women's individual rights to land, and struggles against land acquisition to protect or create a commons? It seems that something counter-intuitive with regard to feminist common sense is being articulated in these contexts, a possibility this paper will explore.

Land rights through custom and tradition in India

There are three kinds of access to land rights in India—through religious Personal Laws to agricultural land, through Forest Acts to forests, and through Customary Laws to agricultural and forest lands occupied by tribal people.

It is important to keep in mind that neither Personal Laws nor Customary Laws are in any pure sense, traditional or indigenous. A large body of scholarship has shown that even up to the eighteenth century across India, there was a considerable range of authorities offering different types of justice, and a multiplicity of scriptural and customary sources of right. The colonial state's efforts to consolidate a body of Hindu and Islamic law to vindicate its claim to be ruling on the basis of the laws and customs of the people, in fact resulted in a body of jurisprudence that modified both 'scriptures' and 'custom' in keeping with official objectives wherever necessary. (For instance, see Derrett, 1968; Nair, 1996; Anderson and Guha, 1998; Singha, 1998).

Similarly, regarding the customary laws of tribal people of Northeast and Central India, while the British claimed to leave them to be governed by their customary practices, in fact traditional communities were reshaped as viable revenue-generating areas (Kurup, 2008), and colonial village heads such as *gaon-burha* were established parallel to traditional chieftains. Colonial control of the Northeast was important for strategic reasons, and Central India was rich in minerals.

It is impossible today therefore, to excavate any practice that is purely indigenous. It is also important to note the continuity of tribal policy between the colonial and post-independence Indian states. The next three subsections look at women's land rights under the three kinds of laws listed earlier.

Women's rights to land in personal laws

Feminist scholars like Bina Agarwal have argued for over a decade and a half, for women's 'independent rights in land' on grounds of welfare, efficiency, equality, and empowerment (Agarwal, 1994: 27). Agarwal has pointed out that it has been easier to push the welfare and efficiency arguments with state planners than equality and empowerment of women. The former is more easily understood within a poverty alleviation framework, she suggests, while the latter kind of arguments run counter to 'deep rooted notions of appropriate gender relations shared by many men who make and implement policy,' for whom more equal gender relations appear as 'threatening to existing family and kinship structures' (1994: 45).

Certainly nothing leads us to think that these attitudes have changed; on the contrary, policymakers continue to express the most appallingly sexist and misogynist opinions quite freely. And yet, in 2005, the amendment to the Hindu Succession Act (HSA) of 1956 which gave women rights to ancestral property, was declared 'passed unanimously' in both houses of the Indian Parliament, first in the upper house Rajya Sabha and then in the Lok Sabha the same year. Several states had already passed such legislation between 1986 and 1994—Andhra Pradesh, Tamil Nadu, Karnataka, and Maharashtra, while Kerala abolished the joint family altogether in 1975.

What did the HSA Amendment Act of 2005 accomplish? Bina Agarwal calls it a landmark (Agarwal, 2005), because it established gender equality on agricultural land and in coparcenary joint family property. The debate on the HSA Amendment Bill in Lok Sabha is intriguing, partly because of the enthusiastic support from many MPs who had clearly not read the proposed amendments with any care, and sometimes made mistaken claims and demands, but even more so because in fact several MPs had very negative responses to the Bill (*Lok Sabha Debates*, 2005). Despite these kinds of views being expressed across party lines, however, the Bill was unanimously passed in the Lok Sabha. Earlier, when the Bill was discussed in the Rajya Sabha, it is reported that 'Only one male member (the rest were women) participated in the discussion that came at the fag end of the day. Some of the members pointed to the low attendance in the House during the debate' (Special Correspondent, 2005).

But there too, the Bill was unanimously passed and the Minister for Law, H.R. Bhardwaj, 'expressed happiness at the unequivocal support given to the Bill by the BJP-led opposition National Democratic Alliance' (Special Correspondent, 2005).

As regards Muslims, the Shariat Act of 1937 that governs Muslims permits agricultural land rights to be governed by custom, as a result of which in many states Muslim women are excluded from ownership of land. There has been an ongoing campaign to end this discrimination along the lines of the 2005 amendment of the HSA (Agarwal, 2005). Christians and Parsis are governed now by the Indian Succession Act which permits ownership rights to ancestral property to women.

But our concern in this chapter goes beyond asking whether women have equal rights to land, to ask *why* women's individual rights to land is so centrally on the agenda of the Indian state, and what the transformation is, that is being brought about in the name of equal rights for women. Let us go back to about a century ago to seek some answers before we return to the moment of 2005.

Producing modern regimes of property under colonialism

Some interesting historical work started emerging in the first decade of this century, on Hindu law reform and codification in late colonial India, a process that has hitherto been debated in feminist scholarship exclusively in terms of enhancement or curtailing of women's rights to property. This work, that of Ritu Birla (Birla, 2009) and Eleanor Newbigin (Newbigin, 2009), for instance, is enabling a reframing of this codification as 'the making of capitalist subjects' (Birla, 2009: 199).

The focus on Hindu law here is largely because through law reforms in the 1860s, colonial officials both created and formalised or codified, 'personal laws,' the effect of which was different on Muslim and Hindu personal law, as Newbigin demonstrates. Koranic shariat law, the 'outcome of the hybrid Company legal system' (Newbigin, 2009: 87), was presented as 'traditional' as well as clear cut and easily applied, under which 'Muslim families were considered to comprise of property-owning individuals, whereas the natural condition of a Hindu family was assumed to be "joint"' (Newbigin, 2009:87). Contrary to later discourses about Muslim law being backwards then, at that point, it was Hindu laws that were considered as requiring reform to bring them into the modern world of individual rights to property.

The impetus towards reform came, argues Newbigin, from conflicts between Hindu professional and mercantile elites on the one hand, and agrarian elites on the other, putting pressure on the Mitakshara coparcenary and 'its system of joint, intergenerational property ownership' through which agrarian elites maintained their authority while for Indian merchants competing with European capital, this focus on 'joint rights and its effect of locking away capital in land' was problematic. Of course, both groups were found in the same families, and younger men gradually opposed joint family living and collective property ownership in the emerging Anglo-Hindu law (Newbigin, 2009: 88).

The movement towards the legal abolition of matriliny in Kerala must be seen as part of the same process. The last vestiges of Nair matriliny that had gradually been delegitimised were finally removed with the Hindu Succession Act of 1956 that gave men equal rights to matrilineal ancestral property. Historian Pravina Kodoth has pointed out that the abolition of matriliny was produced within a narrative of Historical Progress and the newly emerging discourse of individual rights. That is, the end of Nair women's exclusive rights to natal property under matriliny was conducted impeccably in the language of rights—pitting the rights of the 'wife' against those of the 'sister' of the Nair man; the subject of rights was never, of course, assumed to be the Nair woman herself (Kodoth, 2001).

These developments cannot be seen independently of the longer process of turning land into a commodity, which began with the Permanent Settlement of 1793 and culminated in the Land Acquisition Act of 1894; that is, the process through which 'the rule of property' (Guha, 1963[1996]) was sought to be established over heterogeneous practices of land use and land relations, thus creating 'a precise and definitive location of saleable property right' (Sarkar, 2014: 89). We should also note, however, that this process was far from successfully completed by the end of colonial rule, for as Guha argues, the grafting of a capitalist vision of land rights on to the Indian agrarian system without an understanding of the traditions on which it was based resulted in continuing forms of feudal land relations at independence (Guha, 1963[1996]).

The nation state and modernising of property

The independent Indian state thus still needed to address the land question. Let us turn to the debate on the First Amendment to the Constitution in 1951, in which the right to agrarian property was significantly limited by an amendment to Article 31 through which the individual's right to property was made subject to the state's right to acquire property to resolve what Nehru termed 'the land problem.'[9] Government acquisition of land could no longer be challenged on grounds of inadequate compensation and the Ninth Schedule was created, in which land reform legislation was to be placed, protecting it from judicial review. This amendment shows the nation state in the process of establishing a capitalist economy through a 'passive revolution.'[10]

Revealingly, the fact that these reforms were not meant to weaken property rights as such, but only landed property in feudal estates, was spelt out by Finance Minister TT Krishnamachari in a later letter to Nehru during discussions on the fourth amendment in 1954—'We have to move to the left on agricultural land, but moving left in industry will prevent expansion' (cited in Austin, 1999: 104). It is significant that no voice in Parliament explicitly opposed the abolition of *zamindari* (large landholdings). The debate was over whether compensation should be 'just' and 'adequate.' Here was the fledgeling bourgeois state putting in place notions of legitimate and illegitimate property.

Soon, through the Hindu Marriage Act of 1955 and Hindu Succession Act of 1956, far-reaching changes were brought about. These changes are presented as reform of Hindu laws to give women equal rights to property, rights to divorce, and so on. However, it has been convincingly demonstrated by Flavia Agnes (1999) and Madhu Kishwar (1994) that what in fact these legislations achieved was the codification of the vast and heterogeneous practices of communities that were not Muslim/Parsi/Christian, bringing them into conformity with what was assumed to be the 'Indian' and 'Hindu' norm—that is, North Indian, upper-caste practices. This process took away many practices that were better for women in other communities, while giving North Indian, upper-caste women a few limited rights they did not have before.

Capitalist state versus patriarchal family

I would argue that the personal laws on succession and property, such as the Hindu Succession Act, represent a point of conflict between the imperatives of the state and of those of the family. The modern state requires legibility in order to mobilise resources towards capitalist industrialisation, that is, it must be able to 'see' and recognise the forms of property in existence. Towards this end, the institution of individual rights to property is crucial. All forms of property must become completely alienable and transparent to the state—this development is essential for capitalist transformation of the economy. This move is also necessary to make specific individuals responsible for taxation, which cannot be done with common property.

The family on the other hand has its own imperatives of controlling name, descent, and passing on of property, a project disrupted by individual property rights. However, the desire to 'modernise' and to set up such a regime of property rights is also present in sections of the community, leading to debates between 'progressives' and 'conservatives.' It is in the light of this understanding that we must view the gradual granting of land rights to women under Hindu law, all the way up to 2005, when both married and unmarried daughters were given rights to coparcenary property as well. These changes are more than a simple triumph of a feminist perspective—they also represent the establishment of a bourgeois regime of property for the Hindu community at least in principle, which makes land completely alienable by every separate individual owner. In the current climate of widespread resistance to land acquisition, this is a considerable achievement for the state, and for capitalist interests within the community, as it is always easier to pressurise or tempt individual owners rather than communities, to sell land.

We turn now to forest lands and customary land rights in tribal areas.

Forests

Through the Forest Acts of 1865 and 1878, the Forest Department came to control one-fifth of British Indian land area, and overnight, communities that had lived for generations in forests became 'encroachers' on newly enclosed forest lands, and their everyday subsistence activities became crimes—cattle grazing, cutting low hanging branches, gathering leaves, and so on. Other key legislations are the National Forest Policy of 1894, which further regulated rights and restricted privileges of 'users' in forest areas for the 'public good'; the Land Acquisition Act of 1894, which permits compulsory acquisition of land for a 'public purpose'; and the 1927 Act, which remains the main legal basis for depriving forest dwellers of their user rights to forest resources.

There were two main purposes behind these moves—developing forests for the modern timber industry, through 'scientific forestry'; and expanding arable farming 'at the cost of nomadic communities of pastoralists and hunter-foragers' (Sarkar, 2014: 88), for reasons of extraction of land revenue and enhancing export surplus in foodgrains and cash crops (Sarkar, 2014: 88). This process has carried on apace in independent India, with the National Forest Policy of 1952, which focused on protecting forest resources while commercially exploiting minor forest produce, and the Forest Conservation Act of 1980, which placed all forests under the control of the central government. The post-independence state also continued utilising other colonial land acquisition laws for the 'public good' in the name of development.

The Supreme Court has now integrated into Indian environmental jurisprudence the idea of 'the state as trustee of all natural resources' (Rajamani, 2007: 294). Essentially this marks a shift in state policy from the colonial objective of encouraging sedentarisation to dispossessing forest dwellers so that forests can be handed over to private interests for more efficient extraction of forest produce.

During the UPA regime, movements of forest peoples, supported by Left parties in Parliament, were able to get passed the Scheduled Tribes (Recognition of Forest Rights) Act 2006 (FRA, 2006). Since the advent of colonial rule, the usufructuary rights to land of millions of tribals and forest dwellers have remained disputed or unacknowledged due to lack of records of land rights. A Supreme Court judgement in 2001 put the final seal on the extinguishing of such rights when it issued a stay on the regularisation of tribal villages in forest areas. FRA 2006 was militantly campaigned for in order to recognise and formally codify these rights, but interestingly, the rights that are sought to be recorded are not only 'individual rights to cultivated land in forested landscapes' but also collective rights to control, manage, and use forests and its resources as common property. It also 'stipulates the conditions for relocation of forest dwellers from "critical wildlife habitations" only with their "free informed consent" and their rehabilitation in alternative land' (Samarthan, 2012).

It is clear that through the involvement of forest peoples' movements, it is not 'traditional' rights that are being asserted through the FRA 2006, but new forms of collective rights and claims that are being fashioned. These movements represent the powerful presence of thousands affected by the 'brutal violence of the forest bureaucracy' (Ramdas, 2009: 65).

Collective rights are of course not desirable from the point of view of either the Forest Department, which has set up patronage networks through bribery and giving selective permissions to the tribal people to use forest produce, or for supporters of corporate investment-based development (Choubey, 2014). The provision in FRA 2006, making it mandatory to take 'prior informed consent' of Gram Sabha (village council) for any diversion of forest land, is also an obstacle to corporate exploitation of forests. But within 100 days of the first BJP government of Narendra Modi, the Ministry of Environment and Forests passed 240 of 325 projects held up for lack of environmental clearance and it emerged in the media that the government was planning to bypass FRA by using the provisions of Environment Protection Act 1986, which only requires a public hearing for giving permission to any project, not the informed consent of Gram Sabhas. This would not only undermine the Gram Sabha but would establish the dominance of bureaucrats, experts, and politicians on decisions on diversion of forest land (Choubey, 2014).

The FRA 2006 that emerged from movements, and has enormous potential for rejuvenating forests and the collective livelihoods of forest people, can be a threat to expanded regimes of individual property rights amenable to capital, and not surprisingly, is itself under threat under corporate-friendly regimes.

Customary laws

Customary laws is a term used to refer to the bodies of unwritten usages that govern the lives of communities called tribes, in Northeast and Central India. Tribes consider these intrinsic to their identity, culture, and tradition, but of course they have not remained unchanged through time. As noted earlier, although the colonial government formally did not intervene in customary practices, in practice it intervened extensively. Two legislations of 1838 and 1886 facilitated land acquisition by the colonial state and these formed the basis for post-1947 laws that enabled state takeover of tribal lands.

The land tenure system is not uniform over tribal lands. There are different systems in place within both Central and Northeast India. A survey of scholarship in the Northeast shows great diversity. Some tribes have complete community-based ownership with no notion of individual ownership till recently, and others combine individual with clan ownership. Some tribes practise shifting cultivation and so their villages did not have a fixed boundary or name, and communal ownership was the norm among them. Others allot land to each family in return for free labour for about a third of the year. Practices of community ownership were basic to intra- and inter-generational equity as well as the relatively high status of women, because even individually owned land was treated as community resource inherited from ancestors that they could use to meet their needs but had to preserve for posterity according to ecological imperatives (Fernandes and Bharali, 2002).

The argument is not that tribal societies were free of gender hierarchy but that if resources like land, forests, and water bodies are community-owned, women have more of a say in their management. However, the relatively high status it confers on them is based on their role as economic assets in the family, not in society. Most tribal traditions kept a clear separation between the family and society. Women were in charge of the family production and economy while men controlled social power (Fernandes and Bharali, 2002).

A study of five tribes that are at different stages of the interface between customary law and the modern legal system notes that land relations are being modified by several factors—immigration and encroachment but most crucially the changes introduced by the modern legal system. When modern land laws enter such societies through the process of codification, it is found that the result is class formation and a stronger patriarchal ethos. The intervention of individual ownership based laws firsts turn land without an individual title into state property, but this prepares the ground for transferring power from the community to a few elite men who take control of all decision-making and interpreted the customary law to their own benefit, thus deepening and entrenching gender and class inequality (Fernandes et al., 2008).

State policies further strengthen these processes, for example, by giving loans and subsidies for commercial crops only to individual landowning family heads, interpreted as men. Community property-oriented tribes are thus forced to change over to individual title deeds or *patta*s. For example, among the matrilineal Garo of Meghalaya, the state encouraged rubber plantation and gave subsidies and loans to individual owners, thus forcing them to get *patta*s. The administration treated men as family heads and consulted them alone in decisions concerning land use and transfer. Today women continue to inherit land but men wield more political and social power than in the past (Marak, 1997: 60–69. Cited in Fernandes et al., 2008).

Codification and individual rights to land for women are seen as progressive and some tribes are bringing about inheritance rights for women. For instance, the Paite Tribal Council in 2004 introduced provisions in favour of daughters, widows, illegitimate or adopted and other disinherited sons. (Kamkhenthang, 2005, cited in Fernandes et al., 2008: 4). However, two decades ago, legal scholar and activist Nandita Haksar wrote critically of an initiative by Madhu Kishwar to press for individual rights to property for Ho tribal women over community rights. She saw the initiative as uncomprehending of the complex community practices that make up tribal understanding of property and its ownership, and urged rather, the need for a struggle within tribal communities to evolve new customs that are more egalitarian, rather than forcefully introducing from above, individual rights to property (Haksar, 1999).

Haksar's argument is all the more relevant today in the context of accelerated land acquisition by the state in the last few years, now not only for a 'public purpose' but for private capital. The 'progressive' changes in customary laws that tend towards individual rights and now property rights for women must also be seen in the same background that we discussed at length in the context of 'reforms' in Hindu Personal Law.

Let us now return to the present moment.

Property titling for capitalist transformation

In June 2010, a news report noted that Peruvian economist Hernando de Soto, hailed as the 'poor man's capitalist' had arrived in India to help the UPA government to 'merge the informal economy in the slums of the country with the formal or mainstream one' (Chatterji, 2010). De Soto said in this news report that he was invited by Federation of Indian Chambers of Commerce and Industry (FICCI—the tag line on its website is *Industry's Voice for Policy Change*). Among the people in government, he met was the Prime Minister, Manmohan Singh, who was later to present to the Union Minister for Housing and Urban Poverty Alleviation two books written by de Soto, 'for a better understanding of issues relating to urban poverty and slum development' (Chatterji, 2010).

A government official said to a journalist, 'The group led by de Soto will be providing us a methodology for changing the face of the informal economy through routes like property titles and land ownerships.' Another official further clarified, 'De Soto's approach is essentially based on capitalist economic principles. Our government will try to meld them into our socialist objectives.' The news report added, from its briefing, presumably, that De Soto's Institute for Liberty and Democracy(ILD), a Lima-based non-profit organisation, 'has advised governments in many countries to vest slum-dwellers with property rights to maximise the economic use of assets in slums, create organisational forms to increase the productivity of enterprises and *provide identity devices to allow entrepreneurs to operate in expanded markets*' (Chatterji, 2010, emphasis added).

The de Soto agenda has long been recognised by some scholars as a project of attempting to bring about capitalism globally through sustained state intervention. Timothy Mitchell pointed out that de Soto's two books, *The Other Path* (1989) and *The Mystery of Capital* (2000), became 'the most widely cited studies of non-Western economic development in a generation,' and that the Institute for Liberty and Democracy in Peru, which carried out the research presented in these books, has been called the second most influential think tank in the world (Mitchell, 2007).

In Mitchell's rendering, de Soto's argument, based on findings from research in five countries, is that a large amount of their wealth lies outside the formal economy, trapped in forms that cannot enter the market, and therefore cannot be invested to create further wealth. Described as 'dead capital,' this wealth consists principally of land and housing, to which most people in non-Western countries have no formal title registered with the state. Live capital, according to de Soto, is created by transforming the value of material assets 'into abstract forms, which can live an "invisible, parallel life" alongside their physical existence,' This abstract form is credit and capital (Mitchell, 2007: 248–249).

Mitchell points out, using the example of Egypt, one of the countries studied by de Soto, that 'informal property arrangements' have not arisen because of ignorance of notions of private property or because the West did not try to 'export its property system abroad.' On the contrary, in the nineteenth century, Ottoman and European rulers in Cairo launched a series of attempts to transform property arrangements into systems based on an absolute right of private ownership. But Egyptian farmers were able to prevent the complete destruction of livelihoods that absolute property rights entailed because 'Egypt controlled no overseas colonies or Indian territories to which to ship a dispossessed rural population, so could not afford the rates of dispossession that private ownership produced.' Mitchell argues that the position of ordinary Egyptians 'outside' the mechanisms of private property ownership was 'the outcome of a long, often violent, but ultimately relatively successful objection to undergoing the dispossession inflicted on the rural populations of Europe or the complete marginalization or elimination of native populations in parts of the world where settler colonialism was carried through' (Mitchell, 2007: 253).

However, once de Soto's programme was adopted from the late 1970s as part of neoliberal reforms in Egypt, and ILD-drafted legislation pushed through in the early 2000s to bring about a mortgage law, a property titling programme, and new rules for licensing small businesses, the situation changed drastically. The government and the courts began to alter the laws protecting commercial and residential tenants, freeing property developers from the constraint of rent controls. The share of manufacturing in the economy declined, non-oil exports fell, and no significant efforts were made to increase large-scale employment (Mitchell, 2007: 263).

All the evidence from India, Africa, and Latin America go to show that the demand for individual rights to land is a strategy that achieves nothing more than opening up land for capitalist transformation, often via the state. De Soto's programme was promoted powerfully by bodies like the UNDP High Level Commission on Legal Empowerment of the Poor, and in fact India's introduction to de Soto was not in 2010, with his first visit. This High Level Commission, co-chaired by former U.S. Secretary of State Madeleine Albright and Hernando de Soto, with India as one of the founding members, was set up in September 2005 (around the same time as the amendments to the Hindu Succession Act were being passed with such a puzzling lack of enthusiasm, but nevertheless unanimously, in the Indian Parliament).

Individual rights to land and land acquisition

It has been argued by Aditya Nigam that the widespread *continuation* of 'pre-capitalist' forms of production both in agriculture and in non-agricultural sectors is what 'confronts capital's onward march.' Nigam argues that these are actually 'non-capitalist' rather than 'pre-capitalist' forms and 'represent the recalcitrant other of capital and capitalism – that which capitalism must attempt to seize, discipline, control and subsume within its own domain but which constantly escape its logic.' The transformation to bourgeois private property therefore involves and has always involved, he says, 'a violent decimation of all forms of common property and even non-capitalist private property' (Nigam, 2013).

This is evident from the story of land acquisition legislation in contemporary India. In 2013, the Right to Fair Compensation and Transparency in Land Acquisition, Rehabilitation and Resettlement Act (LARRA), was passed, replacing the 1894 Act. Key provisions of this new legislation re-enshrined the state's power to dispossess land for private profit, but ensured farmers a share of the profits that would accrue to capital in the form of higher prices for land and rehabilitation and resettlement benefits. Michael Levien sees this as an attempt to substitute one-time payouts for development. LARRA thus represents the contradiction between the land requirements of neoliberal capitalism and the pressures on the state due to electoral democracy. More importantly, this policy concretises the shift from the state dispossessing land for public sector infrastructure, mining and public sector heavy industry to the state in effect becoming land brokers for private capital (Levien, 2018).

However, corporate interests were not satisfied with this legislation, and with what they called the general 'policy paralysis' of the UPA (which as we saw was constrained in its neoliberal ambitions because of the backing of social movements). The UPA itself diluted many of its provisions through an ordinance later in 2013, and the ordinance has since then been promulgated by the President for the third time in 2015 (that is, without being passed by both houses of Parliament, twice by the government that succeeded the UPA). By this ordinance, the government can acquire land for any private entity without obtaining the consent of affected people and can do so without the precondition of Social Impact Assessments. In addition, even the filing of complaints regarding the state's failure to follow due process now needs the prior consent of the state itself.

Alongside this is the big push towards enshrining individual rights to land, replacing community rights where they existed. We have noted the enthusiasm with which women's rights to land is being promoted by the Indian state. Community rights are also being gradually replaced by individual rights. In March 2018, the Arunachal Pradesh Land Settlement and Records Amendment Act was passed, giving ownership rights to indigenous people of the state of Arunachal Pradesh, who earlier had held lands jointly as a community. The state government said in a statement that echoes de Soto, that with this legislation, 'huge investments are expected, which will augment the economy of the state,' and that with ownership rights, tribal people will be able to lease out their land, and use it as collateral to get loans from banks (Chandran, 2018). We know that none of these benefits actually have accrued in places all over the world where individual land titling has taken place. We also know that individual titles to land make land acquisitions for any purpose easier for the state, and their only purpose is commodification of land.

Michael Levien has starkly defined dispossession as 'state sponsored redistribution of land from the poor to the wealthy' (Levien, 2015). It seems that 'land rights for women' and 'property titles for the poor' are the banners that fly before this process of dispossession leading towards an economy driven by capitalist imperatives.

It is becoming increasingly clear that women's rights to land are an integral part of the agenda of forcibly constructing capitalism through the agency of the state. From the perspective that this chapter offers, all three—the state, the traditional religious community, and the customary community—are equally problematic from the point of view of equitable access to land for women as well as other excluded castes and groups. A truly radical agenda would thus have to challenge all three factors simultaneously—state-led capitalist enclosures of commons, which is part of what Veltmeyer and Petras call the 'new extractivism' (Veltmeyer and Petras, 2014); private individual land ownership; and gendered and caste-based forms of exclusion from land use. This struggle would have to be waged in a context of accelerated decline of agriculture in an era of rampant dispossession.

3 Beyond capitalism

The link between de Soto's programme of property titling and UBI/BIG is that both seek to bring all wealth into the formal economy where it can be available for capitalist speculation. UBI/BIG would replace social security schemes with cash, while property titling is meant to stimulate an economy of mortgage, and all of this is meant to enter the banking system.

Thus, both proposals are either deliberately part of or unwittingly feed into this agenda of formalising all wealth and savings and making them available to capital for mobilisation. In order to move beyond both, we need to reject the capitalist horizon altogether. Here, we can draw on JK Gibson–Graham's insight that capitalism does not encompass all of society, that it is not a complete, closed structure, that multiple non-capitalist practices exist alongside or outside it. Gibson–Graham argue for the need to destabilise the hegemony of 'capitalocentrism' that produces the idea that capitalism is inescapable and omnipresent (Gibson-Graham, 2006).

Weeks and Standing consider 'work' as alienated wage labour, hence the attempts to devalorise it. However, I suggest we need a conception of 'work' as activity that can be performed by all humans and non-humans and retain the term 'labour' for waged or unwaged work involving exploitation and alienation. Everything is work that humans and non-humans do, from singing to swimming to grazing to working on a construction site, to thinking. It is 'alienated labour' if it does not contain elements of self-creation and if it involves exploitation. Developing the idea of alienation away from its humanist form in Marx's *Economic and Philosophical Manuscripts*, we could imagine elements of alienation in unwaged labour (housework, for example) and moments of non-alienation in otherwise exploitative labour such as the music of slaves, of migrant labour, and so on.

The goal would not be to escape work then, but to escape labour, to encourage and be in solidarity with all the ways in which people's activities escape capitalism, or are invisible to it. The goal would be to be in solidarity with struggles of people to build and protect non-capitalist ways of life, collective rights to land and property of different sorts. All over the Global South, such communities and pockets can be found, either actively resisting incorporation into the capitalist order or escaping it.

In the Global North, where capitalism has been established more extensively, the degrowth movement offers a way of rethinking our world:

> Sustainable degrowth is a downscaling of production and consumption. . . . It calls for a future where societies live within their ecological means, with open, localized economies and resources more equally distributed through new forms of democratic institutions. . . . Degrowth proposes . . . a shrinking of the economic system to leave more space for human cooperation and ecosystems.[11]

A truly transformative politics must move away from an individual-centred capitalist regime of property, and towards *collective* forms of property and *use rights* in property. This does not mean an obliteration of rights to property; rather, it would include, for example, protecting the rights of indigenous communities to traditional knowledge, lands, and plant genetic resources against multinational corporations (Onwuekwe, 2004). A feminist politics must learn from the experience of movements for 'commoning,' which work to produce collective use rights which have been extinguished by capitalism—from digital commons to experiments with urban farming (Bollier and Helfrich, 2019)—this is the paradigm for the future.

Notes

1 The number of households *without* a PDS card was 14% in 2012, according to a Government of India report (2016: iv). PDS thus covers most of the population. MGNREGS (legislation passed in 2005) guarantees 100 days of work to unskilled labourers in villages of India. The scheme is also intended to create durable assets (such as roads, canals, ponds, and wells). Employment is to be provided within 5 km of an applicant's residence, and minimum wages are to be paid. On an average, 50 million households have been provided employment every year since 2008, which means about 260 million (considering an average family of five) are covered by it (Salve and Tewari, 2016). These two schemes thus act as a safety net for the most vulnerable sections.

2 On 8 November 2016, the Government of India announced the immediate withdrawal of all ₹500 and ₹1,000 banknotes of the Mahatma Gandhi Series, and the issuance of new ₹500 and ₹2,000 banknotes in exchange for the demonetised banknotes. The objective, it was claimed, was to curtail the use of illicit and counterfeit cash and hit at the 'black' economy. The announcement of demonetisation was followed by prolonged cash shortages in the weeks that followed, which created significant disruption throughout the economy.

3 www.indiabudget.gov.in/budget2016-2017/es2015-16/echapvol1-03.pdf

4 Guy Standing 'The growing Precariat: Why we need a universal basic income' https://singularityhub.com/2015/03/30/the-growing-precariat-why-a-basic-income-is-needed/

5 Ibid.

6 I am setting aside for the moment as undisputed from a feminist perspective, the rights of women to non-landed property in natal and matrimonial families and to the matrimonial home. I consider as undisputed too, the right of women to maintenance upon

divorce, justified by a feminist understanding of the sexual division of labour that makes women in a heterosexual marriage or domestic partnership solely responsible for doing or organising reproductive labour. I make this clarification because several recent court judgements in India have disallowed maintenance to divorced women if they are employed or childless. In other words, women's rights to property in general are not the focus in this paper, but land rights in particular.

7 Presentation at workshop on women and land rights—'Theory & Experiences from the Field: Fostering Rural Women's Access & Ownership to Land and Collectives,' (14–15 May), Jawaharlal Nehru University, Delhi.

8 Presentation at workshop on women and land rights— 'Theory & Experiences from the Field: Fostering Rural Women's Access & Ownership to Land and Collectives,' (14–15 May), Jawaharlal Nehru University, Delhi.

9 *Lok Sabha Debates* 1951: Part II Vol XII Col. 8830.

10 I refer here to Sudipta Kaviraj's well-known development of the Gramscian notion to explain the pattern of development adopted by the Indian state. That is, for a thorough-going bourgeois revolution to be effected, for industrialisation to take place, a domestic market must be built up by reducing poverty in the countryside. This can only be done by effective land reforms, which have been legislated but never effectively implemented because of the influence of landed interests in the coalition of ruling classes. The entire planning process until the 1980s has therefore been an exercise in trying to promote industrialisation without the radical transformation of agriculture (Kaviraj, 1988).

11 The Degrowth website (https://degrowth.org/definition-2/).

References

Agarwal, B. (1994). *A field of one's own: Gender and land rights in South Asia*, Cambridge: Cambridge University Press.

Agarwal, B. (2005). "Landmark Step to Gender Equality," *The Hindu*, September 25. www.thehindu.com/thehindu/mag/2005/09/25/stories/2005092500050100.htm

Agencies (2016). "Deposit of 80% of Banned Currency in Banks Raises Doubts about Success of Demonetization," *The Economic Times*, December 5. http://economictimes.indiatimes.com/wealth/personal-finance-news/deposit-of-80-of-banned-currency-in-banks-raises-doubts-about-success-of-demonetisation/articleshow/55771366.cms

Agnes, F. (1999). *Law and Gender Equality. The Politics of Women's Rights in India*, New Delhi: Oxford University Press.

Anderson, M. and S. Guha eds. (1998). *Changing Concepts of Rights and Justice in South Asia*, New Delhi: Oxford University Press.

Austin, G. (1999). *Working a Democratic Constitution: The Indian Experience*, New Delhi: Oxford University Press.

Banerjee, S. (2017). "A Contentious Proposal," *The Indian Express*, January 14. http://indianexpress.com/article/opinion/columns/poverty-alleviation-universal-basic-income-ubi-direct-benefit-transfer-dbt-black-money-mgnrega-a-contentious-proposal-4473170/

Bello, W. (2018). "10 Years after 2008 Crisis, There's no 'Reforming' Global Capitalism," *Business Standard*, September 21. www.business-standard.com/article/international/10-years-after-2008-crisis-there-s-no-reforming-global-capitalism-118092100162_1.html

Bhalla, S. S. (2017). "No Proof Required: Financing Basic Income for the Bottom 50 Per Cent," *The Indian Express*, January 7. http://indianexpress.com/article/opinion/columns/no-proof-required-financing-basic-income-for-the-bottom-50-per-cent-4462648/

Birla, R. (2009). *Stages of Capital: Law, Culture, and Market Governance in Late Colonial India*, Durham: Duke University Press.

Bollier, D. and S. Helfrich (2019). *Free, Fair and Alive. The Insurgent Power of the Commons*, Canada: New Society Publishers.

Chakraborty, A. (2017). "Is India Ready for a Universal Basic Income Scheme?" *Daily O*, January 12. www.dailyo.in/politics/is-india-ready-for-a-universal-basic-income-scheme-demonetisation-modi/story/1/15062.html

Chandran, R. (2018). "Individual Land Rights to India's Indigenous People Could Be 'Disastrous', Expert Says," *Reuters*, March 15. https://in.reuters.com/article/india-landrights-lawmaking/individual-land-rights-to-indias-indigenous-people-could-be-disastrous-expert-says-idINKCN1GR1U8

Chatterji, S. (2010). "UPA to try 'de Soto Model' for Slum Development," *Business Standard*, June 29.

Choubey, K. N. (2014). "'Red Carpet' in Forests," https://kafila.online/2014/09/28/red-carpet-in-forests-kamal-nayan-choubey/

Derrett, J. D. M. (1968). *Religion Law and the State in India*, London: Faber and Faber.

De Soto, H. (2000). *The Mystery of Capital: Why Capitalism Triumphs in the West and Fails Everywhere Else*, New York: Basic Books and London: Bantam Press/Random House.

De Soto, Hernando (1989) The Other Path: The Invisible Revolution in the Third World Harper Collins

DNA Correspondent (2016). "Fake Aadhar-Linked Ration Cards Issued, Government Orders Inquiry," *Daily News and Analysis*, November 26. www.dnaindia.com/india/report-fake-aadhar-linked-ration-cards-issued-government-orders-inquiry-2277037

Dreze, J. (2017). "Universal Basic Income for India Suddenly Trendy. Look Out," *NDTV*, January 16. www.ndtv.com/opinion/decoding-universal-basic-income-for-india-1649293

Fernandes, W. and G. Bharali (2002). "Customary Law-Formal Law Interface: Impact on Tribal culture," in Subba, T. N., J. Puthenpurackal, and S. J. Puykunnel eds., *Christianity and Change in Northeast India*, New Delhi: Concept Publishing Company.

Fernandes, W., M. Pereira, and V. Khatso (2008). *Tribal Customary Laws in Northeast India: Gender and Class Implications*, Guwahati: North Eastern Social Research Centre. http://ncwapps.nic.in/pdfreports/Customary%20Law.pdf

Financial Times Editorial (2016). "Universal Basic Income is a Bad Idea," September 27. www.financialexpress.com/opinion/universal-basic-income-is-a-bad-idea/392868/

Friedman, M. (1962). *Capitalism and Freedom*, Chicago and London: University of Chicago Press.

Gatade, S. (2005, March 18). "Interview with Ms. C.K. Janu, Leader of Tribals in Kerala," www.sacw.net/Nation/gatade18032005.html

Gibson-Graham, J. K. (2006). *The End of Capitalism (As We Knew It)*, Minneapolis and London: University of Minnesota Press.

Guha, R. (1963/1996). *A Rule of Property for Bengal: An Essay on the Idea of Permanent Settlement*, Durham: Duke University Press.

Gupta, S. (2018). "Women and Land Rights in India: Towards a Democratic and Gendered Formulation of the Land Question," in Jha, P., A. Kumar, and Y. Mishra eds., *Labouring Women: Issues and Challenges in Contemporary India*, Hyderabad: Orient Blackswan.

Haksar, N. (1999). "Human Rights Layering: A Feminist Perspective," in Dhanda, A. and A. Parasher eds., *Engendering Law: Essays in Honour of Lotika Sarkar*, Lucknow: Eastern Book Company.

Hayek, F. (1981). *Law, Legislation and Liberty, Volume 3: The Political Order of a Free People*, Chicago and London: University of Chicago Press.

Jhabvala, R. (2016). "India's Time for Unconditional Cash Transfers," *The Financial Express*, May 17. www.financialexpress.com/opinion/indias-time-for-unconditional-cash-transfers/257046/

Kaviraj, S. (1988). "A Critique of the Passive Revolution," *Economic and Political Weekly*, vol. 23(45/47), 2429–2433, 2436–2441, 2443–2444.

Khera, R. (2016). "A Phased Approach Will Make a 'Basic Income' Affordable for India," *The Wire*, December 20. https://thewire.in/88350/basic-income-phased-approach/

Kishwar, M. (1994). "Codified Hindu Law. Myth and Reality," *Economic and Political Weekly*, August 13 vol. 29(33), 2145–2161.

Kodoth, P. (2001). "Courting Legitimacy or Delegitimizing Custom? Sexuality, Sambandham and Marriage Reform in Late-Nineteenth Century Malabar," *Modern Asian Studies*, vol. 35(2), 349–384.

Kurup, A. (2008). "Tribal Law in India: How Decentralized Administration Is Extinguishing Tribal Rights and Why Autonomous Tribal Governments Are Better," *Indigenous Law Journal*, vol. 7(1), 87–126.

Levien, M. (2015). "Dispossession, Development and Democracy," *The Hindu*, February 4.

Levien, M. (2018). *Dispossession without Development: Land Grabs in Neoliberal India*, New Delhi: Oxford University Press

Lok Sabha Debates (2005). "Motion for Consideration of the Hindu Succession (Amendment) Bill, on 29 August 2005," https://indiankanoon.org/doc/842089/

Marak, C. (1997). "Status of Women in Garo Culture," in Sen, S. ed., *Women in Meghalaya*, New Delhi: Omsons Publications.

Mitchell, T. (2007). "Properties of markets," in MacKenzie, D., F. Muniesa, and L. Siu eds., *Do Economists Make Markets? On the Performativity of Economics*, Princeton: Princeton University Press: 244–275.

Nair, J. (1996). *Women and Law in Colonial India: A Social History*, New Delhi: Kali for Women.

Newbigin, E. (2009). "The Codification of Personal Law and Secular Citizenship: Revisiting the History of Law Reform in Late Colonial India," *The Indian Economic and Social History Review*, vol. 46(1), 83–104.

Nigam, A. (2013). " 'Molecular Economies': Is There An 'Outside' to Capital?" in Menon, N., A. Nigam, and S. Palshikar eds., *Critical Studies in Politics: Exploring Sites, Selves, Power*, Hyderabad: Orient Blackswan.

Onwuekwe, C. B. (2004). "The Commons Concept and Intellectual Property Rights Regime: Whither Plant Genetic Resources and Traditional Knowledge?" *The University of New Hampshire Law Review*, vol. 2(1), 65–90.

Panagariya, A. (2017). "No Fiscal Resources for Universal Basic Income: Niti Aayog Chief Arvind Panagariya," *The Indian Express*, January 25. http://indianexpress.com/article/business/budget/no-fiscal-resources-for-universal-basic-income-niti-aayog-chief-arvind-panagariya-4490255/

Rajamani, L. (2007). "Public Interest Environmental Litigation in India: Exploring Issues of Access, Participation, Equity, Effectiveness and Sustainability," *Journal of Environmental Law*, vol. 19(3), 293–321.

Ramdas, S. (2009). "Women, Forestspaces and the Law: Transgressing the Boundaries," *Economic and Political Weekly*, vol. 44(44), 65–79.

Salve, P. and S. Tewari (2016). "How 52 million Indians May Depend on MGNREGA for 20 Years," *Business Standard*, March 3.

Samarthan (2012). "Recognition of Community Rights Under Forest Rights Act in Madhya Pradesh and Chhattisgarh: Challenges and Way Forward," www.undp.org/content/dam/india/docs/DG/recognition-of-community-rights-under-forest-rights-act-in-madhya-pradesh-and-chhattisgarh-challenges-and-way-forward.pdf

Sarkar, S. (2014). *Modern Times: India 1880s – 1950s*, Ranikhet: Permanent Black.

Singha, R. (1998). "Civil Authority and Due process: Colonial Criminal Justice in the Banaras Zamindari, 1781–1795," in Anderson, M. and S. Guha eds., *Changing Concepts of Rights in South Asia*, New Delhi: Oxford University Press: 30–81.

Special Correspondent (2005). "Equal Rights for Women in Parental Property," *The Hindu* August 17. www.thehindu.com/2005/08/17/stories/2005081705461200.htm

Standing, G. (2011). *The Precariat: The New Dangerous Class*, New York: Bloomsbury Academic.

Standing, G. (2013). "India's Experiment in Basic Income Grants," *Global Dialogue*, vol. 3(5), November. http://isa-global-dialogue.net/indias-great-experiment-the-transformative-potential-of-basic-income-grants/

Standing, G. (2015). "The Growing Precariat: Why We Need a Universal Basic Income," *SingularityHub*, March 30. https://singularityhub.com/2015/03/30/the-growing-precariat-why-a-basic-income-is-needed/

Streithorst, T. (2015). "How Basic Income Solves Capitalism's Fundamental Problem," *Evonomics*, December 20. http://evonomics.com/how-universal-basic-income-solves/

Veltmeyer, H. and J. Petras (2014). *The New Extractivism: A Post-Neoliberal Development Model or Imperialism for the Twenty-First Century?* London and New York: Zed Books.

Weeks, K. (2011). *The Problem with Work*, Durham and London: Duke University Press.

Weeks, K. (2016). "A Feminist Case for Basic Income: An Interview with Kathi Weeks (Interview with Katie Cruz)," *Critical Legal Thinking*, August 22. https://criticallegalthinking.com/2016/08/22/feminist-case-basic-income-interview-kathi-weeks/

INDEX

Note: Page numbers in *italics* indicate a figure and page numbers in **bold** indicate a table on the corresponding page.